WRITE TO TV

Praise for *Write to TV*

"Martie Cook imparts a tremendous amount of knowledge in a way that is both easy to understand and entertaining. It is like having a mentor in book form." — Christopher Crowe, writer, *The Last of the Mohicans*

"I think this is about the best book on writing for television out there. I hope it sells like crazy because television will be better for it." — Peter Dunne, Emmy and Peabody Award-Winning Television Producer (*CSI: Crime Scene Investigation, JAG*), Writer (*Melrose Place, Dallas, Knots Landing*), and Book Author (*Emotional Structure* — Quill Driver Books)

"In her new book *Write to TV*, Martie Cook gives the fledgling writer an insider's view of the TV industry and breaking into the writing game. Using her wit, candor and years of hard-won experience, Martie reports back from the TV trenches and breaks down everything it takes to make it as a writer. We learn the secrets of a winning spec, how to find an agent and what to expect when you do finally land that first big job. It's all here. She even covers what your script cover should look like. And it's all in a fun, personal, practical guide. Where was this book when I was starting out?" — Manny Basanese, Writer/Producer *The Steve Harvey Show* and *The Wayans Brothers*

"*Write to TV* is a must read for anyone even thinking of becoming a TV Writer." — Walter Klenhard, writer/director, numerous movies of the week.

"Martie has done a terrific job in laying out a practical, nuts-and-bolts approach to TV writing. She got it exactly right. Any aspiring writer should read this book before diving into the cold, show business waters. As an added bonus it can also be used as a flotation device." — Marc Warren, Executive Producer, *Full House, Even Stevens*, and *That's So Raven*

"Martie Cook has put together a wonderful resource for anyone interested in writing for television. It's thorough, filled with great anecdotes and helpful tips and covers the whole spectrum of TV writing. I am always looking for up-to-date resources for my students — finally, there is one book that has it all! Teaching writing is no easy task, but Martie Cook has figured out a way to guide readers through the process and still make it fun. The information gathered here is invaluable to anyone looking to enter the industry — it's even helpful for those of us who have been in the industry for years!" — Pam Wheaton Shorr, Lecturer, Department of Film and Television, Boston University

"Finally, a practical approach to the business of TV Writing, seamlessly mixed with the art of writing. A critical tool for anyone who wants to succeed as a television writer" — Alan Barnette, Executive Producer, *Faith of My Fathers*

"*Write to TV* takes you inside the minds of writers, producers, and network suits in this brutally honest book. A "must read" for anyone who has the dream of making it in Hollywood. I wish I had read this book 20 years ago!" — Glenn Meehan, VP of Development, 44 Blue Productions

"At last, someone who has 'been there & done that' has written a serious and informed guide about the world of television writing. Martie Cook's *Write to TV* is a nuts and bolts guide that is absorbing, lively and concise. Offering everything from behind the scenes basics, to writing for different television formats, to how to get an agent, this truly great book accomplishes the triple task of being informative, entertaining and well-written." — Jean Stawarz, Associate Professor of Screenwriting at Emerson College, writer, *Powwow Highway*

"*Write to TV* is chock-full of invaluable tips and personal stories, plus practical advice from the best in the TV writing business." — Anne Zeiser, Director of National Strategic Marketing, WGBH/PBS

WRITE TO TV
OUT OF YOUR HEAD AND ONTO THE SCREEN

Martie Cook

ELSEVIER

Amsterdam • Boston • Heidelberg • London
New York • Oxford • Paris • San Diego
San Francisco • Singapore • Sydney • Tokyo

Focal Press is an imprint of Elsevier

Acquisitions Editor: Elinor Actipis
Project Manager: Paul Gottehrer
Assistant Editor: Robin Weston
Marketing Manager: Christine Degon Veroulis
Cover Design: Alisa Andreola
Typesetter: Charon Tec Ltd (A Macmillan Company), Chennai, India
         www.charontec.com

Focal Press is an imprint of Elsevier
30 Corporate Drive, Suite 400, Burlington, MA 01803, USA
Linacre House, Jordan Hill, Oxford OX2 8DP, UK

Recognizing the importance of preserving what has been written,
Elsevier prints its books on acid-free paper whenever possible.

Library of Congress Cataloging-in-Publication Data
Application submitted

British Library Cataloguing-in-Publication Data
A catalogue record for this book is available from the British Library.

ISBN 13: 978-0-240-80876-5
ISBN 10: 0-240-80876-2

For information on all Focal Press publications
visit our website at www.books.elsevier.com

06 07 08 09 10   10 9 8 7 6 5 4 3 2 1

Printed in the United States of America

Working together to grow
libraries in developing countries

www.elsevier.com | www.bookaid.org | www.sabre.org

ELSEVIER   BOOK AID
            International   Sabre Foundation

For my parents, who took me into their home and hearts. Adoption is a beautiful thing.

"I like to start with something that troubles me — for example, I did a short-lived show called *EZ Streets* which was told from the point of view of the cops and the criminals. The impetus for the show had nothing to do with either — it was the first Gulf War. My friends at the time were all talking about this villain Saddam Hussein and saying how we should go kick his ass. I agreed he was certainly a villain, but wondered how we'd chosen that particular villain to fight — especially when there were so many like him around the world who we were actually supporting. I was troubled by the fact that, as Americans, we made quick decisions about people like that — good or bad. So I decided to do a show where I would give you good guys and bad guys, and then make you like the bad guys and dislike the good ones. Then as soon as you were comfortable with that, I'd make you like the good guys and hate the bad. America apparently wasn't half as interested in this as I was, but I eventually explored the same question with *Crash*. In general, I like asking myself questions that make me uncomfortable, questions that have no easy answers. And when I find something that really makes me nervous, I know I have something I want to write." — Oscar winner Paul Haggis *Crash*, *Million Dollar Baby*, and Creator, Executive Producer, *The Black Donnellys* on how to approach story.

CONTENTS

ACKNOWLEDGMENTS   xix
INTRODUCTION   xxi

PART I   How Hollywood Works   1
Chapter 1   AN OVERVIEW OF THE TV INDUSTRY   3
              It's Called Show Business for a Reason   4
              Technology is Changing the Face of Television   6
              Product Integration   6
              The Role of Production Companies, Studios, and
                 Networks   7
              The Difference Between Network and
                 Syndication   7
              What are Television Sweeps?   9
              Staff Writing vs. Freelance Writing   9
              Do You Have To Live In L.A.?   10
              Writing For Existing Shows is Your First Step   10
              What is a Spec Script?   11
              Choosing a Spec Script That Will Work
                 For You   11
              Studying the Show Before You Write   13
              Purchasing a Sample Script of the Show
                 You Want to Write   14
              Why Two (Sigh!) Specs Are Better Than One 15
              Writing is Rewriting   16
              The Reason Your Spec Probably Won't Sell   16
              Declaring Your Major (and Minor)   17
Chapter 2   GETTING YOUR SCRIPTS READ   18
              Plastering the Town With Your Work   18
              The Initial Meeting   19

	The Invitation to Pitch	20
	What Happens If They Buy Your Story?	21
	Will You Write the Teleplay?	22
	Odds Are They Won't Steal Your Ideas	23
	How Much Will You Make and When Will You Get Paid?	24
	Where Does it All Lead?	24
PART II	Comedy	25
Chapter 3	SITUATIONAL COMEDIES	27
	What it Takes to Write Comedy	27
	Check List For Funny	29
	How Sitcom Writing Staffs Work	29
	The Make-up of a Sitcom Staff	29
	Multi-Camera vs. Single-Camera Shows	31
	A Week in the Life of a Staff Sitcom Writer	32
	How a Freelancer Fits In	36
Chapter 4	DEVELOPING YOUR SITCOM STORY	37
	Getting Started	37
	The Importance of a Good Story	37
	How to Create an Original Story	38
	Making Original Stories Work For Existing Shows	38
	Finding An Original Spin	40
	Study Up	42
	Beating Writer's Block	42
	Stories to Stay Away From	43
	Getting the Poop	44
	Physical Comedy	45
	Sight Gags	45
	"A" Stories, "B" Stories, and the Occasional "C" Story and "D" Story	45
	Getting Feedback	46
	Checklist For Story	46
Chapter 5	SITCOM STRUCTURE	48
	The Importance of Story Structure	48
	Traditional Two-Act Structure vs. Modern Three-Act Structure	48
	Creating Twists	49
	No-Fail Sitcom Structure	50
	Example of Structure	52
	Teasers	53
	Tags	53
	Checklist For Story Structure	54
Chapter 6	OUTLINING YOUR SITCOM STORY	55
	Why You Must Break Your Story Down Act-By-Act, Scene-By-Scene	55

	What a Good Outline Should Accomplish	56
	Good Writing is Key	56
	Format Matters	57
	How Long Should an Outline Be?	57
	Sample Outline for Sitcom	58
	A Few More Rules	60
	How Multi-cam shows Differ in Format	61
	Reading Your Work, Out Loud	62
	Getting Feedback on Your Outline	62
	A Word About Covers	63
	Checklist For Story Outline	65
Chapter 7	SCRIPTING YOUR SITCOM	66
	Formatting Your Sitcom Script	66
	The Difference Between a First Draft and a Shooting Script	66
	Formatting the Single-Cam Script	68
	Sample Format For Multi-Cam Scripts	72
	Scene Writing From Beginning to End	75
	How Many Jokes Should You Have on Each Page?	76
	Setting Up Jokes and Paying Them Off	76
	Why Smart Jokes Will Get a Bigger Laugh	76
	Where Do Good Jokes Come From?	77
	Incorporating Universal Humor	78
	Should You Avoid Jokes That Could Be Considered "Offensive"?	78
	Beware of Jokes That Center Around Current Topics	79
	In Comedy, Three's a Charm	79
	Runners	79
	Alliteration	80
	Comedy That Goes Against Character	80
	Putting the Audience in a Superior Position	80
	Don't Forget to Button	80
	The Dreaded Punch-up	81
	Watch Where You Step	81
Chapter 8	OTHER KINDS OF TV COMEDY	82
	Writing For Animation	82
	Writing For Late Night	84
	Sketch Writing	86
PART III	Prime Time Drama	91
Chapter 9	PLOT-DRIVEN DRAMAS	93
	Why *Law & Order* Thrives and Survives	94
	Ripped From the Headlines	94
	The Importance of Creating Authentic Worlds	95

	Getting the Facts: How to Research Cops, Lawyers, Doctors, and Others	96
	Colleges and Universities	97
	The WGA	97
	Creating Powerful Protagonists and Antagonists	98
	Building Conflict and Jeopardy	98
	One-Hour Dramatic Structure	99
	Scripts For Cable Vary Slightly	100
	How To Structure Your Plot-Driven Drama	100
	How Index Cards Can Help (And Why Studios Order So Many)	100
	Checklist For Plot-Driven Drama	101
Chapter 10	CHARACTER-DRIVEN DRAMA	102
	All About People	102
	Everything In Your Life Isn't Fit For the Screen	102
	How to Dramatize Personal Experience	103
	How Structure For Character-Driven Dramas Differs From Plot-Driven Dramas	106
	Why Colored Index Cards Are Key	107
	Continuing Storylines From Week to Week	107
	Checklist For Character-Driven Drama	108
	The Dirt on Soaps	109
Chapter 11	FORMATTING FOR PRIME TIME DRAMA	110
	Sample Outline For Prime Time Drama	110
	Scripting Your Prime-Time Drama	112
PART IV	Creating Original Series	117
Chapter 12	THE TELEVISION PILOT	119
	Reasons Why You Shouldn't Write a Pilot	119
	One Reason Why You Should Write a Pilot	120
	How Pilot Season Works	121
	Network Schedule: Friend or Foe	122
	Why Some Cable Networks Operate Under a Different Time Clock	123
Chapter 13	FINDING AN ORIGINAL PREMISE	125
	Networks Long For Longevity	125
	Knowing the Market	125
	Tapping Into Future Trends	126
	Adding Your Own Point of View	128
	A Tall Order: Introducing Characters and Premise All in One Episode	129
	Premise Pilots vs. Non-Premise Pilots	129
	Big Love	130

Know What's Out There   131
Sample Treatment for a Pilot   131
Kyle's Turn   132
Creating a 13-Week Episode Guide   133
First Pages   134
Riding Coattails   140
Checklist for Pilots   141

PART V   Made-For-TV Movies   143

Chapter 14   MADE-FOR-TV MOVIES   145
                Hallmark Is the Benchmark   145
                Target Audience for MOWs (Think Pink)   146
                Most Common Types of MOW Stories and
                    Why They Work   147
                Stories to Stay Far Away From   149
                Breaking into the MOW Business   149
                Adapting True Stories   149
                Protagonist vs. Antagonist   150
                Bringing Novels to the Screen:
                    How to Get the Rights   151
                Should You Write a Mini-Series?   154
                Don't Make Your Two-Hour a Four-Hour   154
                Structuring Your MOW   155
                Stories that Can Double as Feature Films
                    and MOWs   156
                Classic Three-Act Structure   157

PART VI   Characters   161

Chapter 15   CREATING COMPELLING CHARACTERS   163
                Character Broken into Threes   163
                What is Backstory?   164
                Character Bios   164
                Why It's Important For The Audience to
                    Like At Least Some of Your Characters   165
                Some of the Finest Characters Are
                    Not Human   166
                Creating Characters With Opposing
                    Viewpoints   167
                Minor Characters Matter   168
                How To Write Quirky Characters (And Why
                    Audiences Love Them)   169
                Twenty Questions To Ask Yourself About Each
                    Character   170

PART VII   Dialogue   171

Chapter 16   WRITING DIALOGUE THAT DANCES ON
                THE PAGE   173
                First and Foremost: Dialogue Comes From
                    Character   173
                Keeping Dialogue Where it Belongs   173
                The Rhythm of Dialogue: How To Avoid Long,
                    Rambling Speeches   174
                The Use of Slang in Dialogue   174
                Right-On Dialogue: Wrong!!   174
                Watch Out for Names   175
                Why Using Dialogue To Reveal BackStory
                    Can Be Deadly   175
                Stay Off the Phone!!   175
                What To Do When All of Your Characters
                    Sound Alike   176

PART VIII   How to Pitch your Comedy, Drama, or Movie
                of the Week   177

Chapter 17   HOW TO GET A PITCH MEETING   179
                Who Will Be in the Room?   179
                Why it's Essential to be Early   180
                Dress for Success   180
                How Many Ideas Should You Pitch?   181
                The Order of Your Stories   182
                How Much Detail Should You Give?   182
                Practicing Your Pitch   183
                Controlling the Room   183
                A Couple of No-nos   184
                The Use of Index Cards and Note Pads   184
                Reading the Room: Why No Usually Means No   185
                Going With the Flow When the Story Starts to
                    Change   185
                Be Prepared for Questions   186
                Example of a Pitch   187
                What To Do if They Don't Buy Anything   187
                The Pros and Cons of Putting Your Pitch
                    on Paper   188
                Respecting the Big Foot   188
                Practice Makes Perfect   189

PART IX   TV News Magazine Shows   191

Chapter 18   WRITING FOR TV MAGAZINE SHOWS   193
                "There's Always Going to be News"   193
                It Takes a Special Breed   194

	Is it News or Entertainment?	195
	Why So Many TV Magazine Shows?	195
	The Power Structure of a TV Magazine Show	195
	Writing vs. Producing	196
	The Power of Enterprising Your Own Stories	197
Chapter 19	A MOCK ASSIGNMENT	198
	Getting the Right Angle	198
	Producer Means Boss	198
	You Can Up the Emotion by Using Real People	198
	Why You Need at Least One Expert	199
	How to Find Experts	199
	A Story on J.K.Rowling, Please: Where Do You Begin?	200
Chapter 20	THE SHOOT	202
	Before You Go	202
	Working With Talent vs. Working Solo	202
	Taking Care of Your Crew	203
	Once You Arrive at the Location	204
	What to Do While the Crew Sets Up	204
	When You Do the Interview	205
	When Talent Does the Interview	206
	One Camera or Two?	207
	Getting B-Roll is Key	208
	The Importance of Natural Sound	208
	B-Roll for the J.K. Rowling Story	209
	Do You Need A Stand-Up?	210
Chapter 21	WRITING THE SCRIPT	211
	Sorting Through Your Tapes	211
	What Is Timecode, and Why It Will Save You	211
	What Is a Sound Bite?	212
	Picking The Right Sound Bites To Tell Your Story	212
	What Is Track?	213
	Making Sure Video and Sound Lock Up	213
	When You Don't have the Video	214
	How to Write Your Script	214
	If You Care to Give it a Try	217
	Checklist For TV News Script	220
Chapter 22	IN THE EDIT BAY AND BEYOND ...	221
	Preparing For Your Edit	221
	Working With an Editor	221
	Bringing Your Story in on Time	222
	Getting Story Approval	223
	Writing Powerful Leads and Tags	223
	Ethics in Television News	224
	Other Things You May be Asked to Do	226

PART X   Reality Television   229

Chapter 23   WRITING FOR REALITY TELEVISION   231
                Reality Television is Not New   231
                Why Reality Television is Here To Stay   232
                Why Americans Have Become
                    Reality-Obsessed   233
                Documentary vs. Game Show   233
                Reality is a Producer's Game   234
                Real Compelling Characters   235
                How to Write a Treatment for a
                    Reality TV Show   236
                The Ethics of Reality Television   236

PART XI   Children's Television   237

Chapter 24   WRITING FOR MUNCHKINS AND
                RUGRATS   239
                What Good Children's Programming Should
                    Accomplish   240
                Brand Loyalty   240
                Dual Audiences   242
                Content is Key   242
                Selling Your Children's Show   243
                The One-Minute-Thirty-Second Grind   244

PART XII   The Business Side of Television   249

Chapter 25   HOW TO GET AN AGENT   251
                Why You Need an Agent   251
                What Agents Actually Do   252
                How Much Does an Agent Cost?   252
                Don't Pay People to Read Your Work   253
                Referrals Are the Way to Go   253
                Why Writers Can Be Protective
                    About Their Agents   253
                Choosing an Agent Who's Right for You   254
                Los Angeles or Bar Harbor? Does
                    It Matter Where Your Agent is?   254
                Agents Who Take Unsolicited Scripts   255
                Do You Need a Manager?   256
                Entertainment Attorneys   256
                Querying Agents   256
                Sample Query Letters: Good and Bad   257
                Making Sure You Are Ready   259

	Patience is a Virtue	259
	Should You Put Your Script on Web sites?	260
	Checklist For Getting An Agent	260
Chapter 26	THE WRITERS GUILD OF AMERICA	261
	What Is the Writers Guild Of America?	261
	How Do You Become a Member?	261
	Key Things The WGA Can Do For You	262
	How Residuals Work	262
	What is Arbitration?	263
	In the Event of a Writers' Strike	263
	How to Protect Your Work	264
	Miscellaneous Guild Benefits	264
Chapter 27	WRITING TEAMS	265
	Should You Get a Writing Partner?	265
	The Pros of Partnerships	265
	Being Responsible For Someone Else's Career	266
	The Cons of Partnerships	266
	How To Choose A Writing Partner	267
PART XIII	How to Get Your Foot in the Door	269
Chapter 28	HOW TO GET WORK AS A TELEVISION WRITER	271
	Why You Need a Plan (And a Back-up Plan)	271
	The Importance of Internships	272
	Contact Everyone You Know and Tell Them What You Want	272
	Entry Level Jobs That Can Lead to Your Writing Break	273
	Ways To Uncover Entry-Level Jobs	274
	Resumés and Cover Letters	275
	How to Write Your Resumé	276
	Sample Resumé	277
	How to Write a Killer Cover Letter	278
	Five Paragraphs to a Good Cover Letter	280
	Sample Cover Letter	281
	Generating Informational Interviews	282
	When a Company Says They're Not Hiring (Baloney!)	282
	The Power of Overnighting Your Resumé (Even If You Live One Block Away)	283
	Brushing Up On Phone Etiquette	283
	Why It's Important to Get the Assistant's Name	283

	How and When to Use Voice Mail	284
	How and When to Use E-Mail	285
Chapter 29	GETTING THE INTERVIEW	287
	Preparing For the Interview	287
	Controlling the Interview	288
	Confidence is Key	288
	The Power of Snail Mail Thank-You Notes	289
	Placing the Dreaded Follow-up Call	289
	Turning a "No" Into a "Yes"	290
Chapter 30	CONGRATULATIONS, YOU'VE GOT THE JOB … NOW WHAT?	291
	Some Tasks May Not Make You Smile	291
	Even the Most Mundane and Menial Tasks Can Lead to a Break	292
	Finding a Mentor	293
	Taking Responsibility For Your Goof-ups	294
	Remember Your Goal: Get a Writing Schedule and Stick To It	295
	How Long Should You Stay in an Entry-Level Job?	295
	Planning the Next Step	296
Chapter 31	THE POWER OF NETWORKING	298
	Keeping in Touch is Job Number Three	298
	Order Your Own Personal Note Cards (You'll Need Them)	298
	Stock Up On Business Cards	299
	Creating Your Own Little Black Book	299
	The Importance of Sending Holiday Greetings	299
	How to Do Lunch	300
	Who Do You Invite?	300
	Taking the Lead	301
	When and How To Ask For What You Really Want	301
	Who Pays?	301
	Should You Bring Your Spec Scripts?	302
Chapter 32	OTHER THINGS THAT CAN HELP YOU SUCCEED	303
	Get Yourself Out There as Quickly as Possible	303
	Writing Buddies	303
	How to Turn Up Contacts When You Think You Don't Have Any	304
	Attend Seminars and Conferences	305
	Enter Your Work In Contests	305
	Using Technology to Get Work Seen	305
	Use Your Talent to Help Others	306
	Learn to be a Good Critic	306

Off to See the Wizard (Or Five Months
     to My Dream Job)   306
Not Giving up on What You Want   308
A Word To Women   308
Take Care of Your Mind and Your Body   309
Oh, the Places You'll Go! The Warmth and
     Wisdom of Dr. Seuss   309
Some Final Thoughts   310

SOME LEFTOVER PEARLS   311

INDEX   313

ACKNOWLEDGMENTS

My life and career have been blessed by a seemingly endless parade of smart, talented, and generous people. Many thanks to:

Micki Dickoff, my college professor, who taught me that television is power and with that power comes responsibility and accountability.

Nancy Fawcett who changed everything.

Marilyn Osborn who called every day at 5 a.m. to see if I was up writing — and then called back five minutes later to see if I really was up writing.

Anne Zeiser, Manny Basanese, and Glenn Meehan, always there, answer in hand.

Mentors Bill and Kathy Greer, Al Burton, Adrienne Armstrong, Lee Aronsohn, Marc Warren, Tom Towler, Gail Hickman, Libby Beers, Walter Klenhard, Joel and Neva Cheatwood, Jim Johnston, Marty Ransohoff, and the late, great Harry Tatelman.

Jan Roberts-Breslin who suggested I might be a good person to write this book.

Kate Taylor, Paul Serafini, and everyone in Children's Television at WGBH for your constant commitment to providing quality programming for our children; and to Amy Podolsky for always finding me such great stories.

The Emerson College Administration: Jacqueline Liebergott, Linda Moore, Grafton Nunes, Michael Selig, Barbara Rutberg, and Sherri Mylott for your continuous support of my teaching and of my creative work; and to my colleagues in the Visual and Media Arts Department who make coming to work a joy.

Robert Fleming and the American Comedy Archives for the valuable resources and support provided in connection with this book.

My editors, Becky Golden-Harrell, always encouraging, never pressuring; and Elinor Actipis, for always listening and coming through.

The many people I interviewed for this book, all of who so generously and graciously shared their time and television wisdom. I am forever grateful.

Tom Kingdon, Jean Stawarz, Peter Dunne, Brian Dunnigan, Ross Murray, and Joseph Osmann who reviewed my work. I appreciate your thoughts and enthusiasm.

Marilyn McPoland and Sasha Cartullo for the quick answers to my last minute requests.

Family and friends who gave me a get-out of jail free card from all social commitments while I hibernated to write this book. It will be great to see you all again.

INTRODUCTION

WHAT YOU NEED TO KNOW FROM THE GET-GO

Shortly before I turned sweet sixteen, I begged my mother to take me on a trip to Los Angeles. Most girls my age had their sights set on the junior prom. I was thinking about my future career as a TV writer.

Why my mother actually agreed to this crazy cross-country jaunt is still somewhat of a mystery to me. Whatever her reason, a few months later we left our small Cape Cod town, hopped on a westbound 737 and headed for Southern California. Once there, we drove along the Sunset Strip, strolled the Hollywood Walk of Fame, and marveled at the footprints outside Grauman's Theatre. A few days later, we took the Universal Studios tour. I remember standing in the hills above the studio, looking down at the glimmering soundstages through a thick haze I would later come to know as smog. I was in heaven. "Some day I am going to work here," I declared.

"Are you?" she asked in a way that said "I'll believe it when I see it."

Thirteen years later, I was back at Universal on Stage 42, this time as a writer, watching my first show, an episode of *Charles In Charge* being taped. The dream had come true.

If it sounds like becoming a TV writer was easy, the truth is, it was anything but. In the 13 years between high school and the sale of my first script, I worked harder than I have ever worked in my life. I went to college, earned a degree, moved 3000 miles away from family and friends, and got my foot in the door by working entry-level production jobs at Columbia Pictures and Universal Studios. For 6 long years, I paid my dues: getting people coffee, taking phone messages, fetching lunch, Xeroxing, and typing. And that was just to pay the bills.

In order to get my writing career up and running, every day my alarm would blare at 5:00 a.m. I'd stumble out of bed in the early morning darkness, turn on my computer and write for 2 hours before going to work. On weekends it was more of the same. I turned down invitations to beach parties and barbecues and instead drove to my office where I wrote and rewrote, feverishly perfecting script after script in hopes of catching the attention of producers and agents. There were days — lots of them — when I thought I would never catch a break.

If it was hard to find work as a television writer then, it is, perhaps, 1000 times more difficult now.

You may be wondering, how can this be? Gone are the golden days of television in which there were three networks that produced limited programming, and therefore comparatively limited opportunities for TV writers. Today, cable television is exploding, and it's all about original programming. Companies like HBO, Showtime, Lifetime, and Disney are churning out series after series, movie after movie. All of these programs have to be written by someone, right? The answer is yes, and that's the good news.

The bad news is, that while the need for television writers has dramatically increased, the competition for jobs has never been so fierce. Enter the office of any agent, producer, or studio executive on any given day and it is almost certain to be piled floor to ceiling with scripts from writers hoping to find work. This should come as no surprise. Television writing is both lucrative (A 1-hour network script currently goes for $30,145) and fun (who hasn't secretly fantasized about putting words into Tony Soprano's mouth?).

And let's not forget the fame factor. Not so long ago, TV viewers didn't give an owl's hoot who wrote the shows they watched. Today, writers like Larry David, Marc Cherry, and J.J. Abrams are as much household names as the actors who bring their characters and dialogue to life. Add to this the fact that, when done well, television writing actually looks *easy*. Thus hoards of people, from the recent college graduate to the untrained couch potato think they can do it.

In addition to the inexperienced writers, the industry is also overcrowded with established writers who have long lists of credits and accolades. When hit series like *Frasier* and *Seinfeld* go off the air, the writers from those shows almost always move on to other programs. If that weren't bad enough, feature film writers also now hunger for a piece of the television pie. Once upon a time, television writing was considered inferior to feature film writing. TV writers were quietly — and sometimes not so quietly — thought of as hacks, while feature film writers were put on pedestals and branded "artists." Today the barriers between the two are almost nonexistent. With fewer and fewer theatrical releases, feature writers are flocking to television like never before. Megatalents like Alan Ball (*American Beauty*) think nothing of picking up an Oscar and waltzing off of the stage into series television (*Six Feet Under*). This is partly because companies like HBO and Showtime have become well known for producing programs that are innovative, groundbreaking and more often than not, oh so risqué. TV has also developed a reputation as a place where writers can actually get projects made. Impossible as it may be to get a new TV series off of the ground, it's still a heck of a lot easier than getting a feature film produced.

What this all boils down to is that television writing has not only come into its own, it's become downright hot. Writing for the small screen has suddenly become the cool thing that nearly everyone wants to do. However competitive you imagine it to be, it is probably a hundred thousand times more so.

But, there is more good news. Despite the intense competition, Hollywood is always open to — make that searching for — a fresh voice with a cutting edge point of view. And the truth is, new writers break into the TV industry every day. So how do you bull your way through all of the competition and stand out amongst the pack? First, you must master your craft. You must learn to create dynamic stories that border on the outrageous rather than the bland, while at the same time are character specific and match the feel, style, and direction of the show. Next, you must come to realize that in today's competitive marketplace, it is not nearly enough to just be a great writer. In order to get work produced, you must also develop a keen understanding of the business side of television writing.

In the pages that lie ahead, I will teach you how to craft smart, original scripts and teleplays. I will educate you in how the TV business operates, and I will offer proven tips on how to best get your work off of your computer and into the hands of agents, producers, and executives. Like an Olympic coach trains a prizefighter, I will push you to your outer-most limits. The journey will be difficult. I will sugarcoat nothing. You will probably get frustrated many times along the way. And when we are finished, the only thing I can promise in absolute good faith is that, script in hand, you will be ready to step into the ring. Beyond that, there are no guarantees. Lesson Number One: The industry is full of really great writers, most of who are out of work.

Now, that we are clear on what I bring to this relationship, let's talk about you. In order for us to succeed, there are things you must bring to the table as well — things I cannot teach you. First, you must reach into the very depths of your soul and come up with an unfailing commitment to both yourself and to your TV writing career. Here and now, you must promise to write every day, even if it's only a page. Excuses don't interest me. We can all find a gazillion reasons not to write. At the end of the day, excuses only stall the dream.

Next, you must vow to live life to its fullest. On one hand, the TV industry reaches out to young writers — on the other hand, young writers are often criticized for churning out scripts that are void of emotion and lack a definitive point of view. To truly be a successful television writer you must extend your scope and vision further than your own backyard. You can't write what you don't know. So get out and explore the planet. See firsthand how other people live. Volunteer at soup kitchens, hospitals, homeless shelters, nursing homes, and crisis centers. It may not be glamorous, but it will make your writing rich.

You must also develop a strong sense of self. Writing, like all art, is subjective. The plain and simple truth is that not everyone is going to love everything you write. Sometimes the criticism will be valid, sometimes downright ridiculous. Either way, it's not going to feel good. As you put your work out there, you may knock on a hundred doors, and they may all slam in your face. At a core level, you must believe in yourself and in your talent with such vigor that you are able to pick yourself up, brush yourself off, and find the courage and confidence to knock on door number one-oh-one.

As much as you will need your ego to succeed, you must also keep it in check. TV writing may be fun, and if you achieve any kind of success, people will probably fawn all over you. But when all is said and done, you must remember that it is, after all, only entertainment. Lesson Number Two: Writing for television is not nearly as noble as finding a cure for cancer or stomping out world hunger, or a whole bunch of other things.

You may be scared, wondering if you can actually do this. I don't have the answer to that. I can only say that you won't know for sure unless or until you try.

A week after I was hired to write the episode of *Charles In Charge* I ran into Bill Greer, the show's supervising producer and head writer. Standing outside the Universal commissary in the blinding California sun, he asked me how the script was coming. "Okay," I told him, hoping he didn't notice that my nose was starting to grow. The reality was, 7 days into script, and I was still on page 1. My moment of truth had finally arrived, and I was paralyzed by self-doubt and an overwhelming fear of failure.

"I hope I can do this," I remember muttering. "I've never really written anything before."

Sensing my apprehension, Greer quietly put his arm around me, smiled reassuringly and replied "Neither did Shakespeare…until the first time."

PART I

HOW HOLLYWOOD WORKS

1
AN OVERVIEW OF THE TV INDUSTRY

The one constant about television is that television is constantly changing. The way the business operates today won't be precisely how it works tomorrow.

Understanding what drives television as an industry can be almost as important to your career as writing a solid script. In the same way insurance salesmen stand around the water cooler talking about new state regulations, as a writer you must be in the know about the entertainment industry. You must possess a wealth of knowledge of where television has been in the past, where it stands today, and perhaps most significantly where it is headed in the future. On any given day, topics like what shows are hot, what shows are not, and who the show runners are and where they came from (as in what shows they used to run) must roll off your tongue like a second language.

Staying on top of this ever-changing picture can be more than a challenge. The best and easiest way to stay current is to read the industry trade journals, namely *Variety* and *The Hollywood Reporter*. These daily magazines are delivered to studio and network executives as well as to writers and producers and directors. Nearly everyone in the business from the most seasoned professional to the newest intern reads these papers faithfully every day. So should you. It is here that you will find up-to-date information on the industry in which you plan to become employed. You will discover precious tidbits like recent deals that have been made, TV shows that have been picked up, TV shows that have been canceled, who is suing who and why, TV ratings, who's been hired, who's been fired, and hundreds of other pieces of important information that will help keep you in the know. The last thing you want is to find yourself in the company of industry insiders and you can't join the conversation because you are uninformed.

"Come to Hollywood. Go to as many parties and events as you can. Stay somewhat sober so that when you speak, people can understand your words. Then rub elbows with as many people as physically possible. Remember … don't go to parties with people who are plumbers and mechanics. They really won't help your writing career. Also get the industry trades: *Variety* or *The Hollywood Reporter*. If you can't afford to buy them,

> steal them. Read the articles. Know what's going on in the business. Remember the names of people you read. These people will be at these parties and events. Talk to them with the knowledge you get from these trades. Compliment them. They will love you. They may remember you. They may hire you. Oh, and have a spec script or two in the wings that you can send them in case they ask." — John Frink, co-executive producer, *The Simpsons*

If you live in New York or Los Angeles, *Variety* and *The Hollywood Reporter* are relatively easy to get your hands on. If you live outside of these two cities, you can get a subscription either by mail or online. You should also make a habit of reading the *L.A. Times* Entertainment and Business sections. If you don't have time to do this every day, you should at least make a valiant attempt to read them on Sunday. Again, they are loaded with industry news. And since you are in a reading mode, plan to devour the same sections of *The New York Times* — and while you are at it, be sure to make *The Wall Street Journal* part of your routine as well. Knowledge is power. If you are to succeed as a television writer, you can't live in a shell. It is imperative you are up to date with what is going on in your industry, and that includes even the seemingly minor stuff.

At the risk of overwhelming you, while I have recommended certain sections in the above papers, the truth is that you should read at least one major newspaper cover-to-cover every day. If you absolutely don't have time to do that, then make sure that you catch at least one TV newscast per day. Turn on the local news while you are getting ready for school or work. Flip on CNN while you are eating dinner. Television is a reflection of society and the way we live our lives. To succeed as a writer, not only do you need to know what is going on in the big, bad world around you, but you also need to have an opinion about it — and you need to be prepared to put that opinion forward in a clear, concise way at any given moment. Good scripts have definitive points of view. How can you have a point of view on something you know nothing about?

In addition to your writing, you will also need to be up to speed on current events in order to carry on intelligent conversations with people in the industry. There tends to be a huge misconception among young, wannabe writers that those in the entertainment business (Californians in particular) are a bunch of shallow, not-so-bright people who sit around all day waxing their surfboards and bodies. Let me assure you — just the opposite is true. While every industry has its share of morons, I have found the majority of people who work in entertainment to be incredibly smart. They are up to date with what's going on in the world around them. These are people who know the names of their senators and congressmen and how to reach them. Do you? If not, it's time to get on the ball.

IT'S CALLED SHOW BUSINESS FOR A REASON

Most writers will tell you that the entertainment industry today is about 30% "show" and 70% "business." Like every other major corporation around the globe, studios and networks exist for one reason and one reason alone — to make money. The same way Ford profits by selling cars, and Coca-Cola makes money off of its soft drinks, studios and networks make money off of their shows. If a show isn't bringing in revenue, it will be canceled.

Television shows, often along with careers, live and die by what are known as the Nielsen ratings. Nielsen is the primary industry-approved company that gathers important data on what shows America is watching. In analyzing those numbers, it is also easy to see what America isn't watching. The tricky thing about Nielsen ratings is that, while technology tells us what shows people are tuning in to see, there is no real effective way to gauge whether viewers actually like or dislike the programs they choose. Ironically, when all is said and done, this amazingly creative industry is driven by math. The bigger a show's ratings, the more advertising dollars that show generates. This is the reason super bowl ads are notoriously sky high.

> "I have a tremendous respect for the audience. I believe the audience knows what they want, and I believe television is a reflection of that. If you respect the audience and respect what they want, it's easier to create programming." — Lucie Salhany, former chairman, FOX Broadcasting Company; founding president and former CEO, United Paramount Network (UPN)

Once upon a time, if a show wasn't doing well in the ratings, but it had critical acclaim — or the network brass believed in it — the network would stand behind it and keep it on the air, giving it a chance to catch on. Today that is simply not the case. With production costs skyrocketing, if a network doesn't see an almost immediate return on its investment, the show is taken off the air. Likewise, letter-writing campaigns were once considered a powerful weapon that television audiences had at their disposal. If viewers were passionate about a particular show, but it had low ratings and the network decided to cancel it, fans could — and would — write letters by the truckload, asking the network to reconsider. Many of these campaigns were successful in saving several shows from certain death, including *Star Trek* (the original series) and *Cagney and Lacey*.

While letter-writing (and now e-mail) campaigns still happen, the punch they pack isn't nearly as powerful as it once was. You may argue that *Family Guy*, which was canceled and then returned to the air, was a result of such a letter-writing campaign. While letters and e-mails from fans may have contributed to the Griffin's return, insiders will tell you that the show's resurrection was more likely a direct result of its popularity in reruns on The Cartoon Network combined with the release of a *Family Guy* DVD, which sold like hotcakes. Thus, FOX realized the show was a potential gold mine. And this is what it all comes down to. In this day and age, shows must perform financially or they go bye-bye.

No one is immune to this rule, including those programs that are backed by powerhouse producers with proven track records. Case in point: *Arrested Development*. Produced by Imagine Entertainment (Oscar-winner Ron Howard's well-respected company), the show had a cult following, won critical acclaim and garnered Emmy awards, including the highly coveted Best Comedy Series. Sadly, *Arrested Development* had big buzz, but lacked acceptable ratings. So FOX pulled the plug.

TECHNOLOGY IS CHANGING THE FACE OF TELEVISION

Technology is quickly altering how and when America watches television. Television is no longer just about the box in the living room that families gather around like they did in the fifties and sixties. Today, in addition to broadcasts, we now have podcasts, which generally require that content be much shorter in length. As I write this, networks and cable companies are scrambling to make deals here, there, and everywhere to get their content distributed through the various means now afforded by technology. Some writers and producers tend to shy away from technology, preferring to focus only on the creative aspects of the industry. If you are one of these people, I say "wake up and smell the coffee cake." Technology is no longer something reserved for pimple-faced geeks and nerds. Rather, it is something everybody in our industry from the high-powered executive to the just-starting-out intern must be aware of and stay on top of in order to be successful.

> "Have a working knowledge of alternative distribution platforms like broadband, PDAs, and cell phones. Increasingly, all programs are being asked to provide different versions to meet the growing demand for alternative delivery systems. It is the near-term future of our business." — Joel Cheatwood, executive director/program development, CNN

PRODUCT INTEGRATION

For decades, networks have relied heavily on Nielsen ratings to set advertising rates. But experts and insiders agree that big changes loom on the horizon. Devices like TiVo, On Demand, Ipods, and cell phones, and the Internet, which allow viewers to watch programs at their leisure, skipping the very ads that paid for the shows to be made, are all-but-guaranteed to revolutionize the entire television industry.

   While no one knows for sure exactly what the future holds in terms of television advertising, product integration — at least in series television and movies of the week — is a good bet. In the past, writing specific products into scripts has been something writers had to stay away from. If a company didn't pay for advertising, networks were not going to promote their product for free. In the future, advertising dollars may well come from product integration, which will work much as it does in feature films. Just as E.T. liked Reese's Pieces, we may soon discover that the TV characters we have come to know and love possess certain commercial tastes as well. As this book goes to press, there is huge debate in the industry as to whether writers will be forced to advertise products within the context of a story. Instead of the generic line, "I'm gonna get a soda," TV characters in the future may proudly announce, "I'm gonna get a Caffeine-free Diet Vanilla Coke, made with Nutra-Sweet" (okay, that might be an exaggeration, but you get the point).

Most writers are resistant to this idea, feeling as though it cramps creativity and forces them to write dialogue that is neither character-specific nor natural. At the same time, despite the opposition, writers understand that the industry is changing, and if they want to survive, they will have to change with it. That doesn't mean they are taking it lying down. Currently, the Writers Guild of America, along with other Hollywood unions, is in talks about codes of conduct and ethical issues involving product integration. Writers are also investigating the possibility of being paid for by incorporating advertisements in their scripts.

THE ROLE OF PRODUCTION COMPANIES, STUDIOS, AND NETWORKS

Production companies, studios, and networks work hand in hand. Production companies produce the product. Networks air the product. Think of it this way: without production companies, networks would have little if any programming to broadcast. Without networks, production companies would have a difficult time getting their shows in front of an audience.

No doubt you have heard of the major studios with giant, internationally recognized names such as Warner Bros., Universal, Paramount, and Sony. What you may not realize is that under the umbrella of these large companies are much smaller production entities with names you probably aren't as familiar with, or maybe even heard of at all. These smaller companies produce the shows in conjunction with the name studio. Most, if not all of the networks also have their own in-house production companies. Until recently, studios were completely independent from networks. Now, because of an FCC (Federal Communications Commission) ruling that eased rules on mergers, the relationship between studios and networks is much more incestuous. It's no longer Universal or NBC. Rather, they are one and the same: NBC Universal. The same is true with ABC and Disney, and CBS and Paramount. As if that weren't confusing enough, even though NBC Universal may now be one conglomerate, every television show that is produced at Universal doesn't necessarily air on NBC. And if that doesn't make you dizzy enough, try adding in the numerous other media outlets that fall under a particular banner. For example, it's no surprise that the Disney Channel and ABC Family are part of the Walt Disney Company.

THE DIFFERENCE BETWEEN NETWORK AND SYNDICATION

In the golden days of television there were three networks — ABC, CBS, and NBC. Today we can add FOX and the CW to that distinguished list. All networks have affiliates. Affiliates are smaller stations in every market around the country. Some affiliates are known in industry jargon as O&Os — meaning they are owned and operated by the network. Others are privately owned either by companies or individuals.

Affiliates broadcast the programs carried by the network with which they are affiliated. For example, you should be able to find the *Today* show on every NBC affiliate in America, but you would never find it on a CBS affiliate. Affiliates make a commitment to carry network programming. However, they have the right to — and will on occasion — back out of this deal if the network offers programming they feel may be inappropriate or could get them fined by the FCC. Though this rarely happens, it occasionally does. Some ABC affiliates chose not to air the historic *Ellen* coming-out episode. While most considered this to be ground-breaking television, some considered it inappropriate. Likewise, several affiliates refused to air Steven Spielberg's Academy Award-winning film, *Saving Private Ryan,* because of indecency concerns — namely violence and language — things that can get affiliates in hot water with the FCC. Along the same lines, some CBS affiliates refused to air 9/11, a top-notch documentary about the September 11th terrorist attacks in New York City because some of the firemen muttered obsenities. (In their defense, who wouldn't, with all they must have seen and dealt with that day?) Surprisingly, despite rave revues, some CBS affiliates stuck to their guns with a steadfast refusal to air, deeming the language to be unsatisfactory for their audiences.

There are certain time periods each day during which most affiliates run network programming. The most lucrative is what's known as prime time. Traditionally, prime time is 8:00 p.m. to 11:00 p.m. Eastern and Pacific and 7:00 p.m. to 10:00 p.m. Central and Mountain Monday through Saturday. (Sunday, it starts one hour earlier). With the addition of FOX and the CW, there is "common prime," which is 8:00 p.m. to 10:00 p.m. Eastern and Pacific and 7:00 p.m. to 9:00 p.m. Central and Mountain (again, it begins one hour earlier on Sunday). Affiliates also tend to carry network programming in the morning, with programs such as the *Today* show and *Good Morning America.* Many will then break for a local newscast and pick up network programming again in the afternoon.

Other blocks of time such as early morning, late afternoon, and early evening are set aside for each affiliate to put whatever it chooses on the air. Most, if not all, stations produce their own newscasts. Some may produce other local programming such as a news magazine or a public affairs show. Due to exorbitant production costs, most affiliates can't afford to produce much original programming — in most cases not enough to fill all the local air time. This is where syndication comes in.

Syndicated programs are shows that have been created and produced by another TV entity and then offered up for sale to local affiliates, independents, and cable stations. Think of shows like *Law & Order, Seinfeld,* and *Friends.* Depending on where you live, you can probably see at least one of these shows on a daily basis. Once a show has reached at least a hundred or so episodes, local stations can buy the rights to air the reruns for a set period of time.

But syndicated programs aren't always reruns. Shows like *Dr. Phil, Oprah, Wheel of Fortune, Judge Judy,* and *Jeopardy* are syndicated, but they continue to produce new episodes. This is known as first-run syndication.

Like the networks, local stations make money on these programs by selling advertising. In syndication, shows may be slightly re-edited from their original formats in order to add extra commercial time.

WHAT ARE TELEVISION SWEEPS?

Television Sweeps are the prime rating periods that networks use to set advertising rates. Sweeps months are November, February, May, and July. You may notice that programming is considerably more exciting during these months. Because so much money is at stake, networks do everything they possibly can to pull in viewers. During Sweeps, you will probably see some of the best television of the season, with very few reruns.

Traditionally, it is during Sweeps that most of the so-called big moments occur on TV. Depending on the show, characters may kiss for the first time, get married, have babies, and even get killed off. Financially speaking, the shows that air during Sweeps are so important to the networks and studios that they will almost always be written by one of the staff writers.

STAFF WRITING VS. FREELANCE WRITING

In series television all shows have writing staffs. These writers come to work Monday through Friday in the same way a lawyer or a stockbroker does. The number of staff writers on each show varies, depending on the show's budget. In addition to staff writers, during the course of a season, most shows will farm out a few scripts to freelance writers. Unlike staff writers, freelance writers are not given offices, nor are they on the studio payroll. Rather, they are paid per script. Most writers start out as freelancers and as they get work produced and build professional writing credits they will then (with any luck) wind up with a staff writing job. While writing on a show is anything but easy, staff writing jobs are considered cushy because of the money and many perks that can come with them. For this reason, staff writing jobs are highly coveted and, unfortunately, there are not nearly enough of them to go around.

> "There's a lot of really fun things about being on staff. You get to sit around all day with really bright, funny people. You make jokes, tell pointless stories, doodle, and there's even people that bring you all of this endless free food. It can be easy to lose sight of the fact that, while this might not be a standard nine-to-five desk job, it's still a job. Executive producers are under a tremendous amount of pressure to keep a show on track. So while you're having all this fun, you also have to stay focused. You must be professional and never lose sight of the fact that you're there to contribute to the room and help keep everything moving." — Manny Basanese, writer/producer, *The Steve Harvey Show* and *The Wayans Brothers*

DO YOU HAVE TO LIVE IN L.A.?

If you want to write for series television, you absolutely, positively must live in the Los Angeles area. This is where the TV business is located. If you are to get a staff writing job, your office will be likely be located at a studio or production company in L.A. Writers who resist Los Angeles will ask about New York. Again, most series television is produced in Los Angeles. Even that handful of shows that are actually shot in New York will often come through Los Angeles-based production companies, and those staff writers are generally represented by Los Angeles-based agents. Not to mention that since most of series television is done in L.A., statistically speaking, your odds of finding work as a writer in La-la-land are significantly higher than they are of finding work in the Big Apple.

> "Don't think you're going to do it from Lebanon, New Hampshire. Get off your ass and get out here." — Jay Leno, host of *The Tonight Show*

You will also find that most agents won't take on new writers who don't live in Southern California. The reason is that in order to get hired, you have to be available to meet with producers and executives. Often these meetings are set up quite quickly. I see many wannabe writers delude themselves into thinking that they can write television from the farm in Iowa, get an agent from the farm in Iowa, and then hop on a plane when necessary to take meetings. This is not close to being realistic. Once you enter the professional writing world, you are competing not only with newcomers like yourself, but also with those who have produced writing credits. With all of these qualified writers right at their fingertips, why would a studio or production company go through the hassle and inconvenience of waiting for an unproven writer to hop on a plane? The answer is they wouldn't.

If you are serious about writing for series television, you should want to move to Los Angeles as soon as possible. By living close to your industry, you will be able to open doors and make connections that could eventually help you sell your first script. You also might be able to land an entry-level job and start learning firsthand how the business works. This could get your writing career up and running faster.

WRITING FOR EXISTING SHOWS IS YOUR FIRST STEP

It's important to understand that no one is going to hire you as a TV writer simply because you want to be one. As with any business, in order to get work, you have to prove that you can actually handle the job. Hollywood is heavily unionized, which makes production outrageously expensive. To cut down on costs, production schedules are usually tight, allowing little, if any, room for error. If a script isn't ready for shooting when it is supposed to be, the cost to delay production can be astronomical. Therefore, most producers will not give out writing assignments to unproven writers without being fairly certain that the writer will not only turn in a decent script, but will turn it in on time. So if you are a new writer without a track record, how do you prove to producers that you can in fact step up to the plate and do a professional job? The answer is you write what is known as a "spec" script. In series television, a spec is the first step to getting work as a writer.

WHAT IS A SPEC SCRIPT?

Simply put, a spec script is a writing sample. You don't get paid to write it; however, if done well, your spec could open doors and generate work for you down the road. Think of a spec script as your calling card. The same way actors and models send out head shots in hopes of gaining future employment, you will use your spec script to find work as a TV writer.

> "Have knowledge of the medium. Watch everything that's on. Then pick a show that is respected for its creative execution. It may not be the top-rated show, but people in the industry respond to it and respect it. And don't say, 'I don't want to watch television.' That's like a banker saying, 'I don't want to count money.'" — Jeff Eckerle, writer/producer *"Law & Order: Special Victims Unit "*

Your first order of business is to come up with a story idea for an existing show. Ideally, your story should use all of that show's main characters, and should utilize as many of the show's regular sets as possible. Once you have the story, you will write a sample teleplay from beginning to end. The goal is to have an end product that mirrors the actual scripts that are produced on that particular show.

CHOOSING A SPEC SCRIPT THAT WILL WORK FOR YOU

When you are deciding which show to spec, there are certain criteria that should be considered in order to choose a show that will work for you. To begin with, the show must be currently on the air in prime time. Don't mix this up with shows that have been canceled and are rerunning in syndication. I can't tell you how many times people have said to me, "The only show I watch is *Seinfeld*. So that's what I want to write." Here is my stock response. First of all, if you want to work as a TV writer, you have to be constantly watching television — and yes, that means more than one show. Secondly, writing a spec for a canceled show is a colossal waste of time. Once a show goes off the air, it quickly becomes yesterday's news. Producers generally won't read these scripts and agents won't sign you on them. You must write a spec for an existing program to show that you are current with what is on the air today.

> "When it comes to choosing what show to spec, you should pick a show that you relate to … not the most popular show that you have no affinity for. It should be a show that is well-known but not oversaturated … and that's a tough one." — Kate Boutilier, screenwriter, *Rugrats* and *The Wild Thornberrys*

Before you jump into the saddle, it is advisable to take a big-picture look at your long-term career goals. Where and how do you see yourself fitting in within the TV industry? To help establish where your sensibilities lie, you might want to think about who you are as a person. Are you someone who is exceptional at making people laugh — or do you possess more of a flair for drama? You may also want to look at the kind of TV shows you are most attracted to. If you tend to watch more drama than comedy, you will probably be more comfortable scripting a one-hour drama than a joke-heavy sitcom. But what kind of drama do you find most appealing? Rough-and-tough crime shows like *CSI* or softer, more character driven vehicles like *Grey's Anatomy*? By writing the kind of show that you really have an affinity for, you will probably struggle less, and in the end produce a stronger writing sample. Be aware that, whatever kind of spec script you choose, it's no guarantee of the kind of show you will eventually end up writing for. The spec that got me the most attention was a *Married with Children*. It was deliciously raunchy and extremely fun to write. Ironically, in the sitcom arena it only got me work on squeaky-clean family shows.

After you make up your mind about what show you want to spec, you need to research it carefully before you start writing. Look closely at how well it is doing in the ratings. While you won't always know for sure if a show is going to be picked up for another season, you can usually make an educated guess. If its ratings are at all iffy, I would steer clear of it. As you are about to find out, writing a solid spec script takes an enormous amount of time and energy. The last thing you want to have happen is to work as hard as you are going to have to work only to find out that once you have finished the show has been canceled and you have to start all over again at square one. If you can find a show that looks like it will be around for a few years, all the better. As long as a show is on the air, you will have a current spec script that can continue to be sent out. Though it happens infrequently, there are shows — usually those that are doing extremely well in the ratings — that networks make commitments to a year or more in advance. These shows tend to be a good bet to spec because it is likely that by choosing one, you will have a writing sample that is current for at least a few seasons.

> "Write a sample. Make sure every word is exactly what you want it to be. Go over it and over it and over it until each line says and exemplifies exactly what you want to say." — Tom Towler, supervising producer, *JAG*; writer, *BTK Killer*

Writing a spec for a brand new show can also be risky. In the first season, shows often struggle to find their voice and identity. Things change as the writers and producers get a feel for who the characters are and where they are going. Also, if the show isn't an instant mega-hit, there may be some producers on other shows who won't be as familiar with it, which can be problematic when it comes to getting it read. Beware of shows that are too obscure for the same reason. Producers have to have a general idea of what the show is and who the characters are in order to evaluate your writing and your script.

Each season a few breakout shows quickly become hits. I commonly refer to these as "the flavor of the month." They are the shows that every writer wants to spec. While there is technically nothing wrong with writing one of these shows, I think it can put you at a slight disadvantage. Let's say you decide to spec a *Desperate Housewives,* which happens to be one of the specs that everyone is writing. When you send it out to an agent, that agent will likely take it home to read over the weekend with 10 other scripts. If 6 of the 10 are *Desperate Housewives* specs, how well do you think the agent will remember your script by Monday morning? The answer is probably not that well. If, however, there were 6 *"Desperate Housewives"* specs, but you wrote a dynamite episode of *Law & Order* your script would have a much better chance of standing out among the pack.

The same thing is true when your agent sends your spec for producers to read. Producers grow tired of reading specs for the same show over and over again. Often the scripts that aren't "the flavor of the month" end up getting writers noticed.

STUDYING THE SHOW BEFORE YOU WRITE

Before you hunker down to write — or even come up with a story for your spec — it is imperative that you sit down and watch the show over and over again. It is virtually impossible to write a stand-out spec script for a show you have seen only once or twice. If possible, you should tape the show. Then play it back repeatedly. Listen to how the characters talk. What is the rhythm of their dialogue? Who are they as people? What do they value? Also, check out the sets. Which ones are used every week? Which ones are used most often? You'd be surprised at how much you miss when you see a show only once. These seemingly minor details will all become major points when you write your spec.

> "The key for any new writer is to produce a great spec script. Pick a show you love. Take the time to research it. Watch it over and over until you get the voice of the characters." — Marc Warren, executive producer, *Full House* and *That's So Raven*

PURCHASING A SAMPLE SCRIPT OF THE SHOW YOU WANT TO WRITE

In addition to taping your show, it is also a smart idea to purchase an actual hard copy of a produced script for the show you intend to write. There are many reasons to do this, the most important being that you are trying to write a script that looks similar to the produced scripts of the actual show. Therefore, you need to get everything right. Having a produced script to refer to will be incredibly helpful. Little things that you may not think about will become key as you write. To give you an example, let's look at the show *Law & Order*. Can you tell me, off the top of your head, how the producers refer to Jack McCoy's office in scripts? Is it "Jack McCoy's office" or "McCoy's office" or "executive ADA's office"? My guess is that you probably don't have a clue. That's okay. However, when it comes to actually writing your spec, you must get it 100% correct. I can all but promise you that as you write, you will come to places that you just aren't sure of. Having a produced script at your fingertips will help ensure that all of your "Ts" are crossed and your "Is" are dotted.

Another reason that it is good to have an actual script is for formatting issues. As you will see once we get going, while there are general rules for formatting a script, each show puts its own, ever-so-slight spin on those rules. By having an actual script, you'll be able to see exactly how the writers of the show handle various issues.

> "Read everything and see everything. Then dig deep into who you are as person, as a character, as a human. What unique point of view can you add to a story? Then forget everything you've seen before you and focus on a story/pitch/idea that only you could tell." — Steve Stark, executive producer, *Medium*; president, Grammnet Producers

There are lots of places that you can buy scripts of shows that have been produced. Generally, they aren't that expensive — usually around $10. Personally, I buy scripts over the Internet from a company called Script City (www.scriptcity.com) because they have a fairly large selection of TV scripts. But anywhere you can find them — as long as they are copies of an actual produced show — will be fine.

It may be difficult to find scripts of newer shows — especially those that are in their first season. If you have decided to spec a new show and you absolutely can't get your hands on one of their scripts, then buy a script that is similar to the show you want to write. For example, if you are scripting a one-hour drama that is plot-driven, an episode of something like *Law & Order* or *CSI* would be a better example than an episode of *The Simpsons*.

Steer clear of downloading scripts from random sites on the Internet. You have no way of knowing who typed the material or how meticulous that person was. In my TV Writing classes, I always require my students to buy a script for whatever show they want to spec. I warn them repeatedly about the dangers of downloading scripts. I explain ad nauseam that people who read scripts for a living have extremely trained eyes. Mistakes are spotted in a heartbeat. Without fail, each semester, one or two students don't heed the advice. At the end of the semester, they turn in their spec scripts and I immediately see places where their format is miles off. When I push them, they sheepishly admit downloading scripts from cyberspace. Don't fall into that trap. Believe me when I say that improperly formatted scripts equal not getting hired.

WHY TWO (SIGH!) SPECS ARE BETTER THAN ONE

I wish I could tell you that once you have finished and polished your first spec script, you can sit back and relax. Unfortunately, you just can't. You now need to write a second spec script. Most agents will want to see at least two writing samples before signing you. Unbelievable as it may sound, there seems to be a tendency among agents to think that if a new writer has one good spec script, it could be a fluke. Before signing you, agents want to be sure that you are someone who can consistently pump out good script after good script. Therefore, they will usually require two samples.

Another reason for needing more than one writing sample is that some producers are more finicky than Morris the Cat. When it comes to television, many have definitive likes and dislikes. You have to give them what they want. If your only sample is a *My Name Is Earl* and the producer who is going to read your work vehemently dislikes *My Name Is Earl*, even if you have written the most brilliant *My Name Is Earl* script in the entire Milky Way, chances are you still won't get hired by that particular producer. Therefore, it's good for your agent to be able to offer up another choice.

When writing a second spec script, it is imperative that you don't spec the same show. You want to be able to demonstrate that you are a writer with huge range. If you are doing comedy and you have written a traditional sitcom like *Two and a Half Men*, it might be wise to try your hand at a single-camera show like *Scrubs* or an animated show like *South Park*. In the same vein, if you are writing drama and your first spec script is a character-driven show like *Grey's Anatomy*, then you might want to try a plot-driven drama like *CSI*. The goal is to prove that you are versatile — put you on any writing staff and you will be able to handle it. That said, if shows like *CSI* are not your cup of tea — and not in the realm of what you feel comfortable writing — then you shouldn't do it because your final product will probably reflect that. In which case, you should choose another character-driven show. Just be sure to look for one that doesn't too closely mirror the spec that you already have under your belt.

Once you have two solid spec scripts, you may want to round off your portfolio with an original sample. This could be a television pilot (see Part IV), a play, or even a short story. At a time when producers and agents are constantly looking for writers with a fresh take on material and a unique point of view, it is quite possible they will ask to see something original before making a commitment to you.

WRITING IS REWRITING

The worst disservice you could do yourself is to think that your first draft is your final draft. A spec script is the most important script you will ever write. Everything is riding on it. Therefore, it is hugely important that you take the time to rewrite it and rewrite it and rewrite it. You need to get it as near-perfect as is humanly possible. If you are a brand new writer and you whip out a spec script in a couple of days – or even a couple of weeks for that matter, I can almost promise you that it isn't as good as it can be.

> "You have to have a total myopic devotion. Writing is such a time commitment. Writing is about rewriting. You're never gonna get there through the first draft. We were willing to — and did — throw out entire drafts two days before taping. If it's on the page, it'll be on the stage." — Max Mutchnick, creator, executive producer, *Will and Grace*

THE REASON YOUR SPEC PROBABLY WON'T SELL

Once a spec script is finally finished, new writers will often be so thrilled with the accomplishment that they will want to shove the script in an envelope and send it off to said show to be produced. Unfortunately, spec scripts almost never get produced and there is a legitimate reason.

If you are Marc Cherry — or anyone on the *Desperate Housewives* writing staff — you know each of the characters intimately. Their voices resonate inside your head day after day, night after night, and even in the wee hours of the morning when you wish they would pipe down so you can get some sleep. You know absolutely every minor detail about their past because you've written it. As a freelance writer, no matter how much you study a show before you write it, you simply won't have the same inside track that the show's writers and producers do. So, if you have written a spec *Desperate*

Housewives, it is quite probable that here and there throughout your script you may have things that are slightly off. It could be a minor story or character point or it could be that your dialogue isn't exactly character-specific. When your agent sends your spec script to the writing staff of *Desperate Housewives,* they will no doubt pick up on the flaws in your script instantly, and they will conclude that you don't know their show.

On the other hand, when your agent takes that same *Desperate Housewives* script and sends it to shows like *Lost* or *Grey's Anatomy,* the producers of those shows may not see the flaws. The reason is that they are so busy writing and producing their own shows that, like you, they may watch *Housewives,* but they don't know it like the back of their hand. So any little bumps in your script will generally go unnoticed by the producers of another show.

> "You never write a spec script with the idea that it's going to be produced. It's not. That's not what you want your spec script to do. Produced shows suck. Yours has to be better than that. You might also shoot for a show that lasts a few years so you don't have to write another stupid spec script. " — John Frink, co-executive producer, *The Simpsons*

While most agents will eventually send your spec script to the show you have written, they usually don't expect much. Neither should you. However, there are lots of other shows out there where you or your agent can submit your work. If your spec script is outstanding, there is a chance you will get hired.

DECLARING YOUR MAJOR (AND MINOR)

In series television, there are comedy writers and there are drama writers. Most writers don't bounce back and forth between the two. Therefore, you must declare yourself as one or the other. This is how your agent will generally sell you.

That said, once you have written two solid spec scripts in either the half-hour format or the hour-long format (and something original,) it might be a good idea then to write a spec for the opposite. So if you've decided you want to write comedy and now have two good samples, I suggest that you spec a drama and keep it in your back pocket. The reason is that most of the time, comedy producers won't read drama specs and drama producers won't read comedy specs. As you will soon see, drama and comedy are, in their own ways, extremely different. Thus, it becomes difficult for producers who work in one area to accurately judge the other. In order to keep all of your prospects open, it is wise to have at least one script in the opposite arena. You have to be ready when opportunity knocks, and in Los Angeles that can happen anytime anywhere. You never know who you might meet at a party or even standing in line at the grocery store.

GETTING YOUR SCRIPTS READ

PLASTERING THE TOWN WITH YOUR WORK

Once you have two solid specs under your belt, your next order of business will be to get an agent (see Chapter 25). A good agent will contact various producers and executives and pitch you as a hot new writer who is about to take off. The agent's goal is to get your work read quickly by people who have the power to hire you. Getting read is the first step to getting produced.

Keep in mind that your agent is one person with many clients. Therefore, it would be a good idea for you also to go through your own list of industry contacts and make phone calls in an attempt to get your work read. Dig deep and contact everyone you know. Call former bosses you once interned for. Get in touch with the Alumni Association of your alma mater and ask if they can put you in touch with any alums working in the industry. Contact friends who know people and ask them to hook you up.

> "Know what you're getting into. There are always stories of the kid right out of college who wrote a spec, got hired on staff, sold a pilot, and got a show on the air right out of the box. It does happen, but so does hitting the lottery. The reality is, you'll be writing numerous specs, facing countless rejections, and wondering if they're still hiring at the Post Office. But if you're absolutely certain you've been chosen by God to write for television and you can't imagine doing anything else with your life, you may just be crazy enough to succeed. Use all the tools at your disposal to get your material to agents and producers. Everyone working in the industry got their foot in the door through some type of connection. If you need to track down your aunt's ex-husband's mother-in-law's best friend who knows somebody who used to work at CAA, do it." — Marc Warren, executive producer, *Even Stevens* and *That's So Raven*

If you feel uncomfortable asking for favors, here's a word of advice: don't. Everybody in the business has asked for help at one time or another. I can assure you with reasonable certainty that there are writers out there who probably aren't half as talented as you, but are more than willing to make the calls that will get them ahead. Getting your first writing assignment and making that jump from wannabe writer to professional writer is extremely difficult. You need to do everything you possibly can to maximize your chances. Putting yourself and your work out there takes courage, I know. But it is a necessary evil on the road to success.

THE INITIAL MEETING

Let's say that one of your spec scripts is *The Office*. Your agent has sent the script to various comedy producers who have agreed to read it. One of the most difficult things to swallow about writing is that it is 100% subjective. You can send the exact same script to 10 producers; 2 or 3 will think it's the best thing they have ever read, while another 2 or 3 will say it's not good enough for the garbage can. The rest will probably fall somewhere in the middle. But those 2 or 3 producers who are fans of your work may contact your agent and request to meet you.

When a producer likes your writing, he or she will take a giant leap of faith and assume that if you can write a professional and funny spec, you can probably write a professional and funny script for their show as well.

For the sake of argument, let's say the producers of *Two and a Half Men* have read your script and want to meet you. What they are really saying is that there is a possibility they will want to hire you, even if it's only to write one script. But first they want to see who you are and what you are all about.

Before you take an initial meeting with producers, it is imperative that you have seen their show. After all, you are hoping to instill enough faith in them that they will hire you to write an episode. You may be thinking, "what's the big deal? The worst thing that can happen is I turn in a not-so-great script, right?" Let me be crystal clear about this so you have a complete understanding of what is at stake for producers when they take a chance on an unproven writer. If you do a less-than-stellar job, the writing staff will have to step in at the last minute and rewrite your script. Some rewriting in television is par for the course, but when it's a "page one rewrite" — meaning they have to scrap almost everything you wrote and start again from scratch — you probably won't be hired back. Production is expensive, with everything being unionized. If a show gets too far behind, the results can be disastrous, both creatively and financially. The only way they will even consider hiring you is if you assure them without a doubt that you can in fact deliver a great script on time. If you haven't ever seen their show, you won't be able to do that. Questions like "Now which guy does Charlie Sheen play?" aren't going to instill confidence. Think of it this way: would you buy a car from a salesman who knew nothing about the make and model you were interested in purchasing? Plan to watch the show as many times as you can before the meeting. If you aren't familiar with the show, research it on the Internet. See if any of the previous seasons are out on DVD. If not, consult your *TV Guide*. You may be able to catch past episodes in syndication. Occasionally, if a show is new enough, producers may well provide you with sample scripts and a few episodes to take home and watch. But if a show has been on the air for a while, they will rightfully expect that you have done your homework and are familiar with it.

Initial meetings with producers (thankfully) tend to be very low stress, because at this point nothing has been offered. It's really just an informal meet-and-greet to see if you click. Usually, you will sit down and have a cup of coffee and the producer will compliment you on your writing and how wonderfully brilliant your spec script is.

After a few minutes of polite chit-chat, the conversation will shift to the show itself. You need to listen very carefully to what is said. They will likely tell you what stories they are currently working on, as well what their current needs are. You should feel free to ask questions about particular kinds of stories they are looking for; or, if they are looking for stories that revolve around a certain character. Often writers and producers may have countless story ideas for one character, but are coming up dry with stories for another character. That's where you can help — and at the same time increase your chances of making a sale. If you know there is something specific they are looking for, you can focus on that area if you get invited back to pitch.

"Your spec script has to be good enough to win an Emmy. You must work harder on it than you will ever work on a script again. That spectacular script will land you an agent, he'll get you some outside episodes, and you'll get your first staff job. You will be ecstatic, and rightly so. Now here comes the important advice: Work as hard as you can on your show; be a team player; eat, drink and sleep your show; but always have your feelers out for your next job. Tell your agent to set up getting-to-know-you meetings with producers of other shows, and network, network, network. Producers put more value on a working writer. It will be a lot easier to line up your next job while you're still on staff than it will be to find a job when you're just another out-of-work writer. More than anything, I wish someone had given me this advice when I was on staff." — Adrienne Armstrong, writer, *Charles in Charge*

THE INVITATION TO PITCH

If all goes well at the initial meeting and the show has a need for a freelance episode, the meeting will probably end with an invitation to come back and pitch. What this means is that you will go home, think up several story ideas for the show, and then come back and pitch them verbally to the producers (see Chapter 17). This meeting, while far from formal, will not be as laid back as the initial meeting. There is a lot at stake for you. If they like one of your ideas, they may buy it, catapulting you from wannabe writer to professional writer.

WHAT HAPPENS IF THEY BUY YOUR STORY?

If the producers decide to buy one of your stories, you will be called back for yet another meeting. This meeting will probably be with most, if not all of the writing staff, and it usually takes place in "the writers' room" or, as writers like to call it, "the room." This is the where the writing staff gathers to work — usually around a conference table.

At this meeting, you will do what is known as beating out or breaking a story. With the help of the writers and producers, you will take the seeds of your original pitch, which was pretty much in broad strokes, and you will start to make definitive decisions about what actually happens in the story. You will start with the first scene and get right down to the nitty-gritty by figuring out where the action takes place and what actually happens in that scene. You will do this for every scene in the story from beginning to end.

Beating out a story is an extremely collaborative process. As each scene is discussed, writers will toss out ideas about what can happen. You should also kick in ideas when you can. This can be horribly intimidating for a new writer. You may feel like the writing staff knows the show better than you do — or worse, you may be afraid of tossing out a stupid idea. That's okay ... do it anyway. Your job as a writer is not simply to write, it is to contribute to the story and to the script as a whole. Don't worry if the staff doesn't go for every idea you come up with. This is all part of the process. Just keep spitting out ideas. If you sit in silence, you are not doing your job. Worse still, what will most likely happen is that the exact same ideas that are dancing quietly in your head will eventually be put forth by another writer. If it's an idea the staff loves, you will be kicking yourself for not speaking up.

> "Half the battle is sitting in a chair and letting your muse come. You start out just typing, but then somewhere the typing turns into writing. You have to earn your muse." — Marilyn Osborn, writer, *The X-Files*; consulting producer, *Touched By An Angel*.

The executive producer (or the show runner) makes the final call on what he or she wants in each scene. It is imperative to pay close attention and follow along with everything that is being decided, as your next step will be to go home and write a story outline. Often when stories are broken, there is an assistant in the room that takes notes, types them up, and sends them your way. But you can't count on it. You should definitely take notes on your own. Once you begin to write the outline, there will be pressure enough. The worst thing that can happen is that you forget things that were decided upon in the meeting because you weren't fully paying attention or jotting stuff down.

If you are doing a comedy and another writer hollers out a funny joke, you should feel free to use it. This is not considered stealing, as you are technically collaborating on the story. Part of a staff writer's job is to contribute to the show as a whole, and that means helping out with other people's scripts.

After the story meeting is over, you will then go home and write a professional scene-by-scene, act-by-act outline. You should do this as quickly as possible without sacrificing the quality of the writing. Unless they are massively behind, most producers would rather see a writer spend a couple of extra days and turn in a good outline than pump up the volume and hastily turn in a mediocre outline that requires tons of work.

As you write the story outline, it is imperative that you spit back everything that was decided in the story meeting. Now is not the time to be a cowboy. A quick way to make producers burning mad is to go home and write an outline that doesn't reflect what was discussed and agreed-upon in the writers' room. Doing it your way will likely end up getting you lost. The end result will be that you turn in a story that doesn't work or a story that the producers don't like. If that happens, you will have risked putting the show behind schedule because the outline will need to be redone. This is not to say, however, that as you write the outline new ideas won't pop into your head. That's fine as long as you call the producers and get the changes approved before you put them in the outline.

Once you have turned in the story outline, the producers will put in the paperwork so that you will be paid. If they end up producing your episode — which they almost always will, unless the show is canceled — you are all but assured to receive story credit both on the script and on the screen.

WILL YOU WRITE THE TELEPLAY?

Usually when producers buy a story from a freelance writer, they will allow that writer to write the teleplay, but this is not guaranteed. Producers have the right to "cut you off at story," which means the actual script will be written by another writer, usually someone on staff. Reasons for cutting you off can vary. If you turned in an outline that was sub-par or veered too far off from what was discussed in the story meeting, they may not want to take a chance on giving you the script. There can also be other reasons for cutting a writer off that have nothing to do with the particular writer. For example, if a show is running behind schedule and they need the script quickly, they may decide to give it to one of their staff writers. Since a staff writer is more in tune with the show than a freelancer, chances are that writer can turn in a more solid script in less time, thus help keeping production on track.

If you are going to write the teleplay, producers will give you notes on your story outline, before they will send you off to write the first draft. The amount of time you actually have to turn in the script varies from show to show. It is usually no more than two weeks, but in extreme cases where a show is massively behind, I have been asked to write a script within two days. Once your script has been turned in, the producers read it and decide if they want to give you notes and ask you to do a final draft. In theory, final drafts should be considerably less work than first drafts. Usually, you are just cleaning up and making little changes here and there. Many times, producers won't even ask for a final draft. Often because of time constraints, they will simply take your first draft and have the writing staff begin to work their magic on it. If this is the case, you will still get paid for the final draft per the Writers Guild of America contract.

> "Be a prolific writer. Write, write, write, all the time, and keep submitting your stuff. You can be the most talented writer and not work — or you can have limited talent and work all the time. This is a hustle job. Don't sit around talking about writing, which is what a lot of people do. Go out and do it." — Eddie Brill, stand-up comedian, talent coordinator, *The Late Show with David Letterman*

ODDS ARE THEY WON'T STEAL YOUR IDEAS

New writers often worry that when pitching ideas to a show, producers will not buy anything, and then a few months later, a strikingly similar story will appear on the air. The question is, how do you protect yourself? The answer is that you really can't. The only foolproof way to make sure that no one snatches your idea is not to put it out there. Of course, not putting it out there means you won't ever become a writer. While I can't guarantee that your ideas won't be stolen, I can tell you that the chances of this happening are probably less than you think. The reason for this is that producers are always looking for talented writers. Therefore, if you have written a knock-'em-dead spec script and you come to the pitch meeting with really great ideas for their show, you will be someone they want to work with. They will not want to offend you by stealing your ideas. Beyond that, producers are more than aware that if they steal your idea, you could sue. The last thing studios and networks want is a lawsuit. Litigation is both expensive and time consuming.

To make sure that your ideas are not inadvertently stolen, there will usually be a writer's assistant in the room during your pitch. That person will write down the date of your pitch and a logline (a sentence or two that embodies the gist of your idea) for each story that you present. I have seen cases where the producers decide not to buy a story idea pitched by Writer A in October, but for whatever reason, they like a similar idea when Writer B walks in with it in December. Believe it or not, they will usually go back and buy the story from Writer A. This is worst-case scenario and, depending on the circumstances, they may ask the writers to share credit. But again, this is rare.

HOW MUCH WILL YOU MAKE AND WHEN WILL YOU GET PAID?

Most studios and networks are signatories to the Writers Guild of America, which means that when it comes to hiring writers, they abide by union rules. When you sell a script, the WGA has etched in stone — or at least the current contract — the requirements for paying writers. Here are the basics:

- Story. Once you have turned in the story outline, you will be paid the WGA minimum for that story. This varies according to the kind of show you are working on: half hour comedies pay less than hour-long dramas because the scripts are shorter. If you are cut off at story, this will be the only payment you receive except for residuals, if applicable.
- Teleplay. If you write the teleplay, in addition to the story payment, you will also receive a check after you turn in the first draft. Another, smaller check will follow for the final draft, regardless of whether you actually write it.

WHERE DOES IT ALL LEAD?

The goal of turning in a strong script is, of course, that the producers will like you and your work so much that when a staff writing position opens, they will see you as a natural fit and hire you. Every once in a great while, a freelance writer will come along with two spec scripts that are so professionally done that he or she will get scooped up by a show before actually making a sale. But for 9½ out of 10 writers, selling a freelance script is the first step to a writing job. Often, it will take a few freelance gigs before you land as a staff writer on a show. In television, it's all about building credits.

PART II
COMEDY

3

SITUATIONAL COMEDIES

WHAT IT TAKES TO WRITE COMEDY

"Does it have to be funny?" While the answer may seem rather obvious, this is a question I am asked repeatedly. Each time, I am a little taken back. The word "sitcom" is actually a hybrid of two words: situational comedy. What this means at a core level is that sitcoms are about funny people in humorous situations. So yes, sitcoms must be funny — hilarious actually — and the people who write them must be amazingly quick-tongued and witty.

While I can teach you how to find stories, format a script, and set up and pay-off jokes, I cannot, unfortunately, teach you a sense of humor. You are either born with one or you are not.

> "Write it down. Write everything down and don't throw anything away. Ask yourself, 'Do I see funny? Do I hear funny?' Be aware that funny exists all the time, all around you … then keep doing it until you get it right. If you don't have a sense of the whimsical or ironical, no one can make you funny. But if you have it, you can polish it and get funnier." — Bill Dana, writer/comedian.

Think about the people in your life. Now, break them into two groups — those that are funny and those that are not. See how easy that was?

Now, it's your turn. Let's do a little soul searching … and let's be painfully honest. The truth is, deep down, you *know* if you're funny. You know because people tell you and they've probably been telling you all of your life. You know because they laugh at your jokes and they look forward to your stories. You know because you are the life of any party. In high school you were probably one of two people: class clown or smart aleck. (Either, by the way, is a perfect fit for a career in comedy writing.) You can find humor in nearly everything, unlike the more serious-minded people in your life who think topics like politics and religion must be avoided at all costs. Most likely the term "politically correct" is not part of your daily vocabulary, and this is a good thing.

In addition to being funny, there are other traits you must possess in order to succeed in the comedy world. First, you must be bold and daring. The comedy business is not for the shy or bashful. When writing jokes, you have to be willing to take chances. Once you get a staff writing job, part of what you will be paid for is to rewrite scripts. This is a group process. All of the staff writers lock themselves in the writing room and go through a script, line by line, punching it up. You will have to holler out jokes on the spot — which can be nerve wracking to say the least. But again, it is part of what you are being paid the big bucks for. If you sit in the room, like a shrinking violet, I promise you won't last long. You have to understand and be okay with the fact that many of your jokes will bomb and never see the light of day, while a few will get a huge laugh and be put into the script. If you are at all shy, you need to get over it quickly. A good way to do this is to take classes in acting or public speaking — or even join an improv group. Anything to get you comfortable sharing yourself and your work with others. In comedy — good, bad, or ugly — you have to be willing to put it out there.

> "Having a thick skin is crucial because on a good day you will be shot down 8–10 times. You also must have some sociability. You will spend 10–12 hours a day in the room with people. I have seen writers whose success or failure was based on how easy or how hard they were to get along with." Bob Daily, co-producer, *Frasier*; co-executive producer, *Desperate Housewives*.

You should know, too, that the writer's room can be raunchy. When you get a bunch of comedy writers locked into a small space, you can't expect the jokes to be clean and politically correct. Some people are offended by these kinds of jokes. That's okay, but if you are one of them, then comedy writing probably isn't for you. If you are going to sit there like somebody's mother, with a disapproving scowl on your face every time someone makes a joke that you feel is inappropriate, you will be scowling all day and half of the night. This will only serve to make everyone around you uncomfortable. Soon, they will label you as someone who isn't much fun, and you will be gone.

You must also be a team player. Comedy writing is an extremely collaborative process; drama writing tends to be a little less so. Thus, you have to be willing to let go of some of your jokes — even the ones you thought were absolutely brilliant — if the writing staff deems them not funny. It's not about your ego, but rather about what's best for the script.

Another important quality you must have as a comedy writer is unlimited patience. Writing scripts that are funny from beginning to end takes an enormous amount of time and brainpower. I have seen skilled writers work from early evening until sun-up, punching up the jokes in a script. One of the notes I see on scripts (and actually write on scripts I am critiquing) is "funnier line," which translates to "write a better joke." Easier said than done. Nonetheless, a big part of writing is rewriting … and as a comedy writer, you have to push yourself — and I mean really push — in order to find the best possible jokes.

CHECK LIST FOR FUNNY

- Do people constantly tell me I am funny?
- Does my sense of humor border on quirky or unusual?
- Do I usually find humor in every situation?
- Am I a risk taker?
- Am I a team player?

If you answered "yes" to the above questions, then comedy writing is probably a good fit for you. If you answered "no" to some or to most of the questions, then I would caution you that you might have a difficult time writing comedy. It might be wiser for you to try your hand at a different kind of TV writing.

> "The number-one thing I wish someone had instilled in me when I was starting out is to be patient. This can be a brutal business under any circumstances, but if you become bitter that you're not 'making it,' sneering at the people who get 'your' opportunities, cultivating a sense of entitlement — forget it. You'll waste a lot of energy and not get any closer to your goals. No matter what kind of genius you think you are, chances are you won't be discovered overnight. But, believe it or not, that's a good thing. Every day you go undiscovered is a day you can spend getting better at what you do — so when you finally 'are' discovered, you'll be that much more ready." — Eric Drysdale, writer, *The Daily Show* and *The Colbert Report*.

HOW SITCOM WRITING STAFFS WORK

Before you jump in headfirst and start writing your spec script, it is important to understand how the sitcom business works. After all, if your professional goal was to be an airplane pilot, you wouldn't just hop into the cockpit, take off, and hope for the best, would you? My guess is first you'd learn all you could about aviation — you'd study important details like the science of how airplanes work, how they fly, how they land, weather patterns, etc. Likewise, it is crucial to understand how the sitcom business operates before you randomly take off.

THE MAKE-UP OF A SITCOM STAFF

All sitcoms have writing staffs. Unlike freelance writers who may only write one episode — and this is usually done out of their home — staff writers are under contract by a studio and/or production company to write and rewrite the show each week. Staff writers have agents who have negotiated a "deal" on their behalf, meaning they have a detailed, written contract that includes a salary, office space, benefits, and whatever other perks an agent can negotiate. Good agents will also negotiate a certain number of scripts for the writer to write. This is important, as each script that a writer receives a "Written by" credit on means that writer is given extra pay. This can add up to significant amounts. Currently, the Writers Guild of America's minimum for a half hour of network television is $20,495. This doesn't include residuals which, over time, can be staggering, if the show goes into syndication.

When you look at the credits on a sitcom (or a drama), you will probably notice a lot of producer titles. What you may not realize is that most producers are actually writers. A producing title means the writer gets more money, has more power, and usually more responsibility. On any given sitcom, you may find the following writer/producer titles, listed in order of rank:

- Executive producer
- Co-executive producer
- Supervising producer
- Producer
- Co-producer

- Story editor
- Term writer

The writing positions above the line carry the most power. Notice the top dog is the executive producer, also known as the "show runner." Most, though not all executive producers are writers. Think of the executive producer as the big boss. He or she is ultimately responsible for all aspects of the show: overseeing the writing, dealing with network and studio executives, casting, keeping the show on budget, approving the final cut of each episode, and everything in-between. The executive producer can hire you or fire you, and make or break your career. Therefore, it is always a good idea to stay in the executive producer's good graces.

> "Writing good scripts is only one part of making it as a staff writer. You've also got to prove yourself in the room. How you operate in the writers' room can make or break you. Each room has its own personality, so it's important to figure out the hierarchy and what works. I always try to figure out what the show runner responds to, in terms of story, character, and jokes. As a staff writer, it's my job to support the show runner and give him or her what he or she needs." — Manny Basanese, writer/producer, *The Steve Harvey Show* and *The Wayans Brothers*.

On a typical writing staff, some of the positions are filled by single writers, some by writing teams. The number of staff writers and their positions is determined by the show's budget and the writer/producer's previous experience.

In addition to these creative positions, there is also a "line producer." Line producers are not part of the writing staff. They take care of the more technical side, handling the day-to-day budget, making sure sets are built, hiring caterers, and overseeing post-production.

As you can see, the lower positions on a writing staff are the story editor and term writer. Story editors were once considered entry-level positions. It was possible to go from a freelance writer directly to a story editor position. Today, that is much harder to do. The bottom rung of the ladder for new writers is a term writer position. What's the difference between the two positions? It really comes down to money.

In addition to a hefty weekly salary, story editors (along with the rest of the writing staff) get paid for episodes they write. Term writers receive only a weekly salary — and with the exception of residuals, which come later — that's it. The weekly salary is more than decent: somewhere around $3500 per week. You may think that, with the job of your dreams and that kind of cash, who cares if you don't get paid for scripts? The answer is *you* will. After the novelty of going to a studio every day and writing comedy wears off, you will look around and realize that every other writer who writes scripts gets paid for them in addition to receiving a weekly salary and you just get a weekly salary. For most writers, the term-writer gig only lasts for one season, and then they are bumped up to story editor. Keep in mind that being a term writer is an entry-level position that will get your foot in the door, give you practical experience, valid writing credits, and a string of new contacts. While you are paying your dues, you will be paid a good salary to learn what can only be taught in the field, and by doing it every day.

> "It's really important to find your voice. A lot of young writers get an idea for what the "formula" for a sitcom script is. They're so concerned about things like how many jokes they have on a page and where the Act Break is that they lose sight of the character. Those scripts always feel constructed and writerly to me. There's no life to them ... no joy. To me, characters are the most important thing. Scripts where the writer manages to enliven a character with a real point of view always stand out." — Manny Basanese, writer/producer, *The Steve Harvey Show* and *The Wayans Brothers*.

MULTI-CAMERA VS. SINGLE-CAMERA SHOWS

Multi-camera sitcoms are usually shot in soundstages before live audiences. The story generally takes place on a few regular sets, with one or two sets added in any given week, depending on the needs of the particular episode. While the traditional, multi-cam sitcom has been around since the days of *I Love Lucy*, there is a school of thought that it may be dying out. The reason for this may surprise you. It's called reality television.

Reality television has, in its own way, spoiled viewers. While we have been used to watching television that takes place on a few sets, shows like *Survivor* and *The Amazing Race* have taken us literally around the world. We have been visually spoiled. Therefore, a TV show that takes place in a character's living room, kitchen, basement, and bedroom can seem awfully dull. Without even realizing it, we feel confined. Single-camera sitcoms like *Scrubs* and *Curb Your Enthusiasm* offer a lot more freedom and creative opportunities for writers because they aren't limited to just a few sets. While single-camera sitcoms do have some standing sets, they also allow writers the flexibility to write scenes that take place outside of these sets. Audiences seem to appreciate this. The one thing that goes against single-camera shows is that they are much more expensive to produce.

A WEEK IN THE LIFE OF A STAFF SITCOM WRITER

Most multi-cam shows tend to operate on a five-day schedule. While writing staffs usually work Monday through Friday (writers may be called in to work an occasional weekend, but this is extremely rare), this does not mean the shooting schedule operates on a Monday-through-Friday schedule. While actual production days vary from show to show, the following is an example of a typical shooting schedule for a multi-cam sitcom.

Day One (Friday)

The first day of production is a "table reading." The writers, producers, studio executives, network executives, cast, and director literally gather in a room around a large table. The atmosphere is relaxed, and table readings are usually catered. As everyone sips on coffee and munches bagels, the cast reads the script straight through from the "Fade In" on page one to the "Fade Out" on the final page. This is a very important day as it is the first time the writers and producers are hearing the script read out loud by professional actors. It is easy to ascertain what jokes work and what jokes fall flat and need to be rewritten.

While the script is being read, the writing staff (along with the director and executives) will scribble notes on their scripts. Once the reading is finished, the actors will either go to the stage and start to bring the script to life or they may go home for the rest of the day and wait for the writers to deliver a new draft. Once the actors have left the room, the writers, producers, executives, and director huddle together for a "notes session." They go through the script page-by-page and discuss what worked as well as what needs to be changed. The studio and network executives have the most power, since, as I mentioned earlier, they own the product. If they insist something be changed, odds are it will be, even if the writing staff disagrees. Likewise, when the executive producer calls for changes, these are also likely to be incorporated. After the notes session, the executives and director leave. It is time for the writing staff to go to work.

Depending on the number of changes (which can be significant on Day One), the writing staff goes back to the writing room and collectively rewrites the script. This can take hours if something just isn't working or they need to come up with some different jokes. Once the script has been rewritten, it is turned over to the script assistants, who make the changes in the computer, proof it, Xerox it, and send the new copy to all concerned, including the cast.

Day Two (Monday)

The cast and director will take the new version of the script and spend the day rehearsing on the stage. Meanwhile, the writing staff is back in the writing offices, doing any number of things. First and foremost, the staff will be feverishly working on getting next week's script ready for the next table reading. Here and there, a writer might be writing the first draft of a future episode that he or she has been assigned. In between, the staff may take pitches from freelance writers who have story ideas they are trying to sell to the show.

Later in the afternoon, the staff will venture down to the stage for a "run through." A run through is just like it sounds: the cast runs through the script from cover to cover. At this point, they probably have not memorized their lines and are still reading from their scripts. But, the show is slowly beginning to take shape, as the director has some of the blocking down. During the run through, the writers and producers sit in chairs at the edge of each set. Every time one scene ends, they literally pick up their chairs and move to the next set, as dictated by the script.

After the run through is over, the actors go home for the day. The writers and producers, however, go into yet another notes session. Just as they did after the table reading, they discuss what worked, what didn't, and what needs to be changed. When the notes session ends, the writing staff once again retreats to the writing room. If the changes are fairly minor, the staff will make them and then go home. If, however, the changes are considerable, they may order dinner and hunker down to start the revision process.

Some shows are in sync: the writers work well together and can make changes quickly. Other writing staffs have been known to work 'til the wee hours of the morning. This usually happens on newer shows or shows that are in trouble, rating wise. In both cases, the writing staff is usually struggling to find the show's characters and/or direction.

Day Three (Tuesday)

The third day tends to be a repeat of Day Two, the only difference is that the show is really starting to take shape. Actors are now probably working without scripts. (If they forget a line, the script supervisor is following along and quickly gets them back on track.) Also, because tape day is looming on the horizon, the number of changes will usually start to drop off. By now the producers and writing staff are pretty much set on the direction of the script. They had better be, as actors are only human and thus not usually capable of memorizing an entire new script in one or two days.

Day Four (Wednesday)

This is known as rehearsal day. It is huge. Throughout the day, the director may split his time between the stage and the "booth," which is a control room where the director and/or assistant director will call the shots and eventually tape the show. The writing staff continues about its normal business of preparing the next script, taking pitches, etc. But then, something a little different happens.

When it comes time for the run through, the producers and writers go down to the stage. But today, unlike other days, they do not sit at the edge of each set. Instead they sit in the seats reserved for a studio audience. Network and studio executives are also in attendance. As the cast runs through the script from beginning to end, the show is actually taped. It is a practice run. While the writers and executives can easily see the action on the stage, they also keep a careful eye on the television monitors that are in front of them. This is crucial, because what they see on those monitors is exactly what the director intends to put on tape for good the following day. This is the last chance to discuss any changes in dialogue, wardrobe, shot composition, or anything else pertinent to the show.

After the rehearsal, there is a final notes session. Everyone must voice any objections now or live with the show as is. For example, let's say you are a staff writer, working on a show with a teenage girl, and the current episode is about the girl going to her prom. But when the girl came onto stage during the rehearsal, she was wearing a god-awful, bubble-gum pink Little Bo Peep-type dress, rather than the short little black number you had envisioned. Now is the time to bring that up. If the executive producer agrees with you, he or she will call the wardrobe person over to discuss a costume change. In the unlikely event that the wardrobe person doesn't have a little black dress in house, she will go shopping that night. The following morning, the producers will have several little black dresses to choose from.

After the meeting, the writing staff may in fact make more changes to the script. But with tape day less than 24 hours away, the changes are usually extremely minor, meaning a little tweak here and there.

Day Five (Thursday)

This is tape day and, without question, it is the most exciting day in the week. Multi-cam shows will almost always utilize a live studio audience. Live audiences are important for any number of reasons. First and foremost, they add real laughter to the production. Secondly, live audiences can boost an actor's performance. If you have ever been to a comedy club and witnessed a comedian tell one bad joke after another, you can feel the energy drain from the room — and also from the comedian. Likewise, if a comedian is on top of the material, audience laughter boosts the energy even higher. The same is true in sitcoms. When the actors hear the laughter and sense the audience likes what it sees, the performances will usually be heightened.

The studio audience will primarily be made up of out-of-towners — people who have come to California to get a firsthand look at Hollywood. (For people who live in Los Angeles, stars and tapings quickly become old hat.) Out-of-towners make great audiences, as TV tapings aren't commonplace on the farm in Iowa or in the mountains of New Hampshire. Therefore, they are seeing something new and they are usually quite jazzed about it.

Multi-cam shows tape in two different ways, depending on the show:

1. They bring in one audience and tape each scene repeatedly until the director has on tape what he or she needs. This means an audience will hear the same lines and the same jokes over and over again. Once a scene is finished, they move on and tape the next scene until they have it right.

2. They tape a show using two separate audiences. The first audience comes in and the show is run from beginning to end. If the actors make mistakes or forget lines, they may redo just that portion of the scene. Once the show has finished taping, there is a break, usually for dinner. The cast and crew eat and relax while a fresh audience is brought in. Then, the show is taped again and the two versions are edited together.

While neither way of taping is right or wrong, I prefer the second way. In my opinion, a fresh audience — though more expensive — helps keep the cast energized. It also allows writers and producers the luxury of making little tweaks, if needed, after the first show.

Utilizing only one audience can be difficult if things don't go smoothly on stage. An audience will have to keep sitting through — and laughing at — the same jokes. If a joke wasn't particularly funny the first time around, it will be less funny the fourteenth time around. Thus the laughter will start to feel forced, which can directly affect an actor's performance. Also, when there is just one audience, the taping will usually run longer. I have gone to sitcom tapings that have started at 5 p.m. By 7 p.m., I am thinking about dinner. By 10 p.m., I am downright irritated — I just want out. If a taping goes too long, the audience will start to piddle out, which again is not good for the actors or for the show. However, for shows that use minors, this can be the more practical way to tape because of child labor laws.

Single-camera shows operate under a completely different time schedule. Because their scenes are shorter and often shot out of sequence, they can actually be setting up and/or shooting two scenes at the same time.

"If you don't at least attempt to reinvent, you shouldn't waste your time. Traditional comedies will always have an audience, but because there are so many of them, why spend your time rehashing old ideas? I think reinvention can come as much from character as from form. Rich, interesting people who have unique and fresh points of view can make an old format seem new again." — Steve Stark, executive producer, *Medium*; president, Grammnet Producers

HOW A FREELANCER FITS IN

Unfortunately, a freelance writer is not usually invited to the table reading or to any of the run throughs or rehearsals. Once you turn in a freelance script, the staff writers take over and handle the revisions. While this may not seem fair, it is actually for your protection. Since you are not technically on the show's payroll, asking you to come in every day would be asking you to work for free. Look at it this way: you are worth more than free, aren't you?

On tape day, however, freelance writers are generally given an invitation (which usually includes a guest) to come and watch the taping of the show they have written. Prepare yourself. This can be a rather nail-biting experience. How much has the script been rewritten since you turned it in? Have your favorite jokes survived all of the rewrites? Has the writing staff added things that deep down you really don't like? At this point there is little you can do about it. What's in the script is in the script and that's what they are going to shoot. You just have to trust that it's going to be good. And usually it is.

Once you arrive at the stage, you will feel very important — and deservedly so. An usher will take you to an assigned seat in the audience. Before the show begins and during breaks in the taping, you will be entertained by a "warm-up" person. This person's job is actually just as it sounds — to get the audience warmed up, ready to laugh, and in good spirits for the taping. The warm-up person will usually be high energy and tell lots of jokes. He or she will also explain what is going on as well as answer questions from the audience. Questions can range from "what's the difference between a producer and a director?" to "who is the star currently dating?"

At some point during the taping, there will be a break in the action — perhaps it is a set change or even a costume change. At this point, the warm-up person who is told in advance where you are sitting, will walk over to you, pull you onto your feet, and introduce you to the audience as the person who wrote the episode. The audience will applaud. You will smile and wave. This is a big and thrilling night for you. They are taping your episode.

DEVELOPING YOUR SITCOM STORY

GETTING STARTED

Now that you have decided that comedy writing is the path you want to take, you already know that your first step will be to write a spec script for an existing show. Once you have chosen the show you want to write, the first step in the writing process is to *study* that show. One of the more foolish questions I get asked time and time again is, "I don't ever watch such-and-such a show, but can I write a spec script on it anyway?" The answer is a resounding no! You cannot write what you do not know. It is impossible to write a good spec script for a show you don't watch. You must commit yourself right here and now to watching whatever show you have chosen *faithfully* each and every week. This will help you get a feel for who the characters are, what they are up to in the current season, what storylines have already been done as well as what sets are used each week. As we discussed, if you want to really be diligent, I would suggest that you tape the show and watch it a few times. You will be surprised what you miss — or even want to go back to when constructing your own story. Having episodes on tape will also be extremely useful later on when it is time to write the dialogue.

THE IMPORTANCE OF A GOOD STORY

Now that you have picked a show to write and studied that show, finding a *good* story is key. I cannot emphasize this enough. Without a good story, you simply cannot have a good script. Think of it this way: when was the last time you walked out of a movie proclaiming, "That was the best movie I have ever seen. The acting was great, the directing brilliant, the cinematography superb — the story stunk, but still it was the best movie I have ever seen." My guess is that you have never uttered those words. The reason being that story is the heart of every script. If your story isn't good, it will be the Domino effect: everything else will ultimately fall. This is true in all scripts, whether for television or film. Coming up with a good story may sound easy, but most writers will tell you that story is the hardest part of a script. With that in mind, please heed this important warning: take time coming up with and constructing your story. In fact, take *lots* of time.

A common mistake new writers make is that they tend to go with the first idea that comes to mind. The reason this usually doesn't work is that if you can think up a story idea in ten seconds, most likely a thousand other writers have thought up the same idea a thousand times before you. In fact, there are probably already many spec scripts floating around with that same idea. To take it a step further, it is very likely that the show's writing staff has also come up with a similar idea. This point will become even more important when you get to the point of pitching story ideas because if the writing staff has heard the idea, they have either rejected it or allowed someone else to write it.

> "Write what you know with voices you've heard all your life. Have the courage to write the truth even if you think you'll be expelled from the will." — Emmy Award-winning actor Henry Winkler

HOW TO CREATE AN ORIGINAL STORY

In sitcoms, the best stories for sitcoms often come from personal experience. Again, sitcoms are about funny people in humorous situations. Usually, they take place in the character's personal life (at home) or professional life (at the office) — or a combination of both. If you look at your own life, you can probably recall a number of funny things that have happened to you as well as to your family and friends at home and/or at work. These stories are unique because they don't happen every day to everyone. This means that when incorporated into a pitch or a script, they will sound fresh — something producers haven't heard before. Don't misunderstand me; this isn't to say that everything funny that happens in your life is worthy of a television episode. However, personal experience is always a good jumping off point.

When constructing stories, it is important to look at the show's characters. Where are they in their lives? Then, think of things that have happened in your own life that might be a good fit for a story. Next, see if it's possible to adapt your real-life experience to fit the show.

MAKING ORIGINAL STORIES WORK FOR EXISTING SHOWS

When I was first coming up with story ideas for *Full House*, I immediately looked at the show's premise. This was a show about three little girls being raised by three grown men (their mother was deceased). After studying the show, I decided I wanted to do an episode where one of the girls might need her mother for something that you really need a mother for. But, since the girls don't have a mother, one or all of the guys would have to step in. I looked at the ages of the three girls and then thought back to my own childhood. What was going on in my life when I was about the same age as D.J., Stephanie, and Michelle? One story in particular came to mind.

When I was about 10 or 11 — Stephanie's age on the show — we had a memorable event at my school. The class was separated by gender: the boys went off with the male gym teacher, while the girls were sent to the auditorium with the school nurse and our mothers. There we watched a movie about our bodies, and all of the wonderful changes we could expect during puberty. After the movie, there was a mother–daughter "tea" (actually juice and cookies), during which the school nurse led a discussion and answered embarrassing questions.

I thought, what a fabulous idea for a *Full House* episode. Stephanie has to go to the movie, but she doesn't have a mother to go with, so therefore one or all of the guys would have to go instead. I could see the men crunched into small chairs, wanting to be invisible while the female discussion went on all around them. The underlying moral of the story — *Full House* always had one — was, of course, that even though Stephanie didn't have a mother, she had three guys who loved her so much they would do anything for her.

A few days later, I took that story idea along with five others, drove to Warner Bros. and pitched it to the producers. Of the six ideas, the one they liked the most was the one that came directly from my childhood. They bought it on the spot, telling me that it was original, something they hadn't heard before. They said that they could easily see the humor and where the jokes would come from.

I left the *Full House* offices that day having sold my first network script. I remember feeling awfully cool. Little did I know that my coolness would be short-lived.

About a week later, I returned to the *Full House* offices where I worked with the entire writing staff to beat out the story. I went home and wrote the outline, and after that, the first draft. Then, I got the call that every writer dreads. It was Marc Warren, one of the show's executive producers. He was calling to tell me that they had decided against doing my script. Apparently, Jeff Franklin, the show's creator and executive producer had read my script and gotten cold feet. Franklin felt that a storyline that dealt with changing bodies was far too sophisticated for the *Full House* family audience. I was crushed.

In retrospect, Franklin was 100% right. I had made a huge mistake. I hadn't completely done my homework. While I had studied the characters and knew all of the sets on *Full House,* I failed to study the show itself. If I had, I would have understood that it was the lead-in to ABC's TGIF line-up. It was an 8 o'clock show that was a clean family comedy — the kind of show that mothers sat down and watched with five-year-olds. While the show had a lot of hugging and a little kissing, that was as far as it went. Therefore, an episode about "changing bodies" was not right for the show, and probably would have gotten complaints from viewers had it made it on the air.

Though the producers at *Full House* scrapped my script, they reworked the original idea and came up with another story that had the gist of what I had wanted to say. The episode is called "Slumber Party." In it, Stephanie is invited to the Honeybees' (the *Full House* version of Girl Scouts) mother–daughter slumber party. Obviously, she can't go because she doesn't have a mother. So one of the guys — Joey — ends up taking her. In his Ninja Turtle pajamas. Comedy ensues.

Because of the Writers Guild of America's rules that only allow a writer to write a certain number of drafts, the producers had to rewrite my episode from scratch. Horrible as it is for me to admit, my first network script was a page-one rewrite, which is not a good thing. As I mentioned, when this happens, the show's writing staff has to step up to the plate and take over. When a writer submits a script that ends up being a page-one rewrite, the show runners usually won't hire the writer back again. In fairness to me, it wasn't completely my fault. After all, the producers bought my original story idea in the first place. Looking back, I think it's because the story I pitched sounded fresh and original — it was something they hadn't heard from the thousand writers who had come in and pitched before me.

I was lucky. The producers were extremely kind to me. They could have taken me to arbitration and asked the Writers Guild to split the credit (see Chapter 26). Instead they gave me sole writing credit on the script and even let me come back and pitch more episodes, some of which they bought. But, if the painful truth be known, not one word nor one joke in the "Slumber Party" script is mine. The lesson I learned was huge. When adapting personal experience, it is imperative to make sure the story works, not only for the characters, but also for the overall feeling and concept of the show.

> "We had a team of writers who wrote as close to our own lives as possible. Our stories came from our relatives and our families, and things that were going on in our culture at that time. Our stories came from everything we observed or read. Then we handed it over to those four extraordinary actors, and the gods just smiled on us." — Norman Lear, executive producer, *All In the Family,* on why the show was such a breakout hit.

FINDING AN ORIGINAL SPIN

There is a theory floating around that there are a small, finite number of stories out there, and that writers just keep regurgitating them. Personally, I don't subscribe to that theory. To do so would be to say that the human imagination is limited. I believe just the opposite — that the human imagination is *limitless*. There are no boundaries to what you can come up with if you really put your mind to it. That said, there are some writers who may not stretch their imaginations as far as they can go. It may be that some aren't as gifted as others — it may be laziness — it may be that old hat feels good. No matter how much I encourage originality, there will always be some writers who come forward with stories we have all heard before. I know because in my early days of writing, I did it.

My first pitch was at *Charles in Charge,* where I had worked for many years as a script assistant. I had gotten friendly with Bill and Kathy Greer, the supervising producers. After writing two spec scripts, the Greers generously decided to see if they could possibly jump-start my writing career by giving me an episode to write.

It was my first pitch, and without a doubt it was my worst pitch. I tried to sell a bunch of tired stories that weren't fresh and original — stories that weren't character and/or show specific. To fully understand the pitch, you must first know the premise. *Charles in Charge* is about three kids whose father is away in the Navy, and for whatever reason, their mother is usually MIA. They live with their grandfather, an ex-Navy man, and they are looked after by a college-age nanny named Charles (played by Prince Charming himself, Scott Baio).

The story I pitched was that the kids are getting older and their grandfather is driving them crazy because he still thinks of them as babies, and always wants to take them to little kid places like water slides and petting zoos. Exasperated, they tell Charles to get Grampa off their backs. Charles suggests that Grampa take a college course to keep his mind sharp. A few days later, Charles, who is a teaching assistant at the local college, is called upon to take over a history class when the professor is at a conference. Suddenly, Grampa shows up — he's decided to take Charles' advice, and has enrolled in the class in which Charles is now the substitute teacher. Of course, the two butt heads and it becomes a power struggle that threatens Charles' job both as a substitute teacher and as a nanny.

You may be asking, what's wrong with that pitch? It has conflict, and the humor is easily recognizable. True. But, here's the problem. This is a story we have heard or seen in one form or another umpteen times. One that immediately springs to mind is an episode of *Family Ties.* In that show, Alex is a substitute teacher in Ellen's class. And guess what? Surprise, surprise — it doesn't work out so well. I have since seen similar stories in numerous spec scripts.

But Bill and Kathy Greer took that old idea and did something different with it. They delved into Grampa's character. Turns out he had been in the Navy during World War II. So we centered the history class on that war. Now instead of conflict merely between substitute teacher and unruly student, the conflict was focused on the inaccuracy of the college textbook. Grampa argued that he had been in the war and that the textbook had many of the facts incorrect. Charles of course had to defend the textbook. With this little added twist, the story spun into an episode about revisionist history. Needless to say, this is not a story we see every day on sitcoms. So, if you find yourself working with ideas that seem familiar (and you may), let me challenge you to really push yourself to spin that old-hat idea into something more original.

> "I'll want to meet any writer who doesn't bore me and finds a quirky
> and inspired way to tell a story, even if it's familiar. Make me laugh.
> Make me think. Write from your own experiences and unique perspec-
> tive. Make me want to get in a room with you and figure out what's
> going on inside your demented brain." — Marc Warren, executive pro-
> ducer, *That's So Raven* and *Cory In The House*

STUDY UP

As you work on your own story, you should be watching as much comedy as
you possibly can. Inhale it all. Watch the sitcoms that are on now, and you will
get a good feel for the current trends in programming. And don't turn your
nose up at past hits — those beloved shows that can be easily found on *Nick
At Night* and *TV Land*. There is a lot you can learn from these programs. They
are called "classic" for a reason — they have stood the test of time. Thirty, forty,
fifty years later, and some of them are better in reruns than much of what's
being produced today. So study shows like *All In the Family*, *I Love Lucy*, and
The Mary Tyler Moore Show. You will find rich, multi-dimensional characters.
Notice the original stories — they all come from character. The same is true
with jokes. The challenge I put before all of my students is to write comedy
that isn't just funny today, but will be funny in years to come to generations
that aren't even born yet. Trust me, this is not an easy thing to do.

You should also keep an eye on some of the comedy being produced by our
friends across the pond. Nowhere on God's green earth can you find a group
of people that are any funnier than the Brits. It's no wonder that some of the
most successful sitcoms in American television comedies have roots in Great
Britain. *All in the Family* was based on the British series, *Till Death Do Us Part*,
Three's Company on *Man About The House*, and, of course, *The Office*, to name
just a few. It should come as no surprise to learn that the Brits also hold the
record for the longest-running sitcom: *Last of the Summer Wine* is currently in
its 27th season.

BEATING WRITER'S BLOCK

It happens to all writers at one point or another — writer's block sets in. No
matter how hard you try, you just can't seem to come up with anything good.
In fact, you can't even come up with anything *bad*. You stare at your computer
screen or the blank pages of a notebook. Nothing. So, what do you do? All
writers handle writer's block differently. Some blast music or watch TV,
some take walks — some even resort to mindless work like dusting and vacu-
uming. You have to find what works for you. Rather than a mindless activity,
I recommend you choose something more proactive — something that might

actually jump-start your story. I suggest you journey to the places stories reside — meaning a trip to your local bookstore or library. Here, as you wander around, you may well come across a book or an article that gives you an idea.

The season following the "Slumber Party" episode, I was invited back to pitch at *Full House.* I was more than a little gun-shy, since my last experience there had been so disastrous. This time, I really wanted to come up with a story that worked. But, nothing was coming to me. I realized that staring at blank pages hour after hour was getting me nowhere. So, I went out to get some air and clear my head. I soon found myself in a bookstore. I went to the TV section and began to browse. I came across a book about *The Brady Bunch.* The similarities between that show and *Full House* were incredible. Like *Full House, The Brady Bunch* was a Friday night, 8 o'clock show on ABC about a nontraditional family (in the sixties, stepfamilies were not nearly as common as they are today). Like the Tanner family, the Bradys were squeaky clean, and there was usually a small but important lesson to be learned each week.

As I began to browse the book, I noticed there was an episode guide at the back. I began to skim it. One show sang out to me. It was a story about Bobby, the youngest male Brady, who, because of a fall, developed a fear of heights, so the family had to help him overcome it.

I knew *Full House* was looking for some stories for Michelle. I thought about where little Michelle was in her life and what kinds of things she might be doing. At the time, Mary Kate and Ashley Olsen were about five years old. Mmmm … might they be learning to ride a bike? What if Michelle was learning to ride a two-wheeler, fell off the bike, and was afraid to get back on?

I need to be extremely clear. I did not steal from that *Brady Bunch* episode. Nor do I advocate plagiarism in any way, shape, or form. If you were to put the *Brady Bunch* episode next to the "Easy Rider" episode of *Full House,* you would see that there is nothing similar about them, except perhaps the underlying theme, which comes from an age-old adage: if you fall off the horse, you gotta get right back on.

Which brings me to my next point: *Bartlett's Book of Quotations* is also a good cure for writer's block. It will open up your mind to lots of different story themes. Likewise, it is commonplace for writers to keep stacks of old *TV Guide*s around and skim them as a way to get ideas. Again, we are not stealing, we are simply jump-starting our minds.

STORIES TO STAY AWAY FROM

There are some story ideas that you should avoid both in a spec script and in a pitch. First, and most importantly, you don't want to do a story that changes any elements of the show. Don't write a spec script where you marry off two of the main characters. Likewise, don't have any of the main characters become pregnant. There are two main reasons for this. First, if these kinds of milestones are going to occur on a show, it is the decision of the producers. They are discussed in-house at considerable length — and then, because it's a special episode, the story and script are usually given to a staff writer, and the episode will almost always air in a Sweeps month.

You should also stay away from stories with obvious endings. One I hear pitched regularly is that the X family is contemplating moving. What's wrong with that story? It's completely predictable, as I know how the story ends before it even begins. The family is not going to move. Why? Because as a freelance writer, you know better than to write a spec script that would, in reality, mean the show had to pony up the money for brand new sets. And if your story ends with the family actually moving when producers read your spec, it won't make a lot of sense because they will know that the family hasn't moved. They are still in the same old house with the same old sets.

While we are on the subject of sets, be sure to avoid stories that will take the characters out of their usual environment. Part of writing a spec is to prove that you can write the show as it is. The challenge of writing for a sitcom — especially multi-camera — is using existing characters and existing sets. Even if you are doing a single-cam show, there are still certain sets that are used each week. The audience gets comfortable with these sets. If your spec relies on too many new sets, producers might think twice about hiring you as they may doubt your ability to tell a story within the confines of their show. It may seem like no big deal to add a new set here or there, but actually it is. Sets cost a lot of money — especially if they are only going to be used for one episode. So, if, in the back of your mind you were thinking about a spec that sends the show's characters on vacation, or to a marriage retreat or any place that would require the main action of your script to take place away from the standard sets, you should probably rethink that idea.

I suggest that in a multi-camera show, you should use no more than one swing set. A swing set is a set that is not used regularly, but rather constructed for a particular episode. The temptation here may be for you to argue with me. You are probably thinking, "But the show I want to write often uses more than one swing set." This might be true. When you get on staff of that show, you can use as many swing sets as the producers and the budget will allow. For now, you have to remember that you are writing on spec. Part of that job entails showing producers that you can write for existing sets and characters.

GETTING THE POOP

Before you start to construct your story idea, I recommend checking out the show's Web site to see if it lists episodes that have already been done. The last thing you want is to invest the amount of time and energy that it takes to write a good spec script, only to find out that your story idea has already been produced. If the show doesn't list its episodes, you might try calling the production offices. Explain that you are a freelance writer doing a spec, and ask them (beg them if need be) to send you a poop sheet (episode guide). I can't guarantee that they will. Some shows are of the mindset that they don't have the time to send this information out to everyone that asks (which is true), while others may have a policy of not sending in-house information out to the general public. But, it is also possible you might get a nice assistant to take pity on you and he or she will agree to quietly slip the episode guide in the mail to you.

PHYSICAL COMEDY

Whenever possible, it is good idea to incorporate physical comedy into your story and script. But, here is the hard part. Physical comedy has to work for the characters and for the show. It can't be slapsticky. What worked for the *Three Stooges,* while funnier than funny, simply won't translate to most of today's shows.

The key to writing good physical comedy is to keep it simple. Many new writers tend to over-think physical comedy and it comes across as convoluted and, in the end, not very funny. Another common mistake I see is for a writer to add physical comedy just for the sake of a laugh. The scene has nothing to do with the story. If your story doesn't naturally lend itself to physical comedy (and not every story does), it is better to leave it out. Putting it in just to say you did will ruin the track and flow of your story.

Still, if you can think of a way to add some physical comedy to your script, you increase your chances of having a really funny spec, which in the end will make you stand out as a writer. Learn to write physical comedy well, and actors will love you. Actors tend to like physical comedy as it challenges them to do more than just deliver funny lines.

SIGHT GAGS

A sight gag is something that is funny simply by being. For example, an actor dressed in a hilarious costume. He or she walks onto the stage dressed as a banana or a hot dog. The actor doesn't need to say a word, but the audience howls. Sight gags aren't required in scripts, but like physical comedy, if you can think of any that are a natural fit for your story, you will be one step further ahead of the pack.

"A" STORIES, "B" STORIES, AND THE OCCASIONAL "C" STORY AND "D" STORY

The main story that you choose to explore in your sitcom is known as the "A" story. It is the primary story of your episode. Think of it as the blurb that will appear in *TV Guide.* In addition to a strong "A" story, most sitcoms have "B" stories as well. A "B" story is a secondary story that runs throughout the episode. Depending on the sitcom and the number of main characters, there may be "C" stories and "D" stories as well.

There are a few reasons that sitcoms utilize secondary stories. First, if you look at the opening credits of a sitcom, you will see the entire cast. In some sitcoms, this can be a fair number of people. All of these actors are being paid hefty salaries to be on the show. Therefore, it would be foolish not to use all of them each week. Secondly, the television audience is primed each week to welcome all of these characters into their homes. It's what they tune in for. Imagine if you turned on *Desperate Housewives* one week and the only house-wife to come across your screen was Susan. Wouldn't you be a tad disappointed — perhaps even annoyed?

It is extremely difficult, especially in shows with larger casts, to incorporate everyone into one large, dynamic "A" story, thus the reason there are "B" stories. Secondary stories can also help heighten the tension by presenting another story to cut away to.

In addition to your "A" story, you will have to write a "B" story — and depending on whether or not your show calls for it, a "C" story and a "D" story. Be sure that each story utilizes different characters. If you are going to write a spec *Two and a Half Men* and your "A" story centers on Charlie and Alan, then you might want to think of a "B" story that focuses on Jake and Judith. See how easy that is?

Now, you try it. Write one sentence that encompasses your "A" story. Then write a sentence for your "B" story, and, if applicable, your "C" and/or "D" stories.

GETTING FEEDBACK

Once you have your story ideas, it is always good to get some feedback before proceeding. The best people to ask for feedback are people who know the show. Whatever show you have decided to write, my guess is that you know other people who watch it. In fact, you probably already discuss the show with them every now and then as a topic of conversation.

Feedback can be a godsend in a couple of ways. First, it can let you know whether or not you are on the right track. Do the people you are telling the stories to think they are funny and right for the show? Second, as you discuss your ideas, you will be surprised how people will chime in and offer you different ways to go that will vastly improve your story. It's the old "two heads are better than one" theory.

CHECKLIST FOR STORY

- Is my "A" story fresh and original?
- Is my "B" story (and if applicable "C" story and/or "D" story) equally fresh and original?
- Do my stories work for the characters *and* for the show as a whole?
- Are my stories funny? Can I easily see where the jokes and humor lie?

- Have I used all of the main characters?
- Have I used all (or most) of the standard sets?
- Have I discussed my story with people who regularly watch the show?
- Have I researched what episodes the show has already done?
- If possible, have I incorporated physical comedy?
- If possible, have I included sight gags?

If you answered "yes" to all of the above, fasten your seat belt. We are ready to move on to the difficult task of structuring your story.

5

SITCOM STRUCTURE

THE IMPORTANCE OF STORY STRUCTURE

Quite simply, structure is one of the most important elements of your script. It is the glue that holds your story together. Think of structure as how you choose to tell your story. What happens in each scene and what is the order in which it happens? Let me warn you that structure is one of the hardest things to do. It takes time, energy, and boatloads of patience. You probably won't get it right the first time. You may not get it right the second time. Most likely you will need to rework your story several times. Don't get aggravated by this — it is a normal part of the writing process, one that is difficult for even seasoned writers.

I often see new writers work at story structure, get frustrated, and give up. They say, "I couldn't figure it out and it was taking too much time, so I just did it my way." This is a colossal mistake. The television industry isn't Burger King. You can't have it your way. Structure exists because it works. Those in the industry understand story structure because they live it every day. If your story is structured incorrectly — or worse still not at all — they will hear it in your pitch or read it in your script and they will automatically think of you as a pedestrian writer because you haven't conquered one of the most fundamental elements of TV writing.

TRADITIONAL TWO-ACT STRUCTURE VS. MODERN THREE-ACT STRUCTURE

For the most part, sitcoms have always been structured in two acts. An act is a series of scenes that tells a story. For multi-cam shows, an act consists of approximately four to seven scenes. Single-cam shows are different. There will be more scenes, as scenes in these shows tend to be shorter. In classic two-act sitcom structure, the first act is the setup of your story. It is where you get your character(s) into hot water. The second act is the resolution. It's where you get your character(s) out of hot water. The acts should be approximately (doesn't have to be perfect) the same length.

In the middle of your script, there is what is known as an Act Break. A strong Act Break is key to a good story. Think of it as a mini-cliffhanger. Something big must happen. The reason is that in network television, Act Breaks coincide with commercial breaks. Commercial breaks give the audience a chance to veer away from your show. They can (and often do) pick up the remote to see what else is on. But, a good Act Break will always bring the audience back because they will want to see what happens and how the characters get out of hot water.

It is no secret that in the past decade networks have struggled to get and to keep an audience. This is difficult to do, since cable television has opened up tons of new stations that are vying for (and getting) their share of viewers. In order to win, networks will try almost anything that feels different. While shows were once almost always structured in two acts, these days some shows follow a three-act structure. To make it easy, you can think of the three acts as the beginning, middle, and end. As with two-act structure, each act should be approximately the same length, and the first and second acts should have strong Act Breaks.

Typically, a show is consistently written in two-act structure or three-act structure. In other words, shows don't mix-and-match by doing two-act one week and three-act the next. It is too confusing for an audience.

When you are writing a spec script or pitching an episode, you should structure your story in whichever format your particular show follows. How can you be sure how many acts your show has? It's easy. Watch the show for a few weeks. Does it have one mini-cliffhanger and commercial break that comes about halfway through? Then, obviously, that show is following classic two-act structure. But, if the show has two mini-cliffhangers and two commercial breaks, then the show is following the more modern three-act structure. A word to the wise — be sure, when studying a show, that you are watching it in prime time rather than in syndication. As we have discussed, shows that go into syndication often have more commercial breaks added. If, for any reason, you aren't clear on how many acts your particular show has, you can also look at the actual show script that is now in your possession. Act Breaks are written in, so it will be easy for you to figure out.

The one exception to two-act or three-act structure is shows that are on commercial-free networks like HBO and Showtime. These stories do not have Act Breaks, but rather go from beginning to end. If you are writing or pitching one of these shows, you don't have to worry about creating strong Act Breaks.

CREATING TWISTS

The worst stories in the world are linear stories. In television, linear stories simply don't work. They are, for lack of a better term, boring. The best stories are those with twists. A twist is something the audience doesn't see coming. In other words, the story seems to be going in one direction, and then something happens that spins the action into a different direction. Twists catch the audience off guard, keeping them engaged and entertained. Think of it as a roller coaster ride. How fun would it be to ride a roller coaster that didn't go up and down with drops that seem to come out of nowhere? The answer is, not much fun at all. It is the same with story. Be forewarned, coming up with twists can be difficult. But, it is something you must do in order to have an exciting story and ultimately an awesome script.

NO-FAIL SITCOM STRUCTURE

I am going to give you the recipe for no-fail sitcom structure. If you follow this to a tee without deviating, I promise you no one will be able to say your structure is incorrect. Here are the main things you need to do:

- Begin each act on the "A" story
- End each act on the "A" story
- Weave in the "B" story (and then the "C" story and "D" story, if applicable)
- Have a clear-cut beginning, middle, and end for all stories
- Put all stories in all acts
- Put all main characters in all acts
- Develop strong Act Breaks that leave your character in jeopardy
- Escalate the jeopardy in the beginning of each act
- Create a twist in the second-to-last scene
- Resolve the "A" story in the final scene

Begin Each Act on the "A" Story

It is important to keep in mind that your "A" story is your primary story. Therefore you need to make it a priority and give it the most focus and time. You should always start each act on your "A" story. Don't beat around the bush, and don't waste precious time. In Act One, you need to get us hooked on your "A" story; in subsequent acts, you need to keep us hooked on your "A" story.

End Each Act on the "A" Story

Your Act Breaks must fall on your "A" story. Again, this is the primary story and the reason we have tuned in. We are not going to be as vested in your secondary stories because they aren't as big. Thus, a mini-cliffhanger centered on a "B" story or a "C" story will not be enough to bring us back after the commercial break(s).

Weave In the "B" Story (and then the "C" Story and "D" Story, if applicable)

Once you have clearly established your "A" story, you can weave in your secondary stories. In some shows, secondary stories are completely separate scenes that cut away from the main action. Sometimes, the secondary stories walk into the main action. Of course, you should do it however your particular show does it. The important thing is to give the most time to the "A" story, then the "B" story, then the "C" and/or "D" story.

Have a Clear-cut Beginning, Middle, and End for All Stories

Each story should be able to stand on its own with a clearly defined beginning, middle, and end. You don't want to start or dabble with a secondary story and then just let it drop. The audience will walk away feeling gypped because they don't know the resolution.

Put All Stories in All Acts

It is important that you include scenes from all of your stories in each of your acts. You don't want to wait until the second act to set up a "B" story. Likewise, it would be a mistake to start a story in Act One and then never return to it.

Put All Main Characters in All Acts

Whenever possible, you should try to get all of the main characters into each act. Characters are the main reason that audiences tune in each week — these are the people they invite into their homes, so you want to be sure to deliver what they are looking for. Also, you want to make sure that all of the main characters are involved in one of the stories — be it the "A" story or one of the secondary stories — and these stories should all be moving forward in each act toward the resolution.

Develop Strong Act Breaks that Leave Your Character in Jeopardy

I can't emphasize this enough. Something significant must happen at the end of each act that will make the audience yearn to know how the character is going to get out of the tight spot you have placed him or her in. An act must build to this moment. At the Act Break, your character must be in the doghouse.

Escalate the Jeopardy in the Beginning of Each Act

When we come back from the commercial break, you must now escalate the jeopardy. Just when we think the character can't get in any deeper, he or she does something that makes the situation all the worse. Also, once you have put the character in jeopardy and the audience has patiently waited through a commercial break to see what happens, you don't want to put them off by going immediately to the "B" story.

Create a Twist in the Second-to-Last Scene

The best-written sitcoms have a twist in the second-to-last scene of the show. The story will be going one way, and then, out of nowhere, something happens that spins the show in a new direction on its way to resolution. Not all scripts do this, because coming up with a good twist can be extremely difficult. Nonetheless, if you can figure out a good twist in the second-to-last scene, you will be ahead of the game.

Resolve the "A" Story in the Final Scene

Your "A" story is your primary story. Once you have resolved the "A" story, you have given away the keys to the candy store. The show is over. Therefore, it is hugely important to hold off on the resolution of the "A" story until the final scene of the final act.

EXAMPLE OF STRUCTURE

Below is an example of how to structure your sitcom. It is only an example. Your story will probably be structured a little bit differently as you will have to come up with your own story sequence and structure, based the needs of your stories.

ACT ONE
Scene One (start "A" story)
Scene Two (start "B" story)
Scene Three (back to "A" story)
Scene Four (start "C" story)
Scene Five (back to "A" story; character(s) in jeopardy)
ACT BREAK
ACT TWO
Scene One (continue "A" story; escalate jeopardy)
Scene Two (continue "B" story)
Scene Three (continue "A" story)
Scene Four (resolve "C" story)
Scene Five (resolve "B" story)
Scene Six (continue "A" story with twist)
Scene Seven (resolve "A" story)

Out of twelve scenes notice that seven revolve around the "A" story. Clearly, it is the primary story. Three scenes are set aside for the "B" story and two for the "C" story. Once you have established your "A" story and all of your secondary stories, you can place them in any order that makes sense, as long as you start and end each act on your "A" story and give that the most time and attention.

As I have stated, there are exceptions to every rule. I am telling you what works for most shows. You will know by studying the show you want to write how that particular show works. For example, *The Simpsons* tends to start on the "B" story. So, if you were writing a spec for that show, you would obviously want to start on the "B" story just like they do.

TEASERS

A teaser (also known as a "cold opening") is the first few minutes of a show before the main credits. Its purpose is very much like it sounds: to tease the audience and get them immediately hooked into the show, thus beating out the competition right from the get-go. At the top of every hour and/or half hour, much of the TV audience has clicker in hand, flipping around to see what's coming on. Which do you think the audience would find more interesting: the main credits of a show or a small, hilarious little section the show? Of course, most people would prefer the latter. Networks bank on that.

Teasers vary from show to show. In some shows, the teaser has nothing at all to do with the main story. It is completely separate. In other shows, the teaser actually helps set up the show. Most shows are consistent: they either do a teaser each week or they don't. Occasionally, you might find a show that varies from week to week, but this is really the exception to the rule.

Should you include a teaser in your spec script? The answer is, it depends on the show you are writing for. Remember, you are trying to make your episode look exactly like the show you are writing. Therefore, it is imperative to do exactly as they do. If they have a teaser every week, then you should definitely write a teaser. If the show you are writing for does not have a teaser, then putting one in would look like you don't know the structure of the show. In those rare cases where it could go either way, I would recommend doing a teaser. It's another opportunity to get a chunk of funny into your script.

TAGS

A tag is a little two to three minute segment that comes at the end of a show after the final commercial break and right before the end credits. In some ways, you can think of a tag as the opposite of a teaser. The thing that makes tags and teasers different is that while a teaser can set up a story and in essence be part of the first act; a tag should never resolve the story. Rather, it should be a separate block that stands completely on its own. You should never end your "A" story in a tag — it should always be wrapped up in the last scene of the final act. The reason this is important is that when a show goes into syndication, it often gets edited a tad differently in order to add in more commercial breaks so that local TV stations can increase revenue. In this case, the tag may not be shown.

Tags can be small extensions of the story — or they can be as simple as using some outtakes of the show. Should you include a tag in your spec? Like teasers, the answer is, only if the show you are writing regularly uses a tag.

A few words of caution. When trying to determine how many acts your show has, don't confuse teasers and tags for Act Breaks. For example, there may be a commercial after the teaser or before the tag, but those aren't Act Breaks. Remember, acts are longer than two or three minutes, and at the act break something significant happens that leaves the audience wanting more.

CHECKLIST FOR STORY STRUCTURE

- Does each act begin and end on the "A" story?
- Have I given the most time to the "A" story?
- Are the secondary stories woven in, each with a clear-cut beginning, middle, and end?
- Do my Act Breaks leave the character(s) in jeopardy/hot water?
- Have I escalated that jeopardy at the beginning of the next act?
- Do my acts feel fairly even in terms of time and material?
- Have I included teasers and tags if applicable to my show?

If you answered "yes" to all of the above questions, congratulations! It is time to begin outlining your script.

OUTLINING YOUR SITCOM STORY

WHY YOU MUST BREAK YOUR STORY DOWN ACT-BY-ACT, SCENE-BY-SCENE

In the professional world of television writing, once a writer has been assigned a story, the first thing he or she does is to write an act-by-act, scene-by-scene story outline. You can think of a story outline as a blueprint to the script. In the same way that a builder wouldn't blindly start construction on a new house without solid plans etched in stone, professional writers don't sit down to write a script without the story being laid out in full detail. If the story doesn't work, the script won't work. It's that simple. Therefore, producers insist on having a story outline, broken down act-by-act, scene-by-scene, before the writer begins the script.

In writing your spec, it is highly advisable that you write a story outline just as a professional writer would. First of all, it's good practice. Perhaps more importantly, an outline is all but guaranteed to save you time and aggravation. Over the years, I have witnessed many a promising young writer enter the writing process with the words, "I don't need an outline. I know what I'm doing." The writer then spends several months hammering out the script. Inevitably, once the script is finished and people start reading it, mistakes are found, and holes are pointed out that the writer hadn't considered. All of the hard work goes down the drain and the writer has to go back to square one and reconstruct the story. A lot of precious time and effort has been wasted.

Don't delude yourself into thinking that as a first-time writer you can skip the outline phase and go right to script. Comparatively speaking, the story is harder to write than the script itself. Let's go back to the construction analogy. Which house would you rather live in: one built on a whim by a builder with just a vague idea of what he hopes the house will look like when it's complete — or one built by a builder who has followed a set of plans designed by a qualified architect? Obviously, the builder without a plan risks wasting lots of time and ending up with a big mess, whereas the builder with a definitive set of plans will probably be finished faster and have fewer problems. It's the same with writing an outline. The writer who writes without a plan risks getting lost along the way. On the other hand, once you have your story outlined, and you know where you are going, writing the script is not nearly as difficult, nor as daunting.

WHAT A GOOD OUTLINE SHOULD ACCOMPLISH

In a nutshell, a good outline should give an overview of the main action of the story. On work for hire, writers and producers should be able to read an outline and be completely clear on what is going to happen, when it's going to happen, and how the story will evolve and resolve.

An outline is broken down act-by-act, scene by-scene. Within each scene, the writer tells where the scene takes place (on what set), and when it takes place (day or night). The writer then describes the main beats (points or actions) that occur in each scene, from the moment we enter that scene until the moment we leave it. Outlines are always written in present tense, with as little dialogue as possible. If, for example, you have a really funny joke, you can and should put it in the outline, but avoid adding dialogue just to add dialogue. Again, an outline is a blueprint of your story. Writing dialogue comes in the script phase.

You should also steer clear of the huge temptation to direct your script by writing in camera angles. Remember, you are the writer, not the director. The director will be more than capable of choosing his or her own shots. So, only add shots in an outline (and script) if they are 100% pertinent to the telling of your story. A word to the wise: if you are going to add shots or use any type of TV lingo, be sure you are using it correctly. Many a day, I have seen outlines and scripts that are overloaded with direction that doesn't make any sense. It's as if the writer feels that by using television jargon producers will think he or she is a professional who fits right in. You won't fit in if you have used the language incorrectly. In fact, just the opposite will happen.

GOOD WRITING IS KEY

A good outline should read like a good novel. The same is true of your script. I don't mean that it should be written in the same style as a novel, but rather that the writing is so crisp, the story so compelling that a reader will not be able to put it down until the very end. A well-written outline shouldn't be all flowery and wordy. Here, less is more. You are looking to describe the action in your story with as few words as possible. The key is to find the precise word or words for what you are trying to say. For example, does the character merely "enter" the room — or does he "slink" into the room — or does he "bull" into the room? Choosing just the right verb for what you want a character to do not only makes the read accurate, it makes it all the more interesting and more exciting.

In writing an outline, you definitely want to think back to high school English. Varying your sentence structure can greatly improve the read.

Avoid run-on sentences. Use proper punctuation and grammar. It matters. You are a writer. This means that everything you write — outlines included — must be written well.

FORMAT MATTERS

When it comes to writing outlines and scripts, there are certain rules for formatting that writers must adhere to. More and more, I notice young writers who, when it comes to format, are either sloppy or lazy — or sloppy *and* lazy. Somehow, they seem to be under the impression that format doesn't matter; as long as the material is good, agents and producers don't care how it is presented. They are dead wrong. Unfortunately, what these writers don't understand is that agents and producers will never know how good the material is because they won't bother to read it. They will get to page one, realize they are dealing with an amateur, close the script, and that will be that.

Professional writers follow industry standards. What this means is that when you work as an agent or a producer or anyone else in the business, you read scripts all the time. Your eye becomes very well trained to spot even the smallest error or deviation from standard format. So, when a script or an outline comes across your desk that is formatted any old way, it immediately screams one of two things: either the writer is pedestrian and doesn't know how scripts are written — or the writer knows, but doesn't care. Neither scenario bodes well for the writer.

HOW LONG SHOULD AN OUTLINE BE?

Perhaps one of the questions I am asked most often is, how long should an outline be? Unfortunately, this is a question for which I don't have a specific answer. I am more about quality than quantity. The most important thing about your outline is that it is well-written — that the story is properly laid out so that it is clear what the problem is, what is at stake for the characters, and what the resolution is.

There is no set number of pages, and in fact the actual length of an outline can vary depending on the story, and how many scenes are involved. When writing a traditional multi-cam sitcom, you will probably have fewer scenes than a single-camera comedy does, though in a multi-cam sitcom, the scenes will probably be longer. If I had to make a rough estimate, I would say 5 to 10 pages, depending on how many scenes are involved.

In terms of quantity, the one thing you really need to look out for is that you don't have too many scenes. Keep in mind that the next step after your outline is to write the script. So everything in the outline will need to be translated into action and dialogue. If your outline has too many scenes and those scenes are too long, you will have a difficult time getting it all into the script.

Typically, a multi-cam show comes in at around 45–48 pages, while a single-cam show comes in at around 30–35 pages. It is important that you bring your script in at around these numbers because that is industry standard. Often, young writers have problems cutting things. Get used to it. Cutting scripts is something you will do every day once you become a professional writer. Also, rest assured that once a script is cut for time, it will ultimately read a lot better.

You should also make sure that your acts are fairly balanced both in the way of scenes and length. It doesn't have to be perfect, but if you have three scenes in one act and fifteen scenes in another act, you are on the wrong track.

SAMPLE OUTLINE FOR SITCOM

What follows is an outline of the first few scenes of a single-camera sitcom called *People Employed by the State of New York to Fight Crime in the 1940s*. The outline was written by Steve Pinto, a student in my Writing Television Pilots class at Emerson College. It is reprinted with Steve's permission. Give it a read, and when you are finished, I will point out some of the more important formatting issues.

<u>ACT ONE</u>

FADE IN:

<u>INT. POLICE STATION – NIGHT</u>
It is 1940s New York and the retirement party for BULL HAUSER, one of the most respected and oldest members of the police force. Bull stands at the makeshift podium, tears streaming down his face as he, filled with emotion, tells all of his co-workers what working there all of these years means to him.

Everyone begins to cry and the emotion reaches its fever pitch when BEESLEY LYME, the assistant to famed crime lord DWAYNE MONTEGUE, arrives on the scene and lets all of the party-goers know that Dwayne is in fact not dead. He is alive.

Having been Bull's life's work, Bull is in disbelief about the rumor of Montegue's living status. He looks to his loving family for support. This is interrupted when the lights go out in a flash.

When they come back on, DWAYNE MONTEGUE, the crime boss of New York, stands in the middle of the room, with three cronies on his side.

He tells Bull that he is going to commit a crime right now, and that Bull will be forced back onto the force because of it. He takes Bull's son Charlie and casually walks him out of the room, as Bull and the other police officers yell "NOO!!!!" and others call for help. They don't actually chase after him though. As soon as Dwayne is out of the room, they run after him.

<u>INT. DWAYNE MONTEGUE'S CAR – LATER</u>
As Dwayne and company drive away from the police station, "Moon River" from *Breakfast at Tiffany's* plays on the car CD player (blatantly disregarding that there were no CD players in the 1950s). Dwayne looks off, obviously affected by the music. One of his cronies straight up asks him why he always insists on listening to this song, and follows it up by asking if this beautiful song is representative of a guarded secret that reveals a soul that Dwayne once possessed. Dwayne looks at him and closes his eyes.

<u>EXT. BY THE RIVERSIDE – 40 YEARS EARLIER</u>
Dwayne, as a young strapping gentleman, stands by the riverside with the woman of his dreams. They stand facing each other, holding each other's hands. The moonlight glistens off the water. Things suddenly take an unbearable turn for the worse when the young woman tells Dwayne that she doesn't think this is working, leaving Dwayne all alone … and cold. Inside and out. As Dwayne looks around, trying to figure things out after this traumatic event, a miracle happens.

A strand of moonlight, coming down from the sky, reflects through overhanging trees in such a way and into the river in just a way that the word CRIME is visible on the surface of the water. Dwayne says out loud that he realizes, because of the moon and the river, what his destiny is.

Notice, right off the bat, Steve tells us what act we are in. The words "ACT ONE" are in capital letters, centered, and underlined. You should follow this rule, and note that the same will be true when you get to subsequent acts.

Next come the magic words "FADE IN" in caps, followed by a colon.

From there, Steve starts to write his story, scene-by-scene. The writing is quick and casual. This is a story. It must move.

Let's look at his first line: "INT. POLICE STATION – NIGHT." This is known as a scene heading or slugline. It is in all caps and underlined. Scene headings are important, as they give us quite a bit of information about where and when the scene takes place. When writing a scene heading, the first question you want to ask yourself is, where does the action take place — inside or outside? In Steve's story, the first scene will take place inside a police station. The word "INT." means interior. If the scene takes place outside, as some of his later scenes do, the scene heading starts with EXT., which means exterior or outside.

After the interior or exterior, you then want to list the specific set. In Steve's story, it is obviously a police station. So INT. POLICE STATION means that the scene takes place inside a police station. A word to the wise when listing sets: make sure that you are consistent. Once you have named a set, if you go back to it later in your outline and script, make sure you use the same scene heading. Otherwise, it can get confusing.

Now that you have added the set to the scene heading, you want to tell us what time of day the scene is taking place. You don't have to be exact. Just give us a rough idea, by using words like "DAY" or "NIGHT," or slight variations such as "MORNING," "AFTERNOON," "EVENING," "DAWN" or "DUSK". Note that the set and time of day are separated by a hyphen, which has one space on each side. At the risk of sounding picayune — which I admittedly am — be sure to be consistent in the use of hyphens. Often writers will use a combination of hyphens and dashes in the slugline. Again, this is slop, and a lack of attention to detail. Be a perfectionist. It is the underlying principle of good writing.

After the scene heading, Steve writes what happens in the scene. Scene descriptions should be brief but poetic. In other words, write what you mean quickly, but write it well. A few things to note: because this is a single-camera sitcom, it is written film-style. Therefore, each time a new character is introduced, that person's name appears in capital letters. This rule applies only to the first time we see that character. Also, notice how Steve breaks the action into several small paragraphs. Not only does this make the outline easier to read (huge paragraphs can be difficult on the eyes), but it helps with the flow of Steve's writing. When you have particularly long scenes, look to break them into smaller paragraphs. A good place to break is where the action or emotion shifts or changes.

From the first scene, Steve begins to move though his act, each scene pushing the story forward until eventually he arrives at the big Act Break moment. When the act is finished, the words "FADE OUT" go to the left of the page. Steve then skips a space (or two) and officially ends the act, with the words "END OF ACT ONE," which are in capital letters, centered, and underlined.

A FEW MORE RULES

In outlines and scripts, stay away from bold and italics. If you want to put emphasis on something — especially in dialogue — underline it, like this. If you are underlining more than one word, do each word separately like this.

When writing scene description, you never want to refer to the reader as "you." Instead, television writers use "we," which incorporates both the reader and the writer. So, rather than writing "you see the gun behind his back," the proper lingo is "we see the gun behind his back."

Be sure that you have a scene heading for where the action takes place. Sometimes, new writers forget this important detail. For example, let's say the scene heading is INT. BEDROOM – MORNING. Bill and Mary are lying in bed, watching television, when the doorbell rings. Mary volunteers to get it. The next action has Mary opening the door, and in walks Mary's mother. They have a whole conversation. But, the writer forgot to change the scene heading to INT. LIVING ROOM – MORNING. Think of it like this: your scene heading tells the director where the action takes place, and thus where the cameras should be set up. Until you tell the director (and everyone else) that you are changing location, no one is going to move.

In scripts you can capitalize words, even in mid-sentence, to emphasize sounds or if you want to be sure that something stands out.

Each time you begin a new act, you must start on a new page.

You should always include page numbers. In television scripts, the page number will be in the upper right hand corner. The number will be followed by a period. (e.g., "13.").

Each page of your outline must end in punctuation. If the last sentence on the page doesn't fit, then go to the next page and begin the new sentence there.

One last thing: unlike books, scripts and outlines have two spaces between sentences. This applies to both scene description and dialogue.

HOW MULTI-CAM SHOWS DIFFER IN FORMAT

You will see in the next chapter that the format for multi-cam scripts is significantly different than single-cam scripts. In terms of outlining, however, they are pretty much done the same way. The only real variance is that in multi-cam outlines, scenes will be assigned either a letter or a number. So let's say, for the sake of argument, that Steve's pilot was a multi-cam sitcom. His first scene would then begin like this:

SCENE A

INT. POLICE STATION – NIGHT
It is 1940s New York and the retirement party for Bull Hauser, one of the most respected and oldest members of the police force. Bull stands at the make shift podium, tears streaming down his face as he, filled with emotion, tells all of co-workers what working there all of these years means to him.

Notice in this case, Bull's name is not in capital letters. That's because in multi-cam scripts, character names are not generally capitalized. Another thing that multi-cam shows do differently is that, after the first scene, they add a reference as to how much time has passed since the previous scene. Keeping with the idea that Steve's script is a multi-cam show, here is how his second scene would look in outline form:

SCENE B

INT. DWAYNE MONTEGUE'S CAR – SAME NIGHT –
A LITTLE WHILE LATER
As Dwayne and company drive away from the police
station, "Moon River" from *Breakfast at Tiffany's* plays
on the car CD player (blatantly disregarding that there
were no CD players in the 1950s). Dwayne looks off,
obviously affected by the music. One of his cronies
straight up asks him why he always insists on listening to
this song, and follows it up by asking if this beautiful song
is representative of a guarded secret that reveals a soul
that Dwayne looks at him and closes his eyes.

READING YOUR WORK, OUT LOUD

I always tell writers that they should read their work out loud — and this includes outlines — before handing it in to anyone. This advice is seldom taken. I know, because I constantly get outlines where a word is missing, sentence structure isn't varied, the same verb is used repeatedly, etc, etc. On the occasions that I actually hear these writers read their work out loud, I watch in quiet amusement as they catch their own typos and mistakes, and find themselves stumbling over their own words. If a writer can't read his or her own outline smoothly, how do you think a producer will ever make it through? There is something about reading your work out loud that allows you to really hear it. I can promise you that if you do this, you will immediately realize where things are off, and thus you will be able to give it another pass before sending it out.

GETTING FEEDBACK ON YOUR OUTLINE

Once you have finished your story outline, it is imperative that you get feedback before diving into the script. Again, this is where you will likely learn if your story is working. It is ideal to get feedback from people who understand television writing. However, if that isn't feasible, look for people that watch the show you are writing. Tell them up front that you want them to be honest in their critique of your work (and when they are, don't make them feel badly about it). The danger in giving your work to family and close friends is that they may be reluctant to tell you the whole truth if they think it might hurt your feelings. You need to make them understand that if your story isn't working, you would rather hear it from them now rather than from producers and agents later.

For me, the general rule of feedback is to remember that everyone has his or her own opinion of what's good and what's not. At the very least, you should look for feedback from three people before moving forward. If two out of three or all three make the same comment about something, you should definitely take note. This is a red flag that something isn't working. If three people out of three people all come to the same conclusion, chances are so will agents and producers. Now is the chance to change things.

However, if people are pointing out different things, then you should listen and consider what they have to say. If it works for you, great. Go ahead and incorporate whatever it is and you will probably have an even better outline and script. If it doesn't interest you, you obviously don't have to use it. Remember, whoever is reading your work is doing you a favor, so try to listen to the criticism without being argumentative. There is nothing worse than a defensive writer.

The one danger in receiving feedback is that some people may look at your story and have an entirely different approach. This can make you rethink the entire story. Be careful about this. There are a gazillion ways to tell a story. You have picked the way that you want to tell it. Just because someone has a different way doesn't mean that way is better. It could be that it is just a different path. Of course, if that approach is definitively better, then it might be worth making the change.

A WORD ABOUT COVERS

When doing an outline or script, you should use a cover page. Again, there are industry standards for how covers are done, and I don't suggest you deviate from them. Covers should be on white paper and the type should be black ink only. Stay away from fancy fonts (even if the actual show uses one) and from adding any kind of pictures or cartoons or anything else that you think is funny. Professional writers rely on the written word. Period.

A cover page should include the name of the show in capital letters. This should be centered on the page and underlined. Then, skip a space and write the title of your episode. This should be centered and put in quotes using upper and lower case letters. Skip another space and center the words "Written By." Then skip another space and center the two most important words: your name.

To better demonstrate what I mean, let me give you an example, using Steve's pilot episode. Here is what Steve's cover page would look like:

<u>PEOPLE EMPLOYED BY THE STATE OF NEW YORK TO FIGHT
CRIME IN THE 1940S</u>

"This is the Episode Where the Series Begins Because of
Complications Between the Good Guys and the Bad Guys"

Written By

Steve Pinto

This information starts about a third to halfway down the page. If this were a professional outline — in other words, you had been hired to do it — you also want to include the words "Story Outline" and the date in the lower right-hand corner. If it were a professional script instead of an outline, you'd write "First Draft" or "Final Draft" and the date down in the lower right-hand corner. When it comes to spec scripts, however, I do not believe in putting a date on the cover. Dates are important on work for hire, because they leave a paper trail, should there be any legal issues. But for spec scripts, I think dates can be detrimental. Let's say your agent starts to send out the script, but you don't get work right away. Six months later, when the agent is still sending the script to producers, they will see the date and know that your work has been out there for a while, yet no one has hired you. In its own way, it sends a subliminal message that the script must not be that great.

If you are sending your script out, you should put your contact information in the lower right-hand corner, so that people will know how to contact you, should they wish to discuss your work. Once you get an agent, your personal information, such as address and phone number, will be replaced by your agent's contact information.

Before sending your work out, you should always register it with the Writers Guild of America (see Chapter 26). When you do, you will be given a registration number. Many writers put this number in the lower right-hand corner of the script. While I always register my work before sending it anywhere, I do not ever list that it is registered on my script cover. A writer for whom I have a great deal of respect once cautioned me against this. He said that successful writers steer clear of this practice because it sends a message to people reading it that you don't really trust them. Professional writers don't walk in the door expecting their work to be stolen. They expect producers to do well by them and to treat them fairly. I agree with this philosophy, and have come to realize that most working writers don't add the WGA disclaimer. The bottom line is that if someone is going to steal your idea, they are going to steal your idea, and I am sorry to tell you that most likely they won't be deterred by a WGA registration number.

CHECKLIST FOR STORY OUTLINE

- Is your outline written in the present tense?
- Did you use all of the show's regular characters?
- Have you refrained from unnecessary dialogue?
- Did you add jokes if you have them?
- Have you steered clear of overusing camera angles?
- Did you vary sentence structure?
- Does each act begin on a new page?
- Does each page end with punctuation, rather than in mid-sentence?
- Did you spell-check your outline?
- Have you read your work out loud?
- Have you given your work to at least three people for feedback?
- Have you made changes to the outline based on that feedback?

If you answered "yes" to all of the above, then you are finally ready to begin writing your script.

SCRIPTING YOUR SITCOM

FORMATTING YOUR SITCOM SCRIPT

As with the outline, if you want your script to be read by anyone in the industry, you absolutely, positively must put it in proper format. Beware: there are many rules to formatting a script. While it is definitely possible to type your teleplay in Microsoft™ Word or similar programs, if you are serious about becoming a television writer, you may want to invest in some scriptwriting software. Though not cheap, this software formats your script to industry standards with just a few simple keystrokes. In the end, it will save you much time and aggravation. If you are a student at a college or university, you can often find deals that will allow you to purchase the software at a discounted rate, sometimes up to as much as 50% off. I would only recommend buying this software if you are 100% certain that you want to be a television/film writer. It becomes an expensive venture unless this is a path that you are sure you want to follow. There are many different scriptwriting software programs available. The one that most writers seem to prefer is Final Draft®. This program is also compatible with the Writers Guild of America Script Registry, which will allow you to register your work online before sending it out.

THE DIFFERENCE BETWEEN A FIRST DRAFT AND A SHOOTING SCRIPT

As I mentioned earlier, it is important to purchase a script of the show for which you are writing. You should follow that show's format to a tee. That said, there are a couple of things you might find confusing, as it is possible the script you bought will be a "shooting script."

You already know that in television writing the script goes from the writer's first draft directly to the writing staff, who make their own revisions. This is the version that goes to the Table Reading. Both versions of this script are generally on white paper and completely clean — starting on page one and ending on whatever the last page happens to be.

Once the script goes into production, it becomes known as a shooting script. The writing staff starts to make changes. Any changes that are made are denoted by an asterisk (*), which appears in the far right-hand margin of the page. The asterisk is to alert both the actors and the production team that changes have been made to what was originally written or planned. These asterisks will only appear on scripts that are in production or have been produced. In your spec scripts, you won't need to worry about this.

When revisions are made to shooting scripts, each set of changes goes out on a different colored paper. Each show has its own variation on color rotation. Sometimes, after a few days, actors end up walking around with scripts that are rainbow-colored rather than the original white, as they will often insert only the new pages with changes into the script.

A shooting script can, on occasion, have "A" pages. Let's say, on page 19, the producers made changes, and the changes didn't all fit onto the page. In that case, there would be an "A" page, so the order would be page 19, page 19A, page 20. The actors would then toss out the old page 19 and replace it with the new pages 19 and 19A This isn't something you need to be concerned with for your spec. You should start on page 1 and continue through to the end in numerical order.

Another thing you want to be wary of when looking at a shooting script is the page count. You may notice that it has fewer pages than that which I have told you are acceptable. Therefore, you may think your multi-camera sitcom only has to be about 36 pages, rather than around 45 because the staff writers only write 36 pages. This is not the case at all. Shooting scripts start out at the normal page count. But as the week progresses, they are cut for time. When producers go into post-production, it is crucial that they have more than 22 minutes (the actual length of a half hour show once commercials are added) worth of film. An edit is really the final rewrite of the show. Things will be cut — jokes that didn't work, a line an actor may have stumbled on, etc., etc. Thus, the writers have to write more than what will eventually be used to give the director and executive producer choice in post. They don't, however, want to go into an edit with enormous amounts of extra stuff because the edit will end up being more costly both in terms of time and money. To reach a happy medium, part of the writing staff's job is to cut the script as they go through the rehearsals and see things that are not exactly working.

If you buy a shooting script, you may notice a couple of odd pages at the front that include a cast list, a production schedule, and a breakdown, and you may wonder if you need to include them in your own script. The breakdown is hard to miss: just as it sounds, it breaks down the scenes in terms of scene heading, which characters are in the scene, and the corresponding page numbers of the scene to the actual script. In a spec script, you don't have to worry about including any of these elements. They are only done for shows that are in production. Likewise, once a show goes into production, it will be assigned a production number. Since your spec script is only a writing sample, it doesn't have a production number, therefore you don't have to worry about including one.

FORMATTING THE SINGLE-CAM SCRIPT

Since you are already familiar with the first act of Steve Pinto's single-cam pilot outline, let's take a look at Steve's first four pages and see how he transformed his outline into the actual script. Notice right off the top that he has added a scene that was not in his original outline. The scene is an exterior, which sets the mood and tone of the piece. He has also put in a Narrator. The scenes are reprinted with Steve's permission.

<u>ACT ONE</u>

FADE IN:

EXT. NEW YORK CITY STREETS – NIGHT

New York City. 1947. Smoke billows up from the sewers, mixing with a light snowfall to fill the streets in a grey haze. Black and white photography captures it in all of its ... grittiness.

A narrator, with a voice maybe even more manly than Robert Stack's, begins to speak, his words filled with importance.

> NARRATOR (V.O.)
> New York City. 1947. Smoke billows
> up from the sewers, mixing with a
> light snowfall to fill the streets in a
> grey haze.

A black stretch limousine slowly makes its way through the empty streets. Following the car, we see a poorly executed rendition of this time period; antique vehicles, several buildings seemingly made out of cardboard, a Starbucks that was supposed to be cut out of the frame but wasn't.

> NARRATOR (V.O.)
> It was December. A lot like any other
> stinkin' night in this stinkin' town,
> but not.

The limousine pulls to the side of the road and parks right in front of THE POLICE STATION.

> NARRATOR (V.O.)
> Because on this night, underneath
> the surface of gaiety and safety,
> there was an undertone of unsafety.
> An undertone of not being safe. An
> undertone of ... crime.

The limo sits, still running, its lights piercing through the snow.

As we leave the limo and head towards the police station, a delightful party is happening inside on the second floor. From outside of the window. we can see that streamers and frilly things hang from the ceiling, along with a banner that reads "BULL HAUSER – YA GOT HIM – HAPPY RETIRE-MENT." All attention seems to be focused on one man who holds a microphone in his hand. His beard is massive.

INT. POLICE STATION – CONTINUOUS

The man with the disgusting beard is BULL HAUSER, 65, and grizzly as hell. He stands at the podium, in the middle of his speech. His wife, CHRISTINE, half his age, stands with their two children, CHARLIE, 9 and TOOTIE, 6, by his side. He is very openly emotional.

> BULL
> I am a man. Through the web of lies
> and conspiracy, I stuck to my guns.

Bull's boss, DENVER, 39, makes his voice heard.

> DENVER
> Pun intended!

The crowd explodes in laughter.

> BULL
> Oh, Denver. You are a hilarious man
> and a wonderful boss. I have enjoyed
> your humor and guidance.

Denver makes a fist and brings it to his chest, touched.

> BULL (cont'd)
> What I am trying to say is that I
> believed in myself. Believed in justice.
> Let that be a lesson to all of you, all
> of you trying to make a differ ence in
> this sometimes wretched world. You
> can make a difference, as I have. I
> believed that Dwayne Montegue, who
> was the evil racketeer I chased for
> fifteen years, unsuccessfully, until I
> killed him last week, was evil. Justice
> found Dwayne Montegue, ladies and
> gentlemen. It found him.

The crowd cheers.

> BULL (cont'd)
> I am ready to retire because I have
> nothing left to do. This man, who was
> my life's work, is dead. Yet I feel alive
> for the first time. Because he is dead.

He pumps his fist in the air.

> BULL (cont'd)
> God damn it. Yes! My work is done!

Just as he says this last line, out from a rather film noir/shadowy part of the room steps BEESLEY LYME, a mildly eccentric gentleman.

> BEESLEY
> Or is it?

The crowd gasps and turns as Beesley, who nobody knew was in the room, slowly saunters towards the exit.

> BEESLEY (cont'd)
> He's alive.

Beesley starts to chuckle aloud while looking wide-eyed at everyone in the room.

> BEESLEY (cont'd)
> Yes. He is alive.

Lyme's smile widens. Everyone is shocked. Speechless. This is really shocking stuff.

> BEESLEY (cont'd)
> Ta ta.

He steps out of the room, leaving the room cold. Mortified. Upset even.

> BULL
> God damn it. Why would Beesley
> Lyme, Dwayne Montegue's right-hand
> man, be here right now? Why?
> I thought I killed Montegue.
> What's the idea?

> DENVER
> (gritty)
> That Beesley Lyme is nothin' but grime.

EXT. NEW YORK CITY STREETS – MOMENTS LATER

Beesley makes his way out of the police station, and heads towards the limousine, opening the door and getting inside.

                     NARRATOR (V.O.)
             In fact it was true. Beesley was not
             lying. The undertone of doom going
             around the city was there because
             Dwayne Montegue was alive. Not dead.

Amidst the snow, the driver exits the limousine, and slowly
walks towards the opposite side, opening the door. The
song "Moon River" plays softly inside the car.

Notice how the outline and script begin the same way. ACT ONE is in capital letters, centered, and underlined. Then, a space is skipped and the words FADE IN.

The first thing we see is the scene heading. In single-cam scripts, it is in capital letters, but it is not underlined.

Directly beneath the scene heading is the action line(s) [sometimes referred to as "business" line(s)]. This is where you want to set up what is happening just as we enter the scene.

Here are a few formatting things that you should note. See how the character names all line up, regardless of how many letters are in the character's name. This is the correct way to write a script. Sometimes new writers think the names should be centered. This is incorrect. If you aren't using a script program, which will automatically set up the format for character names, then you should use the "tab" key rather than the "center" key. The same goes for dialogue, which all lines up at the left dialogue margin. Again, you do not want to use the "center" key at all.

As you can easily see, the characters and dialogue do not extend out in either direction as far as the action lines do, but rather, they seem to be indented right and left. This is hugely important. One of the biggest mistakes that new writers make is that they overextend the dialogue margin on the right side of the page. This is a big issue, because it means that if your script were put in proper format, you would actually have more pages than it appears you do, which of course, affects time.

At the very end of Steve's outline, he uses "parens" (short for "parentheticals") to give a character direction in how to say the line. It is remarkable to me that this is the first time he does it. Young writers often find it hard to resist using parens as a way to instruct actors how to do their jobs. In addition to annoying actors, too many parens actually ruin the read of your script. It is better to use them sparingly. The information contained in parens should be short and sweet. A few words at the most. If you find you have more than that, you should put the information into an action line. Do not use parens at the end of a character's speech; this also goes in an action line, as does stage direction that is meant for another character.

You may have wondered what the abbreviations were in parentheticals next to the character's name. V.O stands for voice over, meaning the narrator isn't present reading the script. O.S. stands for off screen, which signals that we hear the character, but don't see him on screen. CONT'D indicates that the character's dialogue continues, even though there may have been action in between the lines.

While we are on the subject of continuing dialogue, in both single- and multi-cam shows, you must end each page on punctuation. You never want to break a character's line in mid-sentence. So, as you are typing, if you come to the bottom of the page and the character's dialogue isn't going to fit, you must add (MORE) after the character's last line on the page. When you get to the next page, you must add (cont'd). Let's say that Bull's speech came toward the end of a page. This is how it would break onto the next page:

BULL

What I am trying to say is that I believed in myself. Believed in justice. Let that be a lesson to all of you, all of you trying to make a difference in this sometimes wretched world.

(MORE)

BULL (cont'd)

You <u>can</u> make a difference, as I have. I believed that Dwayne Montegue, who was the evil racketeer I chased for fifteen years, unsuccessfully, until I killed him last week, was evil. Justice found Dwayne Montegue, ladies and gentlemen. It found him.

See how Steve ended on the word "world." This is because the next sentence would not fit, so he moved it onto the next page. Also notice how the (MORE) is in capital letters and lines up with the character's name.

SAMPLE FORMAT FOR MULTI-CAM SCRIPTS

Format for multi-cam shows differs from format for single-cam shows. Following are the first two pages of a pilot called "Girls Above Sunset," written by Manny Basanese (writer/producer of *The Steve Harvey Show* and *The Wayans Brothers*) and reprinted with his permission. After you have read the teaser, I will point out some of the more important format issues involving multi-camera sitcoms.

1.

"GIRLS ABOVE SUNSET"

COLD OPENING

FADE IN:

INT. IMAGE TALENT AGENCY – DAY (DAY 1)

(Amy, Corey, Noah, Extras)

COREY MAYER, THE MAIL ROOM BOY, ENTERS WITH AMY COOK. YOUNG, BUBBLY AND WIDE-EYED, AMY SEEMS DAZZLED BY THE PLACE.

                              AMY

Thanks for taking time out from the mailroom to

show me around, Corey.

                             COREY

No biggie.

AN AGENT WEARING A HEADSET WALKS BY.

                              AMY

I've never seen so many people wearing headsets.

It reminds me of my very first concert. Janet

Jackson's Rhythm Nation at the Wisconsin Civic

Center. Wasn't it admirable the way Janet used

dance music and lipsynching to stamp out

poverty and racism? I hope one day I can make

a positive difference with my art. I want to be

a screenwriter.

COREY DIRECTS AMY TO A DESK OUTSIDE ONE OF THE
OFFICES.

                             COREY

Right. Here's where you sit.

NOAH GALLAGHER, A SEASONED AGENT, ENTERS FROM
HIS OFFICE.

                        COREY (cont'd)

And here's the agent you'll be working for. Noah

Gallagher, this is Amy Cook, your new temp.

                             NOAH

Please no names. She's a temp. We have a job to

get you started on ... the Tom Cruise meeting.

                              AMY

Oh my God! I'm gonna meet Tom Cruise? I just

love him. And I'm not like Rosie. I really mean it.

                              NOAH

We already had the meeting. Just clean up the

conference room and wash out the coffee cups.

                              AMY

Oh my God! I'm going to get to wash out

Tom Cruise's coffee cup? I love L.A.!

AMY RUSHES OFF HAPPILY.

                                             CUT TO:

Okay, let's start with the slugline. Unlike single-cam sitcoms, in multi-cam sitcoms the slugline is underlined. Notice that right beneath the slugline in parens is a list of all of the characters that appear in the scene. This will be the case in most multi-cam scripts. The only thing that really varies is where the names are placed. You should refer to the sample script you purchased to reference how your particular show does it and then follow suit.

Another issue in the two formats is that the action lines in multi-cam are in all caps. If you are writing a multi-cam script, be sure that all of your action lines are in capital letters. In some multi-cam scripts when an actor enters or exits a scene, the entrance or exit will be underlined. At the risk of sounding like a broken record … again, you must do it whatever way your particular show does it.

Perhaps the biggest formatting difference is that in multi-cam, the dialogue is double-spaced. Young writers often get confused at how single-cam scripts come in at around 30–35 pages, while multi-cam scripts come in at approximately 45–48 pages. Double-spaced dialogue (along with a couple of other formatting issues) makes multi-cam scripts longer. Also take note that there is a space between the character name and where the dialogue begins.

In multi-cam format, when one scene ends, there will be a "transition." This is a description of how we will be taken from one scene to the next. Common transitions between scenes include "DISSOLVE TO:" (shows a passage of time), "CUT TO:" (no passage of time), or "FADE OUT," (fade to black). Transitions should be typed in capital letters and placed in the far-right margin.

Unlike single-cam sitcoms where the scenes follow each other on the same page, multi-cam sitcoms require a new page every time we go to a new scene. In addition, each new scene should begin about a third of the way down the page.

Script writing software like Final Draft will automatically set up correct margins for you. Writers who are not working with this kind of program will often ask about exact margins for scripts. To be honest, I don't believe there are exact margins. I have seen numbers here and there, but they are all a little bit different. Every show really has its own margins. Most shows are similar, but not exact copycats of each other. Here is the easiest thing I can suggest for those who are using tab keys rather than script software: type out your first page. Then, take the first page out of the script you purchased and hold the two up to the light. See how closely your margins match that particular script, and make adjustments from there.

While I am on the subject of margins, let me urge you to resist the temptation to add a couple of spaces here and there in the margins to make your dialogue or action work. This is often a trick of new writers who want to bring a script in on time, but perish the thought of cutting anything they have written. By lengthening margins, they think they are fooling readers and/or producers. This is not the case. People who read scripts every day have a trained eye. They will pick up on your dirty little secret in a heartbeat, and you will look foolish. The script will read long. Develop professional habits now, starting with your spec. Part of your job as a writer is to bring scripts in on time. If you cheat the margins when you are writing professionally, you will be caught immediately. The first thing that will happen when you turn in your script is that the script assistants will put your script through their software program. If you have cheated the margins to make your script appear to be 45 pages when it's really 54 pages, once it goes through their program, the script will be what it is: 54 pages. This will be annoying to the writing staff, who will now have to do the job you didn't do — and that is to cut your script.

SCENE WRITING FROM BEGINNING TO END

In writing a scene, you want to come in at the last possible moment of the main action of that scene. Ask yourself, what is the purpose of this scene? If the main purpose is for a couple to elope, then start with the woman throwing her suitcase out the window. Don't start with her packing and calling all of her friends. Even though that may be what happens in real life, sitcoms are 22 minutes. You have to cut through the frivolous stuff and get to the point quickly. Each scene should have its own beginning, middle, and end.

Wherever you choose to start, be sure to give the actors something to do. No actor wants to just stand there, waiting for the scene to begin — it makes them feel stupid, not to mention that no action is deadly dull on screen. So, don't have the actor sitting on the couch doing nothing. Let him read the paper. Even changing a light bulb would be better than just hanging out, waiting for the scene to begin. If an actor is purposefully waiting for something to happen, then let him pace. There has to be some definitive action.

HOW MANY JOKES SHOULD YOU HAVE ON EACH PAGE?

There are those who will tell you that agents and producers will actually count the number of jokes that you have on each page. I am not certain that this is true, as when I inquire as to what the magic number actually is, no one seems to have an exact answer. So, while I'm not going to tell you to write X number of jokes per page, I will tell you that when writing comedy, each page should have as many jokes as possible — and most definitely, each page should have some jokes. Comedy has a definitive rhythm. In reading sitcom scripts, I quickly become aware if I haven't laughed or at least cracked a smile in the last 30 seconds. I will then flip back to the last joke. If I have to go back even a page, that is too long. The writer has not done his or her job.

> "Never write down to your audience. Sometimes we write a joke that we think is funny. But we think the audience won't get it because they aren't as smart as us. Not true. They will get it." — Bob Daily, co-producer, *Frasier*; co-executive producer, *Desperate Housewives*

SETTING UP JOKES AND PAYING THEM OFF

Watch stand-up comics, and you will see that they set up a joke and deliver the punchline. As if this isn't hard enough on its own, sitcoms writers have to set up jokes and pay them off, while at the same time advancing the story. When you read sitcom scripts and watch them on TV, you will start to notice that jokes have a definitive rhythm to them. Set it up, pay it off, set it up, pay it off …

As you write jokes, there are a couple of things to keep in mind. The setup to a joke is usually a straight (as in not funny) line. In contrast, this makes a good punchline seem all the more hilarious. Sometimes, I see jokes where I know intuitively what laugh the writer is going after, but the joke fails. Nine times out of ten, this is because the setup is wrong. Sometimes, it's only one little word that stands in the way of a joke working. In trying to fix a joke, novice writers will instinctively go straight to the punchline. Keep in mind that a joke is two parts: the setup and the punchline. If you are having problems making a joke work and you feel that the punchline is correct, try to go back and adjust the setup.

WHY SMART JOKES WILL GET A BIGGER LAUGH

For me, the most aggravating sitcoms to watch are those where I hear the setup to a joke and I beat the actor to the punchline. If I already know the punchline, hearing it delivered, even from the most brilliant comedic actor, isn't going to make me laugh. The way to make an audience laugh is not to give them the line they anticipate, but rather to throw them a curve and slam them with something they didn't see coming. This doesn't mean that every idea or joke has to be brand-spanking-new. Someone slipping on a banana peel, which is the oldest joke in the book, is still darned funny … as long as I don't know it's going to happen before the person actually slips.

> "It's the surprise at the end of the line that you didn't expect that makes you laugh." — Al Burton, executive producer, *Charles in Charge*

Writing smart jokes is the hardest thing in the world. It takes enormous brainpower. It also takes extraordinary patience to throw okay-joke after okay-joke into the trashcan. But if you keep pushing yourself to find those brilliant punchlines, you will rise to the top faster than most.

> "A smart joke isn't necessarily a joke per se. It can be a piece of dialogue, a situation, or even a camera angle, but it requires the audience to possess some additional, not commonly referenced bit of knowledge in order to be funny." — Lee Aronsohn, executive producer and co-creator, *Two and a Half Men*

WHERE DO GOOD JOKES COME FROM?

Good jokes generally come through character. Let's look at *Curb Your Enthusiasm*, which happens to be my current favorite sitcom. All I have to do is see Susie come on screen and I know I am in for a laugh. Whatever is going to come out of her mouth will undoubtedly be funny. Now, for the sake of argument, let's take some of those fabulously funny Susie lines and try to imagine them coming out of any other sitcom character on TV today. In that context, they aren't quite so funny, are they? That's because the best jokes come directly from character.

Character lines are not ever interchangeable. As you write, you really need to get into the character's head. Think how that character would think. Look at the character's flaws and weaknesses … these places are often a treasure chest in which to find good jokes.

> "I think a joke is good if you can find some part of it that relates to you. If a joke gets just one fool laughing, it's good. If a joke gets a lot of fools laughing, it's great." — John Frink, co-executive producer, *The Simpsons*

INCORPORATING UNIVERSAL HUMOR

There are some situations that nearly everyone on the planet can relate to. Take, for example, the classic episode of *Seinfeld* where the gang went shopping, forgot where they parked, and spent hours wandering aimlessly around a huge parking garage looking for their car. Who among us has not had a similar experience? When it happens to us, we feel both stupid and frustrated. So, watching the same thing happen to Jerry, George, Elaine, and Kramer is funny stuff. It's funny because we get it. At some point in our lives, most of us have been there, done that.

If you can find situations or moments that a vast majority of people can relate to, you are all but guaranteed laughs. But don't over-think it. Keep in mind that sometimes — as the writers of *Seinfeld* proved time and time again — the funniest things have to do with life's smaller moments.

SHOULD YOU AVOID JOKES THAT COULD BE CONSIDERED "OFFENSIVE"?

In this world of political correctness, some new writers worry that they should be censoring themselves, so as not to offend anyone. I believe this to be completely the wrong approach. First and foremost, comedy is not politically correct, and the day that it becomes so is the day that it will cease to exist. In order to stand out as a comedy writer, you have to be a risk taker and be willing to show them in no uncertain terms what you are made of.

That said, you don't want to write a script that is just a stream of racy, dirty, politically incorrect jokes just to show that you can. Don't shock just to shock. Jokes have to fit in with your storyline, and they have to come out of the characters. But if you are at all on the fence about a joke, in terms of it being too offensive, my advice is to take a chance and put it in. Most readers aren't going to cross you off their list on the basis of one offensive joke. On the other hand, bold and chancy jokes can make you stand out. My former writing partner and I once got an agent based on one extremely distasteful joke. The agent said he couldn't believe that two women would actually write "those words" (which by today's standards were nothing) and attach their names to it. The bottom line is this: if jokes are too offensive, they can always be cut, but you will probably make a lot of people laugh and gain a lot of fans beforehand.

> "Today's TV market is so cluttered and competitive that I think buyers are looking for anything that may have a chance of cutting through the noise, and if that requires writing what people might find raunchy and outrageous then so be it. I don't think playing it safe gets anyone too far

these days and there are plenty of instances where making a choice that probably seemed scary at the time has paid off in the end." — David Nichols, executive producer, *Caroline in the City*; co-executive producer, *Grace Under Fire*

BEWARE OF JOKES THAT CENTER AROUND CURRENT TOPICS

If possible, try to stay away from jokes that have to do with current issues or politics that aren't likely to stay on the front page for too long. These things may get a laugh today, but six months from now, they won't be funny and they will make your spec script seem dated.

To illustrate this point, take a look at *Murphy Brown* in reruns. It's not nearly as funny now as it was when it was originally on the air. In its time, Dan Quayle, then vice president of the United States, not knowing how to spell a simple word like potato was funny stuff. Today, not only is it not funny, people barely remember the incident. On the other hand, if you look at the old *Dick Van Dyke* show, you will see that they rarely, if ever reference current events and politics. That show's comedy is timeless, and it is as funny today as it was in the sixties. You may be thinking that I am talking about shows that were on the air years ago. It makes no difference. Jokes centered on current events will grow old much faster than you may think.

IN COMEDY, THREE'S A CHARM

Read and watch TV comedy, and you will soon realize that things happen in threes. Jokes are often set up in three parts, with the third one being the punchline. Let's say two nuns are having dinner at the convent. Nun #1 asks Nun #2, "Sister, what do you secretly pray for?" to which Nun #2 responds, "I pray for world peace, the end of poverty and hunger, and one long, hot night with Ashton Kutcher."

In this case, the first two items, "world peace" and "the end of poverty and hunger," act as the setup. They seem to go hand-in-hand, and they are both perfectly in line with what one would expect a nun to secretly pray for. In this joke, "one long, hot night with Ashton Kutcher" is the punchline. It's completely opposite the two things that precede it, and it is 100% off character for what we'd expect a nun to secretly want.

As you write, look for jokes that can be set up this way. If done correctly, they almost always get a big laugh.

RUNNERS

A runner is a small joke that repeats itself, usually in different ways throughout an episode. Think of it as the joke that keeps on giving. Sometimes, runners can almost feel like "C" stories because they are small, but go throughout the entire story. Sitcoms use runners a lot. If you can, add one to your script, and it will be all the funnier.

ALLITERATION

Comedy writers often rely on alliteration for laughs or at least for smiles. For some (odd) reason the human heart is warmed upon hearing words strung together that start with the same letter or sound alike in terms of syllables. In my *Full House* "Slumber Party" episode, Danny takes Michelle clothes shopping. You tell me which store sounds funnier: "Barbie's Dress Shop" or The "Teeny Tiny Tots Shop"? Obviously, "Barbie's Dress Shop" isn't funny at all. But, the "Teeny Tiny Tots Shop" has a certain funny ring to it. Alliteration rarely provokes knee-slapping laughs, but it does usually put a grin on people's faces.

COMEDY THAT GOES AGAINST CHARACTER

Another sure-fire way to get laughs is to have a character do or say something that is completely contradictory to the character we know. When this happens, it usually catches an audience off guard, prompting a laugh. The key is to make sure that there is a clear and valid reason for the character's behavior. Otherwise it could look like you don't know the character.

PUTTING THE AUDIENCE IN A SUPERIOR POSITION

Another way to get laughs is to do what is known as placing your audience in a superior position. This means that you give the audience information that at least one character doesn't have. As viewers watch that character go about his business, ignorant of whatever it is the audience knows but he doesn't, they will almost certainly laugh. If done correctly, this kind of story setup can be downright hysterical. Whenever possible, look to see what tidbits you may be able to spill to the audience ahead of time, before the character catches on.

DON'T FORGET TO BUTTON

At the end of each scene, make sure you include a "button." A button is a joke, but in this case, it should be one of your better jokes, and it should have a really strong punchline. Buttons transition both reader and viewer from one scene to another. It's the old "leave 'em laughing when you go" mentality. Those few seconds of laughter give us a moment to breathe as we are propelled from one scene into the next. Buttons are extremely important to the rhythm of sitcoms.

After you have written your rough draft, be sure to go back and look at the end of each scene to make sure you have included a really clever button.

THE DREADED PUNCH-UP

Once you have a rough first draft, now you are ready for the hard part. You must go through your script line-by-line, joke-by-joke, and punch up the comedy. No doubt you will find places — perhaps even pages — that are void of jokes. You will also find jokes that you secretly know aren't all that funny. You can't just leave them. Punching up a script is perhaps the most difficult thing a comedy writer has to do. Sometimes, it can take hours, even days, to come up with one line or one joke. I have literally seen writing staffs work from sundown until sunup, punching up a script. It doesn't come easy, even for professionals.

> "In reading specs, one thing that connects the bad ones is that the writer didn't spend enough time. I wrote a spec *Everybody Loves Raymond*, which I spent 4–5 months on. I would randomly open it and see if there was a good joke on that page. If there wasn't, I knew I had work to do." — Bob Daily, supervising producer, *Frasier*; co-executive producer, *Desperate Housewives*

WATCH WHERE YOU STEP

Once you have set up a joke and delivered a punchline, leave it alone at least for a moment. Don't do what is known as stepping on the joke. This is done when a joke is buried within a character's dialogue. The writer writes the joke, but then immediately moves on by giving the character more lines without a break or even a breath. The audience needs these few seconds to digest the joke and laugh. Writers who step on their own jokes do themselves, the actors, and the audience a disservice. Consider it a no-no.

8

OTHER KINDS OF TV COMEDY

WRITING FOR ANIMATION

Many, if not all of us have an affinity for cartoons that can be traced back to our childhoods. So, it should come as no surprise then that when *The Simpsons* hit the airwaves in 1989, it became an instant hit and has remained so ever since. To date, it is the longest running prime time animated series in America. It also currently holds the record as the longest running sitcom in the U.S. This animated series for adults was the brainchild of creator Matt Groening and is actually a spin-off of *The Tracey Ullman Show*. The Simpsons are the antithesis of traditional sitcom families; Homer and Bart have become American icons and together, along with their creators, they have singlehandedly reinvented animation. With sharp shows that followed, like *South Park* and *Family Guy*, animation is currently one of the hottest, most watched forms of television today. This is not likely to change.

> "You want to describe the action in detail, but you also want to leave enough room for the animator's creativity. Animators will add their own comedy and bits. It's very collaborative." — Screenwriter Kate Boutilier, *Rugrats* and *The Wild Thornberrys*

In some ways writing for animation is like writing for traditional sitcoms, and in some ways it is much different. If you browse through an animated script, you will see that it looks very much like a regular sitcom script. Some animated shows are written single-camera film-style, others multi-cam style. Some use three-act structure; others opt for traditional two-act structure.

> "There's very little difference in writing animation vs. a live-action sitcom. The stories still have to be compelling and work to take the characters on a journey. On *The Simpsons*, we have a cartoon wrapped around a family, so we constantly look for real family stories, situations, and

emotions. But I believe any animated show searches for these things. Sponge Bob still cries and laughs and gets jealous and falls in love. He may do it thousands of feet under water but it's these differences that make every show, animated or live action, unique." John Frink, co-executive producer, *The Simpsons*

Perhaps the most significant difference between the two is that with animation, the sky is really the limit in terms of what you can do. Traditional sitcoms are hugely restricted by money, time, and what can be done by human actors. In animation, if a writer can think it, an animator can draw it. Animation writers are lucky in that they don't have to be in the constant mindset of "can the show afford to do this?"

In animation, the process between writer and animator is extremely collaborative. To be successful, the two must work in harmony. In the same way sitcom writers turn over their scripts to a director, animation writers put their scripts into the hands of an animator. In order to do this, animation writers have to translate the vision in their head via scene descriptions. Thus, scene descriptions in animated scripts tend to be more detailed than in traditional sitcom scripts. That said, the true trick for animation writers is to write enough description to get the point across, but not so much that it steps on the animator's own creative vision. Needless to say, this is a delicate balance to strike.

Once the script is finished, the process is different as well. Rather than dealing with actors on a day-to-day basis on a soundstage, actors are brought in to record their voices.

Although some animated shows like *South Park* have a reputation for being able to turn around very quickly, as a rule, animation takes a lot longer to produce. To save money, much of it is done overseas. Thus, it can take many months from the time a script leaves a writer's hands until the show is actually complete and ready for air. In the sitcom world, the process is much quicker. The turnaround time for a sitcom is usually a few weeks to a month, depending on whether or not the show is running behind. I have seen sitcom scripts that were turned in and put into production within a week. This is rarely the case with animation.

"Most of the differences I deal with come in the production of the animated show vs. the live-action sitcom. Animation tends to have a much longer time span from table read to aired show. We read a script, record it, and then move on to other shows until that first show comes back in the form of story boards, animatics, and color versions over the course of nine months. We're able to fix the writing, animation, and voice acting during this time period. Most live-action shows table read on one week day and film/tape the show five days later. The writing and acting has to be fixed in a much shorter time frame. So *The Simpsons* should be roughly 270 days better than all other television, right?" — John Frink, co-executive producer, *The Simpsons*

In addition to the so-called hip shows like *South Park* and *The Simpsons*, if you really want to write animation, you should not overlook the whole Saturday morning cartoon deal. This can be a good place to get the lay of the land. Often these shows are packaged as two cartoons within one half hour block. This kind of writing is so specialized that it has its own union, The Animators Guild.

Another interesting trend that is emerging is that some toy companies are starting to get into the animation game by taking some of their top-selling toys/characters and hiring writers to write animated scripts that are then produced and sold on DVDs. If done well, sometimes these shows are picked up by various broadcast entities and aired. A good example of this is Hasbro, which took their popular "My Little Pony" characters and brought them to life through animation. Unfortunately, this kind of work does not fall under the jurisdiction of the Writers Guild of America, so writers who work on these types of programs do not get paid as much. Still, if you can get the work, it is a good thing to put on your resume, in your quest to stacking up writing credits. This kind of work can definitely lead to other things.

> "Most writers direct their movies in their heads as they write, but they have to be careful not to put too much direction in their script as it is normally the director's place to make those decisions. In animation, the writer is expected to call camera angles, to write every color, tone, expression, and even costume. You get to extend yourself creatively. You have to remember: if it is not on the page, the storyboard artist will not know what you mean." — Bonnie DeSouza, writer, *My Little Pony* and *Fish Police*

WRITING FOR LATE NIGHT

Many writers have a goal of writing for late-night television. While there is nothing wrong with this goal, you have to go in knowing that there is limited work available. If you think there are few jobs in sitcom writing, there are even fewer in late night, as there are significantly fewer programs produced in this venue. Still, if you are so inclined to want to work on shows like *The Late Show with David Letterman, The Tonight Show*, etc., the first thing you need to be is topical. You have to ensconce yourself in current events and pop culture. You have to read newspapers (notice the plural). Secondly, these kinds of shows rely heavily on solid joke writing. Look at the monologues; they are completely joke-driven. So you have to get good at writing really smart jokes.

Perhaps one of the most important things you can do to improve your talents in this arena is to get out into a so-called comedy community. Go to comedy clubs regularly and learn from stand-up comics; learn from the good ones, learn from the bad ones. Join improve groups; do whatever you can do to put yourself in the midst of it. When you feel ready, take the plunge and try your hand at stand-up... Get a feel for the rhythm of the setups and punchlines and even the transitions. Get a handle on the timing of jokes. Once you master the art, you will then have to learn how write jokes in someone else's voice.

> "Get as much stage time as you can. The more stage time you get, the better you will be. Only a tiny, tiny percent of people — I'd say 1% — can be really funny really quick. You have to learn how to be yourself, and that's the hardest thing." — Eddie Brill, stand-up comedian, talent coordinator, *The Late Show with David Letterman*

When you are out in comedy communities, you really need to hang around. Get to know comedians who are more successful than you, as well as those who are on equal footing. This is a very tight-knit group of people and belonging is a good first step. If you see someone you think could be helpful, don't hold back. Tell that person what it is you want and ask if he or she can help.

> "You should physically approach the person you're trying to send material to. If you're a normal person, polite, dressed well, and don't appear to be crazy, you have a shot. People want to help young people. They think, 'that person looks like me when I was just starting out.'" — Jay Leno, host of *The Tonight Show*

Writing for late night isn't much different than writing for any other kind of television in that producers don't take unsolicited material. Everything must come through an agent. Agents are difficult to get, and when the arena you are looking to enter is so specialized, it becomes all the harder. Putting yourself in a position to get your work seen is key. If writing for late night is something you are desperate to do, I highly recommend (as I do with other kinds of writing) that you try to get a job in production on one of these shows. I am not suggesting this is at all easy. It isn't. But if you can get your foot in the door, hopefully you will be in a position where you can eventually pitch some jokes or get your material read, and take off from there.

> "When I started on *The Daily Show,* it was such a small enterprise that people were still able to just send in unsolicited packets that might get read. Some were even hired that way, but not anymore. Maybe there are start-ups that would do such a thing, but that's certainly not the case at most of the late-night shows. Most require your packet be sent in by an agent or manager, and the mysteries of how to get one of those are beyond me." — Eric Drysdale, writer, *The Daily Show* and *The Colbert Report*

SKETCH WRITING

Currently, there are very few sketch shows out there. Of course the most obvious one is *Saturday Night Live.* Work in this arena is so limited that it is almost nonexistent. If your goal has always been to write for a show like *Saturday Night Live,* you need to be aware that it is nearly impossible to get hired as a janitor on that show, much less as a writer. I am not trying to be a downer or stomp on your dreams, but I think it's important that you are realistic. If writing for *Saturday Night Live* is the only thing you want to do in life, then I say go for it, because you won't know for sure until you try. Just be sure you have a back-up plan in case it doesn't work out.

As with other television writing, shows like *SNL* will only look at writers who come through an agent. On occasion an unagented writer might squeak through, if he or she comes by way of one of the well-known comedy groups like *Second City* or *The Harvard Lampoon,* but even this is rare.

A professional writing portfolio for a show like *SNL* will usually contain three or four sketches and a couple of commercial parodies, with maybe a monologue of some sort. The work gets passed around and read by the writing staff, who will then decide whether or not to have that person in for a meeting.

> "Nepotism. It's an ugly word that should remain ugly in most cases, but in the world of entertainment it basically runs everything. I'm not talking about cousins giving cousins high paying jobs at the dump, but friends giving friends high paying jobs because they like them. Comedy people want to be around other like-minded comedy people. They form groups, *Second City, The Groundlings, USB Theater,* stand-up communities, college humor magazines, etc. Form a group. Be a part of a group. Be a part of the "I Hate Groups" group. People in the group know you and they trust you or maybe they just like you. When one of you makes it in the door, the door opens for everybody else." — Andrew Steele, head writer, *Saturday Night Live*

While we are on the subject of sketch writing, I would encourage all comedy writers to try your hand at writing a couple of sketches, even if you fancy yourself a sitcom writer with no interest in a show like *SNL.* Having a couple of sketches in your portfolio can put you ahead of the game as, once in a blue moon, producers will ask agents for them. The vast majority of sitcom writers don't bother to write sketches, so if you have some in your back pocket, that might be the thing that gets you in the door someday. I have seen it happen — and more than once.

Below is an example of what a sketch looks like. It is written by comedian Jon Rineman and reprinted with his permission.

THE LSD

INT. KITCHEN

MAN stands by, about to boil some lobsters. Cheesy infomercial music plays.

> MAN
> Boy! I love lobster! Time to get
> these babies cooking!

Man goes to put lobsters into pot, when PITCH MAN enters.

DOORBELL RINGS.

> PITCH MAN
> Not so fast!

> MAN
> Who the hell are you?

> PITCH MAN
> I'm your new best friend!

> MAN
> (Frantically looking around)
> How did you get into my house?

> PITCH MAN
> I came in through the door. And by door,
> I mean chimney! But that's not what
> I'm here to talk about. I'm here to talk
> about lobsters. What would you say if I
> told you that lobsters couldn't feel
> themselves boiling?

> MAN
> I'd say that's wonderful! I'd feel
> much better about boiling them!

> PITCH MAN
> Well, tough luck, Grandma! They
> feel every waking moment of the
> torture that is being boiled alive!

> MAN
> Oh my God, that's horrible!

> PITCH MAN
> Actually, it's great!
> (MORE)

PITCH MAN (cont'd)
Because now, using the excruciating pain being
realized by our orangey-red victims,
you can measure just how dead your
lobster is, and exactly how close its
carcass is to being joyfully consumed!

MAN
Wow, you mean lobsters actually go
through different stages of death?

PITCH MAN
Whoa, how about you shut the hell up!
Because that's exactly what I was going
to say! You can pinpoint exactly how
cooked your lobster is using the new
Lobster Subsistence Decliner...
    (Holds up small machine)
The LSD.

MAN
Are you crazy? You call this
thing the LSD?!

PITCH MAN
Yes, but not because anyone's
trippin' on acid! It's because
they're trippin' up the lobsters
who are trying to survive! The
way it works is, you pick up the
lobster and put him in the LSD.
As the lobster cooks, you'll be able
to see on this meter exactly where
you are in the process of crustacean homicide.

Pitch Man points to the meter.

MAN
Lobsters are crustaceans?

PITCH MAN
Lobsters are dead once their ass hits
the LSD! Take a look!
    (Pointing to meter)
The lobster begins dying by feeling
an intense increase in heat. Then,
in Phase Two, the lobster's pupils
melt, and it loses its sight completely!

MAN

Lobsters have pupils?!

PITCH MAN

I don't even know if they have eyes!
But they've got a lot of explaining to
do at Phase Three, because that's when
they develop a nasty heroin addiction!

MAN

Heroin? Man!

PITCH MAN

At Phase Four, the lobster experiences
sickening, unthinkable twinges and
swelling as its joints become frayed.
Then comes the mild discomfort.

MAN

Mild?!

PITCH MAN

At Phase Five, the lobster is diagnosed
with rheumatoid arthritis! At Phase
Six, it loses the memory of its
seventh birthday! And then at Phase
Seven, the lobster begins to suffer
from Mad Cow Disease!

MAN

Mad Cow?! Oh God! I don't want
to eat a lobster that has Mad Cow!

PITCH MAN

Oh you won't have to! The
Mad Cow is canceled out at
Phase Eight, when the lobster
catches the Bird Flu!

MAN

Oh my God! Isn't that fatal?!

PITCH MAN

No, it's Avian! Just kidding —
Of course it's fatal! And now
that the lobster is dead, you can go
to town enjoying a fine lobster dinner.

MAN
Well, how much does this thing cost?

PITCH MAN
Cost? That's not important.

MAN
Yes! Yes it is!

PITCH MAN
All I can say is, you better buy it,
because anyone who doesn't will
be declared a member of Al Qaeda
and forced to register as an inter-species
sex offender!

MAN
Well, that's pretty rough! I better buy one.
Who should I make the check out to?

PITCH MAN
Oh, don't ask me!

MAN
What? Aren't you a salesman?

PITCH MAN
No! I'm just a guy! A guy who works
at the tollbooths, and really loves his LSD.
Well, I gotta go, but don't forget to buy
your own LSD. LSD — It's the future!

MAN
(Reaching into pockets)
Hey...where the hell is my wallet?!

PITCH MAN
See ya!

MAN
Hey!

Man chases Pitch Man off screen, as "LSD" comes up.

ANNOUNCER (V.O.)
(Sounding unprofessional)
The LSD: Available at the place
next to the thing.

THE END.

PART III

PRIME TIME DRAMA

9

PLOT-DRIVEN DRAMAS

I like to put television drama into two distinctive categories: plot-driven and character-driven. Plot-driven dramas like *Law & Order* concentrate heavily on story. Character-driven dramas like *E.R.* focus more on character.

To illustrate my point, let's look at *Law & Order*. Each episode usually starts with a crime or the discovery of a crime. Every scene that follows builds off of that first scene as we follow the detectives who try to solve the crime, and the prosecutors, who take the accused through the legal system in an effort to bring the perp to justice. Rarely do we cut away from the story in order to go inside the personal lives of the characters.

This isn't to say that that the characters on *Law & Order* aren't well-defined. Take Detective Lenny Briscoe, played (1992–2004) by the late Jerry Orbach. Briscoe was rough around the edges with a quick-tongued, sarcastic wit. The writers made it crystal-clear who he was both as a person and as a cop. Even though they didn't dwell on his personal life, we knew a lot about him. He was a recovering alcoholic. When it came to love and marriage, he was down on his luck, occasionally complaining about his ex-wives, etc., etc. But these character details always came through within the context of a crime story, often as quick one-liners. The writers didn't devote entire scenes to Briscoe's personal life; they didn't follow him to AA meetings and we didn't see him doing battle with the ex-wives over alimony checks.

The same is true with the rest of the cast. For example, we know Lieutenant Van Buren (played by S. Epatha Merkerson) is a feminist who isn't afraid to stand up to the big boys when she is passed over for a promotion she believes is rightly hers. But again, we get bits and pieces of this story in what is almost throw-away dialogue, rather than in centerpiece scenes. The reason is that in plot-driven drama, these kinds of character scenes would only serve to stall the dramatic action of the crime story and frustrate the audience.

A show like *E.R.* is what I would consider to be a character-driven drama. While the backdrop is an emergency room where there is always a lot of action, at its very heart the show is really about the people who work in the ER. It chronicles both their lives at work and their lives at home. It is about the interaction between characters.

Some shows walk a very fine line between being plot-driven or character driven. But usually, it is relatively easy to put a drama into one category or the other.

> "One of the differences between comedy and drama — at least on television — is how much information the audience has at any particular moment and at what point in the story the information is given. In comedy you generally want the audience to have as much information as possible, whereas in drama you frequently want to withhold information from the viewer and reveal it at a point where it'll have the most, well, 'dramatic' impact." — David Nichols, executive producer, *Caroline in the City*; co-executive producer, *Grace Under Fire*

WHY *LAW & ORDER* THRIVES AND SURVIVES

Law & Order first hit the air in 1990, and is easily one of the longest running prime time dramas in the history of television. As if its own success weren't unusual enough, the show has spawned other series, including *Law & Order: SVU* and *Law & Order: Criminal Intent*, which aren't spin-offs, but rather fall under the *Law & Order* banner. The show, which also does phenomenal in reruns, is one of those rare birds that, over time, has undergone cast change after cast change, and the audience doesn't seem to care. As the show enters its 17th season, viewers keep tuning in. This is a tribute to the writing. I believe *Law & Order* to be unequivocally the best-written show on television. Every scene is masterfully structured and propels the story forward. Stories are consistently jaw-dropping, unpredictable, and always loaded with twists and turns. The characters — from the regulars right down to the criminals and victims — are well-drawn, complex, and almost always have an agenda. If you want to write any type of plot-driven drama, you should absolutely study the writing in *Law & Order*. It is television for the intelligent.

RIPPED FROM THE HEADLINES

For plot-driven dramas, one of the best places to find stories is the newspaper. *Law & Order* actually brags that its stories are "ripped from the headlines." This doesn't mean the story that lands in your script should be identical to the one that actually happened in real life. If the story is big enough, the entire country already knows how it turned out. Not to mention that if it were too much like the actual story, you could leave yourself vulnerable to a lawsuit. The key is to take a real story and make it your own by using your imagination and dramatizing it. Take the seeds of what happened in real life and tell it through your own characters, adding in your own plot twists and turns.

You can look at almost any episode of *Law & Order* — old or new — to see how this is done. One that comes to mind was likely drawn from the infamous "Prom Mom" case. In actuality, a girl (who had hidden her pregnancy from her parents) gave birth at her senior prom, put the baby in a plastic bag, and dumped him in the restroom trash can where he died. Then she went back to the prom. In the *Law & Order* episode, the story centered on a pregnant college student who had hidden her pregnancy from her family. With the baby's father at her side, she gave birth in a hotel room. The sensitive teens promptly dumped the baby, and then went back to the guy's fraternity house, where a party was in progress, and they danced the night away like lovers who didn't have a care in the world. In the fictional story, detectives were able to prove a baby had been born due to amniotic fluid found on the sheets. However, there was no body. The episode focused on the detectives finding the baby's body, proving the couple had in fact given birth and committed murder with the help of the girl's father, who we eventually discover had a hand in the cover-up. In watching this episode, there is no doubt what headline the story derived from, yet if you took the real story and put it beside the *Law & Order* story, you would see that they are actually very, very different.

THE IMPORTANCE OF CREATING AUTHENTIC WORLDS

Without a doubt, plot-driven dramas are harder to script than character-driven dramas. The reason for this is that with the plot-driven drama, the writer usually has to create a world where he or she doesn't normally reside. Most writers aren't cops or lawyers or doctors or forensic specialists, etc. However, when you write a script that involves characters that work in these professions, you must become an expert. I cannot over-emphasize the importance of doing the research and getting it right. If you do not, I can promise you that the people who read your script will see holes in it. Once that happens, you will lose credibility as a writer, and more than likely you won't be hired.

I have been asked many times, "don't shows have experts on staff that will take care of the piddley little details?" The answer is "yes." Shows do have consultants at their disposal to check procedures and facts, but this is only for the scripts that are going into production. In other words, staff writers have this luxury. Freelancers do not. You have to come up with the right stuff on your own.

> "I work on a show that's tremendously research-heavy. So I find lots of material from articles I read about operations gone wrong or particularly interesting patients, etc., etc. And I have an entire file full of pages I've torn from magazines or newspapers (or that my mom has sent me in the mail!) over the years, all of which have struck a chord for one reason or another. It's my master-file, and it's where I've pulled some of my favorite ideas." — Stacy McKee, story editor, *Grey's Anatomy*

GETTING THE FACTS: HOW TO RESEARCH COPS, LAWYERS, DOCTORS, AND OTHERS

Some writers love research. I must admit that I am not one of them. However, I force myself to do it and do it well, because experience has shown me time and time again that good research can make the difference between a great story and a mediocre one. While researching professions and procedures can seem a bit overwhelming at first, once you delve in, you will come up with story points and ideas that you never would have thought of, simply because you don't normally live in that kind of world. With each new fact you find, you will get more and more jazzed about your story and script.

> "Research is important because it gives a base from which to start, other than a blank page. It gives you ideas. As I research, I keep a legal pad, and I write down everything that occurs to me." — Tom Towler, supervising producer, *JAG*; writer, *BTK Killer*

There are many relatively painless ways to research various professions that might be in your script, depending on what they are. If it's a doctor or a lawyer you are looking for, chances are you probably already know one. If not, ask your friends if they know of any. Cops are also fairly easy to get in touch with. In larger cities, police have divisions that are dedicated to serving the press. When placing these calls, ask for the Public Affairs Office. Tell them you are writing a script and you have a couple of questions that you would like to ask. Most likely, they will find someone to help you. The same is also true for hospitals, should you be looking for a certain kind of specialist.

When contacting these individuals, be sure to have a short list of questions ready. These experts are professionals who are extremely busy. They aren't sitting at their desk, drinking coffee, waiting for your phone call, and they certainly don't have time to brainstorm your story with you. So be prepared to ask specific procedural questions that will help ensure your script's authenticity.

Sometimes police will let you go on what's known as a drive-along. Not all police departments will let you do this, but some will. Generally, you sign a waiver stating that you know the dangers of going out on patrol as a civilian and that if anything were to happen, you (and your next of kin) would not hold the police responsible. This is a personal choice for all writers to make because, while you will usually be fine, your safety cannot be guaranteed. That said, I know many writers who have done this and come back with extremely rich stories that could not have been conceived simply by sitting in front of a computer screen. I can attest to the value of drive-alongs, as I have had the opportunity to spend an unforgettable night with a special police unit in the heart of one of Boston's most dangerous, crime-ridden neighborhoods. I was with two cops, and we were accompanied by two body guards. Everyone had bullet-proof vests except me. I can tell you that what happens on our streets when the sun goes down defies imagination. It is not the stuff you read about in books and newspapers. If you decide you want to try to do this, I suggest you try doing it in a city if possible. In smaller towns, there is apt to be considerably less action.

If you are looking to specifically research the criminal mind and police procedure, there are a number of good crime reference books out there. I keep a couple on my bookshelf, and am surprised how often I actually refer to them. They cover everything from motive to police investigation and procedure to prosecution. You can find several pertinent medical journals as well. Get into the habit of asking family and friends for reference books as birthday and/or holiday gifts. This kind of information is wonderful to have at your fingertips.

Another great place to get good research is the Internet. The one thing you have to be careful about is making sure that the author of the article is legitimate and that the information is in fact accurate.

COLLEGES AND UNIVERSITIES

If you are having a hard time finding exactly what you need, you may want to try calling a professor who specializes in whatever it is you are looking for. For example, if you have a legal question and haven't been able to track down a lawyer, you might try a law school. Usually, you can find professors by looking in the faculty section of the college's Web site or by calling the school and asking for a specific department. Again, these people tend to have busy schedules, but you may just find a professor in his or her office who is willing to quickly tell you what you are looking for, or at least point you in the right direction. Again, be respectful of that person's time. Keep the questions to a bare minimum, and don't keep calling back like the professor is your own personal consultant.

> "Keep writing. Practice makes, if not perfect, then *better*. You want to be 'in shape,' to have your instrument as finely tuned as possible, in order to take advantage of whatever opportunities happen to come your way. You're going to need that magical combination of talent, hard work, and luck. Read as much as possible. See a reasonable number of movies. Watch just enough TV to edify, inspire, and entertain yourself without setting roots down in the couch." — Don Mancini, screenwriter, *Child's Play* movies; creator, *Kill/Switch*

THE WGA

The Writers Guild of America is another excellent resource for research. You can log onto their Web site (www.wga.org) and look under writer's tools.

There will be a link called "Ask the expert." When you click on this link, a list will come up with phone numbers for experts in almost every field imaginable from the Army to pediatrics. The number listed is for a particular expert — and here is the good news — that expert has already agreed in advance to offer information about his or her field for the purpose of writing authentic scripts. You don't have to be a member of the Guild to use this service.

CREATING POWERFUL PROTAGONISTS AND ANTAGONISTS

Good drama is comprised of protagonists and antagonists. It is very easy to keep them straight. Generally, protagonists are the people we root for. The first three letters of the word describe how we feel about them; we are "pro" these characters. They are usually the heroes or heroines of the story. A well-drawn protagonist will always have a solid agenda and clear-cut goals.

An antagonist is much like it sounds. It is that which antagonizes the protagonist and stands in the way of the protagonist achieving his or her goals. To break it into its simplest form, you can think of it as good vs. evil.

Stories can have more than one protagonist and antagonist in a story. Let's go back to *Law & Order*. Protagonists are the detectives and the district attorneys. The antagonists are the criminals. The detectives and district attorneys want law and order. The criminals stand in the way of them achieving that.

Antagonists do not have to be human. Look at the movie *Jaws*, and ask yourself who the antagonist was. Of course it was the shark. How you play protagonists and antagonists off each other is key in writing a successful drama.

> "Good drama is made by the battle that goes on internally in the protagonist and is brought to the surface through interactions with the antagonist and by forces set against him. Say my hero is in the Army and faced with a decision; he can't kill … that's his internal battle. But will he be able to justify killing when it comes down to saving his friends? It's a drama writer's responsibility to make the internal struggle of the protagonist visible through external actions." — Tom Towler, supervising producer, *JAG*; writer, *BTK Killer*

BUILDING CONFLICT AND JEOPARDY

Good drama revolves around conflict and jeopardy. The best way to build these elements into your script is to give your characters specific goals and points of view that clash. Make sure that each character has an agenda and is willing to do anything it takes to accomplish that agenda. Your antagonist should come between your protagonist and his or her goal. Once this happens, your protagonist must find another way to meet that goal. Whatever it is that your protagonist wants, your antagonist must purposefully and repeatedly step in the way, thus upping the ante, which in turn ups the action and drama.

It's like a game of cat and mouse. In order to create tension, you have to keep raising the stakes. What happens at the beginning of your story looks bleak for your protagonist, and it only gets bleaker as you raise the stakes higher and higher. In the end, one of them, usually the protagonist, achieves the goal and wins.

One of the complaints I have heard about *Law & Order* is that sometimes the antagonists win, and some people find this unsettling. I think this is interesting because it shows that, deep down, people really want the bad guys to get their comeuppance. But at an even deeper level, I believe viewers are somewhat jolted because they have been conditioned to expect the protagonist to prevail. That's what happens in 99% of dramas. When it doesn't happen, people feel like something is a little off. Ironically, part of what makes *Law & Order* so good is that the audience never knows for sure how the show is going to end — until it ends. And that is how it should be.

ONE-HOUR DRAMATIC STRUCTURE

One-hour drama scripts follow a four-act structure, and usually come in at about 55–59 pages. As with comedy, each act must end with a mini-cliffhanger so the audience will hang in there with you through the commercials in order to see what's going to happen next. In a one-hour drama, clearly the most important Act Break falls at the end of the second act. This is where your biggest so-called cliffhanger should come, and it must be a doozy of a moment with huge dramatic impact that holds enormous consequences for your characters.

The reason the end of the second act is so crucial is twofold. First, it generally falls on the half-hour. This is where you stand the greatest chance of losing viewers because they now have other choices. During the first Act Break, they aren't as likely to stray because all of the other programs are already in progress, so they'd have to catch up. But, at the half hour, there are all kinds of new shows beginning, so if viewers aren't totally digging your show, they will flip to something else. This can have major repercussions for you as a writer.

The Nielsen Ratings are not only broken down by the hour, but by the half hour as well. The worst thing that can happen to a drama writer is to have a larger audience in the first half hour than you have in the second half hour. What these numbers suggest to the network is that you had the audience — they tuned in and were ready to watch — but you couldn't keep them. Needless to say, this does not bode well, especially if the network has "delivered" the audience to you by way of a good lead-in.

The second reason that you need a strong second Act Break is that at the top of the half hour the length of the commercial break is double what it is for any other Act Break. This means you need to double the reason for the audience to come back. The best way to ensure that they will hang in with you is to power up the dramatic tension and jeopardy. The idea is to leave viewers hanging, wondering what's going to happen next.

SCRIPTS FOR CABLE VARY SLIGHTLY

More than likely you have noticed that dramas on cable networks like HBO and Showtime run without commercial breaks. Scripts for these shows reflect that in the way they are written. Like the show itself, the scripts go from beginning to end without Act Breaks. If you are writing one of these shows, you should follow the same format that they do. Even if you use that show as a sample for more traditional dramas, the producers will understand the reason you have not put in Act Breaks.

HOW TO STRUCTURE YOUR PLOT-DRIVEN DRAMA

Aside form being roughly the same number of pages and having four distinct acts, plot-driven dramas are structured differently than character-driven dramas. The easiest way to structure your plot-driven drama is to think of it in terms of building blocks.

The first block is the first scene. Often, though not always, in crime dramas the first scene reveals either the crime or the discovery of the crime. Consider that the first building block. Now you have to put another block on top of it, which is the next scene. This might be where the cops search the crime scene and find a clue. That scene would be your second building block, and where that clue takes them would be your third building block. One scene leads seamlessly to another, all eventually building to your Act Break.

Hour-long structure is much more complex than half hour. In plot-driven drama, it is fairly easy to get yourself tangled up along the way. To help you simplify your story, I suggest that your write it out scene-by-scene to the best of your ability, from start to finish including Act Breaks. Then, get out a pad of paper and a pen. Starting with scene one, write down the main action that happens in that scene. Try to fit it into one sentence. Then do the same for your next scene and the next scene after that, all the way through to the end. Now, go back and read the sentences out loud in progression. Do they tell a story? Is this story making sense? Is it moving forward in a way that is dramatic and interesting? If you do this, it will help you find any holes in your story and it should also make you aware of scenes that are redundant.

HOW INDEX CARDS CAN HELP
(AND WHY STUDIOS ORDER SO MANY)

Walk into the office of any drama writer and it is quite possible you will find a large cork board with index cards tacked up all over it. Writers commonly use index cards to help them break stories. Each scene is written on a single index card. The cards are then tacked up in order, usually by acts. This allows the writer to physically visualize how the story is coming together. Let's say the writer is reviewing the story and he realizes that a piece of information was revealed too quickly. He can then take down that index card and reinsert it further into the story. Once the writer is satisfied that all the scenes are where he wants them to be and that the story is working, he can then start to write the outline, by transferring the information on the board into his computer.

CHECKLIST FOR PLOT-DRIVEN DRAMA

- Have I done the necessary research?
- If working off a real-life event, have I used my imagination to make it fictional?
- Do I have strong protagonists and antagonists with clearly defined goals?
- Does each scene build off of the one before?
- Are my Act Breaks strong, especially at the end of Act Two?
- Have I repeatedly raised the stakes and escalated the tension?
- Are all four of my acts relatively even in length?
- Have I included a teaser if the show uses one?

If you have answered "yes" to the above questions, you are likely on your way to developing a good story.

—10—
CHARACTER-DRIVEN DRAMA

ALL ABOUT PEOPLE

In the same way plot-driven dramas are about the story, character-driven dramas revolve human beings. That isn't to say that you don't have to worry about finding a great, dramatic story for the characters — you do. But the driving force of that story will be the characters. Since character-driven dramas are about people, as with comedy, you can use personal experience to come up with unique stories.

EVERYTHING IN YOUR LIFE ISN'T FIT FOR THE SCREEN

While some of the best drama may in fact be born out of personal experience, I feel the need to warn you that everything that's ever happened to you isn't worthy of being placed in a TV script. Sometimes we get so wrapped up in our own lives that we think nothing is more interesting than that which happens to us. This may or may not be true. Frequently, people tell me stories about themselves, adding at the end, "wouldn't that make a great episode of *Desperate Housewives*?" Often, the things they are talking about are not exactly must-see TV. They are more like snapshots, moments in time that are so small, they would not be able to sustain an audience through commercial breaks. These moments feel bigger than they actually are to the person telling the story because they happened to them. So, before you take personal experience and automatically start to build a story around it, ask yourself if the story is really big enough. If not, you may need to make it a "B" story or a "C'" story.

The other big problem in adapting real-life drama to the screen is that sometimes the stories aren't in line with the characters on a particular show. Every story isn't right for every show. If you are going to translate personal experience, it must be relevant to the show's characters, or your script will fail miserably.

Another trap that some writers fall into when incorporating personal experience into a script is that they believe it has to play out in the script word for word, action for action, precisely as it did in real life. This too, can have disaster written all over it. The secret to incorporating real-life experience into drama is to take the seeds of what actually happened and let your imagination run wild. Get inside your characters' heads. You know how you reacted when the incident happened, but how would your characters react if the exact same thing happened to them? They might do things differently than you did, and this may cause a whole new chain of events to occur. As a writer, you must be open to these possibilities. If you adapt real-life experience to a script correctly, it is likely that by the time you are finished, the story will only have minor similarities to the actual real-life events.

> "If you have created really complex, flawed, interesting characters, then those characters will bring the drama with them. Now I am lucky enough to work on a TV show with some really wonderfully crafted characters, so it's often very clear to me who they are, and how they should or shouldn't react to certain situations. I know the kind of drama they bring to the table. The other thing I know to be true goes right back to Screenwriting 101. Imagine your story. Imagine your scene. Now, imagine what the absolute WORST, most horrifically upsetting version of that scene would be for your characters, and write THAT. Because if you temper it, if you write the 'lesser' version of what that scene could be, then you've just sold yourself short." — Stacy McKee, story editor, *Grey's Anatomy*

HOW TO DRAMATIZE PERSONAL EXPERIENCE

After writing what I hoped were two solid comedy specs, I decided to try my hand at a drama script so I would be fully prepared in case an opportunity ever arose for me to get work as a drama writer. I decided to do a spec *Picket Fences*, which in its time was a hot show.

If you aren't familiar with *Picket Fences*, it's one of David E. Kelley's more brilliant creations. The series takes place in the small town of Rome, Wisconsin, and is centered on small-town sheriff Jimmy Brock and his wife, Dr. Jill Brock. Like most of Kelley's work, it's all about quirk. Things in Rome are rarely as they seem. After studying the show, the first thing I did was to think about specific themes I wanted to explore. The dark side of human beings is something that has always fascinated me. I am constantly intrigued when the image that people project publicly is in sharp contrast to who they actually are privately. Once I decided that this was the area I wanted to work with, I needed to find a concrete story. Because I grew up in a small town like Rome Wisconsin, where things aren't always as they seem, I decided that was a good place to start hunting for stories. So I began to call old friends to see if they could throw me any small-town bones that might make a good story for my script. I hit the jackpot with a friend from high school, whom I will call Mary because she would shoot me for using her real name. Here is the story:

One day, Mary arrived home with her two small daughters. I should mention that because she lives in a small town and has a false sense of security, she never locks her doors, even when she goes out. On this particular day, as she pulled in to her driveway, she noticed that the 16-year-old boy who mows her lawn was coming out of her front door. When he saw her, he immediately did an about-face, went back through the house, and slipped out a side door. Mary didn't think much of it until her husband came home a short time later, went into their bedroom, and discovered her underwear drawer dumped in the center of their bed. They knew instantly that they were dealing with a teenage panty thief.

Since this was a quaint and quiet neighborhood with lots of kids, Mary and her husband decided to call the police. When police went to the teenager's house, they confiscated a trunk from his bedroom filled to the brim with ladies' underwear that he had stolen from virtually every woman on the block. Two male cops hauled the trunk to Mary's house, dumped it at her feet, and told her to pick out what was hers. As she did, she realized that she could mentally all but match up underwear to neighbors. She pulled her own underwear out of the trunk, handed them to the police officers, who promptly placed them in a see-through plastic bag, wrote her name across it, and hauled it away as evidence. Several months later when the trial was over, a different set of male cops knocked on Mary's door, plastic bag in hand, there to return the evidence. The ultimate humiliation for any woman.

An underwear thief loose in Rome, Wisconsin, seemed like a perfect fit for *Picket Fences*. But there was no way I could write that story exactly as it happened. While the real-life version was interesting — amusing even — it was not nearly dramatic enough for the small screen. In order to make it more dramatic, I would have to use both the show's characters and my imagination.

When I sat down to hammer out the story, the first order of business was to decide who the thief was going to be and build the story from there. I went through all of the show's characters, but decided that it really couldn't be one of the regulars. Someone who breaks into people's homes, steals ladies underwear, and hides them in a treasure chest has certain, shall we say, character flaws? As a freelance writer, I could not assign these traits to one of the regular characters without altering that character, which, as we have discussed, is a big no-no in spec scripts.

Thus, I realized my thief would have to be an outsider. But, who? Admittedly, my own dark side was intrigued by the idea of a teenage panty thief. So, I decided to keep that part of the story. But, I changed the teenager's character. Instead of being just a nondescript kid who mows lawns, I made him the clean-cut high school hockey star who was admired by everyone. That opened up possibilities, as he could then hang out with the sheriff's son who, on the show, also played hockey.

Once I decided who the thief was, I now had to figure out the rest of the story. I asked myself questions about how the sheriff would go about catching him and what the town would do with this kid once he was caught. I put myself inside Sheriff Brock's head. Based on his character, how would he react? What would be his first move in catching the thief? Was there any way to make the story personal to him, which would raise the stakes and make his drive to solve the crimes all the more urgent? Next, I looked around the town of Rome to see which characters Brock might naturally consider to be prime suspects. On a previous episode, Father Barrett, the Catholic priest, nearly lost his parish when it was discovered that he had a fetish for women's shoes. So wouldn't it make sense that he also might have a thing for ladies underwear as well? Therefore, the rectory would definitely be one of Brock's first stops.

Do you see where I am going? This is how you take the seeds of a story and develop them to a specific show. You have to look at who the characters are, where they are today, and also what they have been up to in previous episodes.

You must also look to heighten the drama. When I looked at how the real teenage thief was caught, it wasn't that terribly dramatic. The cops went to his house, scared him into a confession, and he handed over the goods. In a nutshell, here is how I escalated that drama for my spec script.

Act One opens with Jill Brock, discovering that someone has broken into their bedroom and made off with some of her underwear. This is the latest in a string of robberies where the thief is only after one thing. The women of Rome and their husbands are putting huge pressure on Sheriff Brock to catch this creep. Now that the bandit has hit his house and violated his wife, it's become personal. Brock starts to question suspects, beginning with Father Barrett. Meanwhile, the star of the high school hockey team has become good friends with the sheriff's son. The boys hang out a lot — so unbeknownst to Brock (and the audience), the guy he is looking for is right under his nose.

Act Two continues with Brock tracking the thief, who eventually reinvades the Brock home — this time to get some treasures from Brock's teenage daughter. Stealing personals from Brock's wife was bad enough, but violating his daughter escalates the tension. At the end of Act Two — and remember, this is the most important Act Break — the hockey star is driving the sheriff's son home from a game. In the center of town, they get rear-ended at a stoplight. The car trunk pops open and out pops a box, filled with ladies underwear, which is now strewn all over the main street.

At the beginning of Act Three, all the women of Rome, including the sheriff's wife and daughter, are lined up at the police station, identifying that which belongs to each of them. The evidence is tagged, bagged, and eventually brought to the courthouse and admitted into evidence. Throughout the rest of Act Three and Act Four, the teenager is brought to trial.

While I have obviously left out a lot of the details of my script, the quick version should give you an idea of how I took the seeds of a true story and made it completely fictional by adapting it to the characters on *Picket Fences*. In the first act, the sheriff is drawn in because the crime is personal. The stakes are raised by the townspeople, who put pressure on him to solve the crime. The tension escalates even more when the thief returns to the sheriff's home to steal from his daughter. The end of Act Two features the car accident and the women's underwear strewn all over the street. See how this is much more visual and dramatic than the cops knocking on the door and the kid simply forking over the goods?

Of course, you don't have to use real-life stories when coming up with character-driven drama. You can just as easily look at the characters on the show and create stories that evolve from their characters. Or, you can think of themes that you'd like to explore and adapt those to the characters. You just have to make sure the story works for both the characters and the show.

HOW STRUCTURE FOR CHARACTER-DRIVEN DRAMAS DIFFERS FROM PLOT-DRIVEN DRAMAS

On the surface, scripts for plot-driven dramas and character-driven dramas look very much the same. Both are written single-camera film-style, and both have four acts. Most come in at around 55–59 pages. Structurally speaking, however, these scripts are as different as night and day. As we discussed, plot-driven drama usually starts with an inciting incident and builds one scene on top of the other until its conclusion. There is rarely a "B" story in plot-driven drama and "C" stories are all but unheard of. In character-driven drama, this isn't the case. In many ways, character-driven is structured more like comedy in that there is usually a definitive "A" story and "B" story. Because drama is an hour, there is almost always a "C" story and, depending on the show, a "D" story. These stories are inter-cut with one another. As with comedy, each act should begin and end on the "A" story.

Perhaps the easiest way to structure your character-driven drama is to create each story individually. That way, you can really see each story laid out, beginning, middle, and end, along with twists and turns in between. Once you are confident that all of your stories are working, you can then look at how you want to inter-cut them. It is much harder to look at the script as a whole, and to try to inter-cut stories before you are even sure exactly what direction they will take.

A key to inter-cutting character-driven drama is to take each scene up to a point where something dramatic or interesting is about to happen. Raise the stakes, introduce something new, ask a question. Then, immediately cut away to another story. This helps heighten the tension and keep the audience hanging, desperate to see what happens next.

> "For most writers it's the prospect of telling long-term stories and taking characters through elaborate journeys. It's the prospect of having more creative control. It's the prospect of your work reaching an audience quickly. There is power in the hands of the writer. Who wouldn't want to be a part of that? There is so much good stuff on TV now. People recognize that now more than ever before." — Screenwriter Don Mancini, on why he and other successful feature writers are venturing into TV.

WHY COLORED INDEX CARDS ARE KEY

Colored index cards in character-driven writing can be quite useful, as you can assign one color to each story. Say you choose blue index cards for your "A" story. Now, jot down one or two quick sentences that describe the main action that happens in each scene. Then, choose another color of index cards for your "B" story and do the same. Follow suit for your "C" story, and if you have one, do the same for your "D" story.

Just as you did with the cork board, start to tack the scenes up according to how they happen, act-by-act. By using colors, you can easily see if you have been away from a story too long, or if you are spending too much time on one story and need to cut away to another. You will be surprised how this color-coded system makes any kind of structural errors really stand out much more so than if you just started typing scenes into your computer.

> "Learn how to take notes. You're gonna get a lot of them. The script is the nexus for every project. You're always going to have to be dealing with producers and directors and actors and executives. You have to learn to be diplomatic. You have to control yourself and your craft. You have to listen and mediate between all these points of view, and then produce something honest that doesn't lose the foundation." — Marilyn Osborn, writer, *The X-Files*; consulting producer, *Touched by an Angel*

CONTINUING STORYLINES FROM WEEK TO WEEK

The one difficulty in writing a character-driven drama is that, unlike plot-driven dramas where the stories are often self-contained in each episode, the storylines in character-driven drama frequently continue from week to week. This can make writing a spec script for this kind of show all the more problematic because you don't know where the show is actually going. Also, by the time you get the spec written, rewritten, and out the door, the show has often become dramatically different. So, how do you solve this?

The biggest mistake you can make is to try to guess the direction in which the writers are going to take the show. Even if you are the best guesser in the whole world, chances are that you won't get it exactly right. If you are wrong, and the writers go in a completely opposite direction, your spec script will leave agents and producers quietly scratching their heads, all the while thinking, "this writer obviously doesn't know the show."

Guessing right doesn't always bode well either. Let's say you look into your crystal ball and it is clear to you exactly where the writers are going to take the characters over the course of the season. So your spec script reflects this. The story in your script turns out to be very close to an actual script that makes it onto the air. You might think to yourself, "darn, I'm good." This is true. If you are able to come up with stories that are in line with what the writers are thinking, you are definitely on the right track. Still, don't expect executives to line up and shake your hand.

I once wrote a spec *Wonder Years*. Six months later, the show did a similar episode. Around this time, my agent had sent my spec to an executive at ABC. After reading my script his comment was, "we already did that episode." He all but implied that before writing my script, I must have watched the show and duplicated it with just a few small changes. For this particular executive, it didn't seem to be in the realm of possibilities that I might have just had a similar idea.

To free yourself from these kinds of complications, the best thing you can do is to write what I call a generic script. By generic, I don't mean bland and non-descript; rather, I mean that you should choose a story that could be inserted into the show as it exists today. This means you aren't changing anything or making any assumptions about what is to come down the road. This is the safest way to go. If you write for the show as it stands today and things change, it won't matter. Producers will understand that you wrote your spec during a certain timeframe, and as long as you have everything right in terms of what was going on at that time, you will be fine.

I should probably mention that some shows are extremely difficult to pull off in a spec script. One that many new writers have an interest in writing is *24*. While I applaud their courage, I personally would never attempt to spec this show. In that vein, I would not recommend it as a spec because I think it poses too many challenges for first-time writers. To be sure that I am not being overly cautious, I asked some drama writers what their thinking was on the subject. Most echoed my thoughts, but also added that a show like *24* would be so difficult to spec that if a writer could miraculously pull it off, then that writer would no doubt have a stand-out spec script. While I completely agree with that thinking, I am honestly still skeptical about a new writer's ability to write a good spec for this show because there are so many added complications.

CHECKLIST FOR CHARACTER-DRIVEN DRAMA

- Have I come up with a theme that's appropriate for the show?
- If my story is based on personal experience, is the story big enough to carry an entire episode?
- Have I adapted the event to the characters and to the show?
- Have I dramatized the event so it will play out on the small screen?
- Do I have a clearly defined "A" story?
- Are my "B," "C," and "D" stories equally well-defined?
- Have I inter-cut my secondary stories in ways that will heighten the tension and suspense?
- Do I have strong Act Breaks, especially at the end of Act Two?
- Are all four of my acts relatively even in length?
- Have I included a teaser if the show uses one?

THE DIRT ON SOAPS

On occasion I run across new writers who believe their calling is to write for day time drama (aka "the soaps"). Day time is very different from prime time. First off, like late night and sketch, writing for day time is also quite specialized. In fact, there are only a limited number of agents who represent writers in this arena.

Writing work in day time is difficult to come by. The main reason for this is that once writers get on a show, they tend to stay in their jobs for a very long time. Unlike prime time shows soap operas rarely get canceled, so unless a writer really bombs or leaves by choice (which most don't), the writing staff stays fairly consistent. This is one of the few areas of television where writers tend to be older (many above the age of 40), and this is considered okay. No one is waiting in the wings to put them out to pasture.

Unlike writers in prime time, day time drama writers don't have to live in Los Angeles (or New York). Writer meetings are held via conference call. It is usually only the head writer and the script editor that will go to the set on a regular basis. Outlines and scripts get e-mailed.

Writing day time drama is extremely grueling. Writers tend to churn out one script a week. This might not be so bad except that before they are edited day time drama scripts run anywhere between 80 and 90 pages. The writing staff never goes on hiatus.

If writing for the soaps is something you think you might want to try your hand at, the best way to break in would be to try to get some kind of entry level job on one of the shows. An ideal job would be working in the writers' office on script continuity. That would not only give you the opportunity to learn directly from the writers, it would put you in a position to possibly be given a script. While this is not guaranteed, sometimes when one of the regular writers goes on vacation, new writers will be given a shot at a script. This can lead to more regular work and also to an agent. Breaking in from the outside by submitting a spec script is much, much harder to do.

> "Daytime writing is a hard industry to break into. Most writers in daytime are there for decades. My boss (Lynn M. Latham) once said 'if you write from imagination, you will have material for about a year, if you write from real life, you will have material for a lifetime.' The best thing you can do for soap opera writing is to use real life situations to compel your audience. This is a medium in which the audience connects with the true dramas of everyday life." — Lynsey Dufour, writer, *The Young and the Restless*

FORMATTING FOR PRIME TIME DRAMA

SAMPLE OUTLINE FOR PRIME TIME DRAMA

Drama shows are written single-cam, film-style. The same rules apply in writing one-hour drama scripts as those in single-cam sitcoms.

What follows is the first act of an outline for a prime time drama script called *McClean High*. It is written by Drew Larimore, a student in my Writing Television Pilots class at Emerson College. It is reprinted with Drew's permission. Give it a read, and then we will look at the first few pages to see how Drew went from outline to teleplay.

McCLEAN HIGH

"Not in Kansas Anymore"

ACT ONE

FADE IN:

INT. STACEY HEBERT'S CAR – DAY
LILY HEBERT is driving with her mother, STACEY HEBERT, down a narrow, rural road. Lily is upset — her father has just left the family for a younger woman and so she and Stacey have moved to the Northeast from California to start over. Stacey tries to encourage Lily to be excited about starting her junior year at a boarding school, but to no avail. Lily is dreading the new beginning, longing to stay back in California with her friends. As they arrive at Lily's new school, the camera zooms in on the appearance of the ivy-covered, grandiose McClean Institute for Young Adults.

INT. PRINCIPAL NICK TAYLOR'S OFFICE – DAY
McClean Institute's new principal, NICK TAYLOR, a young man in his late twenties, is busy at his desk writing his welcome speech when his wife, SANDRA, enters.

She is exhausted after a full day of greeting new and returning students and wants to go get dinner with her husband. Nick refuses, convinced he must continue working on his speech. Sandra is disappointed and Nick comforts her, telling her his sun-up to sun-down schedule will come to an end soon, once the school year gets up and running. While in an embrace, the school's benefactress and long-time alumni MELINDA CROSS enters, demanding to speak with Nick. She reiterates how important it is for McClean to shape up its reputation in the academic community and reminds him of her generous allocations, which essentially keep the school functioning.

INT. THE BENDER'S SUV – DAY
SAM BENDER, openly gay, is in the car with his parents. They are nearing the end of their long drive from Louisiana where Sam's father, who is currently governor, plans to run for the Senate. Sam is more than aware they are "dumping" him at McClean Institute to get rid of him for a year so his sexuality doesn't become an issue during the election. His parents proceed to talk politics as they pull up to the school, showing us yet another view of the breathtaking building.

INT. LILY'S NEW ROOM – DAY
Lily comes across her room on the sixth floor and meets her roommate, NIA, a beautiful girl originally from Japan, who has traveled the world.

Relics from all over the globe abound Nia's portion of the room. The girls attempt to make awkward conversation. Lily inquires if Nia's parents dropped her off, and Nia informs Lily she hasn't seen her parents in over two years.

INT. TEACHERS' LOUNGE – DAY
A simple, yet very well-kept area where professors gather to talk over coffee and tea. The new philosophy teacher enters, TREENA SCAPES, who is awkward and younger than most of the other teachers (late twenties), attempts conversation, but it doesn't go so well. Nick enters abruptly, out-of-breath and panicked, asking everyone if any of them speak Latin, as the Latin teacher just quit. Everyone shakes their heads and Nick leaves, looking out of control.

INT. LILY'S ROOM – DAY
Lily continues to unpack as someone knocks on their door.
She turns around to see BRETT BAKER, the school's number-
one football player, standing in the doorway. They make eyes.

                                        FADE OUT.

                      END OF ACT ONE

As you read each scene, you can clearly visualize what is happening and
how the action will play out on screen. Notice Drew only included the broad
strokes, meaning the really important details. His story is easy to follow. We
can see immediately what it is about, who the characters are, and what each
of them is up against. The outline is in prose, absent of all dialogue.

SCRIPTING YOUR PRIME-TIME DRAMA

Now, let's take a look at how Drew transformed his outline into a script. His
first four pages follow.

                      McCLEAN HIGH

                  "Not in Kansas Anymore"

                      ACT ONE

FADE IN:

INT. STACEY HEBERT'S CAR – DAY

STACEY HEBERT and her daughter, LILY, are driving
down a desolate Northeastern road.

                      STACEY
              You know, Lily, it's not going
              to be so bad. I'm sure there'll be
              lots of kids here you can talk to.
              That're probably in the same
              boat you are.

Lily stares out the window, unresponsive.

                      STACEY (cont'd)
              Are you mad?

                      LILY
              About what?

                      STACEY
              The divorce.

> LILY

I just don't know why I had to move
all the way across the country
instead of staying back in
California with all my friends.

> STACEY

Lily, honey, I've tried telling
you. It's because I need space
from your father right now – after
what happened. I need to start
over. Experience something new.

> LILY

So then why didn't _you_ move away and
I stay with Dad?

> STACEY

Because I love you. And because I
need you here right now. With me.

> LILY

Then why are you sending me off to
boarding school?

As they approach the grounds –

> STACEY

Look, see – here we are! It's not
such a bad place. They say with a
diploma from a school like this, you can
get into any college in the country.

Stacy pulls down a driveway, past a sign that
reads: "McClean Institute for Young Adults."

> LILY
> (reading the sign)

McClean Institute? Sounds like a
mental hospital.

> STACEY

You'll like Vermont. They're nice people here.

The car comes to a stop as we see a FULL SHOT of the
McClean Institute for Young Adults. It is a beautiful,
19th-century boarding school with ivy going up and down
its walls. Several students, preppily dressed, are walking
with books in hand through the front doors. The lawn is
impeccably well-kept and the sun shines radiantly.

CUT TO:

INT. PRINCIPAL NICK TAYLOR'S OFFICE – DAY

NICK TAYLOR, the new headmaster at McClean, sits at his desk writing. He is a man in his late twenties, attractive, and clean-cut. Overtly frustrated with what he's trying to write, he mutters several sentences over and over, slamming his fist on the table knowing his work is not satisfactory.

His wife, SANDRA TAYLOR, enters. She is a woman of the same age, sophisticated and beautiful. She knocks lightly on his open door.

Nick looks up.

                    SANDRA
          You driving yourself crazy again?

                    NICK
          Oh, hey.

                    SANDRA
          They're starting to move in. The
          new ones, I think. The returning
          ones have been here all morning.

He continues writing.

                    SANDRA (cont'd)
          You okay?

                    NICK
          What? No. I mean – yes. I mean –
          yeah, I'm okay.

                    SANDRA
          There's only so many times you can
          rewrite that speech, Nick.

                    NICK
          I know.

                    SANDRA
          If you keep ripping it apart
          it'll turn out to be something
          completely different than when
          you started.

Pause.

> SANDRA (cont'd)
> I'm going to get something to eat.
> Wanna come along?

> NICK
> I – I still need to work on this.
> I'm sorry.

Sandra, upset, begins to leave.

> NICK (cont'd)
> Sandra, wait.

He goes to stop her.

> NICK (cont'd)
> I love you. And I love that you're
> here with me. And I love that
> we're doing this together. Because
> I couldn't do it without you.

He takes her hands in his.

> NICK (cont'd)
> Things aren't going to run spick
> and span for a while. They're
> just not. Beginnings are – tough.
> Just bear with me these first few
> weeks. It'll smooth out after that.
> Then we'll have more time to –
> to think about other things.
> I promise. Okay?

They kiss. MELINDA CROSS stands in the doorway
unannounced. Melinda is the school's benefactress, a
woman in her late sixties. She is well-kept and uptight.

If you compare each scene description with the actual scene, you will see that they match in terms of what happens. But the scene is brought to life much more vividly by the dialogue. Notice that the dialogue is casual and very much relaxed, even in the scenes where there is tension, as with Stacey and Lily. This is because that's how people talk in real life.

Drew's outline to script is a good example of how a story in outline form translates into an actual script.

PART IV

CREATING ORIGINAL SERIES

THE TELEVISION PILOT

REASONS WHY YOU SHOULDN'T WRITE A PILOT

Many years ago, when I was just starting out, Manny Basanese, one of my closest friends got a job working as a runner for Herman Rush, the president of Columbia Pictures Television. "This is great," I told him, barely able to contain my enthusiasm. "Now all we have to do is come up with a couple of good ideas for a show. You can pitch them and we are on our way."

Basanese looked at me like I was from Venus. "The president of Columbia Pictures Television isn't going to listen to our ideas," he informed me, explaining that when it comes to buying new shows, studios and networks only deal with writers who have huge, proven track records.

I had a hard time fathoming that if the president of Columbia Pictures Television heard a really great idea for a series, he would discount it simply because it came from writers who were new to the business and didn't have any credits. It turns out Basanese was exactly right.

In order to get a pilot off the ground, you must be a writer with years of experience under your belt. It all comes back to the bottom line: television is a business. Think of it of this way. Let's say Coca-Cola has a job opening for president of the North American division. They get two applications. Candidate "A" has just graduated magna cum laude from the Wharton School of Business, and while enthusiastic, has never stepped foot inside a soft drink company. Candidate "B" graduated from Harvard Business School and has worked for 15 years as vice-president of production for PepsiCo. If you were Coca-Cola, which candidate would you hire to oversee your North American division? Of course you would go with Candidate "B" because he has considerably more experience, and so you would trust that he knows what he is doing and that he could move the company forward.

The same principle applies to television. With new shows, the pressure to succeed is tremendous. There is so much money to be made or lost that networks and studios simply can't take a chance on unknowns.

"We look for originality and fresh voices. In the network game, however, we certainly have to look for writers who have a track record. It is not like a feature film because its success is tied to the exquisite execution of one 110-page screenplay. We need someone who we know can create and tell 100 of these stories and deliver them on schedule. We obviously look for ideas that have depth and growth potential so that they are worthy to stay on for several seasons." — Steve Stark, executive producer, *Medium*; president, Grammnet Producers

Another reason not to do a pilot is that if you don't have the experience to run both the writing staff and the show, someone will be brought in to do it for you. That person may or may not share your creative vision. Many writers — tongue in cheek — compare having pilots made to having a child. It's not a bad analogy. The goal is to create something of which you will be the primary caregiver and nurturer for many years down the road. It's not something you want to put up for adoption.

A good friend who was once an executive at a major production company often spoke about writers who really didn't have the experience to run shows, yet somehow had garnered pilot deals. The result, she said, was almost always the same — both writer and show bombed. This same friend went on to be a very successful writer in her own right and was eventually offered pilot deals of her own. For a long time she turned them down because even after years of being a writer/producer on hit shows, she didn't think she was quite ready for the day-to-day realities of running a show. A lot of people think, "how stupid. How could someone turn down their own show and all of that money?" Actually she was being quite smart. Before stepping up to the plate, she wanted to be 100% certain that she could do the job and that she wouldn't fall on her face in front of the entire country. By biding her time and perfecting her craft, her shot of getting something on the air that will last is, I believe, considerably better than if she had gone for it right out of the gate.

ONE REASON WHY YOU SHOULD WRITE A PILOT

While I have given you lots of reasons not to write a pilot, there is one reason that you should. A pilot can be good ammunition to have in your portfolio. More and more, producers are getting burned out reading spec script after spec script for a particular show, and so they will sometimes ask an agent to send something original. In this case, all the better if you have a pilot script in your back pocket.

I should also mention that, despite everything I have said about having a proven track record, there is a current trend in which networks are seeking out less-experienced writers, with the hopes that they will have fresh ideas — or at least fresh spins on old ideas. Some executives are working hand-in-hand with students at some of the top film schools to see what they can develop. Not to rain on anyone's parade, but I think this trend will be short-lived. The truth is, you simply have to have experience — and lots of it — in order to create and consistently produce a good television series.

HOW PILOT SEASON WORKS

In the television industry there are five seasons. winter, spring, summer, fall, and the most exciting of them all, "pilot season." Pilot season is when writers pitch new series ideas to the networks, and the networks decide which ideas they are going to make into pilots. Though the heart of pilot season really takes place from January through April, it actually starts much, much earlier.

Shortly after July 4th, networks open their doors for writers to come in and pitch ideas for new series. During the months of July and August, executives will hear hundreds of ideas from oodles of hopeful writers. By the time all is said and done, networks will order pilot scripts from only a handful of those writers. Because producing a pilot is so outrageously expensive, only a small percentage of those scripts will make it into production, and an even smaller number will actually make it onto the air.

Hard as it may be to fathom, it takes more than a year from the time a pilot is pitched to the time the show first airs. Here is a rough calendar of how everything times out:

- July–August: Writers pitch new series ideas.
- September–October: After hearing hundreds of ideas, the networks will decide which ones they are most interested in. Deals are made and scripts are ordered. Writers begin work on story outlines and then on scripts.
- Late November: Around Thanksgiving, writers will turn in the first draft of their pilot. Network executives will read the scripts and give notes.
- Mid-December: Writers turn in the second draft of the script, having addressed the network notes.
- January: Upon reading the second draft of all the pilot scripts that have been ordered, networks decide which ones they will dump out of, and which ones they will move forward and put into production.

If networks are on the fence about a certain show, they may order a "presentation." A presentation is a cost-effective way to get a feel for what a show will be without having to risk quite as much money. Rather than shoot the entire pilot episode, a presentation is much shorter. It usually consists of an act or sometimes only a few scenes. Needless to say, as a writer, it is much better to get a commitment to shoot the entire episode. While network executives claim they can get a feel for the concept, characters, writing, etc., offered in a presentation, a pilot is much more effective as they can see a complete story — beginning, middle and end.

- February–April: Hectic and crazy months in the television industry. The pilots that are going into production must be cast, deals must be negotiated, sets must be constructed, and the script is probably still undergoing changes. Then, the show must be shot and edited.
- Early to mid-May: Network executives convene in New York City for what is known as the Upfronts. This is where, one by one, each network unveils its line-up for the new Fall season to advertisers. The hope is advertisers will be so bowled over by what they see that they will race to buy advertising time upfront, hence the term.
- Mid-May–Memorial Day: Once the new Fall season is in place, agents scramble to get writers staff jobs. These few weeks represent the busiest and most anxiety-riddled time for most writers. If you aren't hired onto a show by Memorial Day, it is likely you will spend the year looking for freelance assignments unless something opens up on one of the cable series, which often operate under a slightly different schedule.
- June: Writers go to work on the new season. They flesh out character arcs for the season — meaning they look at where each character will be when the show goes on the air in September, and where each character will be when the show ends in May. They also do story arcs, mapping out the direction of the show for the entire season. Writers also try to get ahead by stockpiling scripts before production begins and everything gets hectic. Most shows can stockpile a few, but generally once production goes into full swing, any jump they may have had usually seems to vanish.
- Late July–August: The actors come to work and the show goes into production.
- September–October: The new Fall line-up hits the air.

So, as you can see, it usually takes more than a year — if the writer is lucky — from the conception of a series until that show actually goes on the air.

NETWORK SCHEDULE: FRIEND OR FOE

Once your show is on the network schedule, you still have one more giant hurdle to overcome: timeslot. The day and time where the network places your show can make or break you. What about the competition? Are you up against an established hit program, which would pull a large chunk of the already fragmented audience away from your show? What is the lead-in, the show that's on directly before yours? Does it do well in the ratings so that your show might pick up some of its audience? Or is it something relatively few people watch, which could make it all the more difficult for your show to find an audience? These things are key indications of how your series will do in the ratings, and they can ultimately make a difference in whether the show stays on the air or gets canceled.

A good example is *Touched by an Angel*. CBS originally put the show on Wednesday evenings. The ratings were dismal. Cancellation loomed on the not-so-distant horizon. But creators John Masius and Martha Williamson must have had an angel watching over them. Somehow the powers-that-be at CBS saw the light and recognized the show's potential. They moved the program to Saturday evenings and saw an increase in the ratings, so it stayed there for a season. Then, Les Moonves took over the network, and in what can only be considered a brilliant scheduling decision, he moved the show to the coveted 8:00 Sunday night timeslot, coupling it with *60 Minutes*. It was as a perfect fit. The show took off — generating huge ratings, and regularly placing in the weekly top-ten most-watched shows list. In its nine-year run, *Touched* became one of CBS' biggest hits. The irony is, it just as easily could have been cancelled.

> "Don't be derivative. Young writers today have a disadvantage because of being bathed in media with the explosion of cable and the Internet. To be original is challenging. The temptation is to be derivative. Young writers should be vigilant and uncompromising with themselves to be original in this epidemic of copycatting." — Rebecca Eaton, executive producer, *Masterpiece Theatre* and *Mystery!*

WHY SOME CABLE NETWORKS OPERATE UNDER A DIFFERENT TIME CLOCK

One of the most important things that networks do is schedule the day and time their programs will air. A huge part of this decision-making process is known as counter-programming, which means sizing up what the competition is doing, and then doing something bigger, better, different, or opposite in order to pull in viewers and win the timeslot. Historically, summer television was always a time of reruns. In fairness to the networks, the audience diminishes in the summer months; families go on vacation, sweltering nights beckon people to little league games, or even to just to their front porch. It makes no difference. All that matters is that in the summer people aren't watching TV like they do in the winter. Still, every year, there are those couch potatoes who want the option of having some kind of television to watch other than reruns.

Not long ago, the cable networks heard the call and seized the opportunity. They began to introduce new shows in the summer, and grateful viewers followed. It may seem obvious, but this seemingly small counter-programming move turned out to be genius. The viewers who were now watching original series on cable and talking about it at the water cooler the next day, were viewers who weren't watching network television, which of course equals a huge loss in revenue. And once the cable networks had the viewers hooked on their shows, the networks had to fight all the harder to win them back. It was an uphill battle, which they didn't always win. Because of this, it is not uncommon now to see new network offerings at scattered times throughout the year, including the summer. However, the heart and soul of the prime time schedule still continues to be unveiled in May and put on the air in September or October.

13

FINDING AN ORIGINAL PREMISE

NETWORKS LONG FOR LONGEVITY

Perhaps the most important thing networks will look for when considering a pilot is how many stories they will be able to get out of the characters and premise. Are these people interesting enough and do they have enough going on that the show can last 10 seasons? Or, are the story possibilities limited?

I hate to keep harping on the expense of producing a pilot, but it is very real and shouldn't be taken lightly. Networks are always on the hunt for the next *Friends* or *Law & Order* that will stay on the air for many, many years. If a show goes off the air, they have to replace it. That means sinking more money into producing another pilot, which is always a crapshoot. Also, the longer a show stays on the air, the better its chances of being sold into syndication, thus increasing profits for years to come.

> "It struck a chord of relatability. The show was not trailblazing. It was about relationships people knew, wanted to know, or liked." — Max Mutchnick, creator and executive producer of *Will & Grace*, on why that show was such a big hit.

KNOWING THE MARKET

When thinking up a concept for a pilot, most writers think primarily about story and characters. Unfortunately, they have skipped the first and perhaps most important step: to study the marketplace and figure out what kind of shows the networks are looking to put on the air. This varies from year to year. Some years, drama is hot, and other years, comedy is hot; sometimes they are looking for more traditional families (if there even is such a thing anymore), other times, it's quirky characters they yearn for; sometimes they want multi-cam shows, other times, single-cam shows. Television goes in cycles. If you are serious about making a sale, you should keep in mind that it's not so much about what you want to write as it is about what they want to buy.

> "There are buying trends that take place every year. If you bring a multi-camera-style sitcom in when they are only interested in single-camera comedies, you are wasting a lot of people's time." — Steve Stark, executive producer, *Medium*; president, Grammnet Producers

You can get a good idea of what the buying trends are in a couple of ways. The simplest way is to faithfully read the trades every day. Also, talk to as many people in the business as you possibly can about where the industry appears to be heading.

Check also to see if there are any breakout shows. Often when one show becomes a big hit, many knockoffs follow. Fifteen years ago, Hollywood wouldn't touch medical dramas. Not until Michael Crichton teamed up with Steven Spielberg's Amblin Entertainment to do a show called *E.R.*, which hit the air the very same week David E. Kelley's *Chicago Hope* premiered. Both shows were hits, and suddenly Hollywood was hungry for medical shows — dramas, comedies, made-for-TV movies — it didn't matter. So, look for trends in a certain type of show that you could perhaps ride the wave on.

TAPPING INTO FUTURE TRENDS

If you can look ahead to future trends and build your pilot at least in part around those trends, you will be a thousand times ahead of the game. Ask yourself, "where will society be in a year or so? What will they be into? What will they value most?"

> "You better know where the 18–34-year-old audience is going because if you don't know that, you don't know anything. It's 18–34 that sets viewing. So you better know them. They set the trends." — Lucie Salhany, former chairman, FOX Broadcasting Company; founding president and former CEO, United Paramount Network (UPN)

Obviously, predicting the future is not easy. Perhaps the best way to help yourself along is to read absolutely everything you can get your hands on. Digest it. See what recurring issues affect of people from coast-to-coast, both big in cities and in one-horse towns. Martha Stewart became rich and famous by watching working mothers and fathers suffer burn-out brought on by long, hectic days at the office and by carting overscheduled kids to birthday parties, soccer practice, ballet, etc. She realized that there would come a time (and it did) when people would yearn to be home. And when they were home, they would want their nest to be a cozy, cheerful place where the entire family could relax and enjoy great meals together.

Cashing-in on trends is something smart and successful writers and producers have been doing for years. Here are a couple of classic sitcoms that fit the bill:

The Brady Bunch

On the surface, this ABC Friday night comedy appeared to be a traditional sitcom about a typical American family. But dig a little deeper and you will see that the Bradys weren't really a typical family, they were in fact a blended family. Mike and Carol weren't just parents — they were stepparents. Show creator Sherwood Schwartz had done his homework, and he realized that this was a new trend. In the days of June and Ward Cleaver, divorce was something people just didn't do. The late sixties brought a time of radical change. It was all about freedom — free love, free sex, and the "you do your thing, I do my thing and if by chance we find each other, it's beautiful" mentality. Once married, some people found the "thing" just wasn't as beautiful as they originally thought, and rather than sticking it out, people started to divorce. Then, they got remarried. Suddenly, Cinderella wasn't the only one with a stepmother. Growing numbers of kids from coast to coast now had both parents and stepparents. You may be thinking, "but Mike and Carol Brady weren't divorced people — they came together as widow and widower." It is highly likely that America wouldn't have warmed up to the Bradys quite as easily had the setup been that they had opted out of previous marriages. Today, blended families are as common as cell phones. But, at the time of *The Brady Bunch*, the concept was just coming into play. Schwartz and the network realized that you don't hit the audience over the head with something they may not be ready for. Sometimes, you have to introduce a concept slowly, give them a chance to inhale it and catch up.

The Mary Tyler Moore Show

Right out of the gate, the theme song asks the show's central question: "How will you make it on you own?" What it was really asking was how Mary Richards, a 30-year-old, single woman with no prospects for a husband, would survive? Thirty-six years later, that may seem like a ridiculous question to you, but in its day, the question was both important and timely. In 1970, the majority of women in America lived in the world of Edith Bunker. In those days, women got married (you were considered an old maid if you weren't off the market and hunkered down in marital bliss by the time you were 25), stayed home, took care of the children, cooked, cleaned, served the husband a nice home-cooked meal every night and made sure he had clean underwear and his shirts were starched. (Gasp!)

But in 1970, the times, they were a-changin'. Gloria Steinem and the women's movement were kicking into high gear. For the first time, women realized they that had choices. In creating *The Mary Tyler Moore Show,* Jim

Brooks and Allan Burns all but had a crystal ball. They possessed genius at a gut level that allowed them to look into the future and see what was in store for women — and for many it was trading in the frying pan for a business suit. Women were learning they could make it on their own without relying on a man to take care of them. And so the "working woman" sitcom was born.

Another sub-genre to be introduced within this show was the workplace comedy, and the idea that people you work with become family. Lou and Mary had a father–daughter relationship. Ted Baxter was the obnoxious brother and Murray Slaughter was the big brother who looked out for Mary, and so on.

> "One error writers make is not speaking with authority or passion. Some people come and read from their pitch notes. Some people stay too long. You should be in and out in 20 minutes and make sure you leave the buyer with a very clear, concise hook as to why this show is right for this time, right now." — Steve Stark, executive producer, *Medium*; president, Grammnet Producers

ADDING YOUR OWN POINT OF VIEW

Once you have studied the market and looked ahead to future trends, you can start to think about the kind of pilot you want to write. What is most important to making your pilot stand out is that you don't simply regurgitate the shows we have already seen over and over and over again. In reading pilot scripts, one problem I see repeatedly is that the writer simply looks at a show that he or she finds hip and, in essence, copies that show. When I say copy, I don't mean steal. I mean that the characters and situations feel strikingly similar. The result is an overwhelmingly stale script. Look at the Larry Davids and the Marc Cherrys and the Aaron Sorkins and the J.J. Abrams. Writers of their caliber have a voice that distinguishes them from the rest of the pack. They bring to life characters who see the world in ways others don't. The key to a creating a knock-'em-dead, stop-'em-in-their-tracks pilot is to bring in your own unique point of view, along with your own distinctive voice. The temptation to imitate other writers may well be lurking in the back of your mind, but I promise giving into that temptation won't serve you the way you think it will. Your pilot script has to be fresh. It has to be you.

> "If you want to really load your gun, write something original. A spec pilot, a spec feature. Show that you can write characters and create worlds from scratch." — Jeff Eckerle, writer/producer, *Law & Order: Special Victims Unit*

A TALL ORDER: INTRODUCING CHARACTERS AND PREMISE ALL IN ONE EPISODE

Writing a pilot script is a lot more difficult than writing a single episode for an existing show. First and foremost, you must introduce the characters and premise. Who is the show about? What do the characters want, and what stands in the way of achieving their goals? Second — and here's where it gets tricky — your pilot must have a good story, and that story should be the jumping-off point for the series itself. Most importantly, the pilot must mirror future episodes. This can be difficult to achieve since none of those other episodes have been written at this point. That's okay; it's all about having a clear vision of the show. Before you write the pilot, you have to know what the show will be from that moment forward.

> "People watch TV in order to see how to live. Having a moral or a point of view makes the program stronger." — Emmy Award-winning actor Henry Winkler

Over the years I have read a good number of pilot scripts, and the biggest mistake new writers make is they forget to include a story. They get so involved with introducing the characters and the premise, and the story eludes them. For example, let's say the pilot is about a married couple who own a bed-and-breakfast in the quaint little town of Waterbury, Vermont. Typically, a new writer might introduce the couple at the front desk, chitchatting. Then, a guy would come in, and with more chitchat, we'd discover he is the caretaker. He would then exit and in would walk the cook … and there would be some more chitchat. But besides revealing who the characters are in the context of the pilot, the chitchat does nothing to move the story forward. There is no jeopardy — nothing at stake for anyone and, consequently, there really are no Act Breaks. It is crucial that you introduce your characters and premise within the confines of a story that is so brilliantly conceived that, like *The Mary Tyler Moore Show* pilot, people will still talk about it more than 35 years later. I'd be lying if I told you this is easy to achieve. It is not. But it is most definitely the goal.

PREMISE PILOTS VS. NON-PREMISE PILOTS

Until recently, most, if not all pilots were premise-driven, meaning a significant event or events occur that sends the characters down a road (which will be the series). In *The Mary Tyler Moore Show*, Mary broke up with her doctor-boyfriend, moved to Minneapolis, and got a job as associate producer in the all-male newsroom at WJM. In *Commander in Chief*, when the president of the United States suffers a brain aneurysm and dies, Vice President Mackenzie becomes the first female president (aka commander-in-chief).

A premise pilot must also foreshadow the kinds of issues and stories that the characters will encounter on a weekly basis. In order for an audience to tune in again next time, they have to have a clear understanding of what they will be tuning in for. These issues were very clearly set up in both *The Mary Tyler Moore Show* and in *Commander in Chief*, as they are in all pilots that are well-written. Though these particular shows, written 35 years apart, couldn't be more different, in some ways there are striking similarities: both are about a strong woman pioneering her way in a job usually, if not always held by men, trying to prove that women can do the job just as well. In both cases, this premise is crystal clear in the pilots.

While premise pilots still get made, there is a current trend which embraces the non-premise pilot. In this type of pilot, there is no event that jump-starts the series. Instead, the pilot episode looks and feels similar to future episodes. Executives are famous for saying things like "the pilot should look like 'episode three.' " I am told the reasoning behind this is that premise pilots confuse an audience when the show is rerun or goes into syndication. Personally, I think the audience is smarter than that.

> "Quickly establish characters, tone, environment, and the series franchise. Rarely do we see the setup premise anymore. Disguise it; make your pilot feel like an actual episode of the show. Introduce characters in smart, indicative ways. Catch them in motion. This is going to be the audience's first impression of your characters, and first impressions count. If the audience doesn't like your characters, you won't get a second chance." — Jeff Eckerle, writer/producer, *Law and Order: Special Victims Unit*

BIG LOVE

One of the best pilots I have seen in recent time is *Big Love*. The night it premiered on HBO, I intended to have it on in the background while doing other things. I was suckered in immediately, and I have been addicted to it ever since. What makes the series such a stand-out? First off, the writers and producers immediately created a world that I knew nothing about, but was 100% fascinated by. If you aren't familiar with the show, it revolves around a family of polygamists in Utah. Bill Paxton plays a man who is married to three women. Between them, they have many children, with more on the way. Everything about this series is captivating.

Part of what it makes it so appealing is the depth of the characters, not only individually, but in how they relate to each other. For example, the three wives can band together and gang up on the hubby when need be. Yet, in the next scene they can be catty women, squawking at each other, completely jealous of one another. Even the sets are different and interesting. From the front, the exteriors are three houses side by side in a quiet neighborhood. Nothing appears out of the ordinary. But In the back, unbeknownst to even the nosiest of neighbors, the three yards all connect to form one big family commune, where the characters can move about both secretly and freely.

The show is 100% risqué. At the risk of sounding naïve, there are times when I say to myself, "I didn't just see what I think I saw, did I?" But it always turns out that I did.

It's no a big surprise that *Big Love* is executive produced by the wonderfully talented Tom Hanks. If you have any desire to write a pilot, I suggest you really study this show. Beginning with the pilot, it does everything good television is supposed to do … and it looks so easy, which, of course, is a tribute to the writers.

KNOW WHAT'S OUT THERE

The good thing about pilots is that there are new ones being made all the time. You should make a habit of taping them and rewatching them a few times. Look at how the characters and premise are set up. Check for unique approaches to things that you have and haven't seen before. Also, buy pilot scripts (you can get them at Script City) and read how successful writers set up their shows.

> "The most common mistake people make while pitching is not 'owning' their concept. Too often people get excited about one element of a series pitch and fail to flush out the other details. A cop that can talk with the ghosts of murder victims to find the murderers may get a network president excited, but there will be no sale if characters, relationships, and story arenas are not provided as well. Television is a business of details: high concept ideas are easy to come by, the people to execute them are not." — Peter Jankowski, executive producer, *Law and Order*; president, Wolf Films

SAMPLE TREATMENT FOR A PILOT

When writing a treatment for your pilot, the most important thing is that you must get across the characters and premise quickly. There is no set format for treatments that's etched in stone, so you have some latitude. Just make sure that you are not writing a scene-by-scene outline. Treatments should be broad-stroked, yet at the same time they should include enough detail so that the reader walks away knowing exactly what the show will be each week.

For the purposes of this book, I have chosen to share with you a pilot treatment for a dramedy written by a student in my Writing Television Pilots class at Emerson College. It is called *Kyle's Turn* and it is written by Matt Smith. Note that the treatment is fairly short, but the writer lets us know what the show is and who it is about quite quickly.

KYLE'S TURN

Kyle's Turn is a one-hour comedy/drama set in the fictional suburban paradise of Mercy, Massachusetts, and centers around a college freshman coming to terms with his homosexuality, as well as the reactions of those within the community around him. It also deals with his family as a whole, showing their everyday trials and tribulations. A seemingly perfect family to the outside world, the show will explore how families perceived this way are crumbling very often in the confines of their own homes.

The lead character is Kyle Bancroft, an 18-year-old studying theatre at Mercy State College. Kyle is a nice kid, complicated like most teens: fun-loving, energetic, sweet, goofy, imaginative, yet at times completely neurotic and self-absorbed. In high school, he was involved in everything from peer advisors to drama club to soccer, but since entering college has focused on the theatre world and trying to get his life in order. He decided to live at home while in school, so his father renovated the large room over the garage and turned it into Kyle's apartment. He gets along well with his family, but the revelation that he is gay creates tension in their outwardly-perfect, upper-middle class household, especially with Kyle's mother, Lorna.

Lorna Bancroft, 47, is a high-strung, socially conscious homemaker who spends most of her time volunteering at bake sales, the garden club, or Mercy's Historical Society. She grew up on the "wrong side of the tracks" with two alcoholic parents, dreaming of what it would be like to have a huge house and a successful family. She now has both of these things and has worked her way up the social chain in Mercy, determined to stay there. She has always tried her best to be a good wife and mother, but her neuroses and constant striving to appear idyllic have drained her family emotionally, so now most of the time they just try to stay out of her path.

Kyle's mother married her high-school sweetheart, Jimmy Bancroft, 24 years ago, but time has drastically taken a toll on their relationship. Jimmy, 47, is the polar opposite of his over-anxious wife. He is a relaxed, low-key, but very successful real estate developer in town, which accounts for the comfortable lifestyle that the Bancrofts enjoy. He is a former baseball player who enjoys watching sports, skiing, boating, and hunting; definitely what you would call a "man's man." Although he loves his family very much, he has been secretly carrying on an affair with Isabel Kingman, who works as a bank teller at Mercy Mutual Savings & Loan.

Kyle has one sibling, an older brother named Rob. Rob Bancroft, 23, works as a rookie police officer in Mercy, and recently moved out of the house and into an apartment of his own. Rob is somewhat dim-witted, giving him a rather Barney Fife quality. Like his father, he, too, is an accomplished sportsman. He is a good older brother; he may not understand what Kyle is going through, but he's still determined to look out for him.

The last member of the Bancroft clan is Kyle's hard-drinking, semi-senile, 66-year-old grandmother Dorothy Sullivan. Dorothy is the type of woman who will say whatever comes into her head without any thought of the consequences or feelings she may hurt. She moved in with the family after the death of her husband, Finn, a year ago. Kyle is the only one that pays her any attention, and he soon catches on that sometimes lack of delicacy is an act to get everyone out of her hair. Her difficult life has made her seem somewhat hardened to the outside world, but she and Kyle have a strange and special bond.

Ava Vintresca, 18, has been Kyle's best friend since they were 3 and in Taste of Honey preschool together. Ava's parents are both teachers working in the Mercy school system: her mother is a bubbly, charismatic woman; her father is gruff and stern. Ava is a sweetheart and always there for her friends, even though her good-natured, yet biting sarcasm often seems perhaps more brutish than loving. However, seeing the length of their friendship, Kyle reacts to this with the same sort of playfulness. Having recently broken up with her needy, long-time boyfriend, she and Kyle are both entering the dating world together — flirty Ava a bit more excited than hesitant Kyle.

Episodes will include storylines involving homophobia, religion, dating, first relationships, therapy, being true to oneself, binge drinking, stalking, eating disorders, infidelity, menopause, cancer, coming out to extended family, unexpected pregnancies, blackmail, wife/mistress confrontations, May/December romances, and even suicide, to name a few. The way the show and the characters are structured will provide outlets for humor despite the serious episode topics.

The show will revolve around the main characters described, with others coming in and out as the season progresses. The focus of the show, however, will be Kyle, exploring both the humor and the pain in coming out of the closet to his family and friends, as well as what it's like to be young, trying to find yourself, and having big dreams in a small, close-minded town. It will break down the stereotypes of suburban families, showing that any sort of Stepford facade is simply superficial. The show will also have the motivating emotional theme of understanding through humor, whether it is in a family, a marriage, or a community. *Kyle's Turn* will help to illustrate that differences can pull people apart as well as bring them together.

As you can see, Matt did a good job laying out the premise, characters, and overall feel of the show. We can easily see what the show is, and who it's about.

After writing the treatment, the writer would do a scene-by scene, act-by-act story outline, which would then be followed by the pilot script. This is the process whether you were doing the pilot on spec or for a network. The only difference is that with a network you would be getting notes and input along the way.

CREATING A 13-WEEK EPISODE GUIDE

One of the first things to cross producers' minds when hearing a pilot pitch or reading a pilot script is whether there are enough compelling stories to sustain a series for years down the road. It is always smart to anticipate questions and have answers in your head should the question ever be asked. With this in mind it would behoove you to create a 13-week episode guide. Count the pilot episode as episode number 1. You don't have to go into huge detail, but rather just a thumbnail sketch of what happens (including B, C, and D stories.) Be sure to use all of your main characters.

> "The most important thing to consider when writing a pilot is whether it leads to a series. Are there more stories to tell with these characters in this environment? If you can't imagine what episode 6, 10, or 14 might be, you may have to rethink your pilot, no matter how good it seems on its own."
> — Lee Aronsohn, creator and executive producer, *Two and a Half Men*

In creating a 13-week episode guide, you will come to see your series much more clearly than you would if you only banged out the pilot. The discoveries that you will make along the way about both the premise and the characters will give you plenty of ammunition for the executive or producer who says, "I just don't see the series here." Half of winning the battle is doing your homework and being prepared.

FIRST PAGES

As I have mentioned, things in Hollywood seem to follow trends. For the longest time, it was almost unheard of for writers to spec a pilot, because the chances of selling it were so slim. There was also an unspoken feeling that executives wanted to have a hand in creating and developing the show with you. So, if you walked in the door with a completely written script, they wouldn't be as likely to bond with it as they would with a script in which they had some creative input and control.

The tide has turned some. Many writers now think the odds of selling a pilot from a solid script are better than selling a pilot from a pitch. The feeling is that in a pitch meeting it is very difficult to introduce new characters, the show premise, and the story for the pilot, and at the same time get across what the show will be each week. But all of these questions can be answered easily in a good pilot script. Writers believe if they can knock out a script that stops executives and producers in their tracks, they have a better chance of making a sale. Plus, the underlying thought is that in some ways executives and producers will secretly be happier because developing a new series from a well-thought-out script is easier than developing it from square one. Executives will still be able to put their creative stamp on it by making changes.

This philosophy makes sense. However, the flip side is that in a pitch, you will be heard all the way through. Executives or producers will usually listen politely to a pitch from beginning to end. It is rare they will stop you halfway through your story to tell you that you aren't holding their interest. The same isn't true in a script. Readers are likely to put a script down if it isn't completely working. Therefore, if you are going to spec a pilot, it is crucial that the characters and story work, and that the writing is fresh and crisp. Your first five pages should really hook the reader in. It is imperative that you quickly set up the premise and characters, ensuring that producers and executives will want to keep reading your script rather than put it down and go to the next one.

Let's take a look at the first five pages of a single-cam comedy pilot called *Merstein's Mansion,* written by Harris Wittels, a student in my Writing Television Pilots class at Emerson College. The work is reprinted with Harris' permission. Watch how fast you understand who the characters are and the show's premise. This is a good example of a pilot that sets up the characters and premise quickly.

MERSTEIN'S MANSION

"Pilot Episode"

ACT ONE

FADE IN:

INT. DINING ROOM – DAY

ANDY MERSTEIN, 25, disheveled and unshaven, hovers over the fancy dining room table. Next to him is MR. MABRY, a lawyer in his mid-forties.

Also at the table is ANGIE MERSTEIN, 17, clad in black "Goth" clothing; MATTHEW, 19, a prima donna actor wearing dark shades; and SEBASTIAN MERSTEIN, 15, puny, clean-cut, responsible.

Mr. Mabry hands Andy a pen and points to a signature line on legal custody papers that sit on the table in front of them. Andy takes the pen and signs. The rest look on with fearful grimaces.

> MR. MABRY
> (to Andy)
> There you go (a la game show host)
> Mr. Merstein. You are now the proud
> winner of three lovely siblings.

> SEBASTIAN
> (to Mr. Mabry)
> Thank you, lawyer guy. You have
> made me feel like a car.

> MR. MABRY
> Cute kid.

> ANDY
> You want him?

                    MATTHEW
    I can't believe Andy is our guardian now.

                    ANGIE
                (to Mr. Mabry)
    Can I call a mistrial? Was this a trial?
    I call a mis-something. Please don't
    put Andy in charge.

                    MR. MABRY
    Sorry, Angie. This was a mis-
    nothing, I'm afraid.

                    MATTHEW
    I'm gonna "miss" everything when
    Andy pawns it all for booze and
    coke.

                    MR. MABRY
    Look, laws are laws.

Mr. Mabry packs up his briefcase and gets up from the
table.

                    MR. MABRY (cont'd)
    It's been a pleasure meeting all of
    you. Now, if you'll excuse me, I
    really must be going.

He heads for the door. Sebastian chases after him and
clings onto his leg for dear life.

                    SEBASTIAN
                (desperately)
    Look, Mr. Mabry ... may I call you
    Mr. Mabry? Do you take bribes?
    What do you want? A trip to Hawaii?
                (then)
    In fact, do you want Hawaii? We're
    very rich. Just take Hawaii — the
    whole thing. It's yours.

Mr. Mabry shakes Sebastian off of him.

                    MR. MABRY
    I'm sorry! There is nothing I can do!
    You are all in his care now.

Mr. Mabry leaves. Sebastian stands in the doorway.

> SEBASTIAN
> (shouting out to him)
> We are all in his doesn't care now!

Mr. Mabry does not respond. Sebastian slams the door and returns to the dining hall, where everyone remains.

> ANDY
> Look, dudes...

Andy pours himself a Jack and Coke and walks out of the room towards the living room.

INT. LIVING ROOM – DAY

Andy strolls in with his drink in hand and plops down on the sofa. The rest enter and stand in front of him.

> ANDY (cont'd)
> I really don't see what you guys
> are so worried about. I'm the
> oldest. The way I see it,
> responsibility is like wine in that
> with age it gets to be so that it is...

Andy takes a swig of his beverage.

> ANDY (cont'd)
> ...good. You know what I'm
> saying?

> SEBASTIAN
> Do you know what you're saying?

A knock is heard on the door. It is opened and then closed. RODRIGO, a mustached Guatemalan man in his fifties wearing a suit similar to Mr. Mabry's, strolls into the living room. He speaks with a thick Guatemalan accent. All of the siblings stop talking and stare at him.

> ANDY
> Mr. Mabry...you're back.

> MATTHEW
> And you're Mexican.

> RODRIGO
> Hello. I am Rodrigo, and I am Guatemalan.

All the siblings except for Sebastian look confused. Sebastian goes to Rodrigo and shakes his hand.

                              SEBASTIAN
          Hi, Rodrigo...
                    (to everyone)
          Everyone, this is Rodrigo.
                    (to Rodrigo)
          Rodrigo, this is...everyone.
                    (then)
          I went ahead and hired Rodrigo as
          our new butler. His resumé and
          background exceeded all the other
          applicants. He's here on a trial
          basis for a little bit. Everyone
          okay with that?

                              ANGIE
          I guess.

                              RODRIGO
          You must be Miss Angie.

                              ANGIE
          I'm going to my room.

Angie exits.

                              MATTHEW
          I'm Matthew.

                              RODRIGO
          And you must be Matthew. It is
          good to meet —

He is cut off.

                              MATTHEW
                    (panicked)
          Christ, I'm late to my audition for
          Oliver! I'd die for this role!

Matthew grabs his car keys and bolts toward the door
SINGING "Consider Yourself" from *Oliver*. He looks back to
everyone and briefly serenades them.

                          MATTHEW (cont'd)
                    (singing in awful Cockney accent)
          ...Consida' yee' self our mate ... consida'
          ye'self paht o' th' famileee...

He exits. Everyone is utterly unimpressed.

ANDY
(a moment. then)
Well, Rodrigo. I'm sorry to waste
your time, but I'm in charge now,
and your services won't be needed.

SEBASTIAN
Shut up, Andy.
(then, to Rodrigo)
Actually, your services are very much needed.

ANDY
Can you quit undermining me?

SEBASTIAN
Andy, we need a new butler!
Randolph died cause he was a
hundred and eighty-seven years old
and I say we give Rodrigo a shot.

ANDY
I don't need some authoritative
figure breathing down my neck all
the time.

RODRIGO
I plan on breathing down no neck,
or any other part of the body for
that matter, Mister Andy. I just
want to help out a bit. I, too, lost
my parents at a young age and know
how hard it can be. I have no plan
of getting in the way. I am very pretty good.

SEBASTIAN
Andy, he's a butler, not a baby-sitter.

ANDY
Well, with Randolph there was no
difference! And the only reason he
was around was because Mom and Dad
hired him before their accident! But it's just
us now!

SEBASTIAN
Exactly! It's just us now! Who's
gonna cook and clean and everything
else? You?

>   ANDY
>   Forget it. Do whatever. I'm only
>   the guardian! I've gotta go pick up
>   something I bought on Craigslist.
>   (bitterly)
>   That okay with you, Rodrigo?

Andy grabs his car keys and storms out of the house.

>   SEBASTIAN
>   (beat)
>   Welcome to our happy home.

>   RODRIGO
>   Everything will be fine. It is like
>   that old saying —
>   (then)
>   "Everything will be fine."

>   SEBASTIAN
>   Okay ... well, make yourself at home.
>   I'm going to finish my science
>   project and go to sleep.

>   RODRIGO
>   Goodnight, Mister Bastian.

In these first five pages, we definitely get a feel for what the show will be. Look at everything we have quickly learned: the Mersteins are filthy rich. Mr. and Mrs. Merstein died in an accident, leaving their three orphaned teenagers in the care of their oldest and most irresponsible child, Andy. The jumping-off point is that, against his siblings' wishes, Andy signs for guardianship of them. But it is easy to see that the real "parent" raising this family and holding them together will be the younger sibling, Sebastian. Rodrigo, the Guatemalan butler, will assist him.

RIDING COATTAILS

Once you have completed your pilot, you may feel euphoric. Your balloon may be quickly deflated, however, when you send out the script and realize that, while people will read it as a spec, no one is dying to make it because you are an unknown writer. I need to warn you that this will likely be the case. If, however, you are still bound and determined to try to get your pilot transformed into a series, then there is one small thing I could suggest, but I have to preface it by telling you that it's a long shot.

Here goes: see if you can hook up with another writer, producer, or show runner who has enough clout in the industry to get a pilot made. The reason this usually doesn't work is that, as we have discussed, it takes writers many years of blood, sweat, and tears to get into a position where a network deems them ready to create their own show. For many writers, this is the ultimate dream. By the time most of them get to this point, they already have their own ideas for series. So the question becomes, why would they want to abandon their own concepts to work with an unknown writer? Not to mention they'd have to share credit and money with you. This is not too appealing to most writers who have reached this level.

That said, if you really have an extraordinary idea that is well executed, you never know what can or will happen, even when the odds are stacked against you. I am a firm believer that as a writer you do the work well, you put it out there, and you keep pushing forward and plugging away no matter what. When you are of this mindset, sometimes things happen in ways you never thought they would.

CHECKLIST FOR PILOTS

- Have you created interesting characters with opposing viewpoints?
- Off the top of your head, can you list countless (compelling) stories that could be told about these characters?
- Does the story in your pilot episode provide a jumping-off point for the series?
- Can you clearly define what makes your pilot unique rather than something we've seen before?
- Does you pilot include an actual story, rather than just introduce characters and premise?
- Have you set up the characters and premise quickly?

PART V

MADE-FOR-TV MOVIES

MADE-FOR-TV MOVIES

Made-for-TV movies have been around since the 1960s. In the 1970s, they were quite popular and tackled a variety of what were then considered controversial issues such as teenage alcoholism and domestic abuse. Until recently, networks broadcast TV movies on a regular basis — some even once a week — leading them to be coined as MOWs (Movies of the Week) in the industry, a term still widely used. Currently (and disappointingly) networks are not making as many movies of the week as they once did.

Since each MOW is self-contained and revolves around a different story and a different set of characters, it is difficult for networks to build a following in the same way they can with a really good series. Additionally, the MOW audience can be fractured among itself because it incorporates many sub-genres, some of which appeal to some viewers, but not to others. For example, I would take a good family drama that revolves around real-life issues over a fluffy romance movie any day of the week. Others may feel the exact opposite. What this translates to is that typically it's much harder to get Nielsen numbers on an MOW than it is with series television.

But if writing TV movies is your passion, don't worry. While the networks may be producing fewer made-for-TV movies, cable networks like Lifetime, USA, and TNT are pumping them out.

> "A concept that is promotable, castable, and can be structured so that the audience (ratings) grows over the two-hour broadcast. Aside from it being socially important and illuminating, a current issue so compelling that everyone in the country is talking about it around the office water coolers the day after the broadcast. Of course, many writers feel a good movie of the week is one they get paid for." — Walter Klenhard, writer/director of numerous TV movies on what makes a good MOW

HALLMARK IS THE BENCHMARK

Hallmark likes to boast about the quality of their greeting cards. What they really should brag about is their Hall of Fame made-for-TV movies. To date, they have produced 227 of them, and the overall quality is consistently unmatched within the industry. In short, Hallmark has set the bar high for what an MOW could and should be. In fairness to cable networks like Lifetime and TNT, Hallmark only produces a few of these movies each year and they sink big money into them, as opposed to the smaller budgets that most TV movies have to operate under.

What makes Hallmark Hall of Fame movies a cut above the rest? The answer is simple. Hallmark movies contain stories that are both original and unusual. They are rarely — if ever — run of the mill, and always told through characters that are courageous and inspiring, steeped in emotional truth. Broken down, the stories are incredibly simple. Here is just a sampling of some of what Hallmark has put on the air:

- *The Magic of Ordinary Days*: During World War II, Livvy Dunn finds herself unmarried and pregnant. Her minister father kicks her out of the house, sends her to rural Colorado, and forces her into an arranged marriage with a farmer. At first the two have little in common. Then, slowly but surely, they fall in love.
- *To Dance with the White Dog*: After 50 years of marriage, Mr. Sam's heart is broken after the death of his wife Cora. Trapped in failing health and loneliness, he seems to be on a downward spiral, when suddenly one day a white dog dances into his life and turns everything around.
- *Rose Hill* (based on Judy Garwood's best-selling novel *For the Roses*): Set in the 1800s, four boys — street orphans — find an abandoned baby girl in New York City and adopt her. The five kids become a family, grow up together, and eventually migrate to Montana where, against the backdrop of the Wild West, this nontraditional family faces a string of challenges that will either pull them together or forever tear them apart.

Should you have any interest in writing made-for-TV movies, I suggest that you study several different Hallmark Hall of Fame movies. You can find them on Hallmark's Web site, in Hallmark stores, or you can rent them at video stores. You will be learning from the best of the best.

TARGET AUDIENCE FOR MOWs (THINK PINK)

If you are a male, the mere thought of watching movies like the ones I've just listed probably makes you want to gag. If you are female, the thought more than likely makes you want to dance. That's because the target demographic for made-for-TV movies is primarily women. You can argue that cable networks like Spike and TNT may indeed make some rough-and-tough films. However, of all the made-for-TV movies that are produced, those are the exception rather than the rule. If you are still unconvinced, think of it like this: how many men do you see standing around the water cooler, enthusiastically chatting up last night's made-for-TV movie? The answer is, probably none. If you listen carefully, however, you will hear women aged 18–80 talking about just that. Because I work in television, people sometimes tend to think of me as a walking talking *TV Guide*. Several times a week, my female friends will undoubtedly ask, "is there a good movie on Lifetime tonight?" They are secretly hoping I say "yes," and horribly disappointed if I say "no." When Lifetime puts out an original, there will be heavy discussion about it the following day.

If you are contemplating writing a made-for-TV movie, you must think pink. Ask yourself, what kind of stories/issues are of interest to women? Can you incorporate a strong female lead character into your story? This is imperative, though thankfully not difficult to do. Let's say you are doing a story on a serial rapist. You can either make one of the victims the person who won't rest until the rapist is caught — or you can create a female cop who won't rest until she puts the sleaze bag behind bars and throws away the key.

Should you be at all tempted to write something that is predominantly driven by heavy male action, half-naked women, or guns and violence — you are undoubtedly barking up the wrong tree. Again, you will have only a few outlets at which to shop your script, and your odds of getting a made-for-TV movie made with this kind of material are slim. You have to think of your target audience. These kinds of stories are not what most women want to watch, and thus not the kinds of scripts that most companies in the MOW arena are looking to buy.

> "Know the network or studio you are trying to sell to. Know the kinds of movies they do, what's been on most recently and what's done well in the ratings. You have to do your homework. If you try to pitch us an all-male period piece, that's not what we're looking to buy." — Libby Beers, vice president of original movies, Lifetime Television

MOST COMMON TYPES OF MOW STORIES AND WHY THEY WORK

There are several kinds of stories that lend themselves to the made-for-TV movie market. As with most television, this market also tends to run in cycles. Usually, a certain sub-genre is really hot for a while, but then the market gets over-saturated, and they stop making that particular kind of story for a time, while moving on to the next hot sub-genre.

Here is a sampling of sub-genres that have found repeated success in the made-for-TV movie arena:

- True crime: Think Ted Bundy, Scott Peterson, and the BTK serial killer Dennis Rader. The good stories usually have a "monster" pitted against sympathetic, unsuspecting victims.

- Novels: Adapting novels into made-for-TV movies is usually a good bet, because novels, if written well, have compelling stories and strong protagonists and antagonists. Perhaps one of the best MOWs I have seen that fits this bill is called *The Pact*, starring Megan Mullaly, based on Jodi Picoult's best-selling, critically acclaimed novel of the same name. This is a simple story about Chris and Emily, two teenagers who grow up across the street from each other and eventually fall in love. This goes over well with both sets of parents who have also been best friends for years. But teenage angst causes Chris and Emily to secretly make a suicide pact, and one fateful evening they go down to the local carousel to end their lives. Emily succeeds, but at the last minute, Chris opts to live. He is later charged with Emily's murder. The story revolves around the two families attempting to come to grips with each other and with what really happened. It is gut-wrenching drama constructed with real and sympathetic characters. Adapting novels for television can produce strong Nielsen numbers as novels come with a built-in audience that has either read the book or heard about it and wants to see the movie.
- Disease of the week: A fairly self-explanatory sub-genre. Stories usually focus on women who bravely fight to overcome some form of physical or mental illness. Films like *Kate's Secret* and *Saving Emily* fall into this category.
- Fem in jep: This popular sub-genre portrays women victimized by men. Stalkers and abusive husbands fall under this umbrella, as do titles such as *A Face to Die For* or *A Face to Kill For*.
- Romance: Often made from novels by writers like Danielle Steele. Titles include *Mixed Blessings* and *Star*.
- Women who have overcome incredible life obstacles: Movies in this category tend to be inspiring. They are usually true and depict women who were dealt terrible hands in life, but managed to beat the odds and triumph. A good example is *Homeless to Harvard*, the true story of Liz Murray who, due to a mother with mental illness, found herself alone and on the street at 15 years old. Despite her horrible situation, she held onto hope, attended school, and eventually got into Harvard. Another good example is *Dawn Anna*, starring Debra Winger, who plays a single mother struggling with a brain tumor. Just as she is recovering, one of her children is killed at Columbine.
- Men behaving badly: Admittedly one of my favorite sub-genres, which includes movies such as *The Babysitter's Seduction* and *The Man with Three Wives*. The titles say it all. Movies in this sub-genre tend to be fairly mindless and have a way of really hooking women in.

Perhaps the most important thing to remember when coming up with a story for a made-for-TV movie is not to make it too complicated. MOWs usually air in the 9 p.m. slot. Most women are tired by this time — they've worked all day either at home or the office or both — and they are looking to relax to something that is smart and stimulating, but at the same time doesn't require too much concentration or brainpower.

STORIES TO STAY FAR AWAY FROM

Stories that don't work for usually MOWs are with stories that are action driven. Surprisingly, comedies don't work as well either. Every once in a while, a network will try a lighthearted romantic comedy — but somehow they just don't hold the same appeal. Stories that have an all-male or mostly-male cast are also no-nos. Likewise, you should not try to turn an old TV show into a movie — as in *Dynasty: The Reunion*. You don't own the rights to those characters, and therefore, you would most likely be sued.

BREAKING INTO THE MOW BUSINESS

As a writer, there are generally two ways that you can break into TV movies. Both involve writing a dynamic movie script.

The first way is to write the script and submit it to an MOW company (through an agent, of course) as something you would like them to consider making. The second way is that you write a script that you don't necessarily think an MOW company will make — perhaps it is a feature script — but it represents a well-structured, well-executed story with compelling characters and raw emotion. This script will serve more as a sample to showcase your talent and demonstrate to executives and producers who you are as a writer. If they like what they see, they may ask you in to pitch — or even better, they may approach you with a movie idea, and if you are interested, they may hire you to write it.

> "Write a spec movie that is a project of passion that's a good example of your writing. Something with emotion, something with drama that escalates and rivets. Something that says, 'I'm a writer you need to pay attention to.' That may not be the script we buy, but it will tell us the kind of writing you're capable of when you pitch other ideas. It's hard to sell a pitch if you don't have a really great writing sample." — Libby Beers, vice president of original movies, Lifetime Television

ADAPTING TRUE STORIES

True stories often make wonderful TV movies. Audiences have heightened appreciation knowing that a story isn't merely the product of a writer's imagination, but rather something that actually happened. But true stories can come with added complications. If the person whose story you want to tell is alive, it is imperative that you obtain the rights to that person's story.

This will be key in helping you to avoid a lawsuit. Even then, writing the script can be tricky, as you will most likely be writing about other real people in that person's life. And even though you have obtained the rights to one person's story doesn't mean that other people who end up in your movie won't file court papers if they think you have made them look bad. This can happen, especially in cases where the story is messy — as in a high-profile murder or divorce — and the parties remain at odds with each other.

If the person you are writing about is deceased, you can breathe a little easier, but not completely. Again, unless you are writing a true-life period piece where everyone is long gone, there may people who decide to sue. If the story involved any kind of court case, you can protect yourself to a degree by making sure that anything you put in your script is in the court documents. So, for example, if your script is about a man who murdered his wife, you would want to go to the courthouse and pour through all of the transcripts. If you find that a witness testified to seeing the man shoot his wife in the head, you can put that in the script. The man would have a hard time coming back and suing you because the testimony was real — not something you made up.

> "There are the legal issues. Make sure that you clearly understand what is real and what you have fictionalized — and be able to document the genesis of every scene." — Walter Klenhard, writer/director of numerous made-for-TV movies

Along those lines, you have to be very careful in terms of sticking to the story as it happened. Often writers think they have a dramatic license to bend the story. While it's true that sometimes things have to be cut or tweaked for dramatic purpose in order to make the movie work, it's not okay to add scenes or things that didn't really happen and present it as the total truth. This is why you will see some disclaimers that read "based on a true story." But, as a writer, you can't use that disclaimer as a get-out-of jail-free card to make up things that didn't actual happen in an effort to improve your story. If you are going to do something that's true, you must stick as closely to the facts as you possibly can.

PROTAGONIST VS. ANTAGONIST

Like all television, Movies of the Week are formulaic. In MOWs, the relationship between the protagonist and antagonist is kicked up a notch. In TV movies — even more so than feature films and hour-long dramas, the protagonist nearly always wins. So, say a woman is being stalked and terrorized by an old flame throughout the movie, and she just can't get rid of him. In order to escape, she decides to go to the one place he'll never find her — her small country cabin in the middle of the woods. Of course, once she's there, who shows up? But the stalker isn't the only one to have followed her there. Just as the stalker is going to harm her, in bursts the detective who has been on the case. He whips out his gun. In the MOW format, there is no way the cop will kill the stalker. This must come from the woman. She is the one who has been terrorized, and the only way we women will feel truly satisfied is if the victim is the one to overcome the bad guy. After investing two hours in her ordeal, we want her to win. It isn't nearly as satisfying if someone else does the deed for her. Especially if that someone is a man.

BRINGING NOVELS TO THE SCREEN: HOW TO GET THE RIGHTS

If you watch made-for-TV movies, you have probably noticed that many of them are adapted from novels. This is something you should never do unless you have the obtained the rights to that novel in writing. If you were to sit down and adapt your favorite novel into a teleplay, a couple of things could — and probably would — happen to you, neither of which would be good. Because you would be taking characters and dialogue that were written by another writer, you would be in violation of copyright laws. Most likely, you would be sued. Also, imagine your embarrassment — and disappointment — if you spent all of the time that it would take to adapt the novel — and you got an executive chomping for it — and then you had to tell that executive that you don't have the rights. The executive would probably be annoyed (and rightly so), feeling that you had wasted his or her valuable time by submitting a script that isn't legally yours to sell.

Getting the rights to a novel is not easy, but it's also not impossible. I wouldn't advise trying to go after the rights to novels of well-known authors like Stephen King and Danielle Steele, as the rights to their books are usually snapped up before the book goes into print. And even if they were available, the rights would cost so much money, you probably couldn't afford them. The same is true with books that have been on *The New York Times* bestseller list. However, you might have a better shot at obtaining rights to books that have been kicking around for several years or those novels that are a bit more obscure.

> "It's an instinctive reaction. It's an emotional reaction. It's like meeting someone you like or finding a house you want to buy. There is a sense of rightness. Beyond that it needs to have great plot and characters. Dialogue is less important. But the plot should be like a freight train. It should start up and keep going … toward the end of the movie it should go faster and faster until you arrive at the station. It doesn't have to be a straight track, but it should pull you along by what will happen next." — Executive Producer Rebecca Eaton, *Masterpiece Theatre* and *Mystery!*, on how to know if a book will translate well to the screen.

If you find a book that you think might make a good movie, look carefully at the book jacket, both inside and out, and jot down any information that you can find about the publisher and the author.

Your next step is to call the publisher. Ask to be connected to the subsidiary or "sub" rights division. Tell whoever answers the phone in that department that you would like to know who controls the theatrical rights to the particular book you are interested in. The person will look up the information for you. Listen carefully — there are a couple of things that he or she might say that could be of great importance to you. It's possible that he or she will tell you the name of an agent or the name of a production company. Both of those are bad news.

If an agent is controlling the rights, that means most likely he or she is doing so on behalf of the author, and will probably want to negotiate for as much money as possible. Additionally, an agent is not likely to fork over the rights to an unknown, unproduced writer. The goal of the agent is not just to get his client money, it's to get the book made into a movie, which would generate even more money and more prestige for the author.

If a production company controls the rights, this too is not great news for you. It means that someone beat you to the punch in thinking the book would make a great movie. It doesn't mean they'll be successful. Be sure to ask the publisher when the contract expires. Write that date on your calendar and then try again at that time.

Another possibility — and this is the best scenario — is that the author controls the rights. I find that dealing directly with authors is a lot more productive. As a writer, you both tend to speak the same language. If an author's novel has been sitting on a shelf for many years without many inquiries, it is possible — depending on how well you sell yourself to the author — that he or she may give you a shot at either a free or very inexpensive option.

You may have to track the author down, which is not always easy. That is why I said to look carefully at the author information on the jacket of the book. For example, the author may live in New York City, but spend summers writing in a cabin in Tinytown, Maine. See if anything gives you a clue — either about the author as a person or where to find the author — such as in small town in Maine in the summer.

Sometimes, you really have to think out of the box and get creative in tracking people down. When I was working for a producer at Columbia Pictures, I once saw a blurb on a book that was coming out in about six months. It was a true story about two Russians who had escaped to the U.S. at the time the Iron Curtain was still firmly in place. The story had lots of action, and mixed with a great love story. I wanted the rights to that book. The problem was — as of that moment — the book had only been published in French, which is a language I don't happen to speak. The book was in the process of being translated to English, but I knew I couldn't wait. If this was as good as I thought, I needed to try to get the rights before it was translated and everyone else was in line for it. So I called the French teacher at my old high school and asked her if she would read the French version of the book and then fill me in on the details. She agreed. Once she reported back and told me that the story was everything I hoped it would be, I was more determined than ever to get those rights.

The problem was, the author controlled the theatrical rights and for some odd reason the publisher didn't have his address or phone number. I kept digging and digging. Somewhere along the way, I found some little blurb that indicated that when the two Russians arrived in the U.S., they had settled in Washington, D.C. Since their name was a Russian one and therefore not common, I figured I would try directory assistance. Bingo. It was that simple. The operator gave me the number. I dialed it, and a man with a heavy Russian accent said, "hello." I immediately began to gush about his story. A week later, he and his wife were sitting across from me — along with the producer I worked for at Columbia Pictures — talking about the possibility of turning their story into a movie. Sometimes, it is the most obvious, simple little clues that can take you where you want to go.

In talking to authors, it's okay to show how passionate you are about their work. They will appreciate your enthusiasm. You should also explain why you think the book would make a great movie. Be sure to tell them a little bit about yourself. Let them know of any connections you may have that would be instrumental in getting the movie made. If money is an issue, it's a good idea to tell them that you can't afford much for the rights, but don't make that the first thing you say. First get them jazzed about you and your commitment to the project. A little passion can go along way. If the book has been sitting on a bookshelf without any interest for a number of years, they may just agree to let you give it a try.

When attempting to get rights to a book or novel you are looking to obtain an "option." An option means that the author (or person who holds the rights to the title) agrees to give you the rights to the work for a set period of time for a certain amount of money that you both agree upon. In some cases, as with more high-profile authors and books, the rights can cost hundreds of thousands of dollars. But it doesn't have to be that expensive. Options can also be free. Usually, they fall somewhere between these two extremes.

Once someone gives you an option to their work, they cannot sell the rights to anyone else until your option expires. This is why having a contract in writing is so important. Let's say, for the sake of argument, that Andre Dubus III (*House of Sand and Fog*) is your next-door neighbor. And somehow, with all of your passion you are able to convince him to give you an option on his next novel. You pay him $1,000 and he signs over the rights for one year. If, the next day, Clint Eastwood called Mr. Dubus and offered him $200,000 for the same rights, Mr. Dubus could not accept. He is legally bound to you and so he would have to wait until your option is up, and hope that Clint is still interested in another year.

A few words of caution about options. If there is no written agreement, it is too easy and too tempting for the author to back out of the deal should a better offer come along. An option doesn't have to be a complex contract — it can be written in a page or two. But, because it is so important, it might be a good idea to spend a few bucks and let a lawyer draw up the contract just to be sure you are fully protected. Again, you don't want to be pitching a novel that you don't have the rights to, nor do you want to waste all of that precious time and energy hashing out the story and sweating over the script only to find the author has backed out of the deal due to a loophole in the contract.

As far as how long the initial option period should be, I would suggest at least a year. You will need time to write the screenplay — or even to go out and pitch the project. You would be surprised in the TV world how quickly a year goes by.

SHOULD YOU WRITE A MINI-SERIES?

At this point in your career, when you are just starting out as a writer, there are a thousand reasons why you should not attempt to write a mini-series. I will give you a select few.

First, in the grand scheme of things, very few mini-series actually get made. Those that do get the green light tend to be enormously expensive. A mini-series can be two nights, if not three or more. The production is usually slicker, often using special effects, and the cast tends to be comprised of big name stars, all of whom get paid (deservedly) a huge chunk of change. Of the mini-series that make it onto the small screen, most will be on during Sweeps and they will be heavily promoted. Again, this is the network's way of casting the bait in order to reel in viewers. The idea is that if they can get an audience hooked the first night, they will be back for the second and possibly a third night as well. With all of this money at stake, networks are not about to entrust two or three full nights of television to a first-time writer. These scripts will usually only go to writers with a proven track record.

Another reason not to attempt a mini-series right out of the gate is that you need to crawl before you can walk and you need to walk before you can run. Concentrate on mastering the art of a two-hour script before you take on four or more hours. Failure to do so will almost certainly result in disaster.

DON'T MAKE YOUR TWO-HOUR A FOUR-HOUR

A common mistake that writers who are just starting out in the MOW field make is that as they begin to write the script, suddenly other ideas pop into their heads. One flash of brilliance leads to another, and before they know it, they are on page 60 and they are only a third of the way through the script. Rather than cutting and making choices, they say, "there's a lot of material here. Maybe I should just make it a mini-series." Wrong. This is not how mini-series are conceived. Not to mention, that almost no one in the industry is going to read a spec mini-series. You are much better off writing a really great two-hour, getting it produced (a big deal in itself), and working your way up as a writer to the point where the networks come to you and ask if you'd consider doing a mini-series. But this is quite a way off on the horizon.

STRUCTURING YOUR MOW

Movie of the week scripts run on average about 110 pages. Traditionally, MOWs followed a seven- act structure. Today, some networks have extended that to an eight-act structure. As with drama and comedy, each act ends with a mini-cliffhanger, raising the stakes and leaving the characters in jeopardy. The biggest Act Break comes at the halfway point, which coincides with the top of the hour, meaning a double commercial break. Though they don't have to be perfectly matched, each act should be approximately the same length. Movies of the week are so formulaic in terms of their structure that I don't need a clock when watching one. I can tell what time it is by what's going on in the movie. Here is how a typical MOW script breaks down in terms of acts:

- Acts One and Two: This is the setup. Who are the characters and what do they want?
- Acts Three through Six: This is the heart and soul of the script. It's where the central conflict plays out.
- Acts Seven and Eight: This is the resolution. How does the story end? Who gets what they want and who doesn't? Who has grown and changed along the way?

Now that you know how a movie of the week breaks down structurally, I would not advise you to write one that way. Instead, I would strongly suggest that you write your MOW as a feature film. The reason is, that if you can get a feature film produced, you will join an elite group of writers. Getting a feature produced is hugely prestigious and it will open more doors for you as a writer than getting a movie of the week produced. You will also make a lot more money. And while I don't want to dwell on the cash factor (writing is about art, not about money), the truth is, if given the chance most of us would rather sell a script for a few hundred thousand.

> "As for an MOW — don't write one. Write a spec feature script, something that could play on the big screen. Think commercially for that first spec script, try to write something that they are always making — Christmas comedy, horror film, romantic comedy — as opposed to Lawrence of Arabia." — Walter Klenhard, writer/director of numerous MOWs

If you can think of a story that could potentially be a feature film, but — here's the key — the story also could work as an MOW, you automatically double your chances of making a sale. You can market the script first as a feature, but if it doesn't sell, you can then shop it in the television world as a made-for-TV movie. The beauty is you won't even have to convert the script to MOW format. Executives and producers in the MOW world will read feature films scripts. If they decide to buy them, they will work with you to develop the script for television.

STORIES THAT CAN DOUBLE AS FEATURE FILMS AND MOWs

If you plan to write a feature film using television as a secondary market in the event your feature doesn't sell, then you definitely want to come up with a story that would work in both arenas. Let's look at a couple of feature films that, had they not been made into features, would have had an excellent shot at being made as MOWs.

- *Fatal Attraction*: This Oscar-nominated thriller almost seems a more natural fit as a made-for-TV movie. Michael Douglas plays Dan Gallagher, a New York City attorney who seems to have it all — great job, beautiful wife and child, nice home — even a great dog. One weekend, while his wife is out of town, he gives in to temptation and beds Alex Forrest (Glenn Close), who works at a publishing house that his firm represents. What he thought would be an innocent and short-lived fling turns into a nightmare. Alex turns out to be psychotic and begins a game of emotional blackmail as she stalks both Dan and his family, threatening to bring down his world at every turn.

  Had it not been for stars like Michael Douglas and Glenn Close, *Fatal Attraction* easily could have been a made-for-TV movie. The original spin on the old story is, of course, a woman stalking a man. What's notable about this is that the seemingly small spin made the movie appeal to men as well as women, as Alex Forrest is every married man's worst nightmare.
- *Ordinary People*: Based on the novel by Judith Guest and directed by Robert Redford, this powerful character-driven drama won four Oscars including best picture, best director, and best screenplay (based on material from another medium). The story centers on the Jarretts, an upper-middle-class family who have been torn apart by the accidental drowning of one son and the subsequent suicide attempt of another. Had it not been for Redford, this story may have well ended up as a made-for-TV movie. The irony is that while the film starred Donald Sutherland, it also cast TV stars Mary Tyler Moore and Judd Hirsch.

CLASSIC THREE-ACT STRUCTURE

If you plan to first put your script out into the theatrical world, then you need to write it as a feature film script. The main difference between a feature script and an MOW script is that an MOW script has the Act Breaks written into the script. You can flip through the pages and see where one act ends and another begins. While features have definitive Act Breaks, they are not written into the script. Yet, industry people will refer to different acts when discussing a script or movie. Just how do they know where one act ends and another begins? It's called classic three-act structure. While not every movie is structured this way, the majority of them are. Personally, I am a believer in three-act structure, especially when you are just starting out. I think it is easy to understand, it works — and it makes writing 120 pages less daunting.

Classic three-act structure is extremely simple to understand. It breaks down as follows:

- Act One (pages 1–30) The setup. Think of it as the beginning. This is where you set the tone and pacing, introduce your characters, their worlds, and their goals.
- Act Two (pages 31–90) The conflict. Consider it the middle. This is the heart and soul of your story. It's where the tension builds and builds and the stakes get higher and higher. One thing after another stands in the way of your protagonists achieving the goals they set for themselves.
- Act Three (pages 91–120) The resolution, or the end. This is where your story resolves itself. We find out who wins and who loses. We also get a glimpse of where the characters go from here.

There are a couple of things worth pointing out. Notice that Act Two is double the length of Act One and of Act Three. If there is one place most writers fall off the wagon, it is in Act Two. You need to make sure that you have enough story, conflict, and jeopardy to hold an audience for approximately an hour. Consider it a red flag when your second act is shorter or equal to your first or third act. Also, the page numbers I have given are rough estimates. Some feature scripts — especially comedies — come in at fewer pages, closer to 105. If your feature comes in under 120 pages, that is fine, but it should not come in over 120. I already know what you're thinking: lots of movies are longer than two hours … look at the stuff Steven Spielberg does, or how about some of those Oliver Stone epics? Let me break this to you as gently as I possibly can: you aren't Oliver Stone or Steven Spielberg yet. Until you attain that kind of notoriety, you have to at least attempt to play by the rules. Also, if you want your feature to double as an MOW, it can't be a gazillion pages. You have to worry about commercial breaks, which take time away from your script.

Classic three-act structure has "turning points" (they can also be called "plot points"). A turning point is an event that spins the action into a different direction. So, your story is going one way, then something happens — an event that changes everything. The result is that the story is now going in another direction. There can be numerous turning points in a script, but in classic three-act structure, there are two places that you absolutely must have them. The first comes at the end of the first act — so anywhere from around pages 25–30. This turning point takes us from Act One into Act Two. The second major turning point occurs at the end of Act Two, right around page 90. You can think of this turning point as the beginning of the end. It takes us out of Act Two and into Act Three where the resolution awaits. Once we are in Act Three, things begin to happen more quickly as the story's momentum propels us toward the end.

Because turning points are so critical to three-act structure, let's briefly look at Callie Khouri's Oscar-winning screenplay, *Thelma & Louise*, which is perfectly constructed within the confines of three-act structure.

In Act One, we meet Thelma (Geena Davis) and Louise (Susan Sarandon). Though friends, they are like night and day. Louise is a waitress with a quiet "seen-it-all, done-it all" kind of sophistication. While she has a boyfriend, she is clearly in charge of her own life. Thelma, on the other hand, is a housewife, married to a sleaze bucket who cheats on her and controls her every thought and move. Without asking her husband's permission, Thelma agrees to accompany Louise on a girls' weekend to a cabin in the mountains. While hubby is at work, Thelma packs everything but the kitchen sink for the trip … including a gun. On the way to the cabin, they pass a roadside dive. Thelma, who never gets out of the house or has any fun, convinces Louise to stop for a drink. Before too long, Thelma is tipsy. Harlan, another sleaze bag, starts to hit on her. When Louise goes to the ladies' room, Harlan dances with Thelma. The combination of booze and spinning around the dance floor makes Thelma sick. She goes outside to get some air. Harlan follows. He pushes her up against a car and attempts to rape her. Suddenly there is a gun at his head. It's Louise, telling him to stop. He does. But, before leaving, he makes a vulgar comment about how he should have finished doing what he was doing to Thelma. This sets off something in Louise who shoots Harlan dead.

Louise killing Harlan is turning point number one. It spins the action into a completely different direction. Up until this point, Thelma and Louise were two women going to the mountains for a weekend getaway. Because of the first turning point, they have now become two women on the run for their lives and from the law.

Throughout all of Act Two, Thelma and Louise are on the run, managing to stay a few steps ahead of the law. They make plans to go to Mexico. The easiest way to get there is to drive straight through Texas. But Louise refuses to go anywhere near the Lone Star state. We later learn that she was once raped in Texas, which further explains her utter distain for Harlan. As Thelma and Louise continue to run, we are introduced to investigator Hal Slocumb, who is tracking them. He is sympathetic to their situation, and tries to get them to surrender. At the end of Act Two, Louise makes a fatal mistake. On the phone Slocum informs Louise that he knows what happened to her in Texas. Louise is momentarily taken aback. She stays on the phone a moment too long, and the cops are able to trace the call. The police now have a handle on exactly where the women are and can move in.

Louise hanging on the phone too long is turning point number two. It spins the action into a different direction. Throughout Act Two, Thelma and Louise had always been able to evade the police. In this fatal flaw, the police are now in a superior position and can move in on the women. This is the beginning of Act Three. It is also the beginning of the end.

The next time you go to the movies or rent a DVD, start to become aware of three-act structure. Once you understand it, it's very easy to see. As I mentioned earlier, it is also a good, clean way for a new writer to attack a feature without getting lost.

> "My best advice is to not listen to any agents or managers or producers who tell you what the studios or networks are looking for. Write from your gut — don't worry about whether it is a 'commercial idea' — write about something that troubles you, something that fascinates you. And make sure you do the research; know that world better than anyone else. Then send your script out and see if anyone wants to make it. If you know your craft, and if it's truly original, your chances of getting it made are much better than if you go off chasing ideas someone else wants to see made." — Oscar winner Paul Haggis, *Crash* and *Million Dollar Baby*, on the best way for new writers to break into the industry.

PART VI

CHARACTERS

CREATING COMPELLING CHARACTERS

Without a doubt, the most important component of any story is the characters. Characters are the force that drives the story forward. They are the element that hooks an audience in. Without interesting, well-defined characters, your story won't work because the audience won't care. Therefore, it is imperative that you create multi-dimensional characters. Multi-dimensional characters are characters with many layers. Like most human beings, they are not perfect. They have flaws and weaknesses that occasionally lead them astray and get them into trouble, yet these same flaws and weaknesses make them relatable.

> "A dynamic character is someone who has an agenda and takes action to further it. Ask yourself, 'What does this person want? What will they do to get it?'" — Lee Aronshohn, creator and executive producer, *Two and a Half Men*

CHARACTER BROKEN INTO THREES

To create complex characters that are multi-dimensional, you must dig deep into your characters' heart and soul. Ask yourself, "what is this person's agenda? What is his point of view?" There are three important layers that need to be defined in order to create a compelling character:

1. Public persona: This is the face your character wears publicly. How does he or she act and react in the presence of others?
2. Private persona: When no one else is present, how does the person think and feel? Very often, the private person and the public persona clash and/or are in sharp contrast to each other. This creates very interesting characters.
3. Incognizant persona: This is who your character really is at his very core. There are things that are happening deep, deep, deep that even he may be unaware of.

WHAT IS BACKSTORY?

Every one of us has a backstory. Consider yours to be everything that has ever happened to you from the moment you were born (and, depending on your life philosophy, you could go back even further) until right now, this second … this moment in time. Everyone has a different backstory. Backstory is what shapes us and makes us who we are as individuals.

Characters have backstories too. Theirs consists of everything that has happened to them up until the moment we meet them on screen. It is important that as a writer you understand the intricacies and complexities of your characters' backstories, because everything that has happened in their past directly contributes to who they are in the present. It's what gives them their all-important point of view. For example, a person who grew up in the inner-city projects, hungry most of the time, probably views the world quite differently than someone who grew up in Beverly Hills. Similarly, a person whose roots are in the Bible Belt probably thinks more conservatively than someone who grew up in San Francisco. Backstory shapes a character's point of view.

Backstory is hugely complex. There are the day-to-day realities that affect a character's viewpoint. These are the relatively small things. Then, there are the life-altering events. These are the big moments in a character's life that change and affect everything. For example, a character who is adopted may have abandonment issues, a character whose parents are murdered may have problems with rage, a character who is fat as a child and constantly picked on in grade school carries feelings of inferiority into adult life.

To illustrate the point further, let's go back to *Thelma and Louise*. Clearly, Louise's backstory plays a huge part in why the women find themselves on the run. Had Louise not been raped in Texas, she likely would not have shot Harlan. Again, keep in mind, that once Louise put the gun to Harlan's head, he stopped what he was doing to Thelma. It was only when he shot off his mouth that Louise blew him away. It is easy to conclude that what Harlan said brought Louise back to her own horrible moment of helplessness. This time, she had all the power and used it by killing him.

In creating characters, it is important to know the small day-to-day things about your character's past. But it is the larger life-altering events that really define a character. Sometimes, as in real life, characters are unaware of how what happened in their past directly affects their point of view and how they react to certain situations.

CHARACTER BIOS

Before you write, you need to take some time to flesh out your characters. I can't stress enough how you must know these people intimately. They must come alive in your head and in your heart. They must talk to you throughout the course of your day, and in the middle of the night. And you must listen to what they have to say.

> "I look for emotional truth. It that's there, it's easy to build character ... I understand that journey." — Emmy Award-winning actor Henry Winkler

Many writers will sit down at their computers and knock out what are known as character bios. It is here that writers make decisions about who a character is and why. They define a character's backstory, including all the important details from the moment a character was born to where he is right before the audience meets him. Most of the fine details of a character's backstory don't get mentioned on screen. It's more for the writer to develop an understanding of what makes the character tick.

Character bios are a good way to get a handle on who a character is, what drives him and why. However, I think there is a danger in knowing too much about your character. I have seen writers who have notebook after notebook filled to the brim with the smallest of character traits and details. Literally, they work months fleshing out each character. Most professional writers don't do this. They get the character basics down, and they come to terms with the life-altering moments that define the character. I have seen many a new writer get hung so up in knowing every little detail about a character that it prevents him or her from actually writing the script. I also believe that writing is about discovery. As you write, you will uncover things about your characters that will be a natural fit. If you have them too etched in stone, you won't be open to possibilities that pop up along the journey.

WHY IT'S IMPORTANT FOR THE AUDIENCE TO LIKE AT LEAST SOME OF YOUR CHARACTERS

I often read scripts that are loaded down with despicable characters. It's one unlikable Joe after another, with virtually no redeeming values. And I wonder to myself, what is the point?

> "There should be at least one character you care deeply about, whose emotional fate you have invested in. There should be a lot of positive elements. The way people watch TV vs. the way they read a book is very different. Once they commit to 15 or 20 pages of a book, audiences will usually stick it out. In TV, they are much more likely to bail if they don't care about at least one character in the story." — Rebecca Eaton, executive producer, *Masterpiece Theater* and *Mystery!*

It is important when writing a script to give the audience someone they can root for, or at the very least bond with. If an audience doesn't like anyone in your script, they will be resistant to the story. And if they don't like your story, it's over. This isn't to say that you can't have dark characters. You can, but you need to even them out by giving them some traits that an audience can relate to. Take, for example, a mafia boss who spends his day ordering executions. When he goes home at night, he watches *Bambi* with his two-year-old — and when Bambi's mother is shot by the hunters, he cries. Now the character has depth, is multi-dimensional and interesting.

Let's look quickly at the character of Hannibal Lecter from *Silence of the Lambs*. Hannibal is a cannibal, which on the surface, makes him a monster. Let's face it; most of us don't have a warm and fuzzy reaction to a guy who likes to devour people. But when Lecter announces that he likes to eat human body parts such as liver with fava beans and a good Chianti, bam! Suddenly there is some depth to him. He doesn't merely want to eat people — he wants to *enjoy* them with a nice side dish over a good glass of wine. Now he is no longer merely a monster, but a character with quirks. We are slightly amused by him, if not completely intrigued.

SOME OF THE FINEST CHARACTERS ARE NOT HUMAN

Not every character you write has to be human. In fact, some of the standout characters in film and television have been nonhuman. The key to creating good nonhuman characters is to give them human qualities and traits, so that people can identify with them. Perhaps the best example of a nonhuman character is E.T. Screenwriter Melissa Mathison set us up to love this ugly little alien from the get-go. Who wasn't tugging their heartstrings the moment the spaceship blasted off, leaving poor E.T. to fend for himself on a planet he knew nothing about? Who didn't share his heartache brought on by homesickness, which we were continually reminded of by his constant desire to "phone home"? And who wasn't secretly amused as E.T. slowly discovered some of Earth's finer things like beer and Reese's Pieces? Despite the fact that E.T. comes from a galaxy far, far away, we had a lot in common with him. This is why his character worked.

> "The only way you can write for a nonhuman character on a situation comedy is to see that character as a person. They have their own individual voice, so they have to be treated the same way you treat the other characters on the show. Sometimes the fact that they aren't human, as on *Alf*, gives them more distinct traits and voices, making them easier to write for than, say, another TV mom. A nonhuman character is simply a more interesting 'person' to write for." — Adrienne Armstrong, writer, *Alf*

Perhaps my favorite nonhuman character in television history is Herman Munster. Herman works because mentally he is the complete opposite of what we expect, based on his physicality. Despite his enormous size and frightful face, Herman is a pussycat. He is friendly and kind, and laughs heartily at his own bad jokes. There is a child-like innocence about him, and in fact he has been known to have a tantrum or two. Herman is also incredibly naïve, having no concept of people's reaction to him. He is always perplexed when strangers walk through walls or jump out windows in fast motion just to get away from him. All of these things make him endearing. While Herman's character may look simple on the surface, it is actually multi-faceted and quite complex. I believe him to be one of the best-drawn nonhumans in television to date.

Other memorable nonhumans include Mr. Ed, Harry (from *Harry and the Hendersons*), Alf, Eddie the dog (*from Frasier*), and the robot from *Lost In Space.*

Children's television is also over-populated with characters that aren't human. Go no further than *Sesame Street* where you will find Oscar the Grouch, Elmo, the Cookie Monster, and, of course, Big Bird.

When creating nonhuman characters, you should approach them like you do human characters. Provide them with an agenda and clear-cut goals and desires. These kinds of characters can be extremely endearing if you give them a definitive point of view and human traits the audience can relate to.

With the exception of those characters in children's television, there are not many other creatures currently on the air. But that doesn't mean there won't be in the future. Again, television goes in cycles. All it takes is one nonhuman character to take off in prime time, and these kind of characters will become the flavor of the month.

CREATING CHARACTERS WITH OPPOSING VIEWPOINTS

In writing scripts, it is imperative that you create characters that have opposing points of view. This will create conflict, which is what drives both comedy and drama.

I believe the best-written show ever in the history of television is *All In the Family.* The characters are all perfectly fleshed out. Even though deep down they love and care about each other, they possess strikingly dissimilar viewpoints, which they aren't afraid to express.

Some of the funniest scenes are between Archie and Meathead. The reason for this is that Archie and Meathead are polar opposites. Let's take a side-by-side look at some character traits for both Archie and Meathead.

Archie	Meathead
Blue collar	White collar
Uneducated	Educated
Republican	Democrat
Christian	Atheist
Prejudiced	Nonprejudiced
Nonethnic background	Ethnic background
Hard-working	Free-loader

The list goes on. It is all but guaranteed that any conversation these two enter into will result in conflict. They can't talk about work, they can't talk about religion, they can't talk about politics. They can't talk about anything without getting into heated disagreements, which eventually become personal.

Imagine if we took the list of traits that we assigned to Archie and gave the exact same ones to Meathead as well. Think about how different their dialogue would be. Archie would talk about what a great president Richard Nixon is. Meathead would agree. In this scenario, where is the conflict? Where is the humor? It becomes nonexistent because these two guys now share the exact same viewpoint. Therefore, nothing they discuss is going to be too interesting. Their conversation, I'm sure you'll agree, is much livelier when Archie and Meathead fight about Dick Nixon. The argument escalates and finally becomes personal, at which point Archie loses patience and tells Meathead to go jump in Lake Pollock (or a similar, bigoted remark).

> "The main reason is the relationship between Sammy and Archie Bunker. Those two opposites got together and sealed it with a kiss. There was a general sense of 'I'm okay, you're okay.' As an audience we knew Archie Bunker and we knew he'd never act on what he said. If we thought he'd act on it … we'd throw bricks through his window. *TV Guide* understood the good intention of that episode and that it fulfilled an important purpose." — *All In the Family* writer Bill Dana, on why he thinks *TV Guide* named his episode "Sammy's Visit," in which Sammy Davis, Jr. kisses Archie Bunker, the 12th best episode in the history of television.

Let's look at *Curb Your Enthusiasm*, another of my all-time favorite shows. Larry (played by Larry David) and his wife Cheryl (played by Cheryl Hines) are a December–May couple. Though obviously in love, their personalities are like night and day. Larry is a Jewish, socially inept, confrontational, sarcastic, eccentric, self-absorbed multi-millionaire. Cheryl, on the other hand is much younger than Larry. She is Christian, an extrovert/social butterfly who cares deeply about the world around her. Put them in seemingly simple situations together and the result is some of the funniest comedy on television. This is because they come to the table with drastically different approaches and viewpoints.

When you are writing characters, be sure they approach most things from different points of view so that you can maximize the conflict, which will in turn escalate the drama and/or comedy. If you need to, make a graph of their personality traits so you can clearly see not just who they are individually, but how they will play out against your other characters.

MINOR CHARACTERS MATTER

While fleshing out major characters, it is important to spend a good chunk of time on minor characters as well. Secondary characters who are well-drawn can really take a script or series to the next level. Though it happens rarely, minor characters can break out and become synonymous with a show. For example, Frasier Crane didn't start as a regular on *Cheers*, but rather he was introduced a few seasons in as a psychiatrist friend of Diane's. The rest is TV history.

Another great example of a minor character breaking out and defining a series is that of *Happy Days'* Arthur Fonzarelli. What started as a comparatively smaller role, "The Fonz" — a leather jacket-clad, motorcycle-riding rebel — quickly became a seventies icon at the hands of the mega-talented Henry Winkler. Yet Winkler himself would probably tell you he had some help. Show creator Garry Marshall resisted the temptation to make Fonzie the stereotypical fifties hood that we have seen time and time again. Instead, Marshall dug deep to create a perfect dichotomy of guy who is super-human, but at the same time super-accessible. A high school dropout, Fonzie was loaded with street smarts. He could get hoards of pretty women with the snap of a finger; and he could start a jukebox with the flip of an elbow. He may have been the coolest guy in Milwaukee, yet he was painfully alone at Christmas. The Fonz could go from being extremely threatening to being completely vulnerable in the blink of an eye. On the surface, many of these traits seem contradictory. But somehow, when thrown together in one character, it worked. Viewers fell in love with him. Had Marshall and the other writers not taken the time to peel away layer after layer and instead gone with the obvious, it is likely The Fonz would not be the household name that it was in the seventies and still is even today. It is also likely that *Happy Days* would not have been as big a hit.

> "He's multi-dimensional … he's cool, but when the jacket comes off he's very human. He's concerned about his friends, distraught over not having parents, he's self-conscious about feeling out of place." — Actor Henry Winkler, on why "The Fonz" was such a well-loved character.

You may think that going the extra mile for minor characters even in a spec script is more trouble than it's worth. I beg to differ. You need to make your script as fresh and as entertaining as possible all the way around, if you want it to be received in a way that will get you work. Characters are a big part of what's going to get you where you want to go. Every one of them matters, no matter how small the role. Look at *Law & Order*. Throughout the course of each investigation and subsequent trial, there are tons of minor characters. Each has a clear-cut agenda and a specific point of view. If the writers on a show of this caliber think fleshing out minor characters is worth the time and trouble, then let me tell you, so should you.

HOW TO WRITE QUIRKY CHARACTERS
(AND WHY AUDIENCES LOVE THEM)

Over the last decade, the term "quirky" has become commonplace when referring to characters. Audiences love quirky characters because they march to the beat of a different drum. Quirky characters work because they are unpredictable. They see the world in ways that the rest of us don't. The result is a character who feels fresh and original. Executives and producers love quirky characters because they usually stand out. Think Adrian Monk (*Monk*) or Susan Mayer (*Desperate Housewives*) or Earl Hickey (*My Name is Earl*). The list goes on.

So, how do you go about creating people who have certain, shall we say, eccentricities? Start by observing the people around you, and I don't mean just family and friends, though certainly that is a good starting place. What I really mean is start to consciously observe people everywhere you go: restaurants, airports, libraries. Everywhere. Listen in to conversations. You will get a wealth of information. Start a notebook, and every time something stands out to you, write it down for future reference. (Don't count on remembering — you won't.) When it comes time to create a character, refer back to your notes. Look through everything. Try mixing different traits from different people in order to create a whole new person. As you are creating characters, just for the heck of it, try going against type, as in a park ranger who has melissophobia (a fear of bears).

TWENTY QUESTIONS TO ASK YOURSELF
ABOUT EACH CHARACTER

Below, I have listed 20 questions to help get you started in creating your own multi-dimensional characters.

1. What does the character look like? (You probably won't use this in a script, but it's a good idea to have a visual in your head)
2. Where was the character born and raised?
3. Relationship to family members?
4. Family economics?
5. Significant friends (including pets)?
6. Religious beliefs?
7. Political beliefs?
8. Hobbies?
9. Profession?
10. Desires and secret desires?
11. Dark secrets?
12. Fears and phobias?
13. Talents?
14. Idiosyncrasies and quirks?
15. Hang-ups (sexual and otherwise)
16. Enemies
17. If the house were burning, what's the one item the character would grab?
18. Secret weapon?
19. Favorite food?
20. What are the significant events that had huge impact on the character's life?

Try filling in the blanks for each one of your characters. As you go, add some questions of your own as they come to you. If you do this thoroughly, you should be on your way to creating some interesting and compelling characters that will eventually take on lives that are all their own.

PART VII

DIALOGUE

WRITING DIALOGUE THAT DANCES ON THE PAGE

For the most part, dialogue is what will move your script along. It is commonly known in the industry — and having read a gazillion scripts I can attest — that most readers will skim action lines. If those lines are bulky, they will skip over them altogether. It is the combination of character and dialogue that tells the story. Therefore, your dialogue must be crisp and rhythmic. Dialogue that is choppy or inconsistent will slow the reader down, and potentially take them out of the story.

FIRST AND FOREMOST: DIALOGUE COMES FROM CHARACTER

The most important thing to remember about dialogue is that it must come from character. This is why I have been harping so on studying the show for which you want to write. You have to know who the character is and be able to get inside his or her head. You have to know character speech patterns, and be ready to fire out dialogue in a voice that is uniquely your character's.

If you get a chance, check out *Law & Order* reruns, particularly those done between 1990 and 2000, when Steven Hill played District Attorney Adam Schiff. If you listen closely to Adam's dialogue, you'll notice that he has a very specific pattern of speech. He never rambles. Rather, he is short and sweet, often speaking only in one-liners. But what he says in those one-liners is smart, powerful, and provocative. You may be thinking, how hard can coming up with one line be? The answer is a lot harder than you may think. These are the kinds of lines that writers spend a lot of time pondering.

KEEPING DIALOGUE WHERE IT BELONGS

When an audience settles in to watch your show, the only thing they will see is what is on the screen. Therefore, steer clear of using the action lines in a script to fill the reader and audience in on what's been going on. Remember, no one is going to have a copy of your script as a companion guide to follow along with at home. Whatever information you want or need an audience to have must come through dialogue or through specific actions by the character.

THE RHYTHM OF DIALOGUE: HOW TO AVOID LONG, RAMBLING SPEECHES

When you think of dialogue, imagine yourself watching a game of ping-pong. Your head follows the ball back and forth, back and forth. Now picture that instead of watching a game of ping-pong, you are watching a conversation. The rhythm is pretty much the same … back and forth, back and forth. Unless someone is telling a story or giving a speech, dialogue isn't usually a monologue.

Start listening to the rhythm of people's conversations. Go to public places where you won't be obvious like the beach or a café, and just listen to how the exchange of information goes back and forth. This is how dialogue in a script should be written.

To understand precisely what I am talking about, open the script you purchased and look at how small most blocks of dialogue are. The smaller they are, the better the read. Sometimes big blocks of dialogue can't be avoided. But if your entire script is that way, you need to go back and chop to make it more conversational.

THE USE OF SLANG IN DIALOGUE

It's okay to use slang in dialogue as long as it matches your character's voice and it works within the context of the show that you are writing for. Obviously, there are certain words and phrases that are considered acceptable on cable networks like HBO, but they are completely unacceptable on network television.

Be sure to use slang consistently. One error I see a lot is characters using slang in one speech and in the very next speech they're using proper English. This is not the way characters talk. Character speech patterns are usually consistent. Characters either speak proper English or they speak slang, but not both.

RIGHT-ON DIALOGUE: WRONG!!

Another pitfall you want to avoid is writing dialogue that hits the nail too squarely on the head. It won't sound natural. Whatever the "it" is, people, as a rule don't usually come right out with it. Let's say a woman thinks her husband is having an affair. The minute he walks through the door, most likely she's not going to blurt out, "I think you're having an affair." She's probably going to be cagier and a bit more subtle. Perhaps something like this:

Wife: Where've you been? It's almost midnight.
Husband: At the office.
Wife: I called the office. You didn't pick up.
Husband: Must've stepped away from my desk. Next time try my cell.
Wife: I did. Five times.
Husband: Must not of heard it. I had a busy night.
Wife: I'm sure you did..

See how the wife says one thing, but she actually means something entirely different. This is known as subtext. What the wife is saying — without coming out and saying it — is that she knows he's cheating on her. Good writing will always contain subtext. It makes the conversation deeper and more interesting as it adds a whole new layer and meaning to the words.

WATCH OUT FOR NAMES

Be sure when you write that you don't overuse character names. In real life, when people talk, they don't continuously tack each other's names at the beginning or end of every sentence. It's good to use character names throughout the script, but do so sporadically and it will sound more natural. This is especially true when only two people are in the scene.

WHY USING DIALOGUE TO REVEAL BACKSTORY CAN BE DEADLY

Perhaps one of the toughest challenges writers face is when they need the audience to have a piece of information, but that information has nothing to do with the conversation at hand. Beware: when you try to insert backstory into a scene or conversation, where it doesn't naturally fit, it will stick out like a sore thumb. It will sound forced and unnatural. If it feels like you're forcing it, you probably are. In that case, you need to stop and look at the script as a whole to try to find a place where you can reveal the information in a more natural way — a way that makes sense to the characters, story, and script.

STAY OFF THE PHONE!!

With the advent of cell phones, it seems the new generation of writers very much likes to write long phone conversations. A piece of advice: unless it is absolutely necessary, don't. Phone conversations come off like monologues, even when they are intercut with another person. Because the characters are in two separate locations, the drama of what they are talking about is significantly lessened. On screen, the shot becomes talking heads, which, as you know by now, is visually dull. Whenever possible, bring your characters into the same space. If that's not feasible, make the phone conversation short and sweet.

WHAT TO DO WHEN ALL OF YOUR CHARACTERS SOUND ALIKE

Once you have finished writing your first draft, you definitely want to go back and read it, out loud. Listen carefully. As you go from character to character, does each sound different? Is each character speaking in his or her unique voice?

It is quite possible that, as you read your first draft, you will discover that some of the dialogue sounds strikingly similar. This is a red flag. Dialogue should never be randomly assigned to whatever character happens to be handy. You now need to go back, line-by-line, and fix whatever is off. The best way to do this is to look at the show and get one character's voice in your head. Now, go through the script looking only at that particular character's dialogue. Make changes accordingly. By not having a mish-mash of voices floating around your head, you are more likely to stay on track. Once you complete the process for one character, repeat the process for every character. Then go back and reread the script from the top. Chances are, it's a lot better now.

PART VIII

HOW TO PITCH YOUR COMEDY, DRAMA, OR MOVIE OF THE WEEK

HOW TO GET A PITCH MEETING

Lining up a meeting to pitch ideas can happen in a couple of ways. The most common is that your agent has sent your spec script around to various shows, and the producers have read your work, liked it, and are anxious to hear your ideas for their show. So they extend an invitation for you to come in and pitch. The other way to generate a pitch meeting is through your own personal contacts. Usually, in this case, producers will have read your work ahead of time as well.

WHO WILL BE IN THE ROOM?

You will usually know the name of at least one person that you will be pitching to, the person with whom you have an appointment. What you may not know in advance is who else will be there. I have had one-on-one pitch meetings with show runners. I have also been led into conference rooms to pitch to entire writing staffs. (Gulp!)

The writer has no control over who will be in the meeting, but hopefully there will be an executive producer, or, at the very least a co-executive producer because you want to pitch to someone who has the power to buy one of your stories on the spot. If you pitch to someone lower on the totem pole, that person will probably not have buying power. He or she will listen, take notes, and then at some point repitch your ideas to the executive producer. While this is better than nothing, it's less than ideal. The person who repitches your story ideas won't necessarily have the same emotional investment in them that you do. Therefore that person may not pitch with the same enthusiasm that you have. This can sometimes make a difference. Another problem with repitched stories is that some of the details can get lost in translation; these very details could potentially make or break the sale. Still, sometimes an executive producer isn't always available at the time of your meeting, and you have to rely on another producer to take your pitch and try to sell a story for you.

WHY IT'S ESSENTIAL TO BE EARLY

If you are a person who tends to run late, I can't impress upon you enough how important it is to be on time for your meeting. In fact, be more than on time … be early.

Running late to anything that's important can be stressful. Racing the clock to a meeting that can jumpstart your TV writing career will make your blood pressure soar. You will start the meeting stressed and discombobulated. Needless to say, under these circumstances, the odds of making a sale decrease. As we discussed, writing staffs are incredibly busy. They do not have time in their day to sit around and wait for you to show up at your leisure. Though they may not verbalize it, deep down they will be secretly annoyed with you for wasting their valuable time. Being late is just not professional.

When going to a pitch meeting, it is a good idea to allow an extra 20–30 minutes for mishaps. Keep in mind that traffic in California is congested and unpredictable. Not to mention that once you arrive at a studio or network, there will be a guard gate. Often, a line forms at the gate, as each person has to stop to identify himself before going through. Once you get to the gate, the guard will give you a map and direct you to the location of your meeting. Production lots can be enormous and sometimes hard to negotiate. It is very easy to get lost. You may have to park several minutes from your meeting location. All of this eats up precious time. So arriving at the studio gates at 10:58 for an 11:00 meeting is a really bad idea. On the other hand, if you show up in the office a few minutes early, no one will fault you. Being early will also give you the opportunity to mentally go over your pitch one final time and to psych yourself up to make a sale.

In the event that something happens where you know you are going to be a couple of minutes late, I would suggest you call the office and let the assistant know that you are running behind and when you expect to arrive. This is also one of the few times I would advocate telling a tiny tale. Believe me when I say the words "I'm stuck in traffic" will be much better received than "I just couldn't get my butt out of bed this morning."

DRESS FOR SUCCESS

A pitch meeting is casual, so you should choose clothes that are comfortable. Remember, this is also a job interview. You are applying for a position as a writer. Therefore, I would stay away from jeans. Shorts are a no-no as well, as are tee shirts with political slogans like "the President stinks," — which may or may not be true — but it becomes a moot point if the person you are pitching to happens to be a fan of the man in the White House.

Just how should you dress for a pitch meeting? Actually, you should dress like a writer. You want to give producers the impression that you are a hardworking writer who just pulled away from a great script to come in and meet with them. So, stay away from business suits — they're for executives, not writers. For men, I suggest a decent pair of pants and a casual shirt. Women can wear pants or a skirt with a blouse or blazer. But please, ladies, heed these words of caution: stay away from blouses that are cut too low or skirts that are cut too high. You are there to sell stories, not sex appeal.

HOW MANY IDEAS SHOULD YOU PITCH?

Pitch meetings are scheduled to last no more than 45 minutes, tops. Finish sooner and you'll get Brownie points. So the question becomes, how many story ideas can you comfortably tell in that hour, leaving room for discussion on each? The answer is that it depends what kind of show you are pitching. Obviously, you can pitch more sitcom ideas in 45 minutes than you can movie-of-the-week (MOW) ideas because an MOW is so much longer and more involved.

> "The biggest mistake some writers make is they don't have the pitch boiled down enough. Before you jump into the pitch, you need a succinct logline — a sentence or a couple of sentences that tell us what your movie is about … what the hook is. We need to see the dramatic progression and the dramatic escalation building to the one-hour block, which is of course key for us. But don't go on too long. Just give us an idea of who the characters are and the main story beats so we can visualize your story. If a pitch goes on too long, you will lose people."
> — Libby Beers, vice president of original movies, Lifetime Television

In addition to pitching stories, you may also want to have a couple of "areas" in your back pocket. An area is the general idea for a story, but the details are not worked out. Consider it a safety net. If you pitch all of your stories without a sale, you can quickly toss out a couple of areas to see if they bite. If the producer indicates that an area is worth exploring, this means that the door is still open. You can go home and develop the areas into full-blown story ideas, and come back again and pitch.

Here is a rough example of about how many stories you can comfortably pitch in one meeting:

Genre	Stories
Sitcom	5–6 plus 1–2 areas
Drama	4 plus 2 areas
MOW	2 plus 2 areas

"It's great to have secondary characters that really score, but in a pitch, you need to show the producers that you can take their primary characters to a place they haven't been before. It's fine if long-lost Uncle Larry returns as Aunt Lauren, but the incident should only serve as a catalyst to conflict and comedy for the primary characters." — Marc Warren, executive producer, *That's So Raven* and *Cory in the House*

THE ORDER OF YOUR STORIES

Over the years I have been asked by many a new writer what order stories should be pitched in. The answer is that you should pitch the best ones first. When you start to tell your first story, you will have the undivided attention of everyone in the room. Each person will make a silent but immediate decision about you as a writer, and whether or not you are right for their show. If your first story is good, even if they don't intend to buy it, they are much more likely to stay with you throughout the entire pitch. Placing your best stories toward the end can be a crucial mistake, because by the time you get to them the producers may have already made up their minds that your stories are mediocre. By that time, they may have already tuned you out.

HOW MUCH DETAIL SHOULD YOU GIVE?

Deciding how much detail to reveal in a pitch is tricky. I subscribe to the "less is more" theory. You definitely want producers to be able to visualize your episode, so it is important to have a clear-cut beginning, middle, and end. You should also include Act Breaks so that they can see the jeopardy and to what extent the stakes will be raised. If it's a sitcom and there are sight gags or physical comedy, you will also want to bring those details out. Still, you don't want to give away everything. The more details you provide, the greater the chance that you say something that someone in the room doesn't like. Once someone says something negative, it is difficult to turn them around. You'd be surprised, but sometimes it's the littlest detail that turns them off from wanting to buy your story.

In pitching sitcoms, I usually focus on the "A" stories. But for each "A" story I pitch, I throw in a "B" story at the end. Usually it is only one sentence and not worked out. I do this because it really doubles the chances of making a sale. Once, at a *Full House* pitch, I was striking out with all of my "A" stories. Luckily, they liked a "B" story enough that they wanted to use it. So, they handed me an "A" story to go with it.

Pitching the plot-driven drama is fairly straightforward — you simply tell the important story points as concisely as you can from beginning to end. With character driven-drama, you have a choice of separating out primary and secondary stories and pitching each one on its own, beginning to end. Or you can pitch the entire episode from start to finish. This really comes down to personal choice. Having listened to many dramas being pitched, I have to say that I lean more toward telling each story individually, as it seems easier to follow. More than once, I have witnessed writers tripping themselves up because they forget an important detail that affects the story later on. Then, they have to stop and go back, which can ruin the flow of the story.

PRACTICING YOUR PITCH

It is critical that you know your stories inside out, and that you can recite them casually, much as if you were telling a friend a story about something that happened to you over the course of your day. The key to being smooth and relaxed is to practice. It isn't enough to write your stories out. You must practice your pitch out loud. I cannot over-emphasize this. There is a big difference in writing a story on a piece of paper and in telling a story verbally. Don't believe me? I will prove it.

Think of your all-time favorite TV episode. Now, walk up to the first person you see and tell the story of that episode. I promise you will be surprised at how much harder this is than you think.

For your own stories, I suggest that you try pitching them to friends. Ideally, those friends should know something about the show, though it's okay if they don't. Just talk your stories through. See if you get lost or, worse, if your friends get lost. If so, this may be a signal that your pitch needs some work.

After you have run through your pitch with friends, continue to practice on your own. Repeat your stories to yourself as you walk down the street, before you go to bed, and again when you are in the shower. Once you have them down, stand in front of a mirror and pitch to yourself. As you do, notice your physical movements. Are you nervous and jiggling all over the place? Are you using your hands to help tell the story? These things can be distracting. Work on telling your stories in a stationary position. You want to look calm and relaxed. Remember, you are trying to instill confidence. Keep in mind, they are potentially not just buying the story; they are also buying the writer, so who you are as a person must shine through.

CONTROLLING THE ROOM

The most important thing you can do in a pitch is what I call control the room. What this means is that from the moment you start your pitch to the moment you end, you engage every single person in that room. This is not about the content of your stories — you've already got that — but rather how you deliver them. One of the easiest and most important ways to keep people interested in what you are saying is by maintaining eye contact. I cannot tell you how many writers tend to lock eyes with the most powerful person in the room. This is a colossal mistake. By isolating one person, you will quickly disengage everyone else. Within moments, their minds will wander to things like what phone calls they need to return or what they might order for lunch. Once they are silently debating tuna or turkey, whole wheat or rye, they are no longer listening to your pitch. You may think that doesn't matter, as long as the top dog is hanging onto your every word. It matters because good executive producers trust their writing staffs. After you leave, they may well ask the other writers and producers for feedback on your stories. When people are with you and enthusiastic about you, they want you to do well and will often go to great lengths to support you. If some or most have zoned out, your chances of making a sale diminish.

Another reason to keep everyone engaged is that as you pitch, it's very possible that if some of the writers like what they hear, they may chime in, and try to make your story all the better, creating a huge advantage for you. But, they can't do that if you have cut them out of the deal.

A COUPLE OF NO-NOS

Whatever you do, do not memorize your pitch. One of two things will happen. Either you will come off as stiffer than the Tin Man, or under the pressure, you will freeze and not remember details. The end result will be the same: your pitch will be a disaster.

Another common mistake some writers make is to read their pitches. This, too, can be deadly. There is no faster way to lose control of the room. You will not be able to maintain eye contact, as your eyes will be focused on the page rather than on the people in the room. Also, your energy level will be diminished because you won't connect to the other people in the room. The key to good storytelling is to know your stories in your heart and to pitch them with enthusiasm, and passion. Don't be afraid to show that you like your stories and that you believe in them. Passion can go a long way in getting producers excited about a story.

THE USE OF INDEX CARDS AND NOTE PADS

No matter how well-prepared you are, it is still easy to get lost in your own pitch. This is usually due to nervousness and pressure. You can be in the middle of telling a story and suddenly you realize you have left out an important chunk or you draw a blank and have no idea where you are going. To prevent this from happening, many writers use either index cards or note pads as a way of keeping on track.

I prefer to use note pads (I like legal pads — they are longer and have more room). I write down each main story idea in bullet points and then place the pad on my lap. This works well because the bullet points act as a road map. If I get lost, I can easily get a quick glimpse at my notes and immediately know where I am and what comes next. With a casual glance, I don't lose eye contact, and more often than not, it is seamless — the producers are totally unaware of my blunder. I recommend bullet points because if you write too much of the story down, you will not be able to find your place as easily, and you may have to stop, read your notes, and figure out where you are. These few seconds of disorganization can take producers out of your story.

Putting notes on index cards is another way to keep on track. I know many writers who prefer this method, but I find it slightly problematic. Index cards are much smaller than legal pads and therefore have a lot less room. By choosing this method, the writer adds another layer to the pitch — and that is to keep flipping the index cards in order to keep up with where you are in the story. If you fail to flip the cards as you go and you end up lost, you will have to stop and flip through the cards to find your place. No matter how fast you flip, you will have momentarily stopped the flow of your story and again you risk losing control of the room. Another reason I am not in favor of index cards for pitching is that, unlike a legal pad, which rests in your lap, you physically have to hold index cards. If you are at all nervous — which you probably will be — your hands may tremble. This is not only distracting, but it can also send a subtle signal to producers that you are not confident.

READING THE ROOM: WHY NO USUALLY MEANS NO

Learning to "read the room" to get a handle on what people are thinking as you pitch is a valuable skill that usually comes with time and practice. As you tell your stories, notice the expressions on people's faces. Do they look enthused and are they maintaining eye contact? If so, you are probably on track in terms of how much detail you are giving. If people look bored or confused, that may be a signal to speed things up a tad.

On occasion, the producers may stop you at some point to tell you this isn't a story they are interested in. The reasons can be numerous; the story you are pitching may not be right for the show or it's a story they have already turned down. The worst thing you can do is argue with them and try to convince them that your version of the story works. This is a battle you will not win. You will only aggravate them. Remember, it is their show … they know even better than you what kind of stories they want to put on the air.

GOING WITH THE FLOW WHEN THE STORY STARTS TO CHANGE

When pitching story ideas, a couple of things can happen. Some producers let you go through your stories from start to finish and they will comment at the end. Occasionally they will stop you in the middle if you hit upon a story that they know they are not interested in. Perhaps the best thing that can happen is that as you pitch, the writers and producers add things here and there.

This is a good sign because it means they like what they are hearing. It is possible that one producer may say something that changes your story, and then another may add on to that. Before you know it, the room is abuzz and you are quietly thinking, "this isn't even close to my idea." At this point, the best thing you can do is smile, nod, and if you can, add to whatever direction they are going in. Remember, these people know their show better than you do, and they know what they want. You may not realize it, but you are on the verge of making a sale.

Some writers might feel disappointed if a story changes too much. Don't get caught up in that. Remember, the goal of a pitch meeting is to walk out with a sale. Even if the producers have made changes, you will still get credit.

> "So many writers come in and apologize for their pitch before they even make it. 'You're probably not going to like this, but—.' 'I know it has some loose ends.' 'This one's not very good, but my agent thought—.' Believe in your product. Or at least convince the people listening that you believe in it. But don't oversell. Volume isn't the same as passion. Tell your story in 2–3 minutes and be prepared to answer questions and expand on your ideas. And don't argue if the producer wants to take the story in another direction. Save your integrity for your novel and sell out cheerfully." — Marc Warren, executive producer, *That's So Raven* and *Cory in the House*

A few times over the years I have had new writers ask, "if I don't like the direction the producers take my story, should I ask to have my name removed from the script?" Let me answer that with a question of my own: why? The goal here is to accumulate credits so that you will be in a position to get a staff-writing job. To turn down professional writing credits (and pay) would be foolish. I've said it before and I'll say it again: television is collaborative. Not to mention that once you establish a relationship with producers and you do a good job, they may well offer you more work. I can promise this won't happen if you send them the message that you don't want your good artistic name associated with their debacle of a script. The best thing you can do is grab every credit you can and do the work well. It doesn't matter if the episode turns out to be just okay. It's the credit that's key.

BE PREPARED FOR QUESTIONS

After you pitch a story, producers might have questions. Perhaps you didn't explain something well enough, or they may see some roadblocks that you hadn't considered. It's important to anticipate things they might ask and to be ready to fire back intelligent answers. Your answers don't have to be perfect. In fact, the solution you propose may not work at all. That's okay. Even if what you are saying isn't exactly right, you may spark an idea in their minds that does work. The idea is to try to offer some kind of viable solution. Learning to think on your feet comes with practice. This is a job interview. Producers want to know that you have a quick and creative mind and that you are going to contribute. Television is collaborative. The worst thing you can do is sit there like a bump on a log, waiting for other people to do your job.

EXAMPLE OF A PITCH

As I told you earlier, one of the first episodes I pitched to *Full House* was called "Easy Rider" and centered on Michelle learning to ride a two-wheeler. The pitch went something like this: kids are making fun of Michelle because she still has training wheels on her bike. So Michelle has decided it's time to learn to ride a two-wheeler. One (or all) of the guys agrees to teach her. At the Act Break, Michelle falls off her bike, gets a bruise, and doesn't want to ride ever again. In the second act, the family must band together in order to get Michelle back on her bike.

See how simple that pitch was? You can easily visualize the story as it unfolds … at least in the first act. The second act, however, was less clear. The producers wanted to know how the family would band together. What specific actions would they take to get Michelle back on her bike? Their fear was that the second act would be stalled by a lack of definitive action. How did I intend to get Michelle back on her bike without the family just talking to her, which would create a series of "talking heads" (i.e., boring scenes)? The room was silent, everyone looking at me, waiting for an answer. One that I didn't have. "Maybe they could bribe her with her candy?" I said, suggesting the first idea that popped into my head. In the script, Joey tries to bribe Michelle with her favorite Disney movie. While I didn't offer them the exact solution, at least it was a place to start.

WHAT TO DO IF THEY DON'T BUY ANYTHING

Sometimes, no matter how much work you do, you will go to a pitch meeting and walk out without making a sale. This has happened to me and it has happened to every writer I know. There can be numerous reasons for not selling: your ideas weren't what they were looking for, other writers have pitched similar stories, etc., etc. It really doesn't matter. The point is you didn't sell a story. When this happens, the best thing you can do is to try to keep the door open. Rather than just saying "thank you and goodbye," reiterate to producers how much you love their show and want to work with them. Ask if it's possible to come back with more ideas. Very often, they will agree. After all, they already like your writing and want to do business with you or you wouldn't be there in the first place. If producers agree to let you come back, see if you can get a sense of what it was about your stories that didn't exactly work so you don't repeat your mistakes. And don't be alarmed if they tell you to call them and pitch over the phone — or maybe even e-mail them a few areas. That's okay; I have pitched by phone before and sold. It's not ideal, but it's still a great opportunity.

THE PROS AND CONS OF PUTTING YOUR PITCH ON PAPER

Some writers type up their story ideas and bring them to the meeting. I have never done this and probably never will. In my mind, a pitch is verbal, and no paperwork is required. When you put story ideas down on paper, I think it is possible you are putting yourself at a disadvantage. If your stories are not perfectly written, or if you have typos or grammatical errors, it could give the producers pause about committing to you as a writer. Also, if you give too much information, you risk that a producer won't like a certain detail and will opt out of buying a story from you.

The one time it could be advantageous to leave written material behind is if you are pitching to producers who are at a lower level and not in a position to buy a story. They will then take your ideas back to the executive producer. As we discussed, they may get details wrong or mixed up. If you submitted stories in writing, there is less chance of this happening, as they may just hand the paper in and not repitch at all. If the stories are well-written, it is possible you will make a sale. So if you feel compelled, you could type up your stories (be sure to include your name and date) and have them in your bag or briefcase. But, this is the only time I would ever leave behind any written work because I think the pros are outweighed by the cons.

RESPECTING THE BIG FOOT

It should go without saying, but I feel compelled to remind you to have respect for both the show you hope to become a part of, as well as for the people running it. I have seen several writers who, because of their amazing talent, were all but guaranteed scripts or staff jobs. Upon meeting with the writing staff, these jobs instantly slipped away due to a definite lack of people skills, common courtesy, and everyday manners. Even if deep down you think that you're too good for a certain show (which at this point you definitely shouldn't), telling producers things like, "gosh, you really need someone like me on your staff because your show is so bad" or "I really belong at HBO, not at this cheesy network show" are just plain insulting and aren't going to get you hired. It may be difficult for you to comprehend now, but once you get into the business you will understand that writers on less-than-fabulous programs don't always realize that their shows are sub-par. They work hard every day, pumping all of their creative energy into the scripts, and in the end, most of them are, if not proud of the work, at least protective of it.

I repeatedly hear new writers say that they want to work on a certain show … and that's it. Their one and only goal. Of course the show they've chosen is always the hippest one on the air. While it's important to have a clear vision of where you see yourself in the industry and what kind of television you'd ideally like to write, you must also be realistic. The truth is that most of what is on the air is mediocre at best. There are only a few so-called "hot" shows out there, and statistically your chances of starting on one are miniscule. There is no room for snobbery here. You have to take whatever you can get and be grateful for the work. Otherwise, you will fall on your face.

> "Get in the door on any show you can — and move on from there. The odds of landing on a great, successful series right out of the gate are tiny. If you are waiting to get on the perfect show, you're going to be waiting a long time." — Bob Daily, supervising producer, *Frasier*, co-executive producer, *Desperate Housewives*

I remember rolling my eyes when my agent called to say he had set up a meeting for me on *Harry and the Hendersons.* I quickly threw together a few lackluster stories and went in to pitch. For every idea I had, the producer cut in with lines like, "Harry wouldn't think that," or "Harry wouldn't feel that." I remember looking at the producer like he was nuts, as the words "it's just a stupid big foot," danced on the tip of my tongue. And therein laid the problem. Harry may have been a stupid big foot to me, but to his writers and producers, he was a vibrant being with heart and soul, and definite likes and dislikes. He was real.

The meeting ended with the producer suggesting that I go home, delve a little deeper into Harry's character, and think up some additional stories more in line with Harry's innermost thoughts and feelings. The door was wide open for me to come back. I never did.

Years later, I clearly understand that the loss of not writing for *Harry and the Hendersons* was mine. The irony is that over the course of my career, I went on to work on shows that made *Harry and the Hendersons* look like darned good television. I have learned to always respect the big foot. I would encourage you to do the same.

PRACTICE MAKES PERFECT

In the event your first pitch doesn't go as well as you hoped, don't worry — you are in good company. Many writers (this one included) look back on their first pitch meeting and cringe. Pitching is an art form, and the ability to do it well usually takes time, patience, and lots of practice.

Each semester in my TV Writing classes at Emerson College, I walk my students through the pitching process. There is one particular article I share with them. In fact, I make them read it aloud. It's called "The Angells" and it is a reprint of remarks made by Les Charles (*Cheers*) at a memorial service for David Angell (*Frasier* and *Wings*). Angell, along with his wife Lynn, perished aboard one of the planes that struck the World Trade Center on September 11th. The article appeared in *Written By* (October, 2001), a monthly publication put out by the Writers Guild of America.

As we sit in classrooms that overlook the splendor of Boston Common, Charles' words resonate through young and eager voices — and the sad irony is never lost on me that we are a mere stone's throw from the old Bull & Finch Pub, now famously known as *Cheers*. In the article, Charles recalls how Angell came to pitch when he and his brother Glen were producers on *Taxi*. The meeting was a disaster. According to Charles, Angell was over-prepared, stayed too long, and all but bored the living daylights out of them. He didn't get the job.

An entire spec script later, Angell once again miraculously found himself sitting opposite the Charles brothers, this time hoping for a gig on *Cheers*. This time they hired him. The fact Angell fell on his face in that first pitch meeting, yet went on to become one of the biggest, brightest, and most-respected producers in television should give hope to all new writers. You don't have to be perfect right out of the gate. It's okay to fail as long as you learn from it.

Charles went on to praise Angell as a terrific human being — someone who never let his enormous success get to his head, who always remembered where he came from, and always gave back to his community. If you can get your hands on this article, I highly recommend it. David Angell may be gone. But for a whole new generation of TV writers, he's still a damned fine role model.

PART IX

TV NEWS MAGAZINE SHOWS

WRITING FOR TV MAGAZINE SHOWS

"THERE'S ALWAYS GOING TO BE NEWS"

Many moons ago, screenwriter Bill Kerby (*The Rose, Hooper*) gave me a piece of advice that I've never forgotten. He was talking about how little work there is for writers in fields like drama, comedy, and features. "But, kid," he said, "there's always going to be news." It turns out he was right.

There are those in the business who absolutely live for news. I am not one of them. This is a personal choice. It really comes down to finding the type of television that you like the best and feel the most comfortable in. I have always had a love–hate relationship with the TV news business. The truth is that, while news may not be my favorite kind of television, I can't tell you how many times working in this arena has paid the bills on the days, weeks, and months I couldn't find work in other kinds of television. News has been my safety net. News can be exciting. Nine days out of ten, it is a pure adrenalin rush, plus you get to travel and meet all kinds of different people.

> "At six or seven at night, the young people are still working hard, still researching. They hang around after most people have gone home. They aren't afraid to show their devotion. They want to try this and try that. Before you know it, a producer or a correspondent needs help with something and asks for a favor. That's how you get on someone's staff. Have an 'I'll do anything attitude.'" — Mike Wallace, *60 Minutes*

For the purposes of this book, I am going to talk mainly about how to work in the TV news magazine arena. Like all programming, news is driven by ratings. The difference is that when a newscast doesn't get a huge audience, they don't cancel it, but rather they fire people and revamp. The principles I am going to talk about in this and the following chapters can easily be applied to all television news, both national and local … alas, a kind of television writing that you don't have to be in New York or L.A. for!

IT TAKES A SPECIAL BREED

The first thing you need to know about working in television news is that you have to be aggressive. You are going to have to go out and get stories — and sometimes you will have to push people's buttons in order to do so. There is no room for the shy in the TV news business. You also have to be mentally tough. TV news isn't always pretty. In addition, you must be a self-starter. Especially at the network level, no one has time to lead you around by the nose. Things will get dumped in your lap, and you have to figure them out on your own. News happens quickly and stories turn quickly. You have to be able to think on your feet. You have to be able to get the story and/or everything you need for the story. Coming back empty-handed is not something news people do.

One of the best stories I ever worked on in TV news was also the worst story I ever worked on. The story was the death of John F. Kennedy, Jr. I was sent as a producer to Martha's Vineyard by one of the national TV news magazines. Kennedy's plane had not yet been located on the bottom of the ocean floor. The mood on the island was incredibly somber, with law enforcement everywhere, and search planes coming and going. There was a feeling among the media that we were simply waiting to bring the world news of yet another Kennedy tragedy.

My first assignment was to get some video of Jackie Kennedy's house. Just to be clear — the news organization didn't draw me a map or even give me an address. As a producer, I am on my own to figure it out. The first thing I did was ask some of the residents. Again, this takes a certain kind of aggressiveness. Imagine how stupid I felt walking up to strangers, asking, "do you know where Jackie Kennedy's house is — and by the way — can you tell me how to get there?" The islanders weren't much help. Overall, they were extremely protective of the Kennedys and at the same time resentful of the massive media invasion.

So, I decided to ask a cop. I figured I had nothing to lose. His answer was clear. "Ma'am," he said, "there are a few things you will never do in your lifetime. Going to Jackie Kennedy's house is one of them."

To which I quickly responded: "Sir, if you knew anything about me, you would know that I will be at Jackie's house within the hour." How I was going to get there, I hadn't a clue. I only knew that somehow I would. Why? Because I was taking a paycheck from a news organization. People were depending on me to get them the footage they needed. Not coming though was simply not an option.

Forty-five minutes later, camera crew in tow, I arrived at Jackie's. In news, if you keep asking the question, sooner or later you will get the answer. In this case, a school bus driver had forked over the directions. But it still wasn't a slam-dunk. State police had turned us away at three separate roadblocks. At the fourth and final roadblock, some nice cop took pity and let us in as long as we promised to behave. To the best of my knowledge, we were the only news crew to get that shot.

That is an example of the kind of aggressiveness you must possess if you want to work in this arena. If you don't have it, choose another line of work because not only will you be unsuccessful, but you will spend a great deal of time feeling downright uncomfortable.

IS IT NEWS OR ENTERTAINMENT?

In recent times, television news has come under attack for being more entertainment than hard-hitting journalism as existed in the days of Walter Cronkite. Critics complain that stories today are fluffier and are often presented tabloid-style. This may have some seeds of truth, but it's not necessarily the media's fault. We live in a very fast-paced world. Information has to be presented quickly and concisely. With the advances in technology, we are used to visual stimulation — and lots of it. Therefore, television news has had to change in order to accommodate the way viewers want to receive their information.

> "I don't believe news and entertainment are mutually exclusive. We don't seem to mind when a restaurant, for example, showcases its wonderful food with an attractive presentation, or a reliable car happens to have a sleek design, or a great autobiographical book is wrapped in an eye-catching cover. Having said that, I think the most compelling news and information is that which impacts my life the most. If it's presented in such a way to create a compelling and entertaining viewing experience, it's the best of all worlds." — Joel Cheatwood, executive director/program development, CNN

WHY SO MANY TV MAGAZINE SHOWS?

Right before the huge influx of reality programming, it seemed that the flavor of the month for networks was the TV news magazine. Nearly every night, you could turn on your TV and find *Dateline* or *60 Minutes* or *20-20* or *60 Minutes II*. The reason? News magazine shows are much cheaper to produce than series television and movies of the week. Networks realized that if they churned out interesting stories that were highly promotable, they could in fact get an audience. The money they make from these shows helps defray the cost of producing comedies and dramas.

THE POWER STRUCTURE OF A TV MAGAZINE SHOW

Let's take a look at how the power structure of a TV news magazine show breaks down. Atop the ladder, you will find several management positions such as vice president, news director, and managing editor, to name just a few. These are the bigwigs responsible and accountable for the overall direction of the show. As a writer, you will probably not encounter these people on a daily basis. In fact, you will rarely deal with them.

On the rung directly beneath management is a host of producer positions, the most important of which is — you guessed it — the executive producer. As with series television, the executive producer is responsible for the overall content of the show. On a day-to-day basis, the executive producer is the big boss. He or she can promote you or fire you — and will always be aware of the kind of work you are doing and how well you are doing it. After the executive producer, there's a show producer, who oversees the nitty gritty operations such as talent, making sure segments are produced, bringing the show in on time, and lots of other key things. Under the show producer are what is known as field producers. These are the people who set up the stories, go on shoots, write the stories, and oversee the edit. Some magazine shows also have writers to write leads and tags and to connect the dots between segments.

WRITING VS. PRODUCING

If you are interested in being a writer on a TV news magazine show, let me talk you out of it. The job you really want to strive for is that of a field producer. This is where most of the storytelling comes into play. As I mentioned briefly, writers on these shows generally write the show itself … not the stories. In order to get to be a producer, you will probably start out as an intern or a production assistant, and you will have to work your way up to becoming a writer. Once you do, my guess is you won't want to stay there long. The novelty of writing leads and tags for other people's stories will wear off quickly. Believe it or not, writing talent intros like "Good evening, I'm Stone Phillips and tonight in an exclusive report, *Dateline* goes undercover to bring you the story of blah, blah, blah…" gets real boring, real fast. Before you know it, you will be chomping at the bit to be the producer who goes into the field, gets down and dirty and brings back the story of blah, blah, blah. In the TV news magazine format, it's a producer's game. The stories happen in the field, not in the studio. This is where the real writing is done. With that in mind, throughout the rest of this section, I will be talking in terms of being a producer rather than a writer. You will quickly see that in this arena, producing is writing. It's all about storytelling.

"News does not happen in a vacuum. Being able to reference the proper context and perspective is an essential part of the writer/producer job description. Typically … every story of any import has a historical context that oftentimes changes the impact of the story completely. In my opinion, one of the major failings of television news in particular is that we too often ignore that context and perspective in presenting the news. In effect, we're asking viewers to form opinions or reactions to stories, issues, and events, without full knowledge." — Joel Cheatwood, executive director/program development, CNN

THE POWER OF ENTERPRISING YOUR OWN STORIES

TV news magazine shows are always in need of good stories. Each week, there are story meetings where the entire staff gathers to discuss potential stories. Part of your job as a producer is to generate story ideas. You should come to every meeting loaded down with articles that you have read in the newspaper or in magazines or on the Internet.

The stories you choose should have national appeal. This is not always easy. Americans tend to think of themselves as one and the same. But the truth is that people who live in Iowa have different interests and issues than those who live in New York City. The things that are important to people in Montana are not necessarily the same things that are important to folks in New Orleans. While every story isn't going to hold the same interest for everyone, you should aim for those stories that will interest the highest number of people.

Don't put forth stories we have seen before, unless you come with a totally different angle that will make it look fresh. For example, if you want to do a story on Mets pitcher Pedro Martinez, we have seen stories ad nauseam about what a fabulous pitcher he is, what his teammates think of him, etc., so stay away from all that. Instead, propose a personal profile: "Martinez, the Man away from the Mound." This story could tell the personal side of Pedro that we really haven't seen before. Things that could be included are what it was like growing up in the Dominican Republic, family, his love of gardening (let's see him talking to his pansies), other hobbies, pets, etc. An interview like this would obviously be shot at his home rather than at the ballpark.

Coming up with your own unique story ideas is not only going to make your bosses happy, it's also going to give you a certain amount of power and control over your work. Usually when you bring a story idea to the table, and the show decides to do it, they will assign that story to you. If you don't bring stories to the table, some will be dumped in your lap — and you may not like what you are given. For example, would you rather do a story on Oscar-winning actress Reese Witherspoon (your idea) or a story on how to battle toenail fungus (their idea)?

The other thing about enterprising your own stories is that your work will probably be better. Human nature dictates that you will put more energy and thought into something that really captivates you vs. something that does not.

> "The most important thing I learned as a producer is that every story is different and not to get complacent and say "same stuff" because it is not "same stuff." Every story deals with different individuals at different times and is therefore different from any other story ever. Look closely and you will see. Don't take the easy road. Look behind the obvious and really report. There was a local Chicago wire service, the Chicago News Bureau, which trained scores of terrific reporters. One of the credoes was. . . "If your mother tell you she loves you, check it out." — Bill Theodore, former NBC news producer and New England bureau chief

A MOCK ASSIGNMENT

GETTING THE RIGHT ANGLE

Once you are assigned a story, the first and most important thing you need to do is to find out what angle your boss has in mind. The same story can be told a thousand different ways. It's not about how you want to tell it; rather it's about how your boss wants it told. As a writer/producer, you are a hired hand. If you work at McDonald's making burgers, you have to make them the way McDonald's specifies. It's the same with TV news. Your boss will almost always have a vision for how your story should be put together. You have to at least attempt to incorporate the elements deemed important.

Sometimes when things get hectic — a common occurrence in TV news — the boss might forget to share his or her vision with you. If this happens, it is important that you tell your boss what you are planning to do. See if he or she agrees or has another take. Some producers may resist this because they feel that their vision is so right-on, that once the story is shot, the boss will love it. I think this can be a mistake. If you bring back a story that is the opposite of what the executive producer intended, it will not be a good thing. There is nothing worse than being called on the carpet with questions about why you didn't ask certain questions or get certain shots. Because of time and money constraints, you will likely not be able to go back and redo it.

PRODUCER MEANS BOSS

Not to scare you, but I feel I should mention that as a producer you are the boss of the story. It is your job to put the story together, to set up the interviews, work with the correspondent, go on the shoot, instruct the crew, write the script, and oversee the edit. Anything that goes wrong is your responsibility. If a shot is off or not there at all, they aren't going to call the cameraman and ask him to explain. They are going to call you because it's your story. You are in charge of everything.

YOU CAN UP THE EMOTION BY USING REAL PEOPLE

The best news stories feature real people. If your story is about identity theft, you could definitely get experts to tell you how to avoid being a victim, and you could have reporters fill in the rest. But there is nothing more powerful or compelling than hearing from an actual victim. It gives the story an emotional force, which viewers can relate to. When they see Jane Smith talk about how she threw credit card bills out in the trash without shredding them, and now she is tens of thousands of dollars in debt because someone stole her identity, viewers get emotionally involved. They subconsciously think, "if it happened to her, it could happen to me."

> "Choosing good subjects to tell your story is the single most important element. You need subjects who leap off the screen with their passion and personality. Even the most dramatic story can be undermined if there is not an interesting, articulate subject to tell it. It seems counterintuitive, but sometimes the person at the center of a story may not be the best person to tell it. When that's the case, you look for strong, supporting voices to help you carry the story. Nothing is more important for a successful piece." — Judy Tygard, senior producer, *48 Hours Mystery*

Finding real people to go on camera can be either easy or difficult. It really depends on the story. Sometimes people pop up when you are doing research. Or, if it's a medical story, you can ask doctors if they have any patients who fit the bill. (For confidentiality reasons, they will have to make the phone calls to the patients for you.) Often, the way to find people is to ask family and friends if they know of anyone who might know of anyone. It is not uncommon when working in a news organization to get e-mails from producers that read, "I'm doing a holiday story on couples who celebrate both Christmas and Chanukah. Does anyone know of a couple who celebrates both and would be willing to talk about it on camera?" It may take some patience, but one way or another you will almost always be able to find a real life person to explore the story.

WHY YOU NEED AT LEAST ONE EXPERT

In doing news stories, it is important to include at least one so-called expert such as a doctor, a lawyer, a scientist, a professor, etc. Experts come in all fields and they give stories credibility because they offer an educated opinion. Let's say you are doing a story on cancer and a new breakthrough in chemotherapy. You can interview patients who have taken the new drug, and they can holler from the hilltops about how it made them well. But an oncologist can tell you why the drug made them well, how it works, and what the downside might be.

HOW TO FIND EXPERTS

Finding an expert is probably the easiest part of your whole story. Experts are usually all-too-willing to speak on camera because it is good publicity both for them and for their company. If you are working for one of the networks, and therefore the story will air nationally, experts all but come out of the woodwork. Many companies have departments set up just to handle media requests. So, if you were doing a story on strokes, you could call virtually any major hospital, ask for Media Relations (or the division that handles media), and tell them what you are looking for. They will do the legwork for you. They will ask you when you want to shoot, where you want to shoot, and possibly some questions about the angle of the story. They will then go find a neurologist qualified to speak about strokes. They will make sure his schedule matches yours — and they will call you back with a time to shoot. One thing you always want to be sure to do is to answer their questions honestly. Don't tell them what you think they want to hear. If it's something that you fear might make them uncomfortable, address it up-front with a disclaimer such as "I don't know how Dr. Jones would feel about this, but I was hoping to do X." You need to have everything on the up and up ahead of time in order to ensure a smooth shoot.

A STORY ON J.K. ROWLING, PLEASE: WHERE DO YOU BEGIN?

Once you know the angle of the story, you can begin to set it up. Let's say your story is on J.K. Rowling, author of the *Harry Potter* books. The executive producer is looking for a personal profile: who is the whiz behind the wizard? The e.p. also wants you to include elements of J.K.'s rags-to-riches life.

The first thing you want to do is make a wish list of people that you will want to interview on camera. If you work at a big enough news organization, they may well provide you a folder loaded with research, which makes it very easy. You just have to sit there and sift through. Often, the research even includes names and contact numbers. Other times, you have to start from square one and do the research on your own. As you go through the research, you will also want to think about locations in which to shoot the story.

So, let's start making a list of people you will want to interview. The first choice is rather obvious. You can't very well do a story on J.K. Rowling without J.K. Rowling. Thus, we shall put her first on the list.

1. J.K. Rowling

Now who? You might be thinking about Daniel Radcliffe, the actor who brought Harry Potter to life, and screenwriter Steve Kloves, who worked closely with Rowling as he adapted her books for the big screen. I say no. Why? Go back to the angle your boss wanted. This isn't a story about how J.K. Rowling's books have become blockbuster movies. This is a personal profile. Therefore, let's see if we can talk to some of the people in her life who might know her private side the best.

2. Family. You could interview her husband, oldest child, sister. Your research will tell you that her mother is dead. Her father would be a good bet … if your research didn't show that their relationship has been rocky. J.K. may not want him in the story. Still it's worth a shot. Be sure to check it out with her publicist.

3. Friends. Does she have a close friend? How about friends from childhood?

4. Acquaintances. If you are looking to include the rags-to-riches thing, how about some of the wait staff at the local Edinburgh cafe where J.K. is said to have written the first *Harry Potter* book while her baby daughter slept?

5. Experts. Even though this is a personal profile, it would still be good to have an expert weigh in. How about her agent or her editor?

Now … how to line all of these people up? First, let's assume that you already have J.K. (With big celebrities, the inquiry will usually have been made before the story is assigned because without the celebrity it all becomes moot.) Family and friends you can probably find with the help of J.K.'s publicist (with whom you will probably be working fairly closely). For the wait staff, find out through your own research or through J.K's publicist the name of the cafe and see if anyone would be willing to go on camera and talk about watching her write, day after day. The agent and editor are easy to find as well. All you have to do is call, tell them who you work for, that you are doing a story on J.K. and you would love to ask them some questions on camera. If you are going to be working with a specific correspondent, always tell them that, too. Names like Diane Sawyer and Mike Wallace get people all the more excited.

Once you have lined up the people you are going to interview, you will need to think about where you want to shoot. Obviously, this will require several locations. Because this is a personal profile, you will really want to go to J.K.'s home in Scotland if she will agree to it. Let's say, for the sake of argument, she will.

While you are in Scotland, you can get her family and then possibly shoot over to Britain to get some of her long-time friends as well. The key is to do as few locations as possible. It takes a lot of time to set up lights, so it wouldn't be feasible nor visually pleasing to just bop from one friend's house to another. Shooting outside can be easier if the weather co-operates. And Edinburgh offers a perfect backdrop for this story — much more visually stimulating than someone's living room. As for the agent and editor, you can get them in their office. Now that you have lined up the people and places, it is time to start preparing for the shoot.

20

THE SHOOT

BEFORE YOU GO

Once you have firm dates and times for your shoots, it is time to really delve in and learn everything you can, especially the most current information on whatever the subject of your story is. So, in the case of J.K. Rowling, read and digest. To make sure you are on top of things, you may want to talk to her publicist to see if there is anything new that you might want to include. You should always look to reveal something we haven't heard before.

You now need to formulate a list of questions that you plan to ask each person you are going to interview. You should also make a list of the video that you want to get. This step is hugely important, as once you get to the location, things can get hectic. If you don't have a road map etched in stone, I can almost promise you will forget things. If you neglect to ask an important question or fail to shoot a specific piece of video that is key to the story, you can't go back and redo it.

Imagine this scenario: You shoot at J.K. Rowling's. You get back to New York and realize that you forgot to ask her something really important. Do you honestly think that the network is going to pay to fly you and a crew back to Scotland? And even if they did, what's to say that J.K. will be game for you to tromp into her house and set up all over again? Not to mention that even if you could get past those two obstacles, once you have left a shoot, it is extremely hard to go back again because you have to match up everything, from what people were wearing to the lighting to the natural sounds in the room. That said, it's much better to be organized and plan what you want to ask in advance. So, get out a legal pad and start to formulate questions.

WORKING WITH TALENT VS. WORKING SOLO

As you formulate questions, it is important to know whether you will be working with a correspondent, and if so, who that correspondent is. On news magazine shows, you will usually work with a correspondent, though there are times that you may have to go to a shoot and do the interview yourself off camera, and then the reporter will voiceover the story, giving the illusion that he or she was present and did the interview.

Working with correspondents is usually a good thing because it gives you a second set of eyes, and you also feel like you have a partner in crime. At the risk of sounding lazy, when you work with correspondents, they end up doing a good chunk of the work, as opposed to what you have to do when you are going solo.

You should always consult with the correspondent ahead of time on the questions. Usually he or she will have done the homework as well and will likely have ideas about what should be asked. You want to be sure you are both on the same page, as you won't have time to iron things out on location, nor do you want to have any kind of disagreement in front of the people you plan to interview.

One thing to keep in mind about working with correspondents is that when the story hits the air, it is the correspondent's face that the audience will see, not yours. Therefore, if a correspondent is uncomfortable with a certain area or wants to rephrase a question, don't take it personally. Part of your job as a producer is to look out for them and to make them look good.

TAKING CARE OF YOUR CREW

When you work on a TV magazine show, you will be assigned a crew that usually consists of a cameraman and a soundman. At the network level, count on them being seasoned veterans. In no uncertain terms they can make or break your shoot. They are required to shoot your interview and whatever else you need. They are not required to put forth any extra creativity if they don't feel like it. Most of them are unionized, so if they don't go the extra mile for you, they will still have jobs tomorrow. The same might not be true for you if you come back with video that's just so-so. Therefore, it is hugely important that you get off on the right foot with them.

My experience is that if you treat the crew well, they will work all the harder for you. Whatever you do, don't show up with an "I'm the boss" attitude. Everyone already knows you're the boss, so there's nothing to prove. When you arrive at the location, there will undoubtedly be lots of equipment to unload. You should offer to help carry stuff in, even if you are female, wearing a skirt and high heels.

Depending on where the shoot is and what time of year it is, offer to get the crew coffee or water. (This isn't always possible, but if it is, do it.) Union rules require that they are allowed a lunch break. That means you need to make sure they get it. Most of the people that work crew in news usually don't whine about lunch, as they are used to tight schedules. So, if you are in the middle of interviewing J.K. Rowling and it's time for lunch, most are happy to finish the job. Depending on what the schedule is, I always try to figure out when and where to do lunch. If there's time to grab something quick at a restaurant, great. If not, I will run out and get my crew food while they break down the equipment and pack it up. I always make sure my crew gets fed and I always pay for it. It's not required, nor will I be reimbursed, but it is my way of thanking them for a job well done. It is also important for them to eat, especially if there is more work to be done after lunch, which there always is. You can't expect people to lift heavy equipment and be creative when they have low blood sugar and their stomachs are rumbling because they are starving.

> "The next generation needs to be more than good writers and good storytellers. As the technology evolves there is a demand for producers who can shoot or edit their own material. The more you can bring to the party, the more marketable you will be." — Judy Tygard, senior producer, *48 Hours Mystery*

ONCE YOU ARRIVE AT THE LOCATION

When you arrive at the location, it is your job to introduce yourself to whomever it is you are supposed to be meeting. Once you get inside, everything will stop and people will look to you for direction. They will want to know where you want to shoot. If I am in a person's home, I always ask them for suggestions, unless I have a real specific reason to be in a specific room. Sometimes people have preferences: there may be a room in which they feel more comfortable or even a room they may not want people to see. Usually when you ask for suggestions, the person will give you a couple of options. I look and mentally decide what I think is best. But before I make a decision, I always consult with the crew. I have a philosophy about television that has never steered me wrong. I believe television production is an extremely collaborative process, and you not only have to trust other people to do their jobs, you also have to trust their expertise. I am certain I can write a script better than the cameraman could. I am equally certain that he knows more about shooting video than I do. So, if he tells me that one room works better than another, I am guessing he is looking at things like natural light, depth of field, etc., the same way the soundman might be looking at an aquarium thinking if it can't be unplugged, the hum is going to be an audio nightmare. Nine times out of ten, I will defer to what my crew thinks is best, even if their choice is different than mine.

WHAT TO DO WHILE THE CREW SETS UP

As mentioned, it will take the crew some time to get set up. Good lighting is important and it is something that can't be rushed. While the crew is setting up, you (and the correspondent) should take the time to establish a rapport with the person you are going to interview. This is key in establishing trust. Trust is an absolute must if you expect the person to divulge any secrets on camera during the interview.

It's possible the person you are interviewing may want to know the questions in advance. If asked, I will usually toss out a few easy ones that hopefully will make them feel at ease. You don't want to give away the keys to the candy store, however. If the person knows every question, he or she will mentally prepare every answer. This takes away from the spontaneity, and the person usually comes across rehearsed and stiff.

Someone who isn't familiar with television interviewing will usually be nervous. All of a sudden, their house is filled with bright lights, a big camera, a bunch of strangers, and perhaps even a big-name correspondent. This can, understandably, make even a calm person anxious. Usually, the fear is that they are going to say something stupid and it is going to go on the air for all of the world to see. You can alleviate these fears by explaining how the process works. Let them know that the interview is going to be edited, so if they make a mistake they can just start again.

Once you have the person you are going to interview feeling as calm and relaxed as possible, take a moment to really look around and make sure everything is the way you want it. Even take a look at the way the person is dressed. Is the look right for your story? I have interviewed lawyers at their homes, and upon arriving, found them in a business suit. If the story is more casual, I will tell them they look great, and then I will ask them if they would mind changing into something that is a bit less formal. If you explain the reasoning, people usually are happy to comply.

In addition to what I want, the camera has preferences as well. Generally colors show up better than black or white. So, if the interview subject is wearing black, white, or a combination, I will let them know they may want to put on something else. Again, if you explain this to people they will work with you. In fact, I often discuss clothing ahead of time. And if I don't, people will sometimes ask. When it comes to being on TV, everyone wants to look as good as possible.

WHEN YOU DO THE INTERVIEW

As previously mentioned, there are times when you, as a producer, will have to conduct the interview. If this is the case, you will sit opposite the person you are interviewing. Since you won't actually appear in the interview and your voice will be edited out, the camera will be positioned behind you, shooting only the interview subject.

You should place your pad with questions on your lap so that you can easily refer to it, with a simple glance down. This is important because you want to maintain eye contact with the person you are talking to at all times. Young writers and producers often think that the most important part of conducting an interview is the questions that are asked. No doubt what you choose to ask your subjects is of the utmost importance. But there is another, equally important skill to interviewing: listening.

At some point in your life, you have probably attempted to tell someone something that's important to you, but you can tell by their body language that they are only half-listening. This doesn't feel good. Well, it won't feel good for the person you are interviewing either, if your head is in your lap as you rummage through your questions or you are staring off into space waiting for them to finish the answer. You want the person who is spilling their heart and soul to you to feel like you are with them, totally focused, hanging onto their every word. It is the only way they will feel comfortable enough to possibly share some of their juiciest secrets.

No matter how well prepared you are or how much research you have done, you don't know everything there is to know about this person. If you did, you wouldn't need to do the interview. When the subject reveals some new bit of information that we haven't heard, it is imperative that you ask follow-up questions. These won't be written down because it's stuff you weren't aware of. This is why listening is so crucial. If you are interviewing a big star and he drops the bombshell that he suffers from clinical depression and often contemplates suicide, your next question can't be, "who did you take to the high school prom?" It may sound funny, but I have seen producers and even reporters who are so focused on what the next question is that they forget to listen to the answers. If the person that you are interviewing discloses something big, and you don't follow up, I can promise you will hear from the executive producer, who will want to know why you didn't ask X, Y, and Z.

To keep on track, I always have a pen in my lap as well. If I hear something that I want to touch on, I maintain eye contact while scrawling a note to myself (just a word or two) so that I remember what I want to touch on. You shouldn't interrupt people when they are talking because you can step on their audio. There is nothing more frustrating when you get to an edit bay and realize that what the person said was significant, but it can't be used because you opened your big mouth and wrecked the audio.

Make sure when people answer your questions that they always answer in full sentences that spit your question back at you. This will save you in an edit bay. If the question is, "do you think aliens actually exist?" and the person merely answers "absolutely," you will have a hard time using that answer because on its own it doesn't contain the reference. But if the answer is "I know aliens exist. I have seen their spaceships in my back yard," now you have an answer that can stand on its own.

After you have exhausted all of your questions, it's always a good idea to see if the person has anything he or she would like to add. This is a way of covering your bases, in case there are one or two things that you may have missed.

WHEN TALENT DOES THE INTERVIEW

When a correspondent does the interview, the process is really the same, except the conversation is between the correspondent and the subject. You are just there to oversee the shoot and make sure that everything goes smoothly. To keep from getting in the way of the correspondent and the interview subject, you should stand off to the side. Usually, the crew will have a monitor, so you can see exactly what is being shot. Keep a notepad with you so that you can jot down things that you want to get or go back to. But whatever you do, do not start shouting out questions. Your correspondent needs to have the rapport with the person, not you.

The only time I will ever interrupt and stop a shoot is if there is a technical problem, because that would mean that the interview or portions of it won't be usable. There have been times when I have been shooting in someone's kitchen and suddenly the refrigerator goes on. It's a slight hum; nonetheless it can make the audio unusable. A good soundman will usually pick up on this immediately; however, if he doesn't, I will stop the shoot and ask him how bad it is. If it's at all questionable, we will unplug the refrigerator. I have stopped shoots here and there and I have been wrong. Whatever I perceived to be a problem wasn't, but that's okay. It's better to be safe than to return to the network with a story they can't put on the air because of technical glitches.

Once the correspondent has finished the interview, he or she will almost always look to you to see if anything has been missed or if there is anything else you want questioned. At this point, it is fine for you to jump in and speak to both the correspondent and the subject with something like, "I thought what you said about X was interesting. Can we touch on that a little more? I'd be interested in knowing A, B, and C about it."

When you interview people, sometimes they will ramble and go off on tangents. If the interviewee has said something interesting and went into a long involved story about it, I might ask for a more concise version. I'd tell the person that what they said was really interesting, but we need to try to shorten the answer a little. This will make the editing process much easier.

ONE CAMERA OR TWO?

For the record, most news interviews are done with one camera. However, with network news magazine shows, there will sometimes be two cameras because the correspondent is usually so prevalent in the story. In this case, one camera is on the person being interviewed, the other camera on the correspondent.

If you only have one camera and are doing an interview with a correspondent, immediately after the interview is finished, ask the person being interviewed to sit tight. The cameraman will swing the camera around so that he is shooting over the interviewee's shoulder. The correspondent will then ask a couple of questions exactly as he or she asked them in the interview. This will give the correspondent a presence in the story. It will also give you some cutaways in the edit bay. You need to make sure that the correspondent phrases the questions in the exact way they were originally asked, or the subject's answers may not match up. In the English language, you would be surprised at how easily one little word that's out of place can really mess things up.

GETTING B-ROLL IS KEY

Now that you have finished the interview itself, there are still some other things you need to do before packing up. The most important is to get b-roll. If you think about what your cameraman has shot, it is the interview. So far, all of the video is a dead-on shot of the person you interviewed and, if the correspondent is present, then there are also dead-on shots of the correspondent. Now it is time to bring your story to life visually. When you put the story together, you are going to want to match up pictures and sound. For the most part, you have the sound, which is the interview. Now, you need to gather video to match that sound. This is known as b-roll.

Before you go out to an interview, you usually will have an idea of some of the kinds of b-roll you want to get. Sometimes though, the interviewee will say something in an interview that you will want to add to your b-roll wish list. You need to get as much b-roll as possible. If you come back short, you will be in a heap of trouble in the edit bay. If you ever look at TV news stories or TV news magazine stories and you see the same shot used twice it is usually because they didn't have enough b-roll. Stories that use the same shot more than once — unless it is intentional for dramatic purposes — are stories that are poorly produced. At the network level, the executive producer will usually call you on this. So, you always want to get more b-roll than you need. When a cameraman tells me that he thinks he has shot enough, I instruct him to shoot more. I am always glad I did.

THE IMPORTANCE OF NATURAL SOUND

In addition to b-roll, you will also want to get what is known as NAT (natural sound) or NAT/SOT (natural sound on tape). Natural sound enhances your piece and makes viewers feel like they are right there in the story. Imagine you did a story on the circus, but you didn't get any natural sound. Just video alone would seem odd, because we know the circus has lots of sounds. Or, if your story involved shots of a funeral, and we could see by the faces of the mourners that some are crying, yet we don't hear them. See how much more real the story would seem with sounds that are natural to the location?

Your NAT/SOTS don't have to be big moments. In fact, sometimes the smaller moments are the most revealing. An example that comes to mind is from several years back in a story about Princess Diana getting media training. As she is being coached at her Kensington Palace home, Prince William and Prince Harry bolt in. They want to watch. Diana agrees, but tells them they need to be quiet. A short time later, William attempts to insert his opinion, to which Diana tells him to shush. The future king of England being shushed by his mother is an interesting piece of NAT because it feels like a very natural, unstaged moment. In those brief few seconds, the audience gained rare insight to this mother–child relationship. While most of us have seen umpteen pictures of Diana and her boys, this was an exceptional glimpse at the two of them interacting.

B-ROLL FOR THE J.K. ROWLING STORY

Let's look at the J.K. Rowling story and list some possible b-roll. Since this is showing the personal side, perhaps the following might work:

- Shots of J.K. interacting with family
- Shots of J.K. at the café where she used to write
- Shots of J.K. in her office
- Pictures of J.K. as a child and with family
- Pictures of J.K. at her previous home in Britain
- Shots of anything related to *Harry Potter* books
- Shots of boxes that contain scribbled on notebooks and napkins
- Shots of awards J.K. has won
- Shots of J.K. reading to her children
- Shots of J.K. talking to wait staff in café
- Shots of J.K. (and kids) out tromping around the Scottish countryside.

That is just a partial list; the full list comes after hearing what she talked about during the interview. When you look at the list, you should be able to see which would have NAT and which would not. For example, reading to her kids and talking to wait staff would definitely include NAT. Old family photos would not.

You may be wondering why I included things like J.K. in her office and her award since this is supposed to be a personal piece. The reason is that even though the piece is a personal profile, there will be no way to avoid talking about *Harry Potter* because that is what catapulted her to becoming an international household name. So, while it won't be the focus, we also can't completely ignore it. Therefore, we need those pictures.

It is important to note that you can't shoot video for things that happened in the past. Yet, when people talk about past events, we need to have visuals. In this case, always ask people ahead of time if they can pull out some old photos. Your cameraman can shoot the pictures while you are at the location. (In the event that the interview is not at the person's home, ask them to bring the photos to the location.) If the cameraman slowly zooms in on it, the shot will be moving and should match up well in your edit.

Another thing to keep in mind about past events is that while you can't go back in time, there is a little trick in restaging them, which is perfectly acceptable in the TV news world.

Let's say that during the interview J.K. talks about when she used to write at the café in Edinburgh. If she is game, after the interview you take her to the café. You sit her at a table, give her a pad and pen, and let her start scribbling. You aren't in any way trying to make the audience believe that this shot happened years ago, which is why it's okay to do it. Somehow when viewers see the shot of J.K. writing at the café, and hear her voice talking about how she used to write at the café, they won't question it. That's because the audio and video lock up.

DO YOU NEED A STAND-UP?

A stand-up is a short piece of video where the reporter looks directly into the camera and speaks. Stand-ups usually come about a half to a third of the way through the story. As a rule, they do not come at the beginning. Because a stand-up is both video and audio, a smart producer will use a stand-up to convey information for which there is no matching video.

Where you shoot your stand-up is key, as a stand-up must fit in visually with your story. If you were doing a story on winter sports, you wouldn't shoot the stand-up in Disneyland because it wouldn't make any sense. Viewers would be pulled out of your story, immediately wondering how the reporter got from the ski slopes in Vermont to Anaheim, California, and why. On the other hand, if the stand-up were done on a moving chairlift or if the correspondent popped on a pair of ice skates and skated around an outdoor rink, those places would make sense.

Let's look at the J.K. Rowling story and see if we can find a place for a stand-up that might work in the story. If I were producing the piece, I might put my correspondent outside one of the cafés where Rowling actually wrote the first *Harry Potter*, or I might simply use Edinburgh as a backdrop.

WRITING THE SCRIPT

SORTING THROUGH YOUR TAPES

When you return from your shoot, the first thing you will need to do is transcribe your tapes. You need to write down every word exactly as it is said and list every piece of video. Most reporters and producers will tell you this is a horrendous job. I can attest. But, as a producer, you need to know exactly what is on every tape. You need to look closely at the video and listen carefully to the audio. There are times when you will find, usually due to technical reasons, that one or the other will not be usable. For example, if an interview was shot outside and a plane went buzzing by overhead, then the audio for those few seconds might be compromised. At the network level you will often have interns and production assistants whose job it is to transcribe the tapes for you. This is a huge help, because you can read the transcriptions and narrow in on what you are going to use. Even then, it is advisable to put the tape in a deck and check it to make sure that what you plan to put on the air looks good and is technically acceptable. You can't count on an inexperienced intern to catch everything.

Depending on how many people you have interviewed and how many locations you have used, it is quite possible that you will literally have several hours of video. If your story is slated at 13 minutes and 30 seconds, that means that you are going to have to choose the best and most relevant 13 minutes and 30 seconds out of everything you have shot.

> "It's that curiosity you show that somehow you want to do it so badly. Frequently, it works out. We all started out that way. We all remember." — Mike Wallace, *60 Minutes*, on how to get your foot in the door.

WHAT IS TIMECODE, AND WHY IT WILL SAVE YOU

To help you keep track of your footage, each tape will have what is known as timecode. Timecode is an exact numeric location of everything that is on a particular tape. When you log your tapes, you will log everything by its time-code, which will make things easy to find when needed. So, let's say you are looking for some video of J.K. Rowling tromping through the Scottish countryside. Rather than have to go through several tapes, you can simply look at your log, pop the tape into a deck, and go right to the footage you are looking for.

This may not seem like such a big deal, but I can assure you it is. When you get into an edit, things get hectic. An editor or an executive producer may ask you for a certain shot or they may ask if the interviewee addressed a certain subject. You can look at the log and pull up the footage instantly. Otherwise, you would have to stop the edit and start digging through tapes. Trust me when I tell you there is no time for this. Edits can be stressful; there is lots of pressure and usually little time. You have to go in completely organized and prepared.

WHAT IS A SOUND BITE?

When you look over the interview portions of your video, you will most likely notice that the questions you asked the interview subject were answered in depth. When you asked J.K. how she created *Harry Potter,* she probably didn't give you a one-sentence answer. Obviously, you won't have time to put everything the person said into your story. Therefore, you will cut a small portion of what was said. This is known as a sound bite. Sound bites should never be long and rambling. They should be concise, no more than 15–20 seconds at the most, and often they are less.

When you think of a sound bite, think of how it was shot. The camera was on the interview subject, which means you have video. Also, the person was wearing a microphone, so you have audio. Sound bites generally have both video and audio. The video is usually just a shot of the person talking, which means when you get into an edit, you will cover some of the "talking head" with some of your more interesting b-roll in order to make the story come alive.

PICKING THE RIGHT SOUND BITES TO TELL YOUR STORY

In putting together your story, the first thing you will do after logging tapes is to start choosing the sound bites you are going to use in your story. Go through each interview, and try to pick out the most relevant things that each person said. Remember sound bites need to be short and sweet. However, if the person makes a good point at the beginning of the sound bite, rambles, and makes another good point at the end, it is possible for an editor to chop out the middle. Likewise, you don't have to start with the first words that came out of the person's mouth. You can cut into a sound bite and start anywhere you choose. Just be careful that when you chop, you don't change the intent of what was said.

Make sure that each sound bite you choose brings up a different point. In other words, don't choose two sound bites from two different people that virtually say the same thing. You will have limited time to tell your story, so every sound bite must give new insight, new information, and a fresh perspective.

WHAT IS TRACK?

Now that you have an idea of what sound bites you are going to use, it is time to write the script. The words that you write are known as "track" or voiceover. Before you go into an edit, a correspondent will enter a sound booth and record the tracks that you have written. Good track gives new information, while at the same time connecting one sound bite to the next. As with sound bites, track should be concise and to the point. It should not ramble. Once the script is written, you should feel a certain rhythm: sound bite, track, sound bite, track.

You do not have to start your script with track. In fact, some of the best stories start with a sound bite, because a good sound bite can really hook an audience in. Whichever you start with — sound bite or track — try to alternate between the two. A TV news magazine script should never be just a series of sound bites back to back. That isn't to say that every now and then you won't put sound bites together without track. I will sometimes string two sound bites together when they directly contradict each other.

For example, let's say the sound bite is of Joe Schmoe, who has been accused of identity theft. His sound bite is "I have never stolen anyone's identity." I might then go directly to another sound bite of a policeman saying, "when we raided his home we found credit cards, drivers' licenses, and banking information for 45 people." Because these statements are so contradictory, they speak for themselves better than any track in between them could.

It is important to keep in mind that track is audio only. When you go into an edit and the editor begins to put your story together, you will hear the reporter's voice every time there is track, but you will only see a black screen. You need to insert b-roll or graphics over track; otherwise your story will have audio over big black holes.

MAKING SURE VIDEO AND SOUND LOCK UP

The hardest thing about writing track is to make sure that you have video to match what you are writing. For example, if you were to write, "before the *Harry Potter* books sold, Rowling was on government assistance." What video would you use to illustrate that? (A better way to get this point out would be through a sound bite.) You must have matching video to cover any track that you write. If you don't, you could find yourself in trouble once you get into an edit. An editor will always ask you what shots you intend to use, and if you don't have any, your story will cease to work at that point. This is your responsibility, not the editor's.

You will want to cover many of your sound bites with video as well. Remember, most of your sound bites are talking heads, the same stagnant shot. To make your story more visually exciting, you will use some of the b-roll to cover what the person is saying. But again, it is crucial that the video and audio lock up. Say that you are doing a story on a teenager who is training to be an Olympic skater. If she says, "it's hard when you fall," and you want to use that sound bite, then it would be good if you had video of her out on the ice doing a jump in which she falls. That video must be inserted at the exact point that she talks about falling.

WHEN YOU DON'T HAVE THE VIDEO

On occasion, there will be video that you don't have. Though this doesn't happen often, you can actually make video by using graphics and special effects. Networks have graphic artists on staff and the capability to do a lot of creative things in this regard. In fact there may be times when you have video, but opt to use graphics and special effects to enhance the production value of your story.

HOW TO WRITE YOUR SCRIPT

As with sitcoms, dramas, and movies, TV news also has a specific format for scripts. You will notice that TV news scripts look nothing like the scripts we have looked at in series television.

TV news scripts are divided into two columns: audio and video. Video always occupies the left side of the page, while audio goes to the right. In the audio column, you will write tracks that lead in and out of sound bites. In addition to typing your tracks, you must also type out the sound bite word-for-word. The idea is that an executive producer or an editor should be able to read the audio column and know precisely what the story is, and how you plan to lay it out.

In the video column, you will list the specific shots that you intend to use over the audio. Try to list the video so that it lines up in a way that matches the audio. This will help ensure that an editor understands precisely what video you want over the audio. When you list the video, you need to list which tape the specific shot is on, and the timecode. You must do this for sound bites as well; if you don't, an editor will have a hard time trying to cut your story together. He or she might have ten tapes that are 30 minutes each. Without timecode listed, there is no way an editor will ever find the shot or sound bite that you want to use.

Here is an example of what a news script looks like:

VIDEO	AUDIO
LIST VIDEO	(TRACK)
TAPE #3	HERE IS WHERE YOU WRITE
03:06:29	YOUR OWN WORDS THAT TELL
J.K. TROMPING IN COUNTRY	THE STORY. TRACK SHOULD
	ALWAYS BE COVERED BY
TAPE #1	VIDEO BECAUSE WHAT YOU
01:25:06	ARE WRITING IS AUDIO ONLY.
J.K. WITH KIDS	TRACK ALSO CONNECTS
	SOUND BITES. A WELL-
TAPE #6	WRITTEN STORY HAS TRACK
06:13:19	THAT LEADS INTO ONE SOUND
J.K. READING TO KIDS	BITE ...
	(SOT)
TAPE # 4	"THE SOUND BITE PICKS UP
04:16:17	WHERE THE TRACK LEFT OFF."
	(TRACK)
TAPE #5	THE FIRST PART OF A TRACK
05::02:09	IMMEDIATELY FOLLOWING A
J.K AT CAFÉ	SOUND BITE PICKS UP WHERE
	THE SOUND BITE LEFT OFF.
TAPE #9	THE TRACK CONTINUES TO
09:12:24	ADD NEW INFORMATION TO

PHOTOS OF J.K. AS CHILD	THE STORY AND THE SECOND HALF LEADS INTO…
TAPE # 11 11:15:20 J.K.'S SISTER	(SOT) "THE NEXT SOUND BITE."
	(TRACK)
TAPE #11 11:21:23 J.K./SISTER HAVING TEA	THE TRICK IS TO MAKE SURE THAT TRACK AND SOUND BITES ARE MIXED. DO NOT WRITE LONG TRACKS …
TAPE # 2 02:15:25 J.K.	(SOT) "THE SAME IS TRUE WITH SOUND BITES."
TAPE # 9 09:26:04 REPORTER STAND-UP	(STAND-UP) YOU MAY ADD A REPORTER STAND-UP TOWARD THE LAST PART OF THE STORY. STAND-UPS ARE GENERALLY USED WHERE YOU DON'T HAVE VIDEO TO GET CERTAIN INFORMATION OUT.
	(TRACK)
TAPE #10 10:03:04 J.K. IN EDITOR'S OFFICE	BE SURE YOUR TRACK AND SOUND BITES DO NOT REPEAT EACH OTHER.

You get the gist. The most important thing to do is to make sure you have listed enough video, and you need to change shots about every 3–4 seconds in order to keep the story visually stimulating. Notice also that the script is in all caps. News scripts are written this way to make it easier on the reporter, especially if the script ends up being put in the teleprompter for a live read.

Once finished, a news script should be in blocks of SOTs and Tracks. This makes it easy for the correspondent when reading the tracks and it makes it easy for an editor as well.

Imagine this scenario: you write the script out, but you haven't put it in blocks. Because it's all squished together, the correspondent misses a track. You don't realize the track wasn't recorded until you go into the edit bay and your editor tells you that it's missing. You may be thinking, "no big deal, just find the correspondent and have him record it." That's a good idea in theory, but what if the correspondent is on a plane to Antarctica to do a story on global warming? You can't count on reporters — especially at the network level — to be waiting around in case you make a mistake. You have to be on top of your game.

IF YOU CARE TO GIVE IT A TRY

If you would like to try your hand at writing a script for a news magazine, I have just the story for you. This was a story I did for local news, but the same story could just as easily aired on one of the network news magazine shows. Of all the stories I have done, this sticks out in my mind as being one of the more unusual. Let me give you the setup, and then we can talk about some game rules for your script.

The story is on the ever-growing trend of pet funerals. In order to set the story up and meet my deadline, I had to find someone whose pet had died and was being buried in the next two days. Here's the kicker: the pet's family would have to agree to allow a news crew to attend the funeral. I called every pet cemetery in every New England state. There were only going to be two funerals that weekend. The first family I called politely declined. I had one shot left.

The second family I contacted agreed to let me do their story. Their German Shepherd named "Pebo" was being laid to rest the following day. I asked them to bring pictures of Pebo by himself and with the family.

The following morning, my crew and I went to the pet cemetery, and interviewed the owner/ funeral director, who gave us an overall view of what to expect. Pet funerals, he explained, were much like human funerals. He showed us an array of urns and caskets, and told us about the latest trends in pet funerals (including the remains of people and their pets sharing a cremation urn for all eternity.).

The funeral director explained that when Pebo's family arrived, his coffin would be opened for a viewing. Then, Pebo's casket would be hoisted onto the back of a golf cart to lead a funeral procession to the cemetery. At the grave site, the owner would say some prayers. The price tag for all of this was about $1500.

While this story may sound ludicrous, as a producer there was one important thing to keep in mind: Pebo's family had done me a big favor by graciously agreeing to let us be part of what was a very sad and personal moment for them. Therefore I had an obligation to ensure that they didn't look stupid when the story hit the air. There was an unspoken trust that I would take care of them, which included instructing my cameraman not to get any close-ups of Pebo. There were kids in this family, and I didn't want to have them watching TV when a promo for the story came on that showed a close-up of their dead dog. I told the cameraman to shoot the viewing from as far away as possible. You could still see a little bit of fur in the coffin, and people would definitely get it. Again, when it comes to a shoot, the cameraman is obligated to follow the producer's instructions. If a shot is missing, it's the producer who will be called on it ... which I was.

Upon seeing the story put together, my executive producer turned to me and said, "Where's the close-up of the dead dog?"

"Didn't get one," I told him, matter-of-factly.

He looked at me like he couldn't believe my words. "Why not?"

"Because I knew if I did, you'd put it on the air."

And that was the truth. By purposefully not getting a close-up, I ensured that the shot couldn't and wouldn't be used. But, again, this is tricky. You have to fight battles and take stands sparingly, because each time you do, you risk getting on the executive producer's bad side.

Okay, now it's your turn. Take this scenario, which is a story about pet funerals. In your case, let's say the deceased is a cat named "Muffy," who belonged to a family with a mother, a father, and a little boy named Johnny. Let's say that you have shot an interview with all of the family members and with the pet cemetery's funeral director. Following is a list of all of the sound bites you have, all of the NATs, and all of the b-roll:

SOTs
- LITTLE JOHNNY
  "I liked Muffy. She was my best friend. I'm sad she got runned over by the big truck. I hope the mean driver goes to jail."
  "I'm happy we're giving Muffy a funeral. Everyone needs a nice goodbye."
  "Sometimes Muffy played ball with me and sometimes she coughed up big hairballs on the rug…"

- DAD
  "I will miss Muffy a lot. She was sweet, ya know? When I think about how every morning I'd put milk in her dish ... the poor little thing. I can still hear her purring. Even now."
  "People say pet funerals are expensive. That may be true. But how do you put a price tag on the unconditional love the animal brought you?"

- MOM

  "Johnny has been so brave. Losing a pet is hard enough on an adult. But for a child, it has to be devastating. I just think little Johnny will be lost without Muffy."

- FUNERAL DIRECTOR

  "I can see Muffy brought this family unending happiness."

  "The tombstones can be engraved with any kind of message you want."

  "I don't think pet funerals are expensive ... not for what you get."

  "We offer a wide variety of services, from cremations to burials. We have caskets lined in silk, and we also have a nice collection of urns to choose from. Our funeral package contains a deluxe coffin, a wake where we present the animal to the family for a final goodbye, a graveside service, music, and some special, special prayers."

  "The price really varies according to the animal. For example, horses cost more than guinea pigs. Guinea pigs cost less than rabbits but more than a goldfish. But, no matter how big or small the animal, the service is always the same. The final farewell is loaded with pomp and circumstance. And that has got to make a family feel good."

  "We have some celebrity pets here. Over under that tree is George Bush's dog. Bless its precious heart and rest its simple soul."

  "We are running a special this month. You can be cremated with your pet. When the pet goes, we cremate it immediately, and then when your time comes, we can put you in the same urn so the two of you can spend all eternity together. It's a very hot thing to do right now. A very nice thing to do."

NAT
- Funeral director saying prayers over funeral music
- Little Johnny sobbing

VIDEO
- Picture of Muffy as a kitten
- Picture of Muffy and Johnny playing ball
- Video of Mack truck with police car and crowd nearby
- Video of Johnny sobbing at service
- Video of pet tombstones
- Video of urns
- Video of pet sympathy cards
- Video of golf cart funeral procession
- Video of little Johnny throwing first shovel of dirt
- Video of Muffy's wake
- Establishing shot of funeral home
- Video of various caskets
- Video of price tags and urns

- Video of tombstone that reads "Presidential Pooch"
- Video of funeral director on phone talking to customer
- Any other photos the family might have
- Any graphics and/or special effects you can create.

This is all you can use to put your story together. See if you can write a story that runs 2 minutes and 30 seconds long (about two and a half pages). You can use two sound bites back-to-back only once during this story. You will not have time to use every sound bite. Some sound bites are too long, so remember to chop them. If you would like to write a stand-up for the correspondent, feel free. Just be sure it goes more toward the end of the story than the beginning. Keep the tone of your story serious; resist the urge to make fun of the subject matter or the people.

CHECKLIST FOR TV NEWS SCRIPT

- Have you mixed track and sound bites?
- Have you covered all tracks with video?
- Have you covered many of the sound bites with video?
- Do you have video to cover whatever track you have written?
- Have you used NAT?
- Is your script in all capital letters?
- Is your script broken into two columns, Video (left) and Audio (right)?
- If you added a stand-up, does it come toward the end of the story?

IN THE EDIT BAY AND BEYOND …

PREPARING FOR YOUR EDIT

Once the script is written, it is time to get ready for your edit. The first step is to get your script approved. On each show there is a producer at a higher level who reads scripts before a field producer goes in to edit. This is to make sure that the story is clear and well laid out. As unpleasant as this process can be — because sometimes you will have to go back and do a rewrite — it really is for your protection. As with series TV, if your script isn't working, your story won't work, which means all of the time you and the editor spend putting the story together will have been wasted.

WORKING WITH AN EDITOR

Once your script has been approved, you can move forward with the editing process. Usually, a specific editor, edit bay, and edit time have been assigned for your story. The first thing you need to do is to check the correspondent's schedule to see when he or she might be able to record tracks. As we discussed, you should do this in advance in case the reporter has to leave town to do another story. If the correspondent won't be around the day that your edit is scheduled, you need to co-ordinate a time when the tracks can be recorded. Plan to sit in on this session with the editor and correspondent. You need to fol-low along on the script and make certain that every track does in fact get recorded. You also want to make sure that you get the proper read. If you are unhappy with the intonation of a track or even the correspondent's energy level, you should ask to have him to redo it.

I feel the same way about editors as I do about cameramen. Some of them are wonderfully creative. Therefore, I never like to breathe down my editor's neck and cramp his or her style. On the day of my edit, I usually take the script and all of my tapes (including track) into the edit bay. I will then sit down with the editor and discuss what the story is, the tone of the story, what I hope to accomplish, as well as any rough spots that I can foresee. If the editor's some-one I haven't worked with previously, I make sure that he or she knows that

I welcome any creative input. Believe me when I say that a good editor can take a good piece and make it great, so you definitely want that person in on the creative process.

After answering any questions the editor has, I usually leave my telephone number and go back to my office. It will take the editor a while to lay down a rough cut, and I like to give him or her the space to do it. Also, rather than wasting time watching an editor push buttons, I can be in my office working on the next story. I will usually check in with the editor every once in a while to see how it's going, or if there are any problems that I hadn't anticipated.

Once the editor has a rough cut, I then go back into the edit bay for many hours. It is astounding how long it takes to edit even a short piece. I have spent 2 days with an editor working on a piece that is a mere 3 minutes long.

The first thing I do when I see the rough cut is to make notes. It's very different to see the script in print, and then to see it cut together. While the editor is playing the rough cut, I follow along with a script to make sure that everything is now in the rough cut. After watching the piece, I ask the editor how long it is. If I am over the allotted segment time, the first thing I have to do is go though with the editor and start cutting things out. This is where solid writing skills really come in to play.

The rest of the edit is spent working with the editor, adding b-roll, special effects, music, and transitions such as dissolves or cuts. Sometimes, it can get tricky if an editor wants to cut the piece a certain way and I don't like the idea. I will usually let him or her have a go at it. Sometimes, I am surprised — it turns out that I like what was done. Other times, I don't like it, and so, as a producer, I have to insist that we do it my way. I approach it sensitively with something like, "I appreciate your coming up with that idea, but somehow it just isn't working for me." You have to remember, you are the boss. An editor is required to edit the piece according to your requirements. But I encourage you to be open to an editor's ideas. In the same way a cameraman shoots video all day — and you work on scripts and stories all day — an editor edits video. Some editors are really very good at it.

BRINGING YOUR STORY IN ON TIME

Unlike comedy and drama, which revolve around one story, TV news magazine shows contain several stories. From the get-go, you will be told by the producer how much time is allotted for your particular story. It is important that you stick to this. One of the hardest things the show producer has to do is to make sure the show comes in on time. Therefore, if your segment is given 13 minutes and 30 seconds, but you bring it in at 7 minutes, you will make the entire show short, and they will have to scramble to find something to fill that extra time. Likewise, if you bring your segment in at 15 minutes, there won't be enough time in the show. Once you see your footage and you start to put together the rough cut, see where you stand. If you are over, but feel that the story warrants it, call the show producer immediately and ask if you could possibly have more time. Be sure to explain the reason why. If the producer agrees … great. If not, you are going to have to chop out 1 minute and 30 seconds.

I don't recommend making a habit of asking for more or less time. Your job as a producer is to bring your story in at the length the show producer requested. While making changes is part of the show producer's job, it does cause extra work for the producer when stories come in other than at the length requested. Do it enough, and he or she won't be happy with you.

GETTING STORY APPROVAL

Once you and your editor are finished with the edit, you will then need to show the completed story to one of the show's higher ups — either an executive producer or one of the show producers — for approval. This can be a nerve-wracking process. The producer will play your story through from beginning to end … at least a few times. You will then be told what works and what doesn't work. The stuff that isn't working in the producer's eyes is stuff that will need to be fixed. Sometimes it involves changing a shot or two. Other times, it is much more significant — as in dropping certain sound bites or even replacing entire sections. (This is why having tapes logged is a good thing.) You may wonder why the producer gave you script approval to begin with if so much was going to change. The truth is that things can look different in script form than they do cut together on the screen.

If a producer asks you to cut something that you feel strongly should stay in, you have the right to state your case. Tell the producer why you feel that a certain sound bite is crucial to the story — or why you are reluctant to replace an entire section. Good producers will listen, but they won't always change their minds. The truth of the matter is that they have more experience than you do — or they wouldn't be in a position of so much responsibility. Sometimes, however, they can be convinced — or you can at least reach a compromise. Be careful not to argue your point too much. Let your feelings be known, but when it's clear that the producer isn't going to change his mind, your argument starts to become a negative. You win some and you lose some — and again it goes back to your being a hired hand. Your job is to bring the story in the way they want it.

WRITING POWERFUL LEADS AND TAGS

Once your story is complete, you will need to write a lead and a tag. Occasionally, the show writers will do this for you, but often it falls on the producer because you are the person who knows the story inside out.

A good lead will introduce the story. It will set the audience up for what they are about to see. It will also let them know which correspondent will be with them throughout the story. Leads should be short — about 20 seconds — and most importantly, they should not step on the story itself. When writing a lead, you want to make sure that you aren't giving away anything in the story, because then the information becomes redundant.

A tag comes at the end of the story. A good tag will contain additional information. It can be an update on what has happened since the piece was shot, or it can point viewers to places they can get more information on the subject. Another way to go about writing a tag is to look for information from your story that you couldn't fit into the script because of time. A tag is a good way for you to still get this information in. For me, the worst tags are when the anchors sit and chit-chat. I feel like it's a waste of time because, almost always, there is more information that can be given.

> "A great television news writer or producer needs to be able to hear voices in his or her head as they write or produce. They need to be able to write or create a program in the voice of their anchor or host instead of their own, which is no small task. How many times have you watched a news program and felt the writing and delivery seemed awkward or bulky, not quite in sync? Most likely that's a program not conceived of with the anchor's voice in mind." — Joel Cheatwood, executive director/program development, CNN

ETHICS IN TELEVISION NEWS

When people watch comedies and drama, they understand that it's fiction. When people watch TV news, though they may be skeptical, they tend to think what they see is true. If you are going to work in TV news, I encourage you to walk through the door with an unshakable sense of ethics. Some viewers will believe whatever you put on the air to be the absolute truth because it's called news. If you are irresponsible, it could mean the difference between life and death.

Here is an example that will bring this point home. As a local news producer, I was once assigned a story on homeopathic medicine. Before I had begun to do the research, the news outlet had already written the promo, which was "Homeopathic Medicine: What You Don't Know Could Kill You." In talking to my executive producer, the story they wanted was to find people who had opted out of traditional medicine in favor of homeopathic methods of treatment. In other words, they wanted me to find a cancer patient who started out with a small tumor, took shark cartilage or something similar, and the tumor has now doubled and the patient may well die. The rest of the story would, of course, be the expert — a doctor who practices traditional medicine — and who would caution patients against using homeopathics.

The problem was that when I started calling reputable hospitals, I could not find a doctor who shared that opinion. In fact, it was just the opposite. Most said that some homeopathics could in fact be beneficial when used in conjunction with conventional medicine. The standard advice from these top-rated specialists was for patients to make sure to tell their doctors exactly what kinds of homeopathics they are taking in order to prevent an adverse reaction that might occur when the homeopathics mixed with conventional medicine.

I went back to my executive producer and told him that I had spoken to 10 doctors, and none shared the angle of the story that we intended to put on the air. He told me to get on the phone and call the 11th doctor — and if need be the 12th — until I found one who shared our point of view and was willing to say so on camera.

Here is how ethic plays into this situation. Let's say I did that and on the 15th call, I found a doctor who supported our theory and was willing to say so on camera. Thus, I would put him on the air and he would spout that homeopathic medicine is bad. Viewers would automatically assume that this doctor represented the views of *all* doctors. They wouldn't know about the 14 doctors before him that had all disagreed. (That would be kept out of the story because it wouldn't support our theory.)

So let me ask you this: what if one of those viewers had cancer and was taking shark cartilage and it was actually helping. But when he saw the story, he discontinued the homeopathic medicine, and eventually died? Am I, in any way, responsible for his death?

If your answer is "no," I beg to differ with you. As a journalist, you have an enormous responsibility to your audience to give them accurate and unbiased information. To put a story like that on the air, knowing what you know, is totally irresponsible. To be clear, I am not talking about legalities — no one is going to come back and sue you for the story — but rather I am talking about ethics. If you want to work in TV news, then you must be completely accountable for what you put on the air.

So, what do you do in a case like this? The first thing you should do is discuss your feelings with the executive producer. Explain what you have found in doing research and what your concerns are for putting the story on the air. If the e.p. tells you that this is the story they want, and you feel that it violates your code of ethics, then ask if it's possible for the story to be reassigned to another producer. Sometimes this isn't possible because there simply isn't another producer available. If this is the case, you may need to make some tough choices. Do you go through with the story or not? I did not, but in doing so, I risked getting fired. But I was at a point in my career where I knew I could get another job. I also knew that there are some things in television that are worth being fired over.

It is a much harder decision when you're just starting out. The best thing you can do is weigh the pros and cons, and listen to your gut. All I can tell you is that if it feels wrong, it usually is.

In addition to having a responsibility to your audience, you also have a responsibility to the people that you interview and put on the air ... no matter what their situation. Over the course of my career, I have interviewed a great number of really cool people. I have also sat across from murderers, drug dealers, rapists, and other people who are so repulsively vile that my skin crawls. But my personal feelings always get pushed aside and I treat everybody equally. I am neither a judge nor a jury. I am a journalist and it is my job to get and give both sides of the story. If somebody doesn't want to talk — even if it's one of the so-called bad guys — I am always honest with that person and inform him that I am going to put the story on the air, whether he co-operates or not. If I only have the other person's side of the story, that's the only side that will make it on the air ... which means it's the only side the general public will hear.

With today's technology, it is actually possible in an edit bay to put words in people's mouths or even switch the order of what they said. This is rarely done, and when it is, it is almost always to insert a word where there may have been an audio dropout. Needless to say, you have an obligation to put forth not only what people say, but also to keep their intent intact. It is a big-no-no to chop somebody's sound bite in mid-sentence if you know that the rest of their sentence changes the meaning or clarifies the beginning.

I have known producers who have gotten in deep trouble for this. In one case, the person who was interviewed called the executive producer to complain that the producer had willfully misrepresented his intent, and he was going to file a lawsuit. The executive producer demanded that the producer give him the raw footage so he could see whether the guy's claims were true. It turned out that the guy was right, and that producer not only got in trouble with the station, her reputation was tarnished because these kinds of things get around.

> "Ethics are absolutely vital in news. Without ethics there can be no belief in what one is watching or reading. There cannot be any conflict of interest nor can there be any appearance of a conflict of interest. Pro teams give out tickets to news outlets ... writer writes truthful pro team story. Can I believe that or did the tickets have something to do with that report? Remember Ceasar's wife ... ". beyond reproach." — Bill Theodore, former NBC news producer and New England bureau chief

OTHER THINGS YOU MAY BE ASKED TO DO

As a staff producer at a network, there are other things you may be asked to cover from time to time. For example, if there is a really big news story, a network may opt to send you out in the field to produce "a live shot." A live shot means that there is no time delay — whatever is happening is being broadcast. Live shots are usually not that difficult (thankfully). As a producer, you show up and make sure that everything is in place. Is the camera crew set up and ready? Is the person that is going to be interviewed all ready to go? If there is talent, have they arrived? Is the satellite link all set? You get the picture. There are a lot of little details, but usually everyone does their job, so there aren't many problems. Of course, if there are, it is your job to resolve them. If you can't, you need to inform the network immediately.

The network will tell you when they are going to come to you. You will usually be on a phone to a producer in the control room in New York. A few moments before they are going to come to you live, that producer will punch up the shot on one of the preview monitors just to make sure they like what they see. Sometimes they will ask for a small change in the shot. If they have the proper feed, they can talk directly to the cameraman. If not, they tell you to relay the message. Sometimes the show producer will be giving you camera instructions while the camera is hot (meaning live). In relaying the message, you have to be careful to do it quietly and without bumping the cameraman, which would cause the live shot to shake. From there, you usually just stay on the phone throughout the interview in case there are any problems or instructions.

Depending on the scope of the story, you may also be asked to track people down and attempt to get them to talk to you on camera. An example of this is a high-profile court case. Once the jury renders a verdict, there are 12 of them that need to be tracked down and asked about it. If the case is high-profile enough, every news entity will be chasing them. Your job is to convince them to talk to whatever network you are with. Though you can't offer money, you can entice them by offering to whisk them away to New York, put them up in a great hotel, etc. You can also tell them that, by agreeing to give your network an exclusive, you will be able to help protect them from the rest of the media that is knocking down their doors.

Another task that might be assigned to you is a stakeout, which is about the most unglamorous job a producer can do. Stakeouts also usually happen in high-profile cases. The media finds out where the person is staying, and they basically wait outside the house or hotel for that person to emerge. This can be tedious-as-tedious-can-be if the person in question doesn't show his or her face for several days. The most difficult thing about stakeouts is that you can't let your guard down. You have to be on your toes and ready to go, the minute the person is on the go. Again, news happens fast, and if you miss it, you can't go back and restage it.

In addition to being assertive, the most important quality that you must have as a news producer is the ability to anticipate things in advance and to think on your feet. A few years back, I spent several weeks working as a freelance news producer for one of the networks covering the Louise Woodward case. (Remember the British nanny convicted of second-degree murder in the shaken-baby death of 8-month old Matthew Eapin?) After the judge reduced her sentence to involuntary manslaughter and set her free, my assignment was to stake out the house where she was staying. It was in a small but affluent Massachusetts neighborhood. I arrived, crew in tow, just after 6 a.m. There was no action all morning. By noon, the network called to say that Woodward was booked on a British Airways flight to London scheduled to depart Boston late that afternoon. They wanted my crew to get video of her in the car on the way to the airport. (We had another crew to get her coming out of the house, and yet another crew waiting at the British Airways terminal.) We did the math on when her flight was scheduled to leave and decided she would probably be heading out at around 2:00 p.m.

This all came a few short months after Princess Diana had been chased to her death by the paparazzi. I looked around at the hoards of media. It occurred to me the police were not about to let all of us get in our cars and chase Woodward to the airport. There was no question they would (rightfully) hold us back. I knew that there was only one road out of this small town. So, with the network's approval, I quickly pulled my crew out of the neighborhood. We waited for Woodward and her entourage closer to the edge of town. Shortly after 2:00, they drove past us: a van heavily surrounded by state police cars, with a couple of local motorcycle cops pulling up the rear. Upon seeing us, the motorcycle cops slowed to a crawl in an effort to put as much time and space between our van and hers. It didn't matter; we knew that two minutes up the road we would cross into the next town, and the local cops would lose jurisdiction. Sure enough, the motorcycle cops were forced to turn back, allowing my crew to get close to Woodward's van. We were the only media crew with her, and we shot her most of the way to the airport. That's an example of how as a news producer, you have to be on your toes, anticipate what might happen, and take appropriate action.

That story may not sound good to you. The idea of stakeouts and car chases turn a lot of people off and with good reason. But I have to tell you, in covering the Louise Woodward story, I never felt like part of the paparazzi. We weren't chasing a celebrity simply to get photos that would make us rich. This was an international murder trial. It was big news. As journalists, it was our job to cover it.

PART X

REALITY TELEVISION

WRITING FOR REALITY TELEVISION

REALITY TELEVISION IS NOT NEW

Reality television is a hybrid that combines the documentary and drama formats. It is unscripted television. Many people believe erroneously that *Survivor* was the first reality program ever to hit the airwaves. This is not even close to being true. Alan Funt first hit the air with *Candid Camera* in 1948, which was followed by a string of reality-driven game shows including *Truth Or Consequences* and *To Tell the Truth*. In 1973, PBS launched the ground-breaking *An American Family*, a 12-part series centered on Bill and Patricia Loud and their five children. The Louds were a real-life family whose problems played out on the small screen. Issues that America tuned in to see included problems within the marriage, and a son, Lance Loud, who is credited as being the first openly gay person ever to be on TV.

There is a whole host of other reality shows that came well before *Survivor* made its big ratings splash. These include shows like *Cops*, which follows real-life police officers out on the street, and even *The People's Court*, which captures the drama and intrigue of people suing and being sued in small claims court. So, while *Survivor* can't be credited with being the first reality program, it can, perhaps be credited with making the genre hot.

> "Television as we know it isn't going to exist in the future. It's going to be a bunch of fragmented networks and the investment in programming is going to drop, so the only way to continue investing a lot in programming is to gather up a lot of distribution sources or have the back end sold when you produce the front end. Or having reality to balance what you're going do with scripted programs." — Lucie Salhany, former chairman, FOX Broadcasting Company; founding president and former CEO, United Paramount Network (UPN)

WHY REALITY TELEVISION IS HERE TO STAY

Big surprise that after the success of *Survivor,* it seemed that every new program to hit the air was a reality show. Some were the absolute pits. Most people assumed that reality was just a phase that would eventually burn itself out. That didn't happen — nor is it likely to. Reality TV is cheaper to produce than series television, and thus, if a show takes off, it can bring a much bigger return in advertising dollars. With the mega success of shows like *American Idol* and *The Apprentice,* why wouldn't networks continue to pump it out?

> "When creating reality programming, we should always think of the audience ... is there an audience for this type of show? What is the promo? How will the network promote the show? What is the budget? Because most reality shows will never play in syndication or get a second run on the network, you need to make all your money in one episode. Like *Extreme Makeover* with Sears ... what is the 'Sears' for you show?" — Glenn Meehan, co-executive producer, *Little People, Big World*; producer, *Entertainment Tonight*

While some reality programming is downright bad, some of it is really very good.

What separates the good reality programs from the bad (besides talent and production value) is that the good ones tap into basic human interests and needs. Most explore a central question, and viewers tune in to see the answer. Let's take a look:

- *The Apprentice*: What if you could have it all? Who in America doesn't want to be as rich and as successful Donald Trump?
- *The Bachelor*: Can you find true love? At a core level, human beings want to believe in love and romance.
- *American Idol*: Who will become rich and famous? Self-explanatory. This is the American dream.
- *Trading Spouses*: Is the grass really greener? When things are mundane, most of us, at some point, fantasize about living someone else's life somewhere else.
- *Survivor*: Who is king of the jungle? This almost goes back to cavemen in that it's survival of the fittest ... and smartest.

As with all television, if you want to create reality programming, don't just regurgitate what we have already seen. Instead, see if you can come up with your own original idea. If you can hit on something that touches basic human needs or desires, you will be ahead of the game.

"Audiences like *The Apprentice* because they share a common bond. Everyone has been hired, most of us have been fired at some point, we have co-workers who are good, and co-workers who are bad and who seem to fail upward…. it's the universal themes in the workplace that the audience relates to." — Jay Bienstock, executive producer, *The Apprentice* and *Survivor*

WHY AMERICANS HAVE BECOME REALITY-OBSESSED

One of the reasons that reality has taken off has to do with America's obsession with fame. Not so very long ago, people only secretly dreamed of being stars. Deep down, most recognized it wouldn't happen; to be on TV, you had to an actor. But reality TV makes it so average people can be catapulted to celebrity. Hollywood has finally become accessible to the average bear. And the beauty of it is that you don't have to be an actor, you don't have to be particularly good-looking — heck, you don't even have to have talent. This is the exact reason that *America's Funniest Videos* has done so well for so long. It gives people a shot at 15 minutes of fame. But reality TV takes that 15 minutes and makes lasting celebrities out of people, and makes some of them very rich. Look at some of these household names: Bill Ransic, Kelly Clarkson, Bo Bice, Trista and Ryan, Rob and Amber. Because these people are real, we can relate to them — even admire some of them. It's the "real" factor that has us hooked. Viewers subconsciously think if it can happen to them, it could happen to anyone.

DOCUMENTARY VS. GAME SHOW

Most reality TV can be broken down into two categories: game and documentary. Examples of game reality shows are *The Apprentice, The Amazing Race,* and *Survivor,* to name just a few. These shows all revolve around various personal challenges and winning a contest. If you look closely at them, they are really game shows that have been taken out of the studio to be played in the field.

With the game show style of reality show, the editing doesn't have to be manipulated because the story is already there. Whatever happened, happened. As a producer, you can't change the outcome of who won or lost, who got voted off or fired.

The second type of reality show is more documentary-driven. Examples are shows like *Real World* and *Little People, Big World.* In these kinds of programs, the editing is much more important in shaping the story. It determines the emotional content of the show. As a producer, you have to take a point of view. Often, scenes will be rearranged from the order in which they actually occurred in order to make a story more compelling.

> "The biggest impact editing makes on a documentary-style show is to take the vast amounts of video shot and cut it down to broadcast length, while still making a comprehensible story. Often you'll hear reality stars complain about how they were edited. What they are really complaining about is the fact that so much of what happened to them had to be cut for time, so their entire point of view was not seen. When the shooting ratio is 40:1, it's true — most of your story is not going to air." — Jim Johnston, executive producer, *Real World* and *Starting Over*

REALITY IS A PRODUCER'S GAME

As with the TV news magazine, reality television is really run by producers. There is very little writing. However, there is still oodles of storytelling. In fact, one of the newer job titles kicking around the industry is story producer. This person takes daily notes from producers or directors and then sorts through umpteen hours of footage, looking for the elements that tie the story together.

> "I never approach reality as reality, but rather as drama. I look at how drama is structured. At the end of the day storytelling is what attracts audiences." — Jay Bienstock, executive producer, *The Apprentice* and *Survivor*

Reality television may be unscripted, but in its own unique way it feels much like a scripted drama ... which may be part of its wide appeal. It's drama, but the characters are real, which makes it all the more thrilling. The storylines often follow the basics of good drama writing. If done right, there should be a clear-cut beginning, middle, and end. Characters must grow or change in some way. Determining where the commercial breaks fall within your storyline is crucial. You have to look at the timing of each act, and make sure you end it in such a way that the viewer will stick around to see the outcome. On occasion, your big scene gets broken up into two acts, and you hang the audience in the middle of the scene.

> "As a story producer you usually have one great scene — a dispute, confrontation, or romantic entanglement — and from there you have to build your story. You search for scenes that set up this big scene, and then you look for the scenes that demonstrate how the characters have changed as a result of this big moment." — Jim Johnston, producer/executive producer, *Real World* and *Starting Over*

REAL COMPELLING CHARACTERS

Look closely and you'll see that good reality TV actually has primary and secondary characters. As with drama, these are the people that make or break the show. To illustrate this point, let's look at the difference between *The Bachelor* and *The Bachelorette*. While both shows share the same concept, *The Bachelor* is decidedly better. The reason is that the primary characters are women ... after the same man. This creates wonderful drama because women are notorious for wearing their hearts on their sleeves; they cry, scheme, manipulate, and get into catfights. The result is fabulously entertaining television. *The Bachelorette*, on the other hand, is a dud. This is because men guard their hearts. Therefore, no matter how great the primary characters are, you simply won't get high-charged emotion and drama.

The Apprentice is a show that has been hugely successful in creating secondary characters. While clearly the Donald is the star (along with the contestants) George and Carolyn have emerged from the backseat with their own distinctive TV personalities. I clearly remember, in the show's early days, watching Carolyn. I thought, "who is this chick? She's a pretty blond who just kind of stands there holding a briefcase." For the life of me, I couldn't figure out what she was all about or how she had risen in the Trump Organization. And then one day it happened. One of the contestants set her off. Her mouth opened and she just put that person away. It was a fabulously bitchy moment that also revealed her intellect ... the kind of "must see TV" that is talked about the next day at water coolers. The producers clearly understood that this was something America wanted more of, because she has been strong ever since. As for George (and his cigars), what's not to love about him? George and Carolyn have evolved as such strong characters that I actually find myself feeling disappointed weeks when they aren't on. Apparently, I will be disappointed a lot in the coming season as the Donald has fired Carolyn. According to published reports, the reason for Carolyn's pink slip was that she was spending too much time as a rising star and not enough time doing the day-to-day tasks that Trump hired her to do. While I have no personal knowledge of how the Trump Organization works, or what Carolyn was or wasn't doing, I will say that from a television perspective, I believe her dismissal to be a mistake. Carolyn will be replaced the Donald's daughter, Ivanka. Though incredibly smart and polished, Ivanka cannot completely fill Carolyn's shoes because of the "bitch" factor. Carolyn could be as bitchy as she wanted to be. Ironically, Ivanka is at a disadvantage. The minute anything nasty comes out of her mouth, America will label her a spoiled rotten brat (which, by the way, she doesn't appear to be) and turn on her. So while Ivanka is certainly interesting to watch, through no fault of her own, she will never be free to stir things up in the same way that Carolyn and George could.

Most reality shows don't set up or utilize these kinds of secondary characters. And I think this is a big mistake because if you get the right people, they can really help build the show's identity.

If you are creating a show, you should try to include secondary characters.

> "Don't encumber the process with too many restrictions, such as attaching a host, producers, and friends. That's what we're here to do. Too many restrictions could tie up a good show. What if the network doesn't want to work with your talent?" — Gary Grossman, partner, Weller/Grossman Productions

HOW TO WRITE A TREATMENT FOR A REALITY TV SHOW

You can sell an idea for a reality show either by pitching it — or by writing a treatment. There is no real standard for treatments in reality television. The key is to get the idea across quickly and concisely. If you decide to pitch your idea, you should try to think creatively as to how you can best get the idea across in an entertaining way.

> "Many times we have a demo/sales reel to show during our pitch meetings. Right now we have a reality/game show that we are taking out. We play the game with the suits." — Glenn Meehan, co-executive producer, *Little People, Big World*; producer, *Entertainment Tonight*

THE ETHICS OF REALITY TELEVISION

In the past few years, I have heard tons of ideas for new reality shows. While most of them are interesting, there are always a handful that shock me by the creator's lack of common decency and morals. One that jumps to mind had been floating around Europe, with no takers (thankfully). Recognizing that it perhaps needed a small tweak (right!), the producers were going to take a closer look at it before trying to sell the concept in America. The show is called *Make Me a Mum.* The lowbrow concept is that men compete, hoping to be the top dog who gets to impregnate a woman who wants to be a mother. The show's producers originally intended to use a microscopic camera to record the fertilization. This is the kind of show that makes me embarrassed to tell people that I work in television.

I have heard concepts that range from giving homeless people a chunk of money to spend, to letting mental patients out of a hospital to see how they react in society without their medication. The list goes on. Let me remind you that if you want to work in reality television, the same rules of ethics apply as they do in any other kind of television. Sometimes it may not seem like they do ... but they do. Reality is not a license for irresponsibility.

PART XI

CHILDREN'S
TELEVISION

24

WRITING FOR MUNCHKINS AND RUGRATS

"Don't talk down to kids; they want to feel as if they are watching up."
—Henry Winkler, author of children's book series *Hank Zipzer*

Of all the different types of television I have had the privilege to work in, I am often asked which is my favorite. I have to say that while comedy is definitely the most fun, without a doubt children's television is the most rewarding. There is nothing like walking out of the office at the end of a (long) day feeling like the work you have done may make a difference in the life of a child.

Children's programming is also by far the most difficult kind of television to create, write, and produce. It is much harder than comedy. In comedy, even if every joke isn't perfect, the audience will usually forgive and stay with you ... at least for a while. In children's programming, the audience is totally impatient and unforgiving. If every aesthetic, every bar of music, every story beat, every piece of dialogue, and every transition isn't completely perfect, the audience will quickly toddle away and nine times out of ten, they won't come back. As a writer/producer, you have to capture a child's attention immediately and then hold it. This is extremely hard to do.

"A certain level of visual stimulation is a necessity. As always, content is key, but you have to find a way to mix the two together. Visual stimulation can open the child's mind to the other aspects of your show and make it easier for solid content to work its way in. There is nothing wrong with education being entertaining. And sometimes to accomplish your educational goals, you need some visual flair. Visual storytelling is paramount nowadays. But the key is to use it to your advantage." —Paul Serafini, supervising producer, *ZOOM* and *Fetch*!

WHAT GOOD CHILDREN'S PROGRAMMING
SHOULD ACCOMPLISH

Good children's programming should be a combination of education and entertainment, sewn seamlessly together so as not to appear preachy. Programs can teach things like math, science, art, literacy, and music; equally important, they can teach crucial life lessons by breaking down racial, social, and gender stereotypes. Additionally, a solid children's show will tap into a child's natural curiosity, encourage creativity, and stretch imagination. Children's programming should be void of sex and violence, and proper language is a must at all times.

Pacing in children's programming is crucial. In order to keep children engaged, segments should not be too long. Learning can be explored through various channels, including song, dance, art, animation, live action, and of course fun characters.

The overall tone of the show is crucial in children's television. Speaking directly to children is absolutely key in creating a successful children's show. Often, there is a tendency for writers to talk *down* to children. As adults, we tend to think kids won't get it. The truth is, more often then not, children understand way more than we give them credit for.

> "You can't make a children's program without teaching. Even if you aren't trying to teach, children are learning aesthetics. If there's music in the show, even if it's not the main focus, you're teaching music. If it's a show with conflict resolution—you are teaching conflict resolution … but it's how you handle it. Are you teaching conflict/resolution in a positive way?"—Kate Taylor, executive producer *Fetch!* and *Peep and the Big Wide World*

BRAND LOYALTY

In programming aimed at adults, the goal is always to create a show that will be around for years. You can put a program like *Law & Order* on the air and, if it is well-written and has a great cast, the audience will remain loyal, coming back season after season.

Building brand loyalty in children's programming is considerably more challenging. The audience is much more fragmented. The reason for this is that content has to be both age-specific and age-appropriate. While a show like *The Wiggles* may be revered by two-year-olds, that brand loyalty is only good for a couple of years. By the time that same child hits four, *The Wiggles* cool factor starts to wear off and the child moves on to the next program. What's interesting to a two-year old will not hold the attention of a five-year-old. Therefore, when creating children's programming, the key is to know the age range of your target audience. While the following age ranges aren't etched in stone, they can be used as a rough guideline to help you zero-in on precisely who you are creating programming for.

- Under 2. Currently, there is controversy about television and this age range. A study released by the American Academy of Pediatrics suggests that children in this category who watch TV can later have attention deficit problems in school.
- Preschool (3 to 5). This is really the heart and soul of children's television. A lot of it tends to be focused on literacy and learning. It prepares kids for school.
- 5 to 7. This age group is commonly referred to as "Bridge Kids." This is a particularly difficult age range. The kids are in school and becoming exposed to lots of different things. They're not "babies" anymore, but they're still clearly children. Therefore, creating programming for them can be more than challenging.
- 8 to 12. These are known as "tweens." This is an area that could always use more good programming. This age range is becoming increasingly independent, and it's important to give them alternatives to some of the real-world pressures they face.

> "To successfully reach tweens, the writer needs to find kid-relatable issues that are emotional entry points for their audience. Never write down to kids. They will spot and reject condescension in a heartbeat. These shows are a safe haven for kids who are constantly bombarded with sexual and violent images. The challenge is to write shows that are smart and funny, while dealing with the constraints of language and content." — Marc Warren, executive producer, *That's So Raven* and *Cory in the House*

One of the most interesting things to keep in mind about age range is that children will often watch one level up from their target group. When I worked as a producer on the PBS show *ZOOM*, the target audience was tweens. I cannot begin to count how many parents would tell me that *ZOOM* was a show their five-year-old watched faithfully. At first I was surprised because some of the content seemed too sophisticated. But the more I thought about it, the more I realized how it made perfect sense. Little kids never want to be little kids … they want to be big kids. Therefore, a five-year-old doesn't want to watch the shows he watched as a baby. He wants to watch the shows that big kids watch. *ZOOM*'s cast had lots of "big kids." That's why little kids liked it, perhaps even more than its tween target audience. For little kids, it's all about keeping up.

"Writing aimed at children should be as smart, as witty, and as thoughtful as writing aimed at adults. Too many shows for kids are either very preachy— 'this is how GOOD children behave'—or dumbed down, as if kids shouldn't hear big words, or be troubled by emotionally complex material. Other sins include being saccharine sweet, or didactic, or cliché-ridden, or boring. The best shows for kids recognize that kids are smart and have interesting inner lives."—Kathy Waugh, head writer, *Peep and the Big Wide World*

DUAL AUDIENCES

Perhaps one of the nice things about children's programming is that parents will sometimes sit down and watch with their kids. A shared viewing experience between parent and child is wonderful, of course. It does, however, add another layer to the mix because it creates a "dual" audience. The challenge for writers and producers is to generate programming that simultaneously operates on two different levels. On one level, it has to be written and produced for kids. But on a whole different level, it should speak to and be interesting enough to hold an adult's interest. Writing for a dual audience takes an enormous amount of creativity and talent. However, writers and producers who have mastered this art form can really create a gold mine.

CONTENT IS KEY

In children's programming, content is perhaps the single most important element. Content can be difficult because children are so impressionable. Everything that goes on the air must be carefully scrutinized. Is the content age-appropriate? Does it send a positive message? Is it void of sex and violence? As a writer or a producer, remember you must also look closely at things like language and even safety issues.

Perhaps one of the things that can be most difficult in terms of creating content is that parents can have vastly different philosophies on child-rearing. Often this goes hand-in-hand with geographical location. I think it is fairly safe to say that parents who live in big cities like New York and Los Angeles are probably overall more liberal than parents who live in places like Alabama or Tennessee. This can get extremely complicated when writing and producing for a national audience.

Take, for example, the PBS children's series, *Postcards from Buster*. The show, created by Marc Brown (*Arthur*), features Arthur's friend Buster, a darling little animated bunny who travels all over the country with his pilot father. Each episode takes place in a different location where Buster meets real (not animated) kids and families, and gets a taste of many different cultures.

The show is to be applauded for celebrating diversity and encouraging tolerance. However, when it comes to content, I am certain that the show's writers and producers must face some difficult decisions. For the sake of argument, let's say on one of his travels Buster meets a biracial family. Across America there are parents who are extremely liberal and want their children exposed to absolutely everything right out of the gate. They are completely at ease with their children being shown that people of different races can fall in love, marry, and have families. But that's only one half of the audience; the other half is at the complete opposite end of the spectrum. They do not want their children exposed to mixed marriages under any circumstances. Finding a happy medium between these two groups can be next to impossible. It also creates an interesting dilemma for writers and producers as to where and when to draw the line. While some parents may not want their children exposed to interracial marriage, other parents may not want their children exposed to same-sex couples, and still others may oppose Muslims or Mormons. So how do you effectively produce a show that promotes diversity if you don't show diversity?

Postcards from Buster is only one small example. The problem of pleasing parents exists on any number of levels. Take the holidays. Not so long ago, writers and producers could easily pump out a Christmas episode or a Christmas special. These days, it's not so simple. While some parents look forward to sitting down with their children and watching shows with Christmas trees and Santa Claus, others find zooming in on one religious holiday highly objectionable. The same can even be said for curriculum. Some parents only want their children to watch programs that are completely educational. Other parents see nothing wrong with letting children watch programs that are entertainment-driven.

The challenge is in meshing these vastly opposing parental viewpoints in order to bring in the greatest number of viewers. Unfortunately, I don't have the answer. I think as a writer or a producer you have to recognize that you can't please everyone—and so you should focus on putting out the best and most appropriate content for your particular show. If you spend your time trying to please everyone, I can almost guarantee that the show will suffer an identity crisis and will most likely fail in the end. At some point, parents have to be partners and take some responsibility. They have to investigate and clearly understand what programs they are allowing their children to watch. If they feel the content isn't right for their child, perhaps they shouldn't tune in.

SELLING YOUR CHILDREN'S SHOW

The best way to sell a children's show is to meet with producers and pitch your concept. Pitches for children's programming can be more creative than pitches for series television. Here are some elements a good pitch might include

- Convey the feel/tone of the program.
- Convey the curriculum.

- Bring along any artwork.
- Create a short demo reel if you can afford it.

As with all television, your chances of actually selling a children's show will significantly increase if you get experience working in this arena. If children's television is where you ultimately want to be, I would encourage you to try get a job on a children's show. This will give you firsthand experience as to how children's programming is produced. It may also open doors for you in terms of knowing producers to pitch your program idea to. Additionally, you should watch and study as many children's shows that are on the air as you possibly can. Tune in regularly to PBS Kids, Disney, Discovery Kids, and Nickelodeon. If you are going to sell a children's show, I cannot over-emphasize how you need to become an expert in this area.

> "There's no such thing as a bad idea, and there's hardly an original idea, and some shows are a conglomerate of ideas. There's new formats, there's old formats. It all comes down to execution. You can have an original format that's badly executed or you can have the most obvious idea in the world and execute it brilliantly." — Kate Taylor, executive producer *Peep and the Big Wide World* and *Fetch!*

THE ONE-MINUTE-THIRTY-SECOND GRIND

To give you an appreciation of just how much time and energy go into a seemingly simple segment of a children's program, I am going to walk you through a story I produced for *ZOOM*. It was the summer of 2002, and America was slowly and apprehensively approaching the one-year anniversary of September 11th. *ZOOM* was planning a one-hour special to help kids deal with it.

Amy Podolsky, the show's researcher, called and said the show wanted to do a piece on kids who had a parent in the military, away fighting the war on terror. The catch was, the parent had to be coming home in the next couple of weeks so we could shoot the actual homecoming. We put feelers out to all branches of the military to see what units might be returning from Afghanistan within the next few weeks. As luck would have it, the U.S.S. JFK aircraft carrier and its protective group of battleships would soon be returning to Jacksonville, Florida, after 6 months at war. The Navy gave us permission to shoot the homecoming.

Deep down, I was glad to be working with the Navy. My father had been a Navy man in World War II. And only 11 months earlier, I had returned to my Cape Cod roots to attend a memorial service for Jerry DeConto, a Navy captain killed at the Pentagon on September 11th. A few years ahead of me in high school, DeConto was the star soccer player with a dynamic personality, and every girl had a crush on him. After high school, he attended the Naval

Academy in Annapolis, worked his way up to the rank of captain, and was given command of the U.S.S. Simpson. At the time of his death, DeConto was in charge of the Navy Command Center; when the plane slammed into the Pentagon, he was working to co-ordinate the Navy's response to the attacks on the World Trade Center. As I began to put the *ZOOM* story together, the tragedy of DeConto and everyone else who was lost that day weighed heavily on my mind.

Once I had the Navy's blessing to shoot the story, my next order of business was to find a child who was energetic and articulate enough to go on camera (*ZOOM* only used kids on camera … no adults) and talk about what it was like to have a parent away from home, actually fighting a war. Again, this was less than a year after September 11th, and the war on terror was an extremely emotional subject … especially for a child. The Navy helped me find a boy whose father was on the U.S.S. Hue City, one of the battleships assigned to guard the massive aircraft carrier.

I arrived in Jacksonville a day before the JFK, met with my crew, picked up a military escort, and went to Naval Station Mayport to meet the child. For the next 8 hours we shot all over the base. The following morning, we tagged along as the boy, his mother, and little brother went down to the docks to wait for his father's ship. Thousands of people — mothers and fathers, sisters and brothers, sons and daughters, aunts and uncles, cousins, and grandparents crowded the streets, each waiting for a loved one they hadn't seen in at least 6 months. American flags were everywhere, as were bands playing patriotic music. My cameraman, who had served in Viet Nam, was thrilled with the pomp and circumstance. He recounted how his own homecoming had been drastically different; there had been no bands or banners — only Americans who spit on him.

Large cement barriers held back the crowd and limited their view of the sea. While waiting for the ships, I spoke to some of the families. They were, of course, elated to have their loved ones returning home, but at the same time, many worried about the future. It was 7 full months before the beginning of "Shock and Awe," but on base there were rampant rumors that the United States had ordered a staggering number of body bags and that the Navy was building jet engines like they were going out of style. For these families, it wasn't a question of whether or not the United States would invade Iraq, but rather a question of when.

A short while later, the military escort pulled me away from the crowd, where I would have a better view of the wide-open ocean. He told me to keep my eyes on the horizon. Within moments, I could make out the vague outline of our ships returning from war. It was hard not to get emotional. As we waited for the ships to reach the port, I happened to glance behind me. In the crowd was a woman holding a baby who couldn't have been more than 3 months old. And then it hit me … the unit had been gone for 6 months.

"Your husband is going to meet his baby for the first time, isn't he?" I asked.

She nodded. Moments later, I watched as her husband got off the ship and she handed him his child. He didn't make a sound, but the tears streaming down his face spoke volumes. Away at war, he had missed so much: the birth of his child, the first cry, the first smile. So many firsts gone forever. At that moment I clearly understood the true sacrifice that military families make in order to protect our freedom. It was a message I wanted to share with children in America.

Back at WGBH, I was excited to get the story written, edited, and ready for air. Then the producers dropped a bombshell: they told me that the 9-11 special was running long, and that in order to come in on time, they needed to cut some stories. While some of the stories were only applicable to September 11th, there were a few stories like mine that could be easily inserted into a regular *ZOOM* episode. Therefore, they had decided to pull my story out of the special and hold it for the upcoming season. But I had so much passion for this particular story and so much respect for the people I had met, that I decided to see if I could change the producers' minds.

I wrote e-mail after e-mail, stating my case, all but begging for my story to be included in the special. This was extremely risky. As a field producer, my job is to get the story in the field. Period. By asking them to reconsider, I was completely overstepping my bounds. But as I have said, passion can be contagious. The producers were gracious; they listened patiently and told me they would see what they could do.

A few days later, Jim Johnston, one of the producers, called and told me that if the story were to work for the September 11th special, there were a couple of things that I needed video-wise to make the piece top-notch. This meant returning to Jacksonville immediately. The September 11th air date was looming. In a few days, the show was scheduled to be fed to PBS affiliates. Time was running out. But reshooting was not nearly as easy as it sounds. The original shoot had been in mid-August on two crystal-clear days loaded with bright sunshine. It was now early September, and the contrast in lighting was huge … not to mention that the boy was now back at school, so the shoot could not take place until late afternoon. This would make it very difficult, if not impossible to match the shots to the video I already had.

The other complication was that I couldn't go back to Jacksonville because the day of the shoot was also my first day as a professor at Emerson College. So I had to give my crew long-distance instructions and hope for the best. If that weren't enough stress, the night before the reshoot, the cameraman called from Jacksonville. He said he didn't know how to break it to me, but Gustav, a category-two hurricane, was sitting off the Florida coast and was due to blow in the next day. I realized then that I had done everything humanly possible to get this story on the air. It was now up to God and the powers of the universe.

The following evening, my cameraman called with the news that Gustav brought rain to Jacksonville. But, oddly he said, when it came time to actually shoot, the sky miraculously cleared. A few days later, I stumbled out of bed at 5 a.m. and turned on my computer. I immediately got an IM from Paul Serafini, one of the show's producers.

He had been up all night, overseeing the final edit on the special. He said he was happy to inform me that my story was in. While I was thrilled, I wasn't completely surprised. I have learned in television (and in life) that when you have passion for something and you commit yourself wholeheartedly to that passion, things often happen that in your wildest dreams you never thought could or would.

For the record, the *ZOOM* story came in at 1 minute and 30 seconds. It took a few days to set up, 3 days to shoot, 1 day to write the script, and 2½ days to edit. When it hit the air, I am sure viewers saw it as a nice little story. But for me, it was much more than that. It was a personal tribute to Captain DeConto, to my cameraman, to the Navy man who cried when he met his child, to those who would be called to Iraq, and most especially to those who would return in flag-draped caskets.

It was my private "thank you" to all the men and women — past, present, and future — willing to put on a uniform and march into hell to protect my rights both as a writer and a woman. Of course, the audience would be privy to none of this. And it makes no difference. All that matters is that in those 90 seconds, I got the message out to kids that those who protect our freedom often do so at great personal cost.

Of all the television out there, I think children's television is by far the best. It is the one place you really can have an impact. You really can make a difference.

PART XII

THE BUSINESS SIDE OF TELEVISION

HOW TO GET AN AGENT

WHY YOU NEED AN AGENT

If you are going to work as a writer in the industry, you will need to find an agent to represent you. Besides your own personal connections, it is the primary way to get your material submitted to shows and read. Networks and studios do not accept unsolicited scripts, and for good reason: they are afraid of being sued. Litigation is too costly and too time consuming.

In the past, I have told many a new writer how to find agent in order to get their work submitted to shows. While most listen, there always seems to be a small handful who finish a spec script and send it off to the show. These writers actually believe that their scripts are so good that producers will make an exception, read their work (risking a lawsuit), and immediately put their script into production. What these writers don't realize is that if your script isn't sent through the proper channels, it won't even be opened, let alone read.

Lots of people out there who want to write television are untrained. So, let's say a writer from Nebraska sends a script to *The Simpsons* in which Marge goes to the dentist. Let's also say that this was the worst script ever written, but down the road, the producers decide to do a story that has Homer going to the dentist. The two stories are apples and bananas. They have nothing to do with each other. But the writer from Nebraska decides to sue, claiming, "my script had a dentist in it. You stole my idea." If you go by this, virtually every topic would be off limits to the producers because there would always be someone ready to file a lawsuit. This is why producers will only accept scripts that come through an agent, manager, or attorney.

Another thing about having an agent is that producers and executives seem to think that it separates the men from the boys and the women from the girls. Agents are people who know scripts. Therefore, if an agent has agreed to represent a writer, the feeling is that the script will be probably be good – or at the very least, professional.

In addition, having an agent allows you to focus solely on the creative side of your career, while your agent handles the business side for you. Most writers I know are not top negotiators and/or business people. That kind of work takes a whole other set of skills that most creative people lack. For this reason, it's good to have someone who can be a real shark when it comes to getting you a good deal.

> "First ... at the very foundation ... there's the question of 'are they talented?' Second ... once I have committed to their well-being and made them successful, will they appreciate the value of what I've done and remain loyal to me? Third ... will I be able to put them in a room with a buyer?"— Richard Arlook, partner, head of motion picture literary, The Gersh Agency, on what he looks at when signing a writer.

WHAT AGENTS ACTUALLY DO

A good agent will be a partner in your career. He or she will strategize about the long-term rather than just about getting one script sold. Agents do a variety of things. First, and most importantly, they will introduce you and your work to the industry. They will attempt to get producers to meet with you and give you a chance. Agents pound the pavement for their clients on a daily basis. They meet with producers and executives over breakfast, lunch, dinner, drinks, Saturday night parties, and Sunday afternoon barbecues, constantly talking you up. Agents send out your scripts and they field offers on your behalf. They will also negotiate your deals. It is a lot of work. If you don't make money, they don't make money since they work on commission. This is why it is hard to get an agent when you are just starting out. From the agent's point of view, it is very difficult to get a new writer up and running. This is because television is all about writing credits.

HOW MUCH DOES AN AGENT COST?

It doesn't cost anything upfront for an agent. However, once you sign with an agency, your agent will take a commission of 10%, which is industry standard. This applies to everything you make, with the exception of residuals. So let's say you sell an episode (story and teleplay) of *Two and a Half Men*. Warner Bros. will send the payments, which eventually add up to the current WGA minimum of $20,956 for story and teleplay to your agent. Your agent deposits the checks into a trust account. The agent's fee is deducted and the agency sends you a check for the difference.

Normally, writers don't mind paying agents if they feel that their agents are working hard on their behalf. It can get a little sticky though, if you feel that your agent hasn't been giving you much time and attention, and so you go out and get the gig on your own through your own connections. It doesn't matter how the work comes to you — whether you line it up or your agent does — as long as you are under contract with an agency, your agent is entitled to the commission.

DON'T PAY PEOPLE TO READ YOUR WORK

Agents do not charge you to read your work. Reading scripts is a courtesy. They are hoping that your script will be phenomenal, that they will sign you and help you build a powerhouse career from which both of you will profit. The rule is very simple: if an agent asks for money to read your script, run. There is a good chance that person is not legitimate.

REFERRALS ARE THE WAY TO GO

Funny as it may sound, most agents are like networks and studios in that they don't take unsolicited scripts. Don't waste your time blindly sending your scripts to different agents, thinking they will be read. They won't.

The best and most common way to get an agent is through a referral. This means that you have a connection to another writer or someone in the industry who is in a position to recommend you to an agent. Referrals can happen in a couple of ways. First, the person who is referring you picks up the phone and sells you as a writer to the agent. This is the best way because the agent is hearing from someone already in the business how talented you are. Then you will send your scripts to the agent, who will give you a read.

The second way is that the person referring you tells you to call the agent and to use that person's name to get you in the door. While this is less than ideal, it's still an in. In this case, call the agent yourself. When the assistant answers, say something like, "I'm calling for Joe Petersen. He doesn't know me, but I have been referred by Bill Olsen. I am a writer looking for representation, and Bill seems to think that Joe and I would be a good fit, so I'd like to talk him about that." The assistant will either put you through or take your phone number. With a referral, you can almost always count on getting a call back. If, for some reason the agent doesn't call you within a few days, don't be afraid to call again.

WHY WRITERS CAN BE PROTECTIVE ABOUT THEIR AGENTS

You have to understand that when a writer refers you to his or her agent, it is a really big favor. Therefore, you never want to tell a writer just casually, "Hey, I've got a new spec script. Would you mind giving it to your agent?" You need to first ask the writer to read your script. The reason this is important is that if your script isn't up to par and the writer gives it to the agent, the agent may second-guess the writer. It may also make it so the next time the writer wants to refer someone, the agent won't be so quick to say "yes."

The best thing that you can do is ask the writer to read your work. Hopefully, he or she will like it. At that point you can say something like, "I'm glad you like it, because I have worked very hard on it. I feel like I am ready to get an agent. Would there be anyone you could possibly refer me to?" That is a better way to go about it, because it doesn't back the writer into a corner if in fact he doesn't want to refer you to his agent. It also opens up other possibilities. Most working writers know various agents. It's possible that they know someone who would be even better for you than their own agent.

> "Beware when an agent promises they can absolutely sell your script or get you work. No one can promise you that. The reality is agents read a lot of great scripts that they think they can sell. Your script may go out to 50 people. You may get 25 meetings. But if nothing comes of them, you may have to go back and write a new script because at that point you are yesterday's news."— Richard Arlook, partner, head of motion picture literary, The Gersh Agency

CHOOSING AN AGENT WHO'S RIGHT FOR YOU

A lot of new writers dream of being signed by some of the bigger agencies like CAA, ICM, and William Morris. Being at one of these agencies may in fact not be the best move for you when you are just venturing out. More than ever, when your career is just beginning, you need an agent who is really going to invest time in getting your work out there and really pushing you as a new writer. Let's say you go with a bigger agency that represents writers on the level of Marc Cherry, J.J. Abrams, and Larry David. How much time do you think the agency will put in working for you vs. working for the other, more established writers? It is very easy for a new writer to get lost in the shuffle at some of these bigger agencies. The only real advantage is that if you are represented by an agency that has show runners, your agent will be able to get your scripts into those hands for a read. Other than that, you might be better off starting at a smaller agency with an agent who has the time and enthusiasm to really get your work out there and get you up and running as a writer.

LOS ANGELES OR BAR HARBOR? DOES IT MATTER WHERE YOUR AGENT IS?

Since the TV business takes place primarily in Los Angeles, it would behoove you to get an agent in L.A. This becomes even more important if you don't live in Southern California, although more and more if you don't live in the Los Angeles area, agents are reluctant to sign you. If you are unable to get an agent in Los Angeles, your next best bet is New York. If you are unsuccessful in either of these cities, I do not recommend going with an agent in another state. The primary reason is that when you are starting out, you probably don't have a ton of connections. Therefore, you need an agent with lots of contacts. If your agent is in East Osh Kosh, how much contact does that person really have with the entertainment industry? The answer is, probably not as much as an agent in Southern California. You need an agent who is out there every day, pounding the pavement for you. This can't be done long distance. I can also tell you that when scripts come in from out-of-state agents, unless they're from a New York agent, they simply don't have the same clout as scripts coming from L.A.-based agents. This opinion may not be right and it may not be fair, but it definitely exists.

> "Know the show you are trying to spec. Know the characters, know the premise, know the kinds of stories they do. A few years back, I took home a pile of spec scripts to read. Most of them were *Frasiers*. I would say 8 out of 10 had stories that revolved around Eddie the dog. *Frasier* wasn't a show about Eddie the dog, it was a show about Frasier Crane."— Beth Bohn, senior vice president, Television Literary Department, Agency for Performing Arts

AGENTS WHO TAKE UNSOLICITED SCRIPTS

If you are not having any luck getting an agent, you can obtain from the Writers Guild of America a list of agents who take unsolicited scripts. While many experts suggest going this route right off the bat, I put it more in the "last resort" category. Good agents are industry insiders who have breakfast, lunch, dinner, cocktails, and attend weekend barbecues with key players in the industry who have the power to hire you. Good agents are hustlers. Their days are jam-packed trying to get their clients work. So, when I come across an agent who has time to poke through the mounds of unsolicited material that must arrive in the office each and every day, I wonder how much time that takes away from selling the clients that are already on the roster.

In fairness to agents who take unsolicited material (and God bless them), it could be that they have assistants who actually work their way through the pile. But it could also be that the agency is new, and thus looking to build a solid clientele. This, too, is a red flag for me. As a writer who is new to the industry, you probably don't bring a lot of contacts to the table. Therefore, you would benefit from having a more established agent.

> "Get a job in production. Being a P.A. or a writer's assistant is a perfect training ground. It allows you to observe the process with people who know what they're doing. It allows you to prove yourself and to get known as someone with unique ideas who's fun to be around. Generally writers who get jobs at the starting level on any show are already known by the staff or show runners. This tends to get you noticed. It can be the first step toward getting an agent."— Beth Bohn, senior vice president, Television Literary Department, Agency for Performing Arts

DO YOU NEED A MANAGER?

If you aren't having any luck getting an agent, you might try to get a manager. Studios and networks will accept scripts that are submitted through managers. A manager acts like an agent in many ways, but there are a few differences that set them apart. In California, agents, like lawyers, are licensed by the state. Managers are not. Agents can negotiate deals, which is something managers legally cannot do. Therefore, while a manager can send out your script and push producers to meet with you and hire you, you will still need to hire an agent or an attorney to negotiate your deal. Unlike agents who receive a standard 10%, managers can set their own rates. You could pay anywhere from 10–20%. That may not sound like a lot, but then you have to add in what you will be paying to an attorney or 10% to an agent. It can end up costing you a lot. However, it may be money well spent if it lands you a job. Additionally, most managers have relationships with agents, so it is quite possible that a manger could help you get signed by an agent, and the two could work quite well together for you.

> "Embrace the agent who tells you what you need to hear as opposed to the agent who tells you what you want to hear."— Richard Arlook, partner, head of Motion Picture Literary, The Gersh Agency

ENTERTAINMENT ATTORNEYS

In the event that you can't get an agent or a manager, you can always hire an entertainment attorney to submit your work. This is also an approved avenue for which studios and networks will accept scripts. An entertainment attorney should be a last resort, however, as they will charge you upfront for any time that they spend working for you. This can add up to a lot of money … especially for a writer who is out of work.

QUERYING AGENTS

While most agents won't take unsolicited scripts, it is possible to get them to solicit your script by writing what is known as a query letter. This is really a marketing letter, where you introduce yourself and your work to an agent and ask that agent to give you a read. Generally, query letters are used more for feature film scripts than for scripts in series television. I have to be honest: I don't have much faith in query letters. In my 25 years in the business, I only recall once ever hearing about a query letter that got someone signed.

However, if you want to give it a try, here is what a good query letter should do: entice an agent to want to read your script. Therefore, you should write a paragraph that talks about your work. Don't go into lots of detail. You just want to whet the agent's appetite. You should also write a brief paragraph about yourself. Bring up anything you can that might be relevant, such as industry experience, awards, connections, or your college degree if you attended a school that is well-thought-of in the industry. You should then come right out and ask the agent if you can send your script. To make it easy for the agent to reply, always include a self-addressed, stamped envelope with your query letter.

When writing query letters, it is important not to appear desperate and/or needy. The key is to present yourself as a professional writer with great writing samples and a seriousness of purpose about getting work in the industry.

> "When you send a script or query letter to a producer or agent, you've only got one shot. If they turn you down, it doesn't matter how good you make it later … they are not going to read it again. Therefore, when a professional rejects your material, you MUST look at that material very carefully before you send it out again. Sometimes they'll give you a reason, like the writing is flat or the characters weren't interesting or different enough. If you're lucky enough to get any kind of critique, you have to listen to it, reread your stuff, and see if there's any truth in it at all. If you find that there is, you have to rewrite before you send it out again. Remember, there are no second chances. If you have sent out 1–15 query letters with no bites, you should sit down and look over your letter again. If it's not getting you anywhere, you may need to rewrite it." — Adrienne Armstrong, writer, *Charles in Charge*

SAMPLE QUERY LETTERS: GOOD AND BAD

Below is an example of a poorly written query letter:

December 1st, 2006

Ms. Zoe Schmoe
The Zoe Schmoe Agency
999 Sunset Blvd., Suite 202
Los Angeles, CA 90039

Dear Ms. Schmoe:

I am seeking representation on my screenplay, *Zachary's Truth,* a small family drama about a troubled 16-year-old boy, who ends up searching for his natural parents. I am hoping you will want to represent me, as I have already sent out 15 query letters to other agents, all of whom have turned me down. They all say that the story doesn't feel fresh or original. I disagree, and I am sure you will, too, once you have read my script.

While I am a banker by trade, it has always been my secret desire to get a movie made. I would love to get out of the 9-to-5 grind and into a more creative profession. I feel certain that *Zachary's Truth* could be my ticket.

I would love to send you a copy of the script. Please let me know if this would be possible.

Thank you for your consideration. I look forward to hearing from you soon.

Sincerely,

Martie Cook

Martie Cook

Now, let's try to rewrite it, making both the screenwriter and screenplay seem more marketable.

December 1st, 2006

Ms. Zoe Schmoe
The Zoe Schmoe Agency
999 Sunset Blvd., Suite 202
Los Angeles, CA 90039

Dear Ms. Schmoe:

My first screenplay, *Zachary's Truth,* is a drama about a deeply troubled 16-year-old adoptee, who is at odds with his adopted family. On the surface, Zach is a punk constantly in trouble at school and with the law. Enter a nonconventional therapist who concludes the only way Zach can be made whole is to find one or both of his natural parents. And so begins the search. When Zach finally comes face-to-face with his natural mother — the one woman he thought could "save" him — he uncovers "the truth" about his past and in the process comes to realize it is better to go through life with a family that loves and wants him, rather than one that does not.

While there have been movies on the subject of adoption, most tend to end with the predictable and heart-warming mother-and-child reunion. Being an adopted child myself, I can tell you in the real world of adoption, this is not always the case. *Zachary's Truth* offers a fresh take on this subject. It is a highly personal story, charged with emotion. I am certain this comes through in the writing, as the script has already placed in the Massachusetts Screenwriting competition and in the prestigious Chesterfield Writers Program, the only two competitions to which I have submitted it.

I feel strongly the timing could not be better for a story that focuses on the complexities of adoption. I am sure you are aware of how many celebrities are adopting children these days, which means the script could be well-received when it comes to casting.

I believe it is a writer's duty to do his or her homework. Thus, I researched several MOWs such as *X* and *Y* that feel similar in terms of emotional content and tone. Most, if not all of these are scripted by writers represented by you. Therefore, I feel certain that you and I share the same sensibility, something that is extremely important to me in choosing an agent. This is the reason I am contacting you.

I would welcome the opportunity to share *Zachary's Truth* with you. Please let me know at your earliest convenience if this is a script you would be interested in taking a look at. I have enclosed an SASE for your convenience.

Thank you for your time and consideration. I look forward to hearing from you soon.

Sincerely,

Martie Cook

Martie Cook

MAKING SURE YOU ARE READY

Perhaps the biggest mistake that new writers make is to send their work out to an agent before it is completely polished and ready to be seen. For some reason young writers seem to have the mistaken impression that agents are there to work with them like writing partners, as in "here is my script, tell me what's wrong with it, I'll redo it and resubmit it to you." First off, you should never, ever submit your work to anyone — especially an agent — before it is ready. People will make judgments about you as a writer, and those judgments will stick. Agents are business partners, not writing partners. An agent will not read your script more than once. Therefore, it is crucial that it is the very best it can be before you send it out.

PATIENCE IS A VIRTUE

Getting an agent — even for writers with credits — is difficult but not impossible to do. Be prepared: it will likely take some time. It is quite possible that you will be turned down more than once before you get signed. Don't take it personally. Writing is a business. It isn't personal, even though sometimes it may feel that way.

Keep in mind that agents, while certainly educated in the business of scripts and screenwriting, are human beings. They aren't always right. The first screenplay I ever wrote took me 1 year to complete. I was working a production job at Universal, which left me little time to write and rewrite. When I finally finished, I sent it to my agent. Here is what she had to say: "This is probably the worst thing I have ever read. If you weren't my client, I wouldn't have bothered to finish it." She went on to tell me that in her opinion none of the script was salvageable, but if I was determined maybe she could recommend a script doctor that I could pay to work with me.

I wanted to cry. Instead, I thanked her for her time and her thoughts. It is important always to be professional. I did not change a word in the script. Instead I went out and shopped for a new agent. That exact same script got me signed at a better agency, placed in national competitions, opened doors to meetings with Academy Award-winning directors, and was eventually optioned at Universal.

So, hard as it may be, try to refrain from feeling devastated if and when agents reject you. The idea is to keep moving forward and to find an agent that understands you and your material … an agent that you really click with. And know that if your work is good and if you keep putting it out there, it is very likely that you will eventually find representation.

SHOULD YOU PUT YOUR SCRIPT ON WEB SITES?

There are a lot of Web sites where writers can post loglines, synopses and/or full scripts. I am not a fan of putting work up on a Web site for the whole wide world to see. Of the many working writers I know, I am unaware of any who got jobs and/or agents by posting their material on the Internet.

Often these sites promise that producers, executives, and agents continuously troll them, looking for new material and undiscovered talent. This may or may not be true, depending on the Web site. Even if agents and producers genuinely do look, after all of your hard work you open yourself up for anyone on the planet to steal your ideas. There is absolutely no way to protect yourself from this.

CHECKLIST FOR GETTING AN AGENT

- Do I have at least two good scripts to show?
- Are my scripts the best they can possibly be?
- If possible, have I asked a writer to take a look at my work?
- Have I registered my work with the WGA?

THE WRITERS GUILD
OF AMERICA

WHAT IS THE WRITERS GUILD OF AMERICA?

The Writers Guild of America, more commonly know by insiders as the WGA, is the main union for television and screenwriters. It is one of the three largest creative unions, including the DGA (Directors Guild of America) and SAG (Screen Actors Guild), in the entertainment industry.

The WGA is broken down into two branches: (1) WGA East, headquartered in New York, is for writers living east of the Mississippi and (2) WGA West, in Los Angeles, is for members living west of the Mississippi.

HOW DO YOU BECOME A MEMBER?

There are very strict rules for getting into the WGA. I could not begin to explain them here, so instead I will refer you to the Writers Guild Web site at www.wga.org. I can tell you, however, that to get in, there is a specifically defined credit system, and you must have accumulated 24 units of credit in the past 3 years. After you have met this requirement, you must then pay a one-time registration fee of $2500. Once you are a member, you will be assessed dues on a quarterly basis, which are based on how much money you have earned as a writer. This seems to be a fair way to do it, as writers who have pulled in mega salaries pay more than writers who are out of work.

If you want to work as a TV writer, eventually you will have to join the WGA. It isn't the kind of thing that you can opt in or out of. Networks and studios are signatories to the Guild — meaning they agree to hire only union writers. There are requirements set in stone as to when you must join, based on the amount of material you have sold. (Again, check out the WGA Web site for the exact rules and regs.) Most writers are eager to get their WGA card. It's really a terrific feeling to know that you belong to the same union as writers like Larry David, J.J. Abrams, Marc Cherry, etc.

Still, every once in a while there is a writer who, for whatever reason, doesn't feel like joining. Rest assured, they will find you. Every episode on every show sends a copy of the writing credits to the WGA. The WGA keeps track of exactly what you have written. When you hit the point where you absolutely must join, they will send the show a letter, explaining that you are not a union member, and that you must join immediately or the show will be in violation of their agreement with the Guild. In this case, the show will tell you to join the Guild or else they will take away the assignment. No studio or network is going to risk being in violation of the agreement for one writer … most especially a new writer.

KEY THINGS THE WGA CAN DO FOR YOU

The most important thing the Guild does is to protect the interests of writers. If it weren't for the Guild, there would be no rules for how producers treated writers or even paid writers. The WGA has an agreement in place with producers, which spells out the rules. In the event producers break those rules, the Guild will go after them on your behalf.

To give you an example: say you have written a show that is in syndication. You are owed residuals. The Guild keeps track of what writers are owed. If you feel that you have not been paid a residual that is due you, you can call the Guild. They will look up the information for you. If it turns out that you are right, that a studio hasn't paid you, the Guild will send a letter demanding payment. But, before they do, they will look for other writers on the show who likely haven't been paid either. The demand letter will go out with several writers' names on it. This is to keep you from having a black mark against your name by a particular studio. If the studio doesn't pay (although they usually will), the Guild can then assess interest and penalties. In the event that this doesn't work, they can take legal action. Now, imagine if you tried to do all of this on your own. The studio would probably ignore you, and if you wanted to sue, you'd have to hire a lawyer, which might end up costing more than the amount you are owed.

The Writers Guild also offers a pension plan and a health plan. There are set rules in place for eligibility, in both of these areas.

HOW RESIDUALS WORK

Residuals are also a bit complicated. You should once again refer to the Writers Guild Web site for a complete understanding of how residuals work. But here is an overall view.

Once a show has gone into syndication, there are certain target markets across the country in terms of residuals. So, let's say that you wrote an episode of *Everybody Loves Raymond* that airs in Philadelphia on September 13. You would be owed a residual. From that point, any of the rest of the target markets can air your show once and you do not get any additional money. However, the minute one of the markets airs your episode for the second time, you are owed another residual. So, basically one run means that it can play throughout all of the markets once.

There are separate rules for residuals in cable television and for foreign markets. You can consult the Guild's Web site to get the specifics.

WHAT IS ARBITRATION?

When two (or more) writers have worked on the same script, arbitration may be necessary to determine who gets what in terms of writing credits. When this happens, both drafts of the script are submitted to the Guild without names on the covers. Three members of the Guild (meaning actual writers or producers) will read each draft and decide how the credit should be divided. In television, the credit is split between the writers often. On occasion, one might be given story credit, while the other is given teleplay credit. Usually producers on a show won't arbitrate freelance writers, but they certainly can if they feel the writer didn't contribute anything. Arbitration can get uncomfortable when it happens between two writers on the same show. It doesn't happen a lot, but it does happen.

IN THE EVENT OF A WRITERS' STRIKE

In the late eighties, the WGA went out on strike. It was nasty and lasted about 6 months. Programming was shut down; people were put out of work — and not just writers. The strike affected everyone employed in the industry, from actors to assistants. Many people lost homes and faced financial ruin. During that time, the producers talked about hiring scabs to write shows so that they could get back into production. There were some unproduced writers who saw this as an opportunity. All I can say is … bad idea.

In the event of a writers' strike, the last thing you want to do is cross a picket line. The writers who have walked off their jobs are fighting to get better working conditions for all writers, and that includes you. When you are eligible to join the Guild, you will reap the benefits that your fellow writers have risked everything for. To swoop in and take their jobs is just plain uncool. It also won't get you very far. Before you know it, the strike will be settled and writers will go back to work. The producers will likely dump you in a heartbeat in exchange for a union writer. And it's not as though your fellow writers at the Guild will be looking for you to join any time soon; no way are they going to count work that was done by scabbing during a strike toward your Guild credits.

A smarter idea is to call the Guild and see if they need any volunteers for making signs or other things of that nature. You might even meet some writers and make some connections.

HOW TO PROTECT YOUR WORK

You should never send your work out without some kind of proof that it is legally yours and the date that it was written. While there is no foolproof way to guarantee that your work will not be stolen (besides not putting it out in the first place), there are a couple of ways that you can protect yourself should you find yourself in this unenviable position. Most writers register their scripts/treatments with the WGA. This service is available to you even if you are not a member of the Guild. The cost for nonmembers is $20. You can register your material either by mail, the Internet, or in person. The registration is good for 5 years and is renewable. The purpose of registering your script is to provide a dated, legal record of when the work was done; should there be litigation, the Guild can provide your registration as evidence.

Another way to protect your work is to copyright the material. For more information on this method, log onto the Web site of the United States Copyright Office at www.copyright.gov.

MISCELLANEOUS GUILD BENEFITS

The WGA has a lot to offer. Much of it is for members only, but there are some things you don't have to be a member to take advantage of. I highly recommend that you visit their Web site often. They have a mentor program that allows you to ask questions of members who have volunteered to mentor young writers. They have a trainee program that you may also want to look into. If you live in New York or Los Angeles, there are numerous events that the Guild sponsors that you don't have to be a member in order to attend. Take advantage of all of this. You have to start meeting and hanging out with writers. You never know where it might lead.

WRITING TEAMS

SHOULD YOU GET A WRITING PARTNER?

As you begin your career, one thing you may want to consider is whether or not you want to work with a writing partner. In the industry, two writers that come together to form one writing entity are known as a writing team. I have worked both on my own and as part of a writing team. Both have advantages and disadvantages. You really just have to weigh the pros and cons and decide what is right for you. I will say, however, that in comedy, I think having a partner can be beneficial, especially when it comes to joke writing.

Being part of a writing team is a lot like being in a marriage. In fact, some writers openly admit that they spend more time with their writing partner than with their significant other. As with a marriage, when it's going good, things are great. But when it's going badly, it can be quite stressful, and getting out is not always easy.

THE PROS OF PARTNERSHIPS

Perhaps one of the biggest advantages to being part of a writing team is that studios often like to hire teams over single writers. The reason for this is that they get two writers for the price of one. It works like this: Shows will budget salaries for each staff writing position. That salary stays the same whether the position is filled by one writer or by a writing team. So, if *My Name Is Earl* has budgeted X number of dollars for a story editor job and the executive producers decide to go with a team, the team will split the weekly salary. They will also split money for scripts and, down the road, residuals. Likewise, writing partners will usually share an office.

One major advantage to being part of a writing team is that you always have someone to bounce ideas off of. This can be extremely beneficial if you have writer's block or are stuck on a story point or a joke. Having someone to brainstorm with, someone who is as committed to finding a resolution, is absolutely invaluable.

Another plus to partnerships is that someone does half of the work, which makes it a lot easier. I have gone to bed and been on page 15 of a script. In the morning, I wake up and miraculously, I am on page 35. While I slept, the writing fairy (my partner) got a burst of energy and plowed through 20 pages. That's not so bad.

You will bring to the table a set number of industry contacts. Because you are just starting out, that number will likely be limited. By having a writing partner, that list should double, as you will now have access to all of those industry contacts that your writing partner has.

When it comes to writing, no doubt you have certain strengths and weaknesses. For example, you may be great at coming up with story ideas, but when it comes to pitching those ideas, you may not be so hot. Or, you may find that you are great at structuring stories, but writing compelling dialogue comes with a great degree of difficulty. Here is where having a writing partner can do you a world of good. The idea is to choose a complementary partner who will balance your strengths and weaknesses. If you accomplish this, your work will improve by leaps and bounds. You will also churn out scripts faster, because the things that you struggled with are no longer a problem.

BEING RESPONSIBLE FOR SOMEONE ELSE'S CAREER

As one half of a writing team, you are not only responsible for your own career, but also for your partner's career. While this may seem to double the pressure, it is actually good pressure. By being responsible to someone else, you may find that you get ahead faster. When you are a single writer, it is very easy to find reasons not to write. Whatever comes along, it's easy to put the writing on the back burner, telling yourself you will definitely do it tomorrow. When you have a partner, you will make an appointment to get together and write. It's not so easy to make the writing secondary, as now it's not just your own career that you are stalling. Being responsible to someone else can be an especially good thing if you don't naturally have a lot of self-discipline.

Perhaps one of the nicest things about being in a partnership is that you aren't in it alone. This can be a real asset on the days when the phone doesn't ring — or worse still it rings and someone on the other end is telling you why they don't want to represent you or hire you. If you are a single writer, this news can be hard to take, and it sends some writers into a tailspin of self-doubt. But misery loves company. When you have a writing partner, you have someone to share your feelings with, and together you can pick yourselves up, and figure out plan "B."

THE CONS OF PARTNERSHIPS

Once you are in a partnership, that becomes your identity. You are no longer known as Barbara Smith, but rather by a combination of your last name and your partner's: "Smith and Jones." And always in that order. If the partnership doesn't work and you decide to go your separate ways, you may have a professional identity crisis.

There can be many reasons for a writing team to break up. The most common seems to be that somewhere along the line one partner feels like he or she is doing more work than the other person and this leads to resentment. Breaking up a partnership is anything but simple. The biggest problem is that since all of the work you have done for however many years was done as a team, you really can't send it out and expect to get work on your own from it. Producers and executives may be reluctant to hire you because deep down, they don't know how your partnership worked. There is a tendency to think that one person may have been more talented, and they aren't going to take your word for it that it was you. The only way to prove your talent is to go out and write a spec on your own or with a new partner. Either way, it is like starting over. For this reason, it is crucial that you don't race into a writing partnership anymore than you would race into a marriage. You really need to know the person you are going to partner with. You need to sit down and talk about your future. Make certain you share the same vision and work ethic. Set up concrete plans for who will be responsible for what.

If you have chosen a writing partner carefully, most likely that person's strengths are your weaknesses. If this is the case, as time goes by, you will rely on that person to do the things that you don't do well. While this may work on the surface and allow you to coast, as time goes by, you won't ever develop those weaknesses, and thus you may never develop your full potential as a writer. This could be problematic if the partnership breaks up and you find yourself going solo.

Another downside of having a writing partner is that producers on a show can like you, but not your partner. More than once, I have witnessed writing teams in which one person was well-liked by the producers and executives, while the other person was despised. In each case, the result was the same: the team eventually got fired. The reason for this is that writing teams are under contract. Therefore, if one goes, they both go. You need to make sure that in addition to being a good writer, your partner also has people skills.

HOW TO CHOOSE A WRITING PARTNER

Choosing the right partner is key to your career. On one hand, you need somebody who thinks along the same lines as you do, and also shares the same values and writing philosophies. On the other hand, you want to make sure you don't choose someone who is your carbon copy. Studios tend to favor diverse teams over teams that have a similar make-up. For example, a team made of a male and female might stand a slightly better chance of being hired than a team made up of two men or two women. The reason for this is that executives feel that a diverse team offers two different points of view. This isn't limited to gender. If you are Caucasian, you may consider hooking up with a minority writer; if you are in your twenties and just starting out, you may consider teaming up with someone a little older and more established.

Before you agree to partner with someone, it is highly advisable to sit down with that person and talk about how the partnership will work. Who will be responsible for what? When will you get together and write? These may seem like unimportant details, but if you are planning to do most of the writing on weekends and your writing partner plans to take weekends off, you will be in trouble. Believe it or not, it is often the little things that lead to resentment and the ultimate break-up of a team.

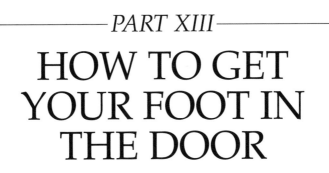

PART XIII

HOW TO GET
YOUR FOOT IN
THE DOOR

HOW TO GET WORK AS A TELEVISION WRITER

"Ideally, you can write your way in. Television is a hungry script monster that needs new product every hour of every day. In television, the writer is king ... and rich. If you have a personality that is a force of nature and an ego that is rock-solid and don't mind hearing no, then become a producer. If you are good at critiquing and/or selling things, try becoming a TV agent ... or selling houses. No matter which way you choose, it will be an uphill climb. If it was easy, everyone would do it. Work hard, believe in yourself ... oh, and work hard. You make your own luck."— Peter Jankowski, president, Wolf Films, executive producer, *Law & Order*

WHY YOU NEED A PLAN (AND A BACK-UP PLAN)

Now that you have learned at least the basics of how to write for television, it is time to formulate a plan for how you are going to get your career going. The most important gift you can give yourself right now is to be realistic. If your plan is to go to L.A. and get a job as a TV writer, that is not a realistic goal. It's a fine long-term goal, but you need a short-term goal as well. I cannot tell you how many writers I have this same conversation with, and they don't take my words to heart because I am telling them something they don't want to hear. They may secretly think that they will be the exception. These same people call me a month later, panicked because they realize how hard it is to get even an entry-level job, let alone get an agent and/or sell a script.

So, let me ask you — what is your short-term goal? Are you going to move to L.A. and try to find work in the industry? Are you going to move to L.A. and wait tables while you keep churning out the scripts? Or, are you going to stay on the farm in Iowa, write scripts, save money, and go to L.A. when you can better afford it? It doesn't matter what your plan is, as long as you have one and you stick to it.

THE IMPORTANCE OF INTERNSHIPS

If possible, you should try to do at least one internship, if not two. Internships are a great way to get your foot in the door. Most are not paid; however, you usually get college credit for doing them.

Internships are important for a number of reasons. First and foremost, they add a layer of professional experience to your resumé. Often when students get out of college they think that student work translates to professional experience. It does ... and it doesn't. While student films and such can certainly get you attention, unless you have won a lot of prestigious awards or your work has somehow generated a lot of buzz, a student film may not land you a job on its own. Once you graduate from college, you are going to be competing for jobs with people who have professional experience under their belts. An internship is a great way for you to start racking up professional credits on your resumé.

In addition to experience, internships give you a professional track record. As a prospective employer, I can make a phone call to your internship supervisor and see what kind of employee you were. Did you show up on time, or were you constantly late? Did you have a good attitude, or were you high maintenance? Did you step up to the plate for the little tasks? Did you follow through on things?

If you play your cards right, an internship can lead directly to employment. While this doesn't always happen, it happens more frequently than you might think. Let's say that you are interning and an entry-level job opens up. If I am the boss, I now have to post the job, sort through a gazillion resumés, set up appointments to interview candidates, check references, hire someone, and then train that person. In the end, the person is an unknown, so he may or may not work out. On the other hand, you are right in front of my face. You know the company; you know how we do business, so I don't have to train you. Plus, you are a known commodity. You have already proven yourself to be a hard worker with a great attitude. So, why would I go through all the trouble of interviewing people when I can just hire you? For this to happen though, you will have needed to demonstrate that you can step up to the plate and get the job done.

CONTACT EVERYONE YOU KNOW AND TELL THEM WHAT YOU WANT

Once you have decided on your game plan, you need to let people know what you are up to. I don't mean in an obnoxious way — but rather, don't be afraid to put it out there. Very often, things come back when you least expect them to. You don't know what will lead to your break, and neither do I. You just have to open every door and see what turns up. Sometimes when you tell someone what you want, they will say, "I know somebody." So, don't be afraid to commit to your goals publicly.

"I know of a lot of would-be writers who supported themselves in non-industry jobs. I think that's a mistake. If your ultimate goal is to make it in Hollywood, you must figure out a way to make yourself into an insider, even if, for the time being, you're a lowly insider. Unless you're heavily connected, that may mean taking jobs that feel a little beneath you just to get your foot in the door. But you learn a lot in those jobs and you put yourself in the path of people who can help you get where you want to go. If your choice is between an executive position at an insurance company and sweeping floors at a studio, I'd pick the studio job." — Manny Basanese, writer/producer, *The Steve Harvey Show* and *The Wayans Brothers*

ENTRY LEVEL JOBS THAT CAN LEAD TO YOUR WRITING BREAK

While you are waiting for your writing to take off, you will most likely need to find a job in order to put a roof over your head and food in your mouth. There are two schools of thought as to what direction you should go: nonindustry jobs or jobs within the industry.

Some people believe that nonindustry jobs such as being a waiter or working in a store are good because they offer flexible hours, which gives you time to write and take meetings. This is true; however, I am a firm believer that, if at all possible, you should try to find a position at a studio or network. There are two main reasons for this. First, by working on a daily basis with people who are writing and producing shows, you will learn a lot more than you will by handing out menus. When I first came to L.A., I thought I knew how to write. Looking back, I realize that I knew a lot less about writing than I thought I did. Working directly for writers (and hanging out with them) is when I actually learned how to write. Through osmosis, I learned how to break stories and how to write and rewrite jokes. In addition, I was privy to mistakes other freelance writers made both in terms of pitching and in drafts of scripts.

The second reason I encourage you to look for a job within the industry is that it's a quick way to develop contacts. Every script I have ever sold has been sold through personal connections — connections I would have never made had I worked at Joe's Diner rather than Universal Studios. With this in mind, I definitely encourage you, if at all possible, to find work within the industry.

Here are some jobs that you may want to investigate when starting out. I have placed them in order of importance.

- Writer's assistant. These jobs are hard to come by, but I think they are the fastest path to becoming a writer. You will have to answer phones, type, and proof scripts. But you will also learn by watching how the pros do it. If you do your job well, and they like you, they may even let you pitch — or at the very least help get you an agent.

- Producer's assistant. Working for a producer is much like working for a writer — as long as that producer is part of the creative force behind the show. However, you could also work for a line producer. This would be okay, though not ideal because you would not be as close to the writers since line producers deal very little with scripts in terms of creativity. Their focus is more on budget and the technical aspects of the show, including post-production.

- Production assistant. There are two kinds of production assistants: those who work in the office and those who work on the set. I have to say it is the office P.A. position that is more beneficial to an up-and-coming writer, because you will be more in touch with the writers and producers. Set P.A.s spend most of their time on the stage, and have more contact with the cast and crew than with the writing staff. As a P.A., you may be asked to do a lot of running around for things directly related to the production of the show — and occasionally you may even be asked to do personal errands. A good P.A. should be high-energy and organized.

If you are unable to secure any of these jobs, then you might try to get a studio job that has high visibility and will put you in daily contact with as many people as possible. For example, you could try the mailroom. Granted delivering mail may not be the most fun job on the planet, but this isn't about fun; it's about getting your foot in the door and paying your dues. By bouncing all over the studio, you will meet a lot of people. You should think of these jobs as stepping stones. When other jobs that are more in tune with what you want open up, you may be among the first to hear.

Another job that puts you in contact with people is in the IT department. For this you definitely need to understand computers and software. But, I knew a guy at Universal Studios who knew every writer on the lot — and he was their personal hero because when they were under deadline and having computer problems, he always came through and saved the day. Through this job and the connections he made, he was able to get many a pitch meeting.

There are oodles of other jobs at studios and networks that tend to sound completely boring. If you are not able to get your foot in the door on some of the more desirable entry-level jobs, you might consider trying to find work in the accounting and/or legal departments. You don't have to stay in the position forever — nor should you. Just get your foot in the door any way you can.

WAYS TO UNCOVER ENTRY-LEVEL JOBS

Uncovering entry-level jobs in the industry can be difficult. Not to scare you, but there are so many people standing in line for these positions, companies don't have to advertise them in newspapers. Studios will often post new positions on various boards around the lot, but that won't do you any good if you aren't already working there.

An industry friend once gave me some great advice that led directly to my job at *Charles in Charge*. It was mid-May, and the networks had just announced their new fall schedules. My friend told me to go through the trades and/or the *L.A. Times* and look for all of the new shows that would be on the air in the fall. (You can now find this info on the Internet as well.) New shows, he explained, need to hire entire production staffs. Those are the places you should target first because you know there are going to be job openings.

The trades and newspapers will list both the production company and the network of the new show. Once a show is greenlighted, production offices are set up almost immediately. All you have to do is call the main number of the studio or network and ask for the show's production offices. You will be put through. When they answer the phone, say something like, "could you please tell me who hires the writer's assistants?" or "who hires the production assistants?" or whatever particular job you are looking for. That is the person you will send your resume to.

RESUMÉS AND COVER LETTERS

The first step in looking for a job is to write your resumé, which you will send out to prospective employers with an appropriate cover letter. Your resumé and cover letter should be thought of as marketing tools. You are marketing both yourself and your skills. Well-written resumés and cover letters can get you in the door and give you the opportunity to convince an employer face-to-face that he or she should hire you. On the other hand, resumés and cover letters that are poorly written and loaded with misspellings, typos, and grammatical errors usually wind up in the trash. So it's important to spend a lot of time preparing both.

Because your resumé and cover letter will be the first impression that a potential employer has of you, I highly recommend that you spend a few extra bucks and get yourself some quality stationery. Matching envelopes are also a must. The goal here is to create a professional image of yourself as a complete and pulled-together package. As for color, white, cream, and ivory are always safe bets, but if you prefer, you can also go with muted tones of blue or gray. Avoid outrageous colors such as lime green and fuchsia. They may be good for party invitations, but certainly not for professional resumés. Some people assume putting a resumé on bold stationery will make them stand out. They are correct — they will stand out, but not in a good way.

No matter how tempting, you should stay away from cutesy gimmicks. They rarely work. I remember once receiving an envelope while I was at Columbia Pictures. I opened it, and a bunch of crumbs went all over my desk. In the midst of the mess was a little ball of paper, all scrunched up. As I unraveled the paper, I realized it was a resumé and cover letter. The cover letter was short and sweet, simply stating, "here it is … in a nutshell." The guy must have placed the resumé in some kind of nutshell. He failed to realize that it would be crushed when it went through the postal machines. The only thing he succeeded in doing was to give me the impression that he himself was some kind of nut. He didn't get hired.

HOW TO WRITE YOUR RESUMÉ

Your resumé should be one page. I sometimes see resumés that are three pages long from people just beginning their careers. If I can get my resumé on one page, after twenty-five years of working in television, so can you. Of course this involves making choices.

While there are numerous ways that you can set up your resumé, I prefer to use bullet points. We live in a time when everyone is out-of-control busy. Resumés that are in paragraph form can be harder to read. With the bullet format, a potential employer should be able to skim your resumé in 30 seconds and get a sense of who you are and what you have accomplished to date.

I am a big believer in starting your resumé with professional experience; some people might suggest you begin with education. While education is important, it is not going to be the reason that an employer hires you. You will be hired for one reason and one reason alone — you have the experience to do the job.

I do not believe in putting down an objective. I think objectives can be extremely limiting. You never know who your resumé will be passed on to, so you want to keep all of your options open. I also do not believe in listing hobbies and interests. As an employer I am not going to hire you because you like to canoe on Sunday afternoons. I am going to hire you because I have a position I am looking to fill and you have the experience to do the job. Additionally, objectives and interests/hobbies take up space on your resumé. I'd rather see this space devoted to something more concrete, like experience and/or awards.

Whatever you do, do not lie on your resumé. I can promise you that you will be caught. It may not happen today or tomorrow, but eventually it will catch up to you. One of the few things you have control of in this industry is your reputation. Once that's gone, it's over. By the same token, you should not undersell yourself on your resumé.

I am often asked by students what they should put on a resumé if they don't have a ton of experience in the field. First off, this is why internships are important. Internships will give you professional experience. I also think you should list jobs that you have had that aren't directly related to the industry. There is nothing wrong with having worked at places like Blockbuster or Pizza Hut while you are in college; in fact, I think it's just the opposite. The fact that you are studying full-time and working shows that you aren't spoiled. It also gives a potential employer another reference to call. Not to mention the fact that you never know what will attract a potential employer. My cousin got her college degree in a field that had nothing to do with television or even communications. On a whim, she sent her resume to one of the major cable networks. The executive who called her in for an interview had been intrigued by the fact that throughout college, she babysat. Apparently, the guy had four kids and he figured if she could go to school during the day and babysit at night she must be hard-working and high-energy. He hired her. So you just never know.

You should also list student work that won any type of award, and any relevant classes you may have taken. Additionally, don't forget to include any kind of special skills you possess.

SAMPLE RESUMÉ

Here is a sample resumé using the bullet format. You can set up your resumé any way you choose, but keep in mind the easier it is to read, the better.

Joe Blow *20 Apple Street * Farmland, Iowa 91405
* (515) 555-9135 * JoeBlow@aol.com

Professional Experience	2006 NBC/Universal Los Angeles, CA Intern • Assisted EXECUTIVE Producer in all aspects of production, *The Office*
	2005 Warner Bros. Los Angeles, CA Intern • Supported writing staff, *Two and a Half Men*
	2004 Iowa Film Commission Des Moines, IA Office assistant • Worked with executive director to bring films into state • Liaison to Hollywood production companies • Assisted film-makers with location scouts
	2002–2003 Ferguson and Foley Des Moines, IA Receptionist • Answered phones • Managed client correspondence • Reorganized filing system
Related Experience	2005–2006 Boston, MA Writer/producer • Wrote and produced 20-minute film, *Magic Mile* • Winner, Kodak Award for Best Student Film • Finalist, MTV competition for Best Student Film

Education	2002–2006 Emerson College Boston, MA
	• B.A., Film/Video
	• Graduated summa cum laude
Skills	Word, Final Draft, Movie Magic, fluent in Spanish and French
References	Available upon request

HOW TO WRITE A KILLER COVER LETTER

If written well, a cover letter can be equal to — if not more important than — your actual resumé. While your resumé lists your experience and skills, a good cover letter explains in detail how that experience directly translates to the job at hand and makes you the ideal candidate.

A cover letter is a business letter. Technically, it is formal, but at the same time it should be conversational. Cover letters should be single-spaced, with two spaces separating each paragraph. Like resumés, cover letter should be one page.

Cover letters should always be addressed to a specific person. Letters addressed "To Whom It May Concern" are a waste of time. If you don't know whom it concerns … then why are you even writing? It is your job to find out who it concerns. Usually, this is fairly easy to do. Simply call the company and ask who hires for the particular job that you are trying to obtain. By sending your resumé and cover letter to an actual person, you will at least know that it is going to get into human hands rather than tossed onto a big pile. You will also have a name, so if you don't hear back in a few days to a week, you know who to follow up with.

Before you begin writing a cover letter, it would behoove you to call the office of the person to whom you plan to send your resumé. Ask the assistant for the correct spelling of the person's name, and if you have any doubt as to the person's gender (i.e., names like Leslie, Cameron, Jamie, etc.), check that as well. Take it from someone who has received more than one letter addressed to "Mr. Marty Cook." Before I read word one, I already have a negative impression of the person applying for the job. By making a mistake in the spelling of my name and in my gender, the writer has actually delivered an important message: he or she doesn't care enough to check the minor details. Television is a detail-oriented profession. If an employer can't trust you to get small details right, how could you ever be trusted with some of the bigger details that go with the day-to-day production of a show? The answer is, they can't. Cover letters with glaring errors are not likely to achieve your purpose, which is getting the job. Chances are you won't even be called in for an interview.

The most common mistake I see in cover letters from young applicants is a tendency to explain why the job would be beneficial to their careers. In writing a cover letter, the most important thing to remember is that it's all about what you can do for them, not what they can do for you; for example. "I'm applying to be a writer's assistant because I want to be a comedy writer and working on a top-rated show like *Two and a Half Men*, where I could learn from talented writers, would be a great first step toward my long-term career goal."

Here's a news flash: while Lee Aronsohn and Chuck Lorre might be flattered that you like their show, they aren't going to hire you so they can jumpstart your comedy-writing career. If they are going to hire you, it is for one reason alone: they have a need for a writer's assistant and you have the qualifications to fill the position.

This means that your cover letter has highlighted previous experience that shows that you know how to type, you understand television production and deadlines, you know how scripts are put together, you can take quick and comprehensive notes in the writers' room, you work well under pressure, you know how to answer phones and take messages, and you have a pleasant personality.

Several years ago, an up-and-coming writer asked if I would look over a cover letter he was planning to send out. The letter was going to a former CEO of two studios, who now owns a well-respected production company. Both the student and the producer were alums of the same university. Because this is the worst cover letter I have ever seen, I have opted to leave out the names of both the sender and the intended recipient.

April 23, 2001

Mr. Joe Blow
President & CEO, _____ Pictures
Studio Address

Dear Mr. Blow:

Everyone in the entertainment industry is sleazy, except for you and me.

Like you, I went to X University, where I studied film and television. I will receive my degree in May, and I plan to move to Hollywood and work in the industry. Here is a sampling of some of my most recent achievements:

- Wrote six full-length screenplays, all which received lots of recognition and awards.
- Produced two films.
- Worked as an editor on three films.
- Served as DP on five films.
- Acted in two films.

Everyone in the entertainment industry is sleazy except for you and me. That's why it would be great for us to work together.

I hope to hear back from you soon.

Sincerely,

Joe Shmoe

Joe Shmoe

In addition to this being a poorly written cover letter, the writer made two colossal mistakes. In the very first sentence of the very first paragraph, he insults everyone in the entertainment industry with the sole exception of the intended recipient. Putting other people down in order to push yourself ahead is a big no-no. You are not going to be hired by telling a prospective employer what is wrong with everyone else. You will be hired by making a case, which tells the employer all the things that are right about you for the job.

The other big mistake the writer makes is that he never asks for what he wants. He basically tells the CEO that he is a jack-of-all-trades. He is a writer, a producer, an editor, a director of photography, and an actor. Now, put yourself in the recipient's shoes. If you were to receive a letter like this, how would you even begin to guess what the writer wanted from you? Is he looking for work as a writer? Or, does he want you to see if you can hook him up with an editor? The problem is this: no one in the industry has time to stop and think about what is going on inside your head. It is your job to communicate quickly and clearly why you are writing and what, specifically, you want.

The writer would have been better waiting until he arrived in L.A. to send the following letter:

> Dear Mr. Blow:
>
> I am a recent graduate of X University, where I studied film and television writing. Despite the heavy competition, my long-term goal is to become a screenwriter. With this in mind, I have just moved to Los Angeles, where I am currently meeting with as many people as possible in hopes of finding an entry-level job in the industry.
>
> I have long been a fan of the movies you produce. Films like X and Y are the exact type of movies I envision myself writing someday. I understand that you are extremely busy, but if there is any way you could possibly spare a few minutes to offer some friendly advice to a fellow alum, I would welcome the opportunity to meet you. As a newcomer both to Los Angeles and to the business, any suggestions you might have on how to get my foot in the door would be most appreciated. I am taking the liberty of enclosing my resumé so that you may get a better idea of what I have to offer in terms of skills and experience.
>
> I will call your office in a few days to see if we might set up a time to meet.
>
> Thank you in advance for your time and consideration.
>
> Sincerely,
>
> *Joe Shmoe*
> Joe Shmoe

FIVE PARAGRAPHS TO A GOOD COVER LETTER

First, be sure that your contact information is clearly visible on the cover letter itself. And remember: a good cover letter should prompt a person to want to meet you. It should be professional, but not stiff. It should flow in a conversational way.

- Paragraph 1: Intro. State the reason you are writing. If you have any connection such as someone who has referred you or you went to the same college, be sure to say that right off the bat. If you are applying for a certain job that you saw advertised, put that in as well as where you saw the posting.
- Paragraphs 2 and 3: This is the heart and soul of the letter. It is where you do your selling. Look carefully at what the job is and what qualifications are needed. Then, go through your resumé and, in these two paragraphs, cite specific examples of past work experience that make you qualified for this position.
- Paragraph 4: Request a face-to- face meeting. Remember no company is ever going to hire you without first meeting you. The goal of sending your resumé and cover letter is to get you in the door so that you can move to that next step. In this paragraph, you want to take the initiative to ask for that meeting.
- Paragraph 5: Tell the person that you will contact his or her office in the near future to see if you can schedule an appointment. This shows that you really want the job and are willing to take the initiative to get it. By adding this, you are really helping yourself, because if the person doesn't call you, then you will be forced to call them (whether or not you want to).

Always thank the person for his or her time and consideration, and end by saying you look forward to speaking with him or her soon.

SAMPLE COVER LETTER

December 1, 2006

Mr. Joe Doe
Executive Producer, *Show Name*
Paramount Television
5555 Melrose Avenue
Los Angeles, CA 90048

Dear Mr. Doe:

Gary Green suggested I contact you regarding the writer's assistant position that is currently available on your show.

As my enclosed resumé reflects, I am the perfect candidate for this position. As an intern on *The Office,* I worked directly with the executive producer, which allowed me access to the writer's room. On occasion, I would fill in for the writer's assistant, so I have a full understanding of how the room works as well a complete comprehension of the day-to-day production pressures. You should know I work extremely well under pressure; little (if anything) rattles me.

My internship at *Two and a Half Men* afforded me the opportunity to work one-on-one with the staff writers, whom I assisted by inputting first drafts into the computer. I also did a lot of proofreading and helped with formatting and preparing scripts to go to the table. I am highly energized and organized. While in college, I worked in the law office of Fergusen and Foley where, in addition to typing and answering phones, I took on the task of restructuring their entire filing system.

I would welcome the opportunity to meet with you to further discuss how my production experience combined with my skills at running a busy office make me a perfect fit for the writer's assistant position. I can be available at your convenience. I will call your office in the next few days to see if we might be able to schedule a time to meet.

Thank you so much for your time and consideration. I look forward to speaking with you soon.

Sincerely,

Joe Shmoe

Joe Schmoe

GENERATING INFORMATIONAL INTERVIEWS

Even if a company doesn't have a job available, it is a good idea to get yourself out to try to meet people in the industry. Usually, I do this by telling people that I'd like to seek their advice. People generally love to give advice because it's nonthreatening and it makes them feel good. The goal is to get people to know you. They really only know you if they have had the opportunity to meet with you. Also, informational interviews can reveal different avenues that you might want to consider. And, if the person likes you well enough, he or she may even refer you to someone else in the business.

WHEN A COMPANY SAYS THEY'RE NOT HIRING
(BALONEY!)

In the event that you call a company to ask who does the hiring for X and you are told, "we aren't hiring right now," don't necessarily believe them. When I applied for a script job at *Charles in Charge,* I called on a Friday afternoon. I was told that they were all staffed. I asked if I could get the person's name anyway, as I would still like to send my resumé in the event something opened up or someone didn't work out. I got the person's name and my resumé was in the Friday 5:00 p.m. mail. I expected nothing. Monday morning, I was called in for an interview. It seems they had so many resumés, they didn't want any more. But since I was politely aggressive, my resumé went in — right place, right time — just as they were starting to interview script people.

THE POWER OF OVERNIGHTING YOUR RESUMÉ
(EVEN IF YOU LIVE ONE BLOCK AWAY)

Every once in a while, a job will come along that seems perfect for you. In these rare cases, you may want to think about sending your resumé and cover letter via an overnight mail service like FedEx. You obviously won't want to do this for every resumé you send out, as it is expensive. But for the job you feel you can't live without, overnighting your resumé can give you an advantage.

Mailrooms in major companies are not generally known for being speedy. In fairness to them, they sort, handle, and deliver enormous volumes of letters and packages each day. A letter that you mail at the post office could take a few days to get to the company. Once in the mailroom, it could take a little longer to get to the person.

FedEx and other overnight mail deliveries are handled differently, because they have a feeling of urgency. When these letters come into a company they need to be signed for, which means someone is accountable. Mailroom personnel will usually deliver overnight mail first thing in the morning or on a separate afternoon run. They will not take chances, as they have no way of knowing if this piece of mail is something a boss is waiting for. The last thing they want is for the boss to call the sender asking for it, only to find that it has been sitting in the mailroom all morning.

Once the overnight mail arrives in the boss' office, many assistants just place the package in the boss' in-box. What this means is that the boss will personally open the package and read your cover letter and resumé. I am not saying this is always the case — or that the read will be anymore than a quick glance. But it is a way to up your chances of getting your resumé directly into the hands of the person who can hire you. The other nice thing about this is that you are sending the employer a message: you want this job so badly you are willing to invest $20 or so to get your resumé there quickly.

BRUSHING UP ON PHONE ETIQUETTE

When looking for a job, you need to have decent phone skills. You should be friendly and energetic. State your name and get right to the point of your phone call. Don't make the assistant ask you 20 questions to figure out the nature of your call. These people are busy. Get to the point. Don't think you are going to outsmart them by dancing around their questions. Assistants are well-schooled in screening their bosses' calls.

WHY IT'S IMPORTANT TO GET THE ASSISTANT'S NAME

Perhaps the biggest mistake you could make is to treat assistants poorly. While assistants may be lower on the totem pole, don't underestimate their power.

They can get you through the door. Several times throughout the course of any given day, assistants have their boss's undivided attention. They will decide how high a priority to make you ... or whether to even mention that you called.

As a former assistant, I can tell you that when people phoned to get a message to my boss and treated me like dirt, I would sometimes "accidentally" forget to write down the message. Oops. Likewise, I often spoke to total strangers who were polished and professional, and who struck up a conversation with me. When I was alone with the boss, I would give those people a push by saying something like, "Joe Shmoe called again. He seems like a really good guy. Maybe you could give him a call back?"

Good bosses trust their assistants implicitly. Many tend to think of their assistant as a reflection of themselves. Often, the feeling is that if a boss hears someone has been abusing their assistant, they simply won't want to do business with that person.

> "Be nice to assistants. First of all, it's the right thing to do. But secondly, assistants often wield a great deal more power than people realize. If you're a jerk to them, they will let their boss know. I know of several instances where a prospective writer has shot himself down for a job or a story pitch by being snotty to an assistant. People generally don't want to work with dinks. So my best advice is, don't be a dink." — Manny Basanese, writer/producer, *The Steve Harvey Show* and *The Wayans Brothers*

When making phone calls, you should always ask for the assistant's name. Most people fail to do this. Not only is getting a name a way of seemingly becoming more personal, but it's also easier to call back an actual person, should your phone call not be returned in a reasonable amount of time. I usually say something like, "Hi, Anne ... it's Martie Cook. You and I spoke last week. I'm trying to get through to Mike about the production assistant job. But I haven't heard back. Is there anything you can possibly do to help me connect with him?" If there is camaraderie between you and the assistant, the chances of getting what you want significantly increase. Remember, the assistant is also going to be looking at you, sizing up whether or not he or she wants you as a fellow employee.

I can tell you the name of every assistant of every writer, producer, or executive I interviewed for this book. I am grateful for all of their help in making sure all of my phone calls were returned.

HOW AND WHEN TO USE VOICE MAIL

If you aren't having much luck getting a call back, you might try calling the person you are trying to reach after hours. Sometimes when assistants have gone home for the day, a boss will answer his or her own phone. If nothing else, you may get the person's voicemail. Most people I know tend to retrieve their own voicemail messages. Thus, if you get a boss' voice mail, it's really like getting a minute or so of their time to state your case.

Here are a few things to keep in mind about voicemail. First, don't ramble. Some voicemail systems are on a timer. The last thing you want is to get cut off and have to call back and do part two. It's really important to be clear and concise. Also, keep your energy level high. Believe it or not, people will form an opinion of you based on how you sound on the phone. Always give your phone number both at the beginning of the message and again at the end. Sometimes (especially with cell phones) there can be dropout. The person might miss one number — and that could be the difference in whether or not you get a return phone call. Also, you do the person a favor because you're giving them a couple of chances to write down your number, rather than having to go back and listen to the whole message again.

"Hi, this is Martie Cook. 781-555-2421. I am calling to follow up on a resumé I sent for the production assistant job. I feel I have all of the qualifications that you are looking for, and I really believe that I am the right person for the job. I would welcome any opportunity to come in and talk to you about it. If you could give me a call back, I'd be most appreciative. Again, it's Martie Cook 781-555-2421. I look forward to talking with you."

Be sure when making these kinds of calls that you aren't too obvious about trying to get the person's voicemail. Calling at midnight is just too weird. You should try any time after 6:00 or 6:30 in the evening — or just before 9:00 in the morning. You can also try during lunch.

HOW AND WHEN TO USE E-MAIL

Using e-mail to contact someone is a little trickier than voicemail. While you can usually figure out the person's e-mail address by looking at the company Web site, e-mails from outsiders are not always well-received. Company e-mails tend to be internal and used for business purposes. So, your sneaking your way in because you haven't gotten a return phone call doesn't always go over well. In fact, more and more companies are adding controls to prevent the general public from sending unsolicited e-mails to their employees. Still, if you feel it is the only possible avenue left to reaching the person, then you should give it a try.

As with voice mail, try to keep it short and sweet. Tell the person why you are writing and what you want. A couple of things to keep in mind. First, get yourself a professional screen name. You may think that a name like SpoiledRottenPrincess@hotmail.com is cute, but think about what it says to a prospective employer.

You also want to make sure that the person can get back to you with as little effort as possible. I am a believer that once you graduate from college you should get an e-mail account that you pay for. I have had experiences with people who use free e-mail accounts, in that I e-mail them and for whatever reason, they never get the e-mail — or they get it a few weeks later. If your e-mail account is free, then you can't complain. You are getting exactly what you are paying for. Nothing for nothing. If, you are paying, however, you can complain about any problems. Usually, there aren't going to be any. It's really important that you get the e-mail if a potential employer answers your e-mail — and it doesn't bounce back to them as undeliverable.

One other thing you want to do is to make certain that your own computer won't prevent e-mail from reaching you because you have the spam controls set too high. Not too long ago, I received an e-mail from a student who was about to graduate. He wanted some advice. I took the time to answer him. Shortly afterward, I got an e-mail back, not from him, but from his e-mail provider, stating that it didn't recognize my e-mail address. Included in the e-mail was a link I was supposed to click on, which would take me to a form to fill out. Once I filled out the form, if the student deemed me appropriate, he'd be in touch. Of course I didn't fill out the form. (Why would I?) Over the next few days his e-mail provider kept sending me reminder notices that the form was still waiting for me. It was really annoying. Finally, the student called, irked that I hadn't responded to his e-mail. I told him that if that was going to be his approach to getting a job, he would likely be unemployed for years to come. When you want something from someone — especially a job — you have to make yourself accessible. No one has time to chase you. If it's too much trouble for someone to get in touch with you, they won't bother.

GETTING THE
INTERVIEW

PREPARING FOR THE INTERVIEW

Being prepared for an interview is the most important step to getting the job. Before I meet with a potential boss, I always "Google" both the company that I am applying to and the person with whom I will be interviewing. In this day and age, with so much information available right at your fingertips, it is unacceptable to walk into a company uninformed, not knowing what it's all about. Not to mention that some of the facts you learn you may be able to weave into the conversation, making yourself look smarter and savvier than the competition.

While we are on the subject, you should understand that "Googling" is a two-way street. You can "Google" a potential boss, but that boss can also "Google" you. More and more employers are using the Internet to acquire additional information on prospective employees. Therefore, do be careful what you write in blogs or post on web sites like myspace.com. My rule of thumb is, if you wouldn't want your mother to read it, you don't want a prospective boss to read it either. What may seem to be cute, fun, and even innocent at the time, may not feel so fun if it kills your chance at a job.

Some people prepare for an interview by trying to anticipate every possible question that could be asked and then coming up with a clever response. I believe this is a mistake. Try as you might, you will never be able to come up with every question that will be thrown your way. By having stock answers, you risk coming off as robotic. There is also the possibility of choking if a question is thrown at you a slightly different way than you anticipated. I think the best way to get a job is to be your natural self. This requires knowing who you are as a person and being confident about what you have to offer professionally. (If you aren't feeling particularly confident, keep this in mind: the person you are interviewing with already thinks you have something to offer; otherwise, you wouldn't have been invited in for an interview.)

> "Be yourself and be honest. Don't always second-guess people and tell them what you think they want to hear. They want the real deal. They want you to be you." — Jeff Eckerle, writer/producer, *Law & Order: Special Victims Unit*

When it comes to an interview, there is no law that says you have to know the answer to every question. I have gotten many jobs where a prospective boss tossed out something I didn't know off the top of my head. My response was a sincere "that's a great question. I'm not sure I know the answer." If I can come up with something quick in the moment, I will toss it out. If not, I will add, "I will have to think about that."

CONTROLLING THE INTERVIEW

After the polite introductions, I will usually take the bull by the horns and say something like, "would you like me to tell you a little bit about myself?" This question is almost always met with a smile and relief. It gives the person behind the desk a chance to sit back, catch some breath, sip the coffee that's been sitting untouched, and listen, rather than going through a list of the same old, dull questions that have been asked repeatedly of other candidates.

By controlling the interview, I accomplish a couple of important things. Right off the bat, I establish that I am a confident self-starter. Both of these qualities are important to prospective bosses. (The last thing any supervisor wants is an employee that will have to be led around by the nose.) Perhaps most importantly, by controlling the interview, I am able to get all of the points out that I wish to make. I can match the job description to my background and talk in detail, with concrete examples of how my experience makes me the most qualified candidate.

CONFIDENCE IS KEY

You are going to be hired for a job for one reason and one reason only: the person behind the desk believes that you have the skills and qualifications to do the job. Therefore it is imperative you look confident in your abilities. If you don't believe in yourself, how can you expect a potential employer to believe in you? It's okay to be nervous deep inside (actually nervousness is good because it means you care); you just don't want the nervousness to show.

The first job I applied for in Hollywood was at Columbia Pictures, working for Marty Ransohoff, a producer who was just starting production on a movie called *Jagged Edge*. Ransohoff was mega-powerful and I wanted the job more than anything. I met him at the studio, where he promptly intimidated the daylights out of me. I was immediately bombarded with questions and comments like, "why should I hire you?" and "you have no experience" and "you know nothing about the film industry." I sat there, my mouth open, at a complete loss to defend my abilities and present my case. Five minutes later, the interview was over.

I left the studio feeling incredibly disappointed. The job had been mine to win or lose — and I was certain I had lost it. I went home, whipped off my business attire, and threw it into a crumbled up ball on the floor. Then I ordered a pizza and ate the whole thing. Just as I was finishing, the phone rang. Ransohoff wanted to see me in his Beverly Hills office immediately. Apparently his vice president of development liked me and had somehow, miraculously, convinced him to give me another shot.

On the 20-minute drive to Beverly Hills, I made a pact with myself that no matter what, I was going to look this man squarely in the eye and give him all of the reasons he would be a fool not to hire me. Somehow, I pulled it off. He gave me the job.

Here's the deal: the guy was just as scary at 2:00 p.m. as he had been at 10:00 a.m. In the 4 hours between meetings, he hadn't changed. I had. Somehow, I had reached deep inside and found the confidence that was needed to sell myself for the position. This turned out to be one of the best jobs I ever had. Ransohoff wasn't a monster after all; rather, he was smart as a whip and taught me tons about feature film writing and production. He had been initially tough on me because he wanted to see if I could handle him. He knew that if I couldn't handle him, then I would never be able to handle the day-to-day pressures that come when a film is in production.

THE POWER OF SNAIL MAIL THANK-YOU NOTES

After an interview, do yourself a favor and send an old-fashioned thank-you note. It is mind-boggling to me how few people seem to do this, as it can really give you a leg up on the competition. First, most people like to receive mail, and thanking someone for their time is always a classy thing to do. It can only make you look good. Second and perhaps more importantly, writing a note puts your name in front of the person again and it also gives you the chance to restate your interest in the job, or to add something that you didn't say during the interview process. Reminding the person that you exist and are still extremely interested in the position can be key, especially if they have interviewed a number of candidates after you. It can help keep you from getting lost in the shuffle.

PLACING THE DREADED FOLLOW-UP CALL

I hate to be the bearer of bad news, but you might send out a ton of resumés and not get a call back from anyone. This may have nothing to do with you or your resumé. It might just not be right place, right time. In any case, you now have to make follow-up calls. These can feel humiliating because you may be thinking deep down that if they liked what they saw, they would have called you.

I have learned not to write scenarios. You have no way of knowing what the other person is thinking. It could be they were on vacation, or they were meaning to call and didn't get to it. Or, it could be they weren't going to call, but somehow you managed to get them on the phone and convince them to give you a shot. A follow-up call is important because it shows you have a real interest. It also keeps your name in front of the person you want to hire you.

TURNING A "NO" INTO A "YES"

Most of the time when people decide not to hire you, they don't bother to contact you and inform you of their decision. Occasionally, you may receive a courtesy letter telling you that they have filled the job, but even this is rare. Still, every once in a blue moon, someone may actually call you to tell you they have decided not to hire you. Your instinct will be to thank them for calling, and then to hang up. This is the worst thing you can do. Once you end the conversation, it is over ... you have let them off the hook.

What is most advantageous to say in this kind of conversation is something to this effect: "Thank you for telling me. I have to admit I am a little disappointed because I really wanted the job, and feel that I have a lot to offer your company." Then go in for the kill. Ask if they will be doing any hiring in the future. Ask if they are aware of anyone else in the company in need of someone with your skills. If not, ask if you can keep in touch and check back every so often. I learned long ago that just because you aren't the first choice for a job doesn't mean you won't eventually get the job, or another one just like it. I have also come to realize over time that it is possible to turn something negative into something positive.

Several years ago, I decided I wanted to work in children's television. I sent my resumé and reel to WGBH, where they were starting up a new children's show called *Zoom*. (The show had been on in the seventies, and then off for many years and they had decided to bring it back.) I received a call from one of the producers politely telling me that they had looked over my reel, and while it was good, there wasn't anything on it directly related to children's television. She told me that I would be competing with producers who had spent lifetimes doing top-notch, well-respected children's shows like *Sesame Street* and *Mr. Rogers' Neighborhood*. There was no way I was going to get the job over them.

I told her that I understood what she was saying, but anyone who knew anything about me knew that if there was anywhere I belonged it was in children's television. I went on to say that I was determined to break into children's TV at WGBH. I asked if there was anyone on any other show she could possibly refer me to. I think my enthusiasm and determination caught her off guard. She agreed that she would at least forward my reel to the producer who would be making the ultimate decision in who to bring on board. For the next 7 years, I worked consistently as a field producer on *Zoom*. It was a great gig.

Turning a "no" into a "yes" isn't easy, and it won't always work. Sometimes people just aren't going to hire you, and that's okay. But you have nothing to lose by trying.

CONGRATULATIONS, YOU'VE GOT THE JOB ... NOW WHAT?

SOME TASKS MAY NOT MAKE YOU SMILE

Getting an entry-level job in the television industry will probably feel really good ... for a limited amount of time. But if you are a true writer, the novelty will wear off quickly. It is possible, even likely, that you will start to feel frustrated because you will probably be asked to do things that you consider beneath you. After all, in your heart, you are a writer, not a gopher, nor a production assistant, nor a script typist, nor a production secretary. You may look at some of the writers and think that you could do a better job. Maybe you could. But the bottom line is they are in their job and you are in yours. You are picking up a paycheck for whatever job you have agreed to do and so you have an obligation both to the show and to the people who hired you to do that job well.

You may not realize it now, but someday when you are further into your career, you will come to understand that most entry-level jobs give you more than a simple paycheck. They give you experience. In exchange for getting lunch and coffee and answering phones, you are actually learning firsthand the ins and outs of television production. This is vital to becoming a writer, especially if you want to run your own show someday. An entry-level job gives you the opportunity to spend five days a week with writers and producers and watch how it is done. This is the stuff that can't be taught in film school or simply by reading books or studying TV shows. By being there, you will learn by osmosis, and one day you will wake up surprised at all the things you actually know.

> "The reality is, you will have crappy jobs. Working for annoying people, that's a given. You'll be asked to do uninteresting things — like Xeroxing, or answering phones, or fetching coffee. You'll be irritated that you're putting your fancy-schmancy advanced degree to use — fetching coffee.

But here's the thing. When you fetch that coffee you have to do it with a smile. And you have to make that the best damn cup of coffee on the face of the planet. You do this because if you fetch that coffee with attitude, roll your eyes, act like you're too 'good' to be fetching coffee, then that's what people will remember about you. Not that you're smart, or talented, or that you have a fancy-schmancy degree from some fancy-schmancy institution. You'll be the ungrateful kid with a bad attitude, the kid who couldn't even handle the smallest task. So if you're smart, you'll handle yourself with grace, and you'll save your grumbling for the drive home. Otherwise, you've just managed to burn a bridge over something as stupid and unimportant as fetching a lousy cup of coffee." — Stacy McKee, story editor, *Grey's Anatomy*

The fastest way to get out of an entry-level job is to do that job better than well. Take on every task, no matter how menial, with enthusiasm. For example, let's say you are asked to pick up lunch for the writers. You do so and deliver it on time. Then, one dodo-brain whines that he asked for cole slaw, not the potato salad that you so erroneously brought back with his sandwich. I am telling you — if it kills you , the correct response is a polite "I'm sorry. I would be happy to go back to the restaurant and get you some cole slaw." You must prove that you are unshakable — an absolute rock that can't be broken under pressure.

Prove that you are reliable and dependable. Show up to work every day with a good attitude. On days you don't have a good attitude, fake one. Demonstrate extreme loyalty to the people you work for. If you want them to take care of you, then you need to take care of them. It's a two-way street, and you have to be prepared to go the extra mile. That means if it's 3 a.m. and the writers are still in the room struggling with a script, stick your head in the door and volunteer to make a fresh pot of coffee. I promise the gesture won't kill you — and it will mean the world to them. It's the little things that people will remember when it comes time to help and promote you … or not.

"No one is successful overnight. My first job was being a receptionist and driving a limo. I delivered bottled water to my boss' picnic. And I did it with a smile. You have to have a good attitude. When we have to work nights or weekends and I see the slightest roll of an eyeball, I know that person isn't going far." — Jay Bienstock, executive producer, *The Apprentice* and *Survivor*

EVEN THE MOST MUNDANE AND MENIAL TASKS CAN LEAD TO A BREAK

Everyone breaks into the business differently, and you never know where or how your break is going to come. The way it happened for me isn't exactly how it happened for my friends, and it will probably be completely different for you. You just have to work hard and be open to everything and everyone.

Case in point: one day while working at *Charles In Charge,* I went up to the Xerox room to copy a script. There was a long line. Bored, I struck up a conversation with the guy behind me. Unbeknownst to me, he was an executive producer. Drama was his thing. I told him I had sold a couple of comedies. He asked if I had any interest in writing drama. Later that afternoon, I schlepped one of my drama specs over to his office. Eventually, he hired me. I often look back on that day, thankful that I didn't have the attitude that I was too high and mighty to Xerox a script.

FINDING A MENTOR

The most important thing you can get out of an entry-level job is a mentor. This is something that can't be forced; it has to happen naturally. A mentor is obviously someone with more experience than you and in a position of power. Basically, your personalities just click. For whatever reason, you genuinely like each other. You have a great deal of respect for what that person has accomplished, and he or she sees potential in you and wants to help push your career ahead.

Mentors are crucial when breaking into TV writing. Depending on their position, they can help you get a break in many different ways. If they have enough power, they can actually assign you your first story or script. If they are a little lower on the totem pole, they can still go to bat for you by telling the powers that be that you have worked hard, you are a good writer, and they would like to help you get a break. This is known as guaranteeing a script. And it is a very big favor.

Selling your first script is so difficult because, as we have talked about repeatedly, producers are often reluctant to give first-time writers a try for fear that they won't come through with a script that is usable. If a writer or producer guarantees your script, what they are saying to the executive producer is that if your script comes in and it's a dud, they will rewrite it and make sure it's in good shape. You may be thinking, "what's the big deal?" In the course of a busy production schedule, a producer who has to drop what he or she is doing to rewrite your script — for which you will get the money and the credit — is definitely doing you quite a big favor.

> "Find yourself some mentors, and learn from their experience ... learn from their successes, learn from their failures. If you aren't in New York or L.A., it gets a little bit harder, but try to strike up a discussion through writing back and forth. Ask for advice, not a job." — Gary Grossman, partner, Weller/Grossman Productions

TAKING RESPONSIBILITY FOR YOUR GOOF-UPS

Once you are in a job, you will have days when you are totally on top of your game, and days when you are not. Undoubtedly because you are human, sooner or later you will make a mistake. It could be fairly minor or it could be more significant. No matter how big or how small the error, my best advice is to accept responsibility for it.

Probably one of the biggest mistakes I ever made in television was as a writer on a magazine show called *Real Life,* which aired on NBC. The show was in the start-up phase. We were about a week away from its debut. We had been rehearsing and working 18–20 hour days, 7 days a week for several weeks. I was bleary-eyed and exhausted. One morning, somewhere around 1:30, the show producer asked me to go into an edit bay and oversee some titles that were being laid into a particular story. He cautioned me to make sure everything was spelled correctly.

A few days later, I noticed the show's two executive producers and the show producer, gathered in an edit bay, all looking fairly annoyed. It didn't take long for me to figure out why. I had screwed up big time. One of the words I was charged with overseeing had been misspelled, and I didn't catch it. That may not sound so bad, but it created a Domino effect. The word had been laid into the story … the story had been placed in a show … and the show had been fed to the network in Burbank. Thankfully, someone at NBC who was more bright-eyed and bushy-tailed than me caught the spelling error … and thankfully, there was time to fix it before the show aired.

None of my bosses mentioned the mistake to me. I'm not even sure they knew that I was the one responsible. But I felt horrible because I knew I was responsible and that I had caused a lot of tired, over-taxed people a lot of extra work. I also felt stupid because I am a writer; spelling mistakes aren't something that a writer at the network-level should make. I remember being so over-tired and humiliated that I just wanted to cry.

Instead, I marched into the boss' office, sat down, and informed him that I was the one responsible for the misspelling. I apologized and told him how bad I felt for all of the work I had caused him, not to mention the embarrassment in front of the network executives. When I entered his office, I think he was fairly annoyed. As soon as I stepped up to the plate and took responsibility for what had happened, he immediately softened.

Whenever I make a mistake at work, I always own up to it, no matter how difficult that is to do. The bottom line is that everyone is human and at some point in time, everyone makes mistakes. What people remember is how you handle the mistakes. If you take responsibility, bosses may not always like what you have to tell them, but ultimately they will respect you for your honesty. But if you are someone who tries to sweep the mistakes under the carpet — or worse still, let a coworker take the blame — people will eventually figure you out. I have also discovered that if you take responsibility for mistakes, then when something happens that you really didn't do, your boss is much more likely to believe you.

REMEMBER YOUR GOAL: GET A WRITING SCHEDULE AND STICK TO IT

Once you get in a position where you are working the long days that a television job demands, or any job for that matter, you will probably find it hard to find the time to write. Many people I know who are working entry-level industry jobs leave early in the morning and don't get home until 8 or 9, and that's on a good night. On weekends, in addition to various social invitations, there are those tedious but necessary chores like laundry, errands, grocery shopping, and paying bills. You will also want some time (and will have rightfully earned it) to relax and have fun. So where does the writing fit in? The answer is, unless you make it a priority, it won't. Before you know it days, then weeks, then months will have gone by and not only will you not have written anything, but deep down it will be nagging at you. The way to avoid this is to open your day planner, look at your week, and physically scribble in an appointment to write the same way you would a doctor's appointment. That's the first step.

The second step is to keep the appointment that you have made with yourself. If possible, try to write at approximately the same time each day. Before long, it will become habit.

"Very important: never invest 100% of your self-worth in your writing career. It ain't worth it. No matter how successful you may become, there's always going to be someone more successful, more talented, younger, luckier, richer. And if that's the only yardstick by which you measure your happiness, you're bound to be disappointed. It seems obvious, but lots of people in show business seem to make this mistake. There's more to life than that. And being a well-rounded person will make you a better writer, anyway." — Don Mancini, screenwriter, *Child's Play* movies, creator, *Kill Switch*

HOW LONG SHOULD YOU STAY IN AN ENTRY-LEVEL JOB?

About 6 months into an entry-level job, you should start to have casual conversations with your boss about your career aspirations. Don't do it too often and don't make it too calculated. When the subject comes up or it fits into the conversation naturally, you can talk about it. If you have been doing a good job, most bosses are going to be curious, if not downright interested, in what you want to be when you grow up.

After a year, I believe it is time to set up a formal appointment to discuss your future. When I say formal, I mean get on the boss' calendar as an appointment, rather than just trying to catch him or her on the fly. If you try to do the latter, the conversation is almost sure to be interrupted by something or someone, and the boss won't feel badly about it because the conversation is casual, not formal.

You can start the conversation by saying something like, "Believe it or not, I've been here a year, and so I thought it might be a good time to check in with you to see how you think I'm doing." Hopefully the response will be that everything is great and that you are doing a fabulous job. At this point, you can come back with, "I'm glad to hear you say that because I am really happy here and I'd like to talk to you about how you think I might fit in, in the future, and when I might be able to take on more responsibility."

If you have an idea of how you see yourself fitting-in down the road, definitely lay it out. But make sure you are realistic. Asking to go from an entry-level job to being a staff writer or producer is not a request most bosses will consider, no matter how much they like you. (Keep in mind, what you ask for will depend on the type of job you are in as well as the position that your boss is in.) You could certainly talk about your desire to be a writer and ask your boss to read one of your specs and, if he or she likes it, would you ever be considered to pitch?

You need to listen very carefully to how your boss responds to your request. He or she may say that you need to be there longer than a year before you start asking to move ahead. That's fair. But see if you can get a timeframe of when it would be okay to reopen the discussion. You may be told that there aren't any more scripts open this season, but that you can possibly pitch next season. Or, you could be told that the job you are in really doesn't have much growth potential. In addition to listening to the words, listen to the body language. If your boss is making a promise for something down the road, does he or she seem sincere or a bit put off and uncomfortable? All of this information is hugely important, even if it's stuff that deep down you really don't want to hear.

PLANNING THE NEXT STEP

Once you have had the conversation, it is time to digest it. At the risk of stating the obvious, if your boss tells you that the job has no growth potential, the first thing you have to do is start to look for another job immediately. You are marking time in a dead-end job. Besides the paycheck, it's wasted effort because it isn't going to get you where you ultimately want to go. You may be upset, but you should be thankful that your boss told you the truth rather than lead you on with false hope for another few years.

On the other hand, if your boss made a future commitment to you, it would behoove you to stick around and see if he or she comes through. Whatever the promise, and in whatever timeframe, go back and remind the boss of the conversation. If you have the initial meeting in October and you are assured that you can pitch story ideas "next season," I wouldn't go marching in on the day the fall schedule is announced; wait until the writing staff comes back to work and settles in. Then, say to your boss, "At the end of last season, you told me I could possibly pitch some story ideas. I'm wondering if that offer is still open."

Here is where things can get sticky. In a perfect world, your boss might say, "Of course. Let me know when you are ready." But there is another scenario: the boss makes excuses about why now isn't a good time, but maybe somewhere down the road. Now you have gone from a firm commitment to a "maybe." This means you have some decisions to make, and you have to be painfully honest with yourself. Do you think the boss is sincere or do you think that carrots are being dangled? While I have preached endlessly about the importance of having a good work ethic and doing your job well, there is a small danger that if you do it too well, some bosses won't want to promote you because they don't want to lose you. What this means is that they are really looking out or themselves, not for you.

Now, you must make some awfully tough choices. Do you stay and see what happens or do you look for another job? I can tell you what you will want to do: you will want to stay and hope for the best. No one likes to job-hunt, not to mention the fact that you have now invested a year and a half in this position. By quitting, in essence, you will have to start over and find another company where you will have to prove yourself all over again. I can't tell you what to do here, because every situation is different. I can only tell you to trust your gut. If it feels like a dead end, then you must get out. So far, you have only invested a year and a half. But in the blink of an eye, those 18 months can become 5 years. People get comfortable in jobs and time goes by fast.

By the same token, you have to be realistic. In today's competitive marketplace, it may take you several years to sell that first script, so hanging around just might pay off. Remember, it took me 6 years to make my first sale.

THE POWER OF NETWORKING

KEEPING IN TOUCH IS JOB NUMBER THREE

While your first priority will be to keep churning out spec scripts and looking for an agent or for work as a writer, and your second job will be the so-called day job that pays the bills and puts a roof over your head, I am now going to add a third job to the mix: networking.

While your parents may have worked for the same company for years on end, the opposite is true in television. Rarely (if ever) do writers and producers spend their whole careers at one studio. Shows get cancelled, writers don't get rehired on returning shows, or their agents find them better gigs. People bounce from show to show, studio to studio, and you must keep up with them, the same way you must keep up with the contacts that you meet at seminars or parties. The worst feeling in the world is to realize that someone you once worked for now has a fabulously powerful position, and could potentially help you, but you don't feel like you can call because you haven't spoken in years. Speaking from the other side of the desk, there is nothing more off-putting than someone who phones only when I can do something for them. You can easily prevent this from happening by taking a genuine interest in other people's lives and careers. But I warn you — keeping up with people takes a lot of time and effort.

ORDER YOUR OWN PERSONAL NOTE CARDS (YOU'LL NEED THEM)

You should get yourself some nice note cards. These are great for jotting quick little notes. For example, if someone has taken you to lunch … send a quick thank you. If you are reading the trades and see that someone you know has been promoted, whip off a quick little note of congratulations to them. These are the things that will make you look classy — and they will also help you stand out among the pack.

STOCK UP ON BUSINESS CARDS

While you are in an ordering mode, you should also get yourself some professional business cards. You will be surprised how many people you are going to meet and how quickly. Before long you will wind up at parties, screenings, and all kinds of industry events, where you will strike up conversations people with whom you will want to stay in touch. You will look so much classier and polished reaching for a business card than scrounging around your wallet or purse and pulling out an old bank receipt to scrawl your contact information.

It is important to think carefully about what information you want to include on your cards. I was once at a party where a guy was handing out cards to anybody who would take one. In addition to his name, address, and phone number, the cards listed him as a TV writer. The moment the poor guy left the room, people rolled their eyes and snickered because everyone knew he hadn't sold anything. There is a feeling that, until you have made that first sale, you technically aren't a television writer … at least not a professional one. It's like someone saying they are a store owner when they really don't own a store, but someday hope to buy one.

If I were just starting out, I would simply list my name and contact information, including my e-mail address and cell phone number. I would choose a card that is both professional and eye-catching in its design and color.

If you don't have the money to purchase professionally printed cards, you can easily design and print your own business cards on your computer. The same is true for note cards.

CREATING YOUR OWN LITTLE BLACK BOOK

The easiest way to stay in touch with people is to create your own personal book of industry friends and contacts. Every few months when you find yourself with a few spare minutes, tear through the pages and search for people you haven't spoken with in a while. Then, give them a call, say that you haven't talked to them in a while, and you're calling to say "hello" and see what they are up to. Not only is this a good way to keep in touch, it is also a good way to keep connected to the grapevine. It is quite possible that the person you are talking with will have been in touch with other people you know and can fill you in. One little call can really keep you on the pulse.

THE IMPORTANCE OF SENDING HOLIDAY GREETINGS

In late August, I can usually be found on the beach, mentally designing my holiday cards. Each year, I send tons of them and I make each one personally. This task is incredibly time-consuming (and trust me, I have no more spare time around the holidays than you do), but worth every minute of effort. In addition to helping me stay in touch and wish my industry friends well, it also gives me a chance to jot a quick thank-you to the people who may have been especially helpful with my career over the past year.

You may be thinking, "why not just grab a couple boxes of Hallmark snowmen, and call it a day?" The answer is, because lots of people send Hallmark snowmen. Go into any office around the holidays, and you are sure to see several of the exact same card. Remember, you are trying continuously to make yourself stand out as someone who is exciting and different. Television is a visual medium. By designing your own cards, you are sending a subtle reminder that you are a creative and unique person who thinks out of the box.

Please heed the following words of caution: most, if not all holidays are centered on religion. Therefore, if you're going to send cards, don't assume that you know someone's religious preference — or worse still that they'd enjoy a card centered on your religious preference. Stay far away from any symbols (including Santa Claus and Christmas trees) that have religious connotations because they could be considered offensive.

HOW TO DO LUNCH

If you know anything about the entertainment industry, you probably know the importance of lunch. Lunch in Hollywood is ceremonious. It's something everyone does. You will constantly hear people say, "let's do lunch."

In Hollywood, lunch is serious business. Most people in the industry do lunch frequently, some do it every day. There are certain "hot spots" where industry people tend to gather. It is not uncommon to go to any one of these restaurants on any given day and see many powerful people dining with other powerful people, including executives, agents, writers, producers, directors, and stars. Lunch is a place where deals and futures get made — or at least discussed.

But lunch isn't something reserved for the rich and famous. People like yourself who are just starting out can also get career mileage by getting into the lunch game. It's a great opportunity to socialize with people in the industry — especially those who are further along in their careers and might be able to offer you some support or advice.

WHO DO YOU INVITE?

After you have been at your job for a month or two, you will probably start to get friendly with people … and this includes the higher-ups like writers and producers. You will find that there are some you just really click with. When you feel comfortable, you should start to ask them to lunch. How busy the show is will determine when you can do it. On some shows, writers get to go to lunch, on other shows they work through lunch and have it delivered. If this is the case, you just have to wait for a hiatus week or — worst-case scenario — at the end of production.

Lunch is a fabulous opportunity for you to get to know people better. Being away from the office, you are much more relaxed. Also, it is complete one-on-one time without the possibility of the phone ringing or people interrupting because they need to talk to you or your lunch mate right away.

TAKING THE LEAD

Once you have arrived at the restaurant and ordered your food, you should start to ask your lunchmate questions. At the beginning, questions can be of a more personal nature (as long as it's respectful): you can ask if they are married, what their spouse does, if they have kids, where they grew up, what part of town they live in, etc. You can then move to questions like how they got to whatever job they are in, what their ultimate career goals are, etc. Listen carefully to what they have to say. They may offer some ideas you hadn't considered.

WHEN AND HOW TO ASK FOR WHAT YOU REALLY WANT

At some point, the conversation will shift to you. After you have asked the person all about their life, it is almost guaranteed that he or she will have similar questions for you. One of the questions will likely be about your career and what you want to do long-term. You should definitely tell the person that you want to be a writer. See what the reaction is. You may be asked what kinds of things you'd like to write … you may be asked what shows you have written specs on. When the time is right — and you will know it instinctively — it is okay to ask the person for advice and/or help. You could say something like, "if you were me, how would you go about getting an agent?" Or you could say, "I know you are incredibly busy, but would there be any possible way that I could ask you to take a look at my spec?" You have to be polite, but I also encourage you to be direct. Sometimes we tend to think that people can read our minds. They can't. One of the biggest mistakes people make is that they don't ask for what they want.

Don't be shy. This is one instance where as long as your request is reasonable, the person will probably say "yes." The mere fact that he or she has agreed to have lunch with you means that the person likes you. People generally try to help people they like. Writers and producers tend to remember how people helped them when they were just starting out, and they are usually willing to pay it back by helping another up-and-coming writer.

WHO PAYS?

When it comes to who pays the bill, I have good news and bad news. The bad news is that it is your responsibility. You invited the person to lunch, and therefore the classy thing to do is to pick up the check. The good news is that nine times out of ten, the person you invited won't allow you to do so. Usually, that person is at a much higher level and often has an expense account, so it can be written off. Even if the person doesn't have an expense account, he is probably well aware of the fact that he is making considerably more money than you. But, you have to put up at least a little fight. If the person says, "I got it," don't automatically say, "okay." Try something more along the lines of, "I invited you and I totally intended to pay." The person will usually say something like, "you can take me when you sell your first script or get your first staff job." Then you can graciously accept the offer and promise to take them the next time. Just be sure to follow through, not because the person is going to be keeping a scorecard, but because it's the right thing to do.

You should also be prepared for the possibility that the other person won't argue with your intention to pay. This rarely happens, but it could. Keep in mind that lunch in Los Angeles is not cheap. This is one time I would advocate borrowing the money from your parents if you don't have it, because you need to make sure that you either have enough cash or enough credit on your credit card. The last thing you want to have happen is for the waiter to snip your credit card into pieces as Steven Spielberg looks on.

SHOULD YOU BRING YOUR SPEC SCRIPTS?

I would not bring spec scripts to lunch. To me, it is too pushy, and seems too calculating — as in the only reason you asked the person to lunch was to get him or her to read your work. You know where this person's office is. If he or she has agreed to read your spec, you can bring it in the next day. The person is probably not going to read it immediately anyway, so one more day won't kill you.

OTHER THINGS THAT CAN HELP YOU SUCCEED

GET YOURSELF OUT THERE AS QUICKLY AS POSSIBLE

If you are serious about being a television writer, you need to get going on it yesterday. I often come across wannabe writers who talk ad nauseam about their plans for breaking into the industry. They are always going to do it after they save some money, or after they live at home for the summer, or after their cat dies, or after a whole laundry list of other things. Life has a way of marching by. Five years whiz by in the blink of an eye, and some of these same so-called writers are still talking about getting into the industry.

The TV industry is a young business especially in comedy. It is much harder to break in when you are 30 than it is when you are 22. So, if you have any inclination that writing TV is something you want to take a shot at doing, the best thing you can do is put yourself out there quickly. I know this can be hard financially, but I also know that when there is a will, there is a way. You can figure it out. Get yourself a roommate … get four roommates if you have to. Do whatever it takes to get yourself out there.

> If you start writing comedy at 19, 20, 21, 22, or 23, and you do it for 7 years and it doesn't work out, you're still only 30. You can at least say, "I tried." Nothing is more heartbreaking than the guy who says, "I always wanted to be a comedy writer, but I just couldn't get out there." — Jay Leno, host, *The Tonight Show*

WRITING BUDDIES

If you have opted to go solo rather than be part of a team, it can be incredibly useful to have at your disposal people you trust, who can read your work and give you feedback before you send it out. There are a couple ways to do this. You could join a writers' group. These are usually fairly small and intimate, and everyone reads everyone else's work and then gets together to discuss it. The thing that is nice about a writers' group is that there is discussion — which means that if someone has an opinion about something in your work, you have the opportunity to see if others share the same opinion before you start changing it.

If there is a negative about being in a writers' group, it is the time commitment. If you are employed, you will have little enough time to devote to your own writing; a writers' group requires you to give undivided attention to other people's work. While there is nothing wrong with this — and actually it works quite well for a lot of writers — you should realize that it is a commitment both in terms of time and energy.

Another way to go is to get a writing buddy. A writing buddy is another writer with whom you can talk out stories and trade scripts. It amounts to one-on-one attention for both of you. While you are working on separate teleplays, you each know the other's work intimately and care about it as much as you do your own. You are there for each other to answer questions, give support, and offer feedback if not on a daily basis, then at least on a weekly one.

A good writing buddy can keep you on track. The nice thing is that with technology, you don't even have to live in the same part of the country. With the help computers, you can shoot scripts back and forth and then rendezvous on the phone to go over notes.

> "The biggest mistake a writer can make is not to finish. I've seen so many writers with promise put it away when it's 30–40% done. If they'd go on and finish, even if it's not salable, they'd have learned so much along the way." — Al Burton, executive producer, *Charles in Charge*

HOW TO TURN UP CONTACTS WHEN YOU THINK YOU DON'T HAVE ANY

If you didn't attend college, and you have racked your brain and come to the conclusion that you really, legitimately don't have any connections to anyone in the business, don't despair. You can always make connections. Start by getting involved with local organizations that deal with film and television. These groups may vary, depending on where you live. If you live in New York or Los Angeles, there are always industry-related events going on. If you live outside of these two cities, you may find local chapters of national groups like Women in Film or the National Academy of Television Arts and Sciences. You should also look at getting involved with your state's film commission.

ATTEND SEMINARS AND CONFERENCES

Start to attend events that attract other writers. There is a wide assortment of seminars and conferences for screenwriters held all over the country. You will need to do some research on which ones might be best for you. The thing that is good about these events is that you not only learn about writing, but you also meet people in the industry. But you need to put yourself out there. Talk to people during a break or at lunch — come home with names and numbers — and stay in touch. It won't do you any good to listen to the lecture and then sit like a bump on a log when it's time to socialize with other industry people.

ENTER YOUR WORK IN CONTESTS

Whenever possible, you should enter your work in TV writing contests. This is a good and easy way to get your work read by people in the industry. Even if you don't win the grand prize, you can still come out ahead. Because writing is so subjective, you never know who your script may attract. I have been a semifinalist in competitions and received calls from producers and agents asking to read my work.

You should be choosy about which contests you enter as you probably won't be able to enter all of them. (Entrance fees can add up.) The best way to choose a competition is to look at the people behind the contest — mainly the sponsors and judges. If you see major studios, production companies, networks, or agents involved, then it's probably a good bet. I am leery of some of the smaller competitions that sound like a one-horse show and boast that the winning script will be read by an industry professional. I do not mean to imply that these are not legitimate, but personally, I would look for something more concrete. I believe it is far better to walk away as a finalist in a well-respected competition like Scriptapalooza or Screenwriting Expo than to walk away a winner in a contest that few people have heard of. Of course, the downside to entering the more-well known contests is that there is a lot more competition, so your chances of placing are slimmer. Still, if you do your homework and master the craft, you should end up with a dynamic script, and this should up your chances.

USING TECHNOLOGY TO GET WORK SEEN

Not so long ago, the only way to get work produced and in front of an audience was to go through the routine channels such as agents, studios, and networks. Thanks to technology, Webcasts, video podcasts and vlogs, it is now relatively easy to get your work in front of potentially millions of viewers. In recent months, many writers and producers have gotten some good mileage and great publicity off work they created with very little, if any, financial backing. This is the good news. You now live in a world where you can use technology to help deliver your art and/or your message. The bad news is that it has not taken long for these avenues to become overcrowded. In many ways, it's like an agent's office … loaded down with a lot of work that isn't good but has to be sifted through in order to find the gems. The sheer volume of people trying to break in this way makes it all the more difficult to stand out in the crowd. That said, if you have a creative idea, and you think you can execute it, then by all means use technology to get it out there. Like everything else, you just never know what can happen.

USE YOUR TALENT TO HELP OTHERS

I am a firm believer that if you have talent, you should use it to help others. Go out and offer your services to the charity of your choice at least once a year. Write a Public Service Announcement or a brochure or whatever it is they need. You will feel great afterward, and you will probably learn something along the way. An added bonus is that you will have some produced work that you can put in your portfolio. I am a firm believer that if you put good stuff into the universe, good stuff always comes back.

LEARN TO BE A GOOD CRITIC

In addition to your own writing, you will be asked constantly to critique the work of other writers. The trick to this is to be both sensitive and honest. It is important to always tell a writer the truth. Holding back — or worse still, saying a script is good when it's bad — can actually harm the writer if he or she listens to you and then puts the work out to the industry. By the same token, you have to learn how to critique in a way that isn't going to hurt the writer's feelings. As much as I try to tell you that writing is a business … it still feels personal to most people most of the time.

In critiquing writing, perhaps the best thing you can do is to say some positive things about the script up-front. Once you have made the writer feel good, you can say things like, "I thought maybe you could use a few more jokes toward the middle" or "I thought Act Three wasn't quite as strong as your other acts." Whatever you do, try to stay away from words like "boring" and "dull." They serve no purpose — and they are words you would not like to hear spoken about your own work. The key is to offer constructive criticism, and whenever possible, suggest solutions to the problems at hand.

OFF TO SEE THE WIZARD (OR FIVE MONTHS TO MY DREAM JOB)

Let's talk about tenacity. It is a must in the television business. When I left Los Angeles to move back to New England, most of the television jobs were local. There was only one network gig in town. It was a new magazine show called *Real Life*. I wanted to be a writer on that show more than anything, and felt certain I had the credentials. But sometimes, even for a writer with credits, it is hard to get noticed by the people who have the power to hire you.

The executive producer on the show was a man by the name of Joel Cheatwood. In October, shortly after the announcement was made that the show would be going into production, I sent Mr. Cheatwood a resumé. I did not hear back. I placed follow-up calls to his assistant, and went through my usual routine of faxing my resumé and also sending it via FedEx. Nothing. Deep down, I knew that the chances he had even seen my resumé were slim to none. His office was no doubt being inundated with resumés from writers and producers from all over the country.

I was determined that there had to be a way to reach this man. But how? Because his office was at the NBC affiliate in Boston, I began to draw up a list of all of the people I knew that might have a connection to him. I looked carefully for anyone who may have gone to the same college as me.

I found a guy named Gene Lavanchy. He was the local sports anchor, so I figured he probably had some clout. Instead of telling him precisely what I wanted, I told him that I was an Emerson alum and I had just moved back from Los Angeles. I asked if I could come by his office, show him my resumé, and seek his advice for how to find television work in the Boston area.

I met with Lavanchy, who graciously looked at my resumé and told me he knew exactly where I belonged. There was a new NBC show getting ready to start up. He said I'd be perfect for it. I asked him how I'd go about getting a job on that show. He said I needed to talk to a man by the name of … Joel Cheatwood. I asked him if he could give me any advice on how to get my resumé through to Cheatwood, who was obviously incredibly busy and probably could wallpaper his office with all of the resumés he'd been receiving. Lavanchy said he'd take care of it.

I guess he did, because a week or so later I received a call from a producer on *Real Life* asking me to come in for an interview. The interview went well — or so I thought. She told me she would be in touch within the next couple of days. I never heard from her again. When I called her, my calls were not returned.

The holidays came and went. One morning in early February, I woke up and decided that enough was enough. This would be the week I would convince Joel Cheatwood to hire me. I didn't have any idea how I was going to make that happen … only that I was determined that it would. Over a cup of coffee, I wracked my brain, trying to think of some back door way to get to him. I felt like there must be something I was missing. I pulled out a newspaper article about *Real Life* that one of my friends had clipped out of the *Boston Globe* several months before. Stupid me … I had skimmed it, but I hadn't really read it. As I read over the article, I discovered that Mr. Cheatwood was married to a TV producer named Neva, who would also be working on the show. I thought back to the day I had gone in for the interview and I vaguely remembered walking by her office. To the best of my recollection, there had not been a secretary outside her door. I realized if I sent my resumé directly to her it was likely she would open it personally. So I fired off yet another resumé and cover letter. My friends rolled their eyes at me and laughed at my "back door" approach.

But it was I who got the last laugh a day later when Neva Cheatwood called and told me she had received my resumé. She wondered how soon I could come in to meet with her and Joel. They had a writing job on a new show they thought I'd be perfect for. The next day, Neva met me in the lobby of the TV station and took me up to Joel's office. I felt like Dorothy … I was finally going to meet the wizard. They hired me on the spot. It was a great job — and I learned tons. I also met lots of great people, many of whom have hired me on other shows.

It was a long walk down that Yellow Brick Road. It took me exactly five months to get in the door. Looking back, there were a thousand places I could have given up along the way: when I didn't get a call back from the three resumés I sent, when my follow-up phone calls weren't returned, when the producer interviewed me and then wouldn't take my phone calls. I have learned that if you refuse to take "no" for an answer, sooner or later it will almost always come back as a "yes."

NOT GIVING UP ON WHAT YOU WANT

I look around at many of the people I went to college with. Some are fabulously successful working in key industry jobs. Others are not in the business at all. So, what makes the difference? It's simple. The people in the business knew what they wanted and were willing to hang in. When one path didn't get them where they wanted to go, they tried another route … and another route … until they got their desired break. But this takes time and can be emotionally and financially draining. The people who are not working in the industry — for whatever reason — didn't want it as badly. The minute you decide it's over … then it's over. By the same token, if you're not happy trudging through all of the muck that you will have to trudge through in order to sell your first script, then you owe it to yourself to ask whether it's worth it to continue vs. finding something that really does make you happy.

A WORD TO WOMEN

While women are making headway in the entertainment industry, the truth is that the business is still run predominantly by men. Therefore, the temptation may be to be cute. Don't rely on that. Cute may get you in the door, but I promise it won't sustain you — and in the long-run it sure as heck won't earn you respect. What will get you ahead in the industry are your brain, your professionalism, and your commitment to your craft.

> "Work hard. Don't try to find a short-cut or be the cutest. Just work hard. It will eventually be rewarded and your talent will take you from there."— Jay Bienstock, executive producer, *The Apprentice* and *Survivor*

And, ladies, while we are on the subject of being professional, let me warn you that there may be days ahead when something happens at work that makes you either so angry or so frustrated that you simply want to burst into tears.

Don't do it.

I think one of the worst things a woman can do is to cry at work. No one wants to deal with it … especially men. Do it enough and people will label you as someone who doesn't have it together. If you are a woman in this business, you have to be tough. So, whatever it is, the best thing you can do is suck it up … at least until quitting time. Once you are alone and on your way home, you can sob to your heart's delight. But, you cannot do it in the work place … not without potentially damaging your reputation.

TAKE CARE OF YOUR MIND AND YOUR BODY

Okay … here is the part where you get to call me square. (And frankly, my dear, I don't give a damn!) Here is the part where I am going to tell you not to use drugs. There is a temptation for people just starting out to want to be cool — and there is often a misconception with new writers that the entertainment industry is populated by a bunch of druggies. I have to tell you that this is not so. I know tons of extremely successful writers, producers, and executives, and I promise you they don't spend their nights on the Sunset Strip shooting up.

Plain and simple, drugs aren't going to get you where you want to go. As a writer, your biggest asset is your brain. Screw that up and you will have no writing career. Worse, you may not have a life. If you follow my advice along with the wonderful advice that everyone who contributed to this book has put forth, there is every reason to believe that you have a solid career ahead of you. But I promise … you can't write scripts from 6 feet under, nor while you're vomiting in rehab. Let me say it again, because it bears repeating: drugs aren't going to get you where you want to go.

OH, THE PLACES YOU'LL GO! THE WARMTH AND WISDOM OF DR. SEUSS

For most television writers, the road to success is filled with tremendous highs and lows and plenty of bumps along the way. Even with the most thought-out career strategy, I am sorry to tell you there will probably be times when things don't go exactly according to plan. Likely there will be days that you want to give up, days when you question why you ever wanted to be a television writer in the first place, days you wonder why you actually thought you could do this. When self-doubt seeps in, it's important to take a deep breath and be extra kind to yourself. I highly recommend the book *Oh, the Places You'll Go!* by Dr. Seuss. It will make you feel good. It will make you smile. It will soothe your soul. It will remind you of just how wonderful and talented you really are. Most importantly, it will encourage you to keep moving forward with your plan.

SOME FINAL THOUGHTS

In talking to the many successful people that contributed to this book, I came to realize that many offered the same solid advice, which I think is worth summing up: work hard, write, get your foot in the door any way you can, write, have a point of view, write, have a good attitude, and write. Nearly all of them believe that television needs to re-invented and that change will only come through fresh, new, pioneering voices. I echo the challenges these writers, producers, and executives have consistently put before you: when it comes to TV writing, be a revolutionist, not a copycat. Come to the table with something to say. Have the courage to be who you are.

I have spent much of this book educating you on the cold, hard realities of the television business. But let me say that there is no greater thrill than walking onto a soundstage and seeing professional actors performing your work. Likewise, the day you finally see your name on the screen beneath the words "Written by" is a day you'll remember when you're 90. In addition to the work itself, television offers many perks. For me, one of the best things about this business is all of the cool, fun, creative, smart, and talented people that I have had the privilege to know and work with along the way.

Television is a small business. Hang around long enough and, sooner or later, you run into all of your heroes. It has taken me 25 years to cross paths with mine. It seems only fitting, then, that I give him the final word:

> "The best advice I could give to new writers is write. It all starts there. It sounds simple, but the act of filling in those blank pages is the hardest thing for writers to do. But if you're able to and willing to do that, find what's closest to your sense of humor or dramatic sensibility. If you like *South Park* and *Earl,* write a couple. Then do everything you know how to do in this world to get that work read."— Norman Lear, executive producer, *All in the Family* and *The Princess Bride*

SOME LEFTOVER PEARLS

"The joke in Hollywood is 'I fly over the middle of the country.' You can't do that. You have to worry about what's between New York and L.A. New York and L.A. are insignificant compared to what the rest of the country wants." — Lucie Salhany, former chairman, FOX Broadcasting, founding president and former CEO, United Paramount Network (UPN)

"Write for the cast, know the cast — be in tune with the actors and write for their strengths." — Emmy Award-winning actor Henry Winkler

"First make sure you're in the right field. Do you remember your own childhood … i.e., is childhood something visceral for you, or something intellectual? If it's the latter, then maybe you want to teach or do research, but I'm not sure you should be making TV! Do you read kids' books? Do you know what makes a good book vs. a dreary one? Ditto with kids TV. Do you watch it? Do you like it? Are you critical of the dreck that's out there? If you think you've got a sharp eye for what's good, and if you really think you can add something vital and/or meaningful to a kid's life, then by all means jump right in!" — Kathy Waugh, head writer, *Peep and the Big Wide World*, on breaking into children's programming

"I think the biggest challenge in animation, or at least our show, is keeping stories grounded in reality. Since going anywhere costs the same as sitting on the couch, it's easy to pitch unbelievable storylines. The challenge is to be able to tell a story where the characters go to these places, but still keep it real and relatable. They can always get bonked on the head, suffer multiple flash-backs, and live out various dream sequences, but you must always be able to come back to the world where the characters live and believe they're that same person again." — John Frink, co-executive producer, *The Simpsons*

"Be educated about the business. Having a great idea for a show is one thing, but having the know-how to execute it is something else. Be as informed as you can. Know the marketplace. Know who your competitors are. Read the trades. Watch programs on the various networks that have kids programming. Make sure you aren't attempting something that has already been successfully tried. This way, when you meet with producers or writers who are already in the business, you come off as someone who has a clear understanding of the world you are trying to enter. And this will up your chances of breaking in to the business dramatically." — Paul Serafini, super-vising producer, *Zoom* and *Fetch*

"Expand your knowledge base! Know the world you live in. Have a sense of history … perspective and context are invaluable when it comes to news judgment. Enter the business without preconceived notion. Broadcast news desperately needs to freshen the existing model. More of the same is not good. The proverbial wheel needs to be reinvented." — Joel Cheatwood, executive director/program development, CNN

"Best thing a creator/producer can do when pitching a show is to tell us where they see it airing. There are over 300 stations, but there aren't 300 for each idea … there's maybe only two or three. So tell us you see your show on Comedy Central or that it would be great for HGTV." — Gary Grossman, partner, Weller/Grossman Productions

"It's all about the subjects, the cast, and conflict. … Can the audience relate to them? Are they likeable? Do they care enough about them to continue to watch each week? Conflict is reality television's drama. Is there enough? Will it keep the audience on the edge of their seats so that they stick with us through the break? You always want to 'jump the break' with some sort of cliffhanger." — Glenn Meehan, executive producer, *Little People, Big World*

"Watch a lot of TV. Find shows you like and study them. Read scripts. See how the script translates to the screen. Study your medium. If nothing else, be familiar with everything that's bought so you get a real sense of what prime time television is." — Jeff Eckerle, writer/producer, *Law & Order: Special Victims Unit*

"*Sesame Street* pioneered format and was cutting-edge in terms of curriculum. It took an advertising model of selling products, but in this case was selling letters and numbers. The puppets were sophisticated and appealed to both children and adults." — Kate Taylor, executive producer, *Zoom* and *Peep and the Big Wide World,* on the enormous success of *Sesame Street*

"Write, write, write. Live, breath the series world— have multiple scripts of your favorite series. When the day comes that you have a meeting with a producer, your passion and work ethic will make an impression." — Walter Klenhard, writer, TV series and MOWs

"Find that story that you can't stop thinking about — that original story that interests you, that story that so resonates that you can't not do it. That will give you the momentum to write and rewrite, to hear feedback, and to be able to take notes on the feedback." — Rebecca Eaton, executive producer, *Masterpiece Theatre* and *Mystery!*

INDEX

9/11, 8
13-week episode guide creation, 133–134
20–20, 195
24, 108
48 Hours Mystery, 199, 204
60 Minutes, 123, 193, 195, 211
60 Minutes II, 195

A
A story, 45–46, 50, 51, 52, 53, 106, 182
Abrams, J.J., xxii, 254, 261
ABC 7, 8, 39, 43, 108
Act Break, 49, 51, 99, 155
after getting job
  goal, 295
  menial tasks, 292–293
  mentor, 293
  planning for the future, 296–297
  promotion, 295–296
  taking responsibility, 294
Agency For Performing Arts, 255
agent, 10, 15, 17, 18, 30, 152
  charge, 253
  checklist for getting, 260
  cost, 252
  entertainment attorney, 256
  e-publishing, script, 260
  location, 254–255
  manager, need for, 256
  need, 251–252
  patience, 259–260
  preparedness, 259
  query letter, 256–257

  referral, 253
  role, 252
  sample querry letter, 257–259
  selection, 254
  unsolicited scripts, 255
Alf, 166, 167
All In the Family, 40, 42, 167, 168, 310
alliteration, 80
Amazing Race, The, 32, 233
American Academy of Pediatrics, 241
American Beauty, xxii
American Family, An, 231
American Idol, 232
America's Funniest Videos, 233
Angell, David, 190
Angell, Lynn, 190
animation, writing for, 82–84
Animators Guild, 84
Apprentice, The, 232, 233, 234, 235, 292, 308
arbitration, 263
Arlook, Richard, 252, 254, 256
Armstrong, Adrienne, 20, 166, 257
Aronsohn, Lee, 77, 134, 163, 279
Arrested Development, 5–6
Arthur, 242
audience
  dual audiences, 242
  likings, 165–166, 169, 170
  for MOWs, 146–147
  in superior position, 80
authentic worlds creation, importance
  in plot-driven dramas, 95

B
b-roll, 208
  example, 209–210
B story, 45–46, 50–51
Babysitter's Seduction, 148
Bachelor, The, 232, 235
Bachelorette, The, 235
backstory, 164, 165, 175
Baio, Scott, 5, 41
Ball, Alan, xxii
Bambi, 166
Bartlett's Book of Quotations, 43
Basanese, Manny, 9, 30, 31, 72, 119, 273, 284
Beers, Libby, 147, 149, 181
Bice, Bo, 233
Bienstock, Jay, 233, 234, 292, 308
Big Bird, 167
Big Love, 130–131
Big World, 232, 233, 236, 312
Black Donnellys, vi
Blockbuster, 276
Bohn, Beth, 255
Boutilier, Kate, 12, 82
Brady Bunch, The, 43, 127
brand loyalty, in children's programming, 240–241
Bridge Kids, 241
Brill, Eddie, 23, 85
Brown, Marc, 242
BTK Killer, 13, 96, 98
Bundy, Ted, 147
Burger King, 48
Burton, Al, 77, 304
button, 80–81

C
C story, 45–46
CAA, 18, 254
cable networks
  counter-programming, 123–124
Cagney and Lacey, 5
Candid Camera, 231
Caroline in the City, 79, 94
Cartoon Network, 5
CBS, 7, 8, 123
character-driven drama
  checklist for, 108
  colored index cards, 107
  day time drama writing, 109

personal experience dramatization, 103–106
and plot-driven dramas, 106
real-life experience, in drama, 102–103
storylines continuation, from week to week, 107–108
characters, 51, 77
  audience attraction, 165–166
  backstory, 164
  bios, 164–165
  composition, 170
  layers, 163
  minor characters, 168–169
  nonhuman characters, 166–167
  with opposing viewpoints, 167–168
  and premise introduction, 129
  20 Questions, 170
  quirky characters, 169–170
  real compelling characters, 235
  sound alike, 176
Charles, Glen, 190
Charles in Charge, xxi, xxiv, 20, 41, 77, 257, 275, 282, 293, 304
Charles, Les, 190
Cheatwood, Joel, 6, 195, 196, 224, 307, 308, 311
Cheatwood, Neva, 307, 308
Cheers, 168, 190
Cherry, Marc, xxii, 16, 128, 254, 261
Chicago Hope, 126
Child's Play, 97, 295
children's programming, 239
  brand loyalty, 240–241
  content, 242–243
  dual audiences, 242
  good programming, 240
  one-minute-thirty-second grind, 244–247
  selling, 243–244
Clarkson, Kelly, 233
classic three-act structure, 157–159
Close, Glenn, 156
CNN, 4, 6, 195, 196, 224
Coca-Cola, 5, 12, 119
Colbert Report, The, 29, 85
cold opening, *see* teasers

Columbia Pictures, xxi, 153, 275, 288
Columbia Pictures Television, 119
comedy, 22, 27, 28
    against character, 80
    alliteration, 80
    animation, writing for, 82–84
    checklist for funny, 29
    checklist for story, 46–47
    checklist for story structure, 54
    checklist for story outline, 65–66
    late-night, 84–85
    physical comedy, 45
    sample outline 58–59, 61–62
    sketch writing, 86
    in threes, 79
    see also jokes
Commander in Chief, 129–130
contests, participation in, 305
Cookie Monster, The, 167
Cops, 231
Cory in the House, 42, 182, 186, 241
counter-programming, 123
    in cable networks, 123–124
cover letters, 275–276
    good cover letter, 280–281
    how to write, 278–280
    sample, 281–282
covers, 63–64
Crash, 159
Cronkite, Walter, 195
CSI, 12, 15
Curb Your Enthusiasm, 32, 77, 168
CW, The, 7,8

D
D story, 45–46
Daily, Bob, 28, 76, 81, 189
Daily Show, The, 29, 85
Dana, Bill, 27, 168
Dateline, 195, 196
David, Larry, xxii, 128, 254, 261
Davis, Geena, 158
Dawn Anna, 148
Deconto, Jerry, 244–245, 247
DeSouza, Bonnie, 84
Desperate Housewives, 13, 16–17, 28, 76, 81, 169, 189
dialogue
    backstory, 175

character names usage, 175
    from characters, 173
    characters sound alike, 176
    phone conversation, 175–176
    rhythm, 174
    right-on dialogue, 174–175
    slang usage, 174
Directors Guild of America, 261
Discovery Kids, 244
disease of the week, 148
Disney, xxii, 7, 244
documentary show, 233
Douglas, Michael, 156
Dr. Phil, 8
Dr. Seuess, 309
drama
    character-driven dramas, 102
    plot-driven dramas, 93
    sample outline, 110–112
    sample script, 112–114
Drysdale, Eric, 29, 85
dual audiences, 242
Dubus, Andre III, 153
Dufour, Lynsey, 109
Dynasty: The Reunion, 149

E
Eapin, Matthew, 227
Eastwood, Clint, 153
Easy Rider, 43, 187
Eaton, Rebecca, 123, 151, 165, 312
Eckerle, Jeff, 11, 128, 130, 288, 312
Ed, Mr., 167
Eddie, the Dog, 167, 255
edit bay, TV news magazine show
    approval, from higher ups, 223
    leads, 223–224
    preparation, 221
    tags, 224
    timing, 222–223
    working with editor, 221–222
Ellen, 8
Elmo, 167
e-mail
    how and when to use, 285–286
Emerson College, 58, 110, 131, 135, 190, 246, 277
entertainment attorney, 256
Entertainment Tonight, 232, 236

entry level jobs, 291
  duration, 295–296
  uncovering jobs, 274–275
  and writing break, 273–274
E.R., 93, 126
E.T., 6, 166
Even Stevens, 18
Everybody Loves Raymond, 262
executive producer, 21, 30, 196
Extreme Makeover, 232

F
Face to Die For, A, 148
Face to Kill For, A, 148
Family Guy, 5, 82
Family Ties, 41
Fatal Attraction, 156
Federal Communications Commission
  (FCC), 7, 8
FedEx, 283
fem in jep, 148
Fetch!, 239, 240, 244, 311
Final Draft®, 66, 75, 278
first-run syndication, 8
Fish Police, 84
Fonzarelli, Arthur, 168–169
For the Roses, 146
FOX, 5, 6, 8, 126, 231, 311
Franklin, Jeff, 39
Frasier, xxii, 28, 76, 81, 167, 189
freelance writing, 9
Friends, 8, 125
Frink, John, 4, 17, 77, 83, 311
Full House, 14, 38–40, 43, 80, 182, 187

G
game show, 233
Garwood, Judy, 146
Gersh Agency, The, 252, 254, 256
Girls Above Sunset, 72–74
good cover letter
  five paragraphs, 280–281
good jokes
  origin, 77
Good Morning America, 8
Google, 287
Grace Under Fire, 79, 94
Grammnet Producers, 4, 36, 120, 126, 128
Grauman's Theatre, xxi
Greer, Bill, xxiv, 41

Greer, Kathy, 41
Grey's Anatomy, 12, 15, 95, 103, 292
Groening, Matt, 82
Grossman, Gary, 236, 293, 312
Guest, Judith, 156
Gustav, Hurricane, 246

H
Haggis, Paul, vi, 159
Hank Zipzer, 239
Hanks, Tom, 131
Happy Days, 168–169
Harry and the Hendersons, 167, 189
Harry Potter, 200–201, 209, 210, 212, 213
Harvard Business School, 119
Harvard Lampoon, 86
HBO, xxii, 49, 130, 188
Hill, Steven, 173
Hirsch, Judd, 156
Hollywood Reporter, The, 3, 4
Homeless to Harvard, 148
Hooper, 193
House of Sand and Fog, 153
Howard, Ron, 5

I
ICM, 254
I Love Lucy, 32, 42
Imagine Entertainment, 5
incognizant persona, 163
informational interview, 282
interview
  confidence, 288–289
  controlling, 288
  follow-up call, 289–290
  getting started, 287
  negative to positive, 290
  preparation, 287–288
  thank you notes, 289
Ipods, 6

J
JAG, 13, 96, 98
Jagged Edge, 288
Jankowski, Peter, 131, 271
Jeopardy, 8
jeopardy escalation, 51
Johnston, Jim, 234, 246
jokes
  about current topics, 79

number of, 76
offensive jokes, 78
origin, 77
runners, 79–80
setting up, 76
smart jokes, 76–77
see also comedy
Judge Judy, 8

K
Kate's Secret, 148
Kelley, David E., 103
Kennedy, Jackie, 194
Kennedy, John F, Jr., 194
Kensington Palace, 208
Kerby, Bill, 193
Khouri, Callie, 158
Kill Switch, 97, 295
killer cover letter
how to write, 278–280
King, Stephen, 151
Klenhard, Walter, 145, 150, 155, 312
Kloves, Steve, 200
Kodak, 277
Kutcher, Ashton, 79
Kyle's Turn, 131, 132–133

L
Larimore, Drew, 110
L.A. Times, 4, 275
Last of the Summer Wine, 42
late-night television writing, 84–85
Late Show with David Letterman, The,
23, 84, 85
Lavanchy, Gene, 307
Law & Order, 8, 13, 15, 93, 94, 95, 98, 99,
125, 131, 169, 173, 271
Law & Order: Criminal Intent, 94
Law & Order: Special Victims Unit, 11,
128, 130, 288, 312
leads, 223–224
Lear, Norman, 40, 310
Leno, Jay, 10, 85, 303
Lifetime, xxii, 145, 146, 147, 149, 181
line producer, 31, 274
Little People, 232, 233, 236, 312
Lorre, Chuck, 279
Los Angeles, 4, 10, 17, 35, 254
Lost In Space, 167
Lunch, how to do, 300

M
made-for-TV movies, 145
action driven stories, 149
classic three-act structure, 157–160
Hallmark, 145–146
mini-series, 154
MOW business, breaking in, 149
MOW structuring, 155–156
novels in screen, getting rights,
151–154
protagonist vs. antagonist, 150–151
stories, as both films and MOWs, 156
sub-genres sampling, 147–149
target audience, for MOWs, 146–147
true stories adaptation, 149–150
two-hour writing, 154–155
Magic of Ordinary Days, The, 146
major and minor declaration, 17
Make Me a Mum, 236
Mancini, Don, 97, 106, 295
Man With Three Wives, The, 148
Married with Children, 12
Marshall, Garry, 169
Martinez, Pedro, 197
Mary Tyler Moore Show, The, 42, 127–128,
129, 130
Masius, John, 123
Masterpiece Theatre, 125, 151, 165, 312
Mathison, Melissa, 166
McClean High, 110–115
McDonalds, 198
McKee, Stacy, 95, 103, 292
Medium, 14, 36, 120, 126, 128
Meehan, Glenn, 232, 236, 312
men, behaving badly, 148
Merkerson, S, Epatha, 93
Merstein's Mansion, 135–140
Microsoft , 66
Million Dollar Baby, vi, 159
mini-series writing, 154
minor characters, 168–169
Mixed Blessings, 148
mock assignment, TV news magazine
shows
boss' intention, 198
example, 200–201
experts, for story, 199–200
real people, 198–199
Monk, 169
Moonves, Les 123

Moore, Mary Tyler, 156
Movie Magic, 278
MOWs (Movies of the Week)
    action-driven stories, 149
    breaking in, 149
    common types, 147–149
    protagonist and antagonist, 150–151
    stories, as both films and MOWs, 156
    structuring, 155–156
    target audience, 146–147
Mr. Rogers' Neighborhood, 290
Mullaly, Megan, 148
multi-cam scripts
    formatting, 72–75
multi-cam sitcom, 32, 57, 61, 74
multi-dimensional characters, 163, 170
Munster, Herman, 167
Murphy Brown, 79
Murray, Liz, 148
Mutchnick, Max, 16, 125
My Little Pony, 84
My Name Is Earl, 15, 169, 265
Myspace.com, 287
Mystery!, 123, 151, 165, 312

N
National Academy of Television Arts
    and Sciences, 304
natural sound on tape (NAT/SOT),
    208–209
Naval Academy, 244–245
Naval Station Mayport, 246
Navy Command Center, 245
Navy, United States, 244–245
NBC, 7, 8, 226, 277, 294
network schedule, 122–123
networking power
    business card, 299
    contacts, 378
    holiday greetings, 299
    how to do lunch, 300
    personal book, 299
    personal note card, 298
    requirements, 301
    spec scripts, 302
    taking the lead, 301
networks, 7, 7–8, 9, 49, 121, 123–124,
    125, 195, 261
New York Times, The, 4, 151
news, *see* TV news magazine shows
Nichols, David, 79, 94

Nickelodeon, 244
Nielsen Ratings, 5
Nixon, Richard, 168
no-fail sitcom structure, 50–52
nonhuman characters, 166–167
non-premise pilot
    vs. premise pilot, 129–130
novels, in made-for-TV movies, 148
    getting rights, 151–154

O
offensive jokes, 78
Office, The, 277
Olsen, Ashley, 43
Olsen, Mary-Kate, 43
On Demand, 6
one-hour dramatic structure, 99–100
Oprah, 8
Orbach, Jerry, 93
Ordinary People, 156
original premise
    13-week episode guide creation,
        133–134
    Big Love, 134–140
    characters and premise introduction,
        131
    first pages, of pilot script, 134–142
    future trends, tapping into, 126–128
    market study, 125–126
    networks longevity, 125
    premise vs. non-premise pilots,
        133–134
    riding coattails, 142
    sample pilot treatment, 131
    writers own viewpoint, 130–131
Osborn, Marilyn, 21, 107
Oscar, the Grouch, 167

P
Pact, The, 148
Paramount, 7
Paramount Television, 281
Paxton, Bill, 130
PBS, 231, 241, 242, 246
PBS Kids, 244
Peep and the Big Wide World (Taylor),
    240, 242, 244, 311, 313
Pentagon, 244–245
*People Employed by the State of New York
    to Fight Crime in the 1940s*, 58–59,
    61–62, 64

People's court, The, 231
PepsiCo, 119
Peterson, Scott, 147
Phillips, Stone, 196
phone etiquette, 283
physical comedy, 45
Picket Fences, 103–105
Picoult, Jodi, 148
pilot
  counter-programming, in cable
    networks, 123–124
  network schedule, 123–124
  pilot season, 121–122
  reasons, not to write, 119–120
  reasons, to write, 120–121
  see also original premise
Pinto, Steve, 58, 68
pitch meeting
  amount of details, 182–183
  attendees, 179
  controlling the room, 183–184
  don'ts, 184
  dressing, 180–181
  example, of pitch, 187
  index cards usage, 184–185
  note pads usage, 184–185
  number of ideas, 181
  order of stories, 182
  practice, 183, 189–190
  preparation, for questions, 186–188
  pros and cons, 188
  reading the room, 185
  respecting the big foot, 188–189
  story modification, 185–186
  timing, 180
  when they don't buy, 188
Pizza Hut, 276
plot-driven dramas, 93
  authentic worlds creation,
    importance, 95
  on cable networks, 100
  and character-driven dramas, 106
  checklist for, 101
  colleges and universities, 97
  conflict and jeopardy building,
    98–99
  facts getting, 96–97
  index cards, 100–101
  Law & Order, 94, 95
  in newspaper, 94–95
  one-hour dramatic structure, 99–100

protagonists and antagonists, 98
structure, 100
Writers Guild of America, The,
  97–98
plot points, *see* turning points
Podolsky, Amy, 244
Postcards from Buster, 242, 243
premise pilot
  vs. non-premise pilot, 129–130
prime time drama
  formatting, 110
  sample outline, 110–112
  scripting, 112–115
Prince Harry, 208
Prince William, 208
Princess Bride, The, 310
Princess Diana, 208, 228
private persona, 163
producer, 196, 197, 198, 205, 211,
  226–228, 236, 242
producer's assistant, 274
product integration, 6–7
production companies, 7
Prom Mom case, 95
protagonists and antagonists, 98
public persona, 163
punch-up, dreaded, 81

Q
query letter, 256–259
quirky characters, 169–170

R
Radar, Dennis, 147
Radcliffe, Daniel, 200
Ransic, Bill, 233
Ransohoff, Marty, 288, 289
Real Life, 294, 306
real-life experience, in drama, 102–103
Real World, 233, 234
reality television, 32, 231
  Americans' obsession, 233
  documentary vs. game show,
    233–234
  ethics, 236
  need for, 232–233
  producer's game, 234
  real compelling characters, 235–236
  treatment, 236
Redford, Robert, 156
residuals, 262–263

resumés, 275–276
  how to write, 276–277
  power of overnighting, 283
  sample, 277–278
rewriting, 16, 19
Rineman, Jon, 86
romance, 148
Rose Hill, 146
Rose, The, 193
Rowling, J.K., 200–201, 202, 203, 209, 210, 212, 213, 215, 216
Rugrats, 12, 82
Rush, Herman, 119
runners, 79–80

S
Salhany, Lucie, 5, 126, 231, 311
sample script, purchasing, 14–15
Sarandon, Susan, 158
Saturday Night Live, 86
Saving Emily, 148
Saving Private Ryan, 8
Sawyer, Diane, 201
scene writing, 75
Screen Actors Guild, 261
Screenwriting Expo, 305
Scriptapalooza, 305
Script City, 14
script writers, 18
  agents, 18
  initial meeting, with producers, 19–20
  invitation to pitch, 20
  payment, 24
  story buying, by producers, 21–22
  story stealing, 23
  teleplay writing, 22–23
script writing, TV news magazine shows, 214–217
  graphics and special effects, 214
  pet funerals, 217–220
  sound bite, 212–213
  tapes, sorting, 211
  timecode, 211–212
  track, 213
  video and sound, 213–214
Scrubs, 15, 32
Second City, 86
Seinfeld, xxii, 8, 11, 78
seminars and conferences, 305

September 11th, 8, 190, 244–246
Serafini, Paul, 239, 246, 311
Sesame Street, 290, 312
Sheen, Charlie, 19
Shock and Awe, 245
shooting script, 66–67
  and first draft, 66
show business, 4–6
show runner, *see* executive producer
show studying, 13
Showtime, xxii, 49
sight gags, 45
Silence of the Lambs, 166
Simpsons, The, 4, 17, 77, 82, 83, 251, 311
single-cam script
  formatting, 68–72
single-camera sitcom, 32, 59, 60
sitcom, 27
  checklist, for funny, 29
  freelance writer, 36
  multi-camera vs. single-camera shows, 31–32
  sitcom business works, 29
  staff writers, 29–31
  writer, five-day schedule, 32–36
  writing, 27–29
sitcom scripting
  alliteration, 80
  audience, in superior position, 80
  button, 80–81
  comedy, against character, 80
  comedy, in threes, 79
  formatting, 66
  good jokes, origin, 77
  jokes, about current topics, 79
  jokes, number of, 76
  jokes, setting up, 76
  multi-cam scripts formatting, 72–75
  offensive jokes, 78–79
  punch-up, dreaded, 80
  runners, 79–80
  scene writing, 75
  shooting script and first draft, 66–67
  single-cam script formatting, 68–72
  smart jokes, 76–77
  universal humor, incorporating, 78
sitcom story, developing
  A, B, C, D stories, 45–46
  feedback, 46
  good story, importance of, 37–38

original spin, finding, 40–42
original stories, for existing shows, 38–40
original story creation, 38
physical comedy, 45
sight gags, 45
stories, to avoid, 43–44
story idea construction, 44–45
study up, 42
writer's block, overcoming, 42–43
sitcom story, outlining
covers, 63–64
feedback, 62–63
formatting, 57
good outline features, 56
length, 57–58
multi-cam shows format, 61–62
planning, 55–56
precise writing, 56–57
reading out loud, 62
sample and rules, 58–61
sitcom structure
example, 52
importance, 48
no-fail structure, 50–52
tags, 53
teasers, 53
three-act structure, 48–49
twists, stories with, 49–50
two-act structure, 48–49
situational comedies, see sitcom
Six Feet Under, xxii
Sketch Writing,
Example, 87–90
Slumber Party, 40, 80
smart jokes, 76–77
Smith, Matt, 131
snail mail, 289
Sony, 7
Soprano, Tony, xxii
Sorkin, Aaron, 128
sound bite, 212–213, 213, 214
South Park, 15, 82
spec, reasons it won't sell, 16–17
spec script, 11–13, 15–16, 302
Spielberg, Steven, 8, 157, 303
Spike, 146
staff writing, 9, 28
stand-up, 210
Star, 148

Star Trek, 5
Stark, Steve, 14, 36, 120, 126, 128
Starting Over, 234
Steele, Andrew, 86
Steele, Danielle, 148, 151
Steve Harvey Show, The, 9, 30, 31, 68, 72, 273, 284
Stone, Oliver, 157
stories, 38–40, 45–46, 98
backstory, 164
enterprising one's own stories, 197
as films and MOWs, 156
good story, importance of, 37–38
idea construction, 44–45
MOW stories, 147–149
order, in pitch meeting, 182
original story creation, 38
to stay away from, 43–44
true stories, adapting, 149–150
story producer, 234
story stealing, 23
studios, 7, 267, 274–275
success tips, 303
clear idea, 308
contacts, with organizations, 304
contests, participation in, 305
Dr. Seuss wisdom, 309
early entry, 303
evaluator, 306
mind and body, taking care, 309
seminars and conferences, 305
talent, 306
technology usage, 305–306
tenacity, 306–308
women, 308–309
writing buddies, 303–304
Survivor, 32, 231, 232, 233, 234, 292, 308
Sutherland, Donald, 156
syndication, 8–9, 30, 53, 262

T
tags, 53, 223–224
Taxi, 190
Taylor, Kate, 240, 244, 312
teasers, 53
technology, 6
usage, 305–306
teleplay writing, 22–23
Television Sweeps, 9, 44

television writer, 271, 303, 309
   approaching people, 272–273
   cover letters, 275–276, 278–282
   e-mail, 285–286
   entry level jobs, 273–274, 274–275
   how to get work, 271
   internships, importance, 272
   need for plan, 271
   overnighting resumés, 283
   phone etiquette, 283
   resumés, 275–276, 277–278
   voice mail, 284–285
   when they're not hiring, 282
   writer's assistants, 283–284
tenacity, 306–308
term writer, 31
That's So Raven, 14, 18, 42, 182, 186,
   241
Thelma and Louise, 158–159, 164
Theodore, Bill, 197, 226
three-act sitcom structure, 48–49
Three Stooges, 45
Three's Company, 42
Till Death Do Us Part, 42
timecode, 211–212
TiVo, 6
TNT, 146
To Dance With the White Dog, 146
To Tell the Truth, 231
Today, 8
Tonight Show, The, 10, 85, 305
Touched by an Angel, 21, 107, 123
Towler, Tom, 13, 96, 98
Tracey Ullman Show, The, 82
track, 213
Trading Spouses, 232
true crime, into made-for-TV movies,
   147
true stories, into TV movies, 149–150
Trump, Donald, 235
Trump, Ivanka, 235
Trump Organization, 235
Truth Or Consequences, 231
turning points, 157–158, 159
TV Guide, 19, 43, 45, 147
TV industry, 3
   first step, to become a writer, 10–11
   in Los Angeles, 10
   major and minor declaration, 17
   networks, 7, 7–8

product integration, 6–7
production companies, 7
rewriting, 16
sample script, purchasing, 14–15
show business, 4–6
show studying, 13
spec, reasons it won't sell, 16–17
spec script, 11–13
staff writing vs. freelance writing, 9
studios, 7
syndication, 8–9
technology change, 6
Television Sweeps, 9
two specs, writing, 15–16
TV Land, 42
TV news magazine shows, 193
   additional work, as producer,
      226–228
   aggressiveness, 194–195
   checklist, 220
   editing, 221–228
   enterprising one's own stories, 197
   and entertainment, 195
   ethics, 224–226
   mock assignment, 198–201
   news, existence, 193
   power structure, 195–196
   sample script, 215–216
   script writing, 211–220
   shoot
      b-roll, 208
      camera, 207
      correspondent, 202–203
      crew, taking care of, 203–204
      interviewing, 205–207
      location, 204
      natural sound, importance of,
         208–209
      preparation, 202
      stand-up, 210
      while crew sets up, for interview,
         204–205
   writing vs. producing, 196
tweens, 241
twists, creation, 49–50, 51–52
two-act sitcom structure, 48–49
Two and a Half Men (Aronshohn), 15, 77,
   134, 163, 277, 282
two specs, writing, 15–16
Tygard, Judy, 199, 204

U

United Paramount Network (UPN),
    5, 126, 231, 311
universal humor, incorporating, 78
Universal Studios, xxi, 7, 273, 274, 277
USA Network, 145
U.S.S. Hue City, 245
U.S.S. JFK, 244
U.S.S. Simpson, 245

V

Van Dyke, Dick, 79
Variety, 3
video and sound, 213–215
Viet Nam, 245
voice mail
    how and when to use, 284–285

W

Wall Sreet Journal, The, 4
Wallace, Mike, 193, 201, 211
Warner Bros., 7, 277
Warren, Marc, 14, 18, 39, 42, 182, 186, 241
Waugh, Kathy, 242, 311
Wayans Brothers, The, 9, 30, 31, 72, 273,
    284
WGBH, 290
Wharton, 119
Wheel of Fortune, 8
Wiggles, The, 240
Wild Thornberrys, The, 12, 82
Will and Grace, 16, 125
William Morris, 254
Williamson, Martha, 123
Winger, Debra, 148
Wings, 190
Winkler, Henry, 38, 129, 165, 169, 239,
    311
Witherspoon, Reese, 197
Wittels, Harris, 135
Wolf Films, 131, 271
women, 127–128, 130, 147, 308–309
    dressing, in pitch meeting, 181
    with incredible like obstacles, 148

Women in Film, 304
Wonder Years, The, 108
Woodward, Louise, 227–228
Word, Microsoft, 278
World Trade Center, 190, 245
Writers Guild of America (WGA), The,
    24, 40, 97–98, 261
    arbitration, 40, 263
    contract, 23
    key functions, 262
    membership, 261–262
    minimum, 24, 30
    miscellaneous benefits, 264
    residuals, 262–263
    script registry, 64
    web site, 97
    work protection, 264
    writer's credit system, 263
    writer's strike, 263
Writer's assistants, 273–274
    importance in getting names, 283–284
Writers Guild of America Script
    Registry, 66
writer's block
    overcoming, 42–43
writing buddies, 303–304
Writing Partners
    how to choose one, 267
writing teams
    cons of partnerships, 266–267
    partner selection, 267–268
    pros of partnerships, 265–266
    responsibility, for other's career, 266
Written By, 190

X

X-Files, 21, 107

Y

Young and the Restless, The, 109

Z

ZOOM, 239, 241, 244, 245, 246, 247, 290,
    311